Macroeconomics:

Understanding National Income, Inflation, and Unemployment

Macroeconomics:

Understanding National Income, Inflation, and Unemployment

Edwin G. Dolan

Assistant Professor of Economics, Dartmouth College,
and Adjunct Professor of Economics, Royalton College

with the collaboration of

David E. Lindsey

Senior Economist
Division of Research and Statistics
Board of Governors of the Federal Reserve System

THE DRYDEN PRESS

Hinsdale, Illinois

TO
EDWARD BASTIAN
and his tradition of excellence in teaching

EGD and DEL

Editorial production services by Cobb/Dunlop, Publisher Services, Inc.
Picture research by Marcia Kelly
Cover and text design by Caliber
Typesetting by Applied Typographic Systems

Grateful acknowledgment is made to the following people and organizations for the use of
    photographs:
Chase Ltd., Washington: Arthur Okun (p. 107)
Culver Pictures: Thomas Malthus (p. 307), David Ricardo (p. 335), and Adam Smith (p. 10)
Harvard University News Office, Cambridge: Joseph A. Schumpeter (p. 421)
Historical Pictures Service, Chicago: John Maynard Keynes (p. 121), Alfred Marshall (p. 36),
    John Stuart Mill (p. 116)
United Press International: Arthur F. Burns (p. 172), Milton Friedman (p. 206), Friedrich A.
    von Hayek (p. 28)

Preface

Economics in Today's World

The economics profession, as we who pursue it know, is strongly counter-cyclical. Like suppliers of shoe repairs or intercity bus travel, suppliers of economic analysis enjoy a boom whenever the economy goes into a slump. In the sixties, students drifted away from economics in search of "relevance." Today we do not have to go around telling students that economics is relevant—our rising enrollments show that they already know it is. Our job now is not to disappoint them. They come to our principles courses with simple, practical concerns and questions. We must be equipped to address those concerns and questions. That is what this book is all about.

Inflation and Unemployment

The number one concern that draws students to the principles course is the problem of inflation and unemployment. When I first sat down to write this book, I had a survey at hand that showed inadequate treatment of inflation and unemployment to be the number one source of dissatisfaction with existing textbooks. To do the job right, it was clear that the presentation of macroeconomics had to be built from the ground up with the economic concerns of the seventies in mind. The traditional Keynesian income determination model, tried and tested through many editions of traditional textbooks, could serve as a starting point, but only that. You as an instructor had to be given a way to teach principles students the things that we in the profession have learned in the past few years about how our economy works—about the importance of inflationary expectations, about the role of money in the economy, about unemployment and the process of job search, and all the rest. These ideas are too important to be reserved for those few students who pursue economics into intermediate and advanced courses. Unfortunately, they are also too complex just to be tacked on to the traditional model by inserting a chapter on "contemporary macroeconomic issues." In this book, instead, the modern theories of inflation and unemployment are built right into the core of the analysis. The result is a text that is simpler, more straightforward, and easier to teach than anything you have ever seen.

Here is how it is done. First, Chapters 5 to 7 introduce the most important terms and concepts of macroeconomics, including the key concept of macroeconomic equilibrium. Chapters 8 to 13 then present conventional national income determination topics in a way that never muddles the key distinction between real and nominal values. That puts us in a position to ask the most important question of all: how is it determined what part of any change in nominal national income will take the form of a change in real income and employment, and what part will take the form of pure inflation?

This question is answered in a unique set of four chapters that builds on what the student has now learned. First, Chapter 14 discusses four traditional explanations of inflation and unemployment: the crude quantity theory, the Keynesian theory of inflationary gaps, the Phillips curve, and cost-push theories. It is shown how each of these ideas contains a part of the truth, but not the whole truth. Chapter 15 then takes up the economics of "the new unemployment," not neglecting the contribution that microeconomics has made to our understanding of unemployment in recent years. Next, Chapter 16 integrates the four incomplete theories of Chapter 14 into a whole. The four "crude" theories are seen to fit together almost like pieces of a jigsaw puzzle. This chapter uses a completely original graphical exposition of the theory of inflationary recession. It is this graphical presentation that brings this theory, often seen only in complex mathematical form, down to a level even simpler than the familiar "Keynesian cross" analysis that revolutionized the textbooks of a generation ago. Finally, Chapter 17 discusses contemporary controversies in macroeconomic policy, including wage and price controls, fine-tuning vs. policy rules, and indexing.

Chapter 17 also begins with a brief, entirely verbal and intuitive recap of what has gone on in Chapters 15 and 16. This gives the book a valuable two-track flexibility since Chapters 14 and 17 can be read as a coherent sequence by themselves if desired. The short track through this material makes it possible to cover the essentials of inflation and unemployment theory even in a one-semester course. But even if the short track is taken, this textbook still says more on these vital topics than anything previously available.

The Role of Government

A second way in which this book tries to meet the interests and concerns of today's students is the treatment of the role of government in the economy. In the changing political and economic climate of the seventies, Americans are taking a closer and more critical look at government than ever before. Economics textbooks of the past often reflected a bland acceptance of the way government performed its economic role, attributing dissenting views to an insignificant minority. Now it is the majority who are discontent. Today no aspect of our government's policies toward inflation, unemployment, growth, or international trade escapes critical reexamination.

The Cases

No matter how well a textbook presents general principles, those principles by themselves are not enough. A time-honored doctrine tells us that each generalization should receive a specific illustration, just as each illustration should lead to a generalization. In this book, numerous short case studies are included to tie principles to reality. Many of these cases illustrate general statements about economic policy with specific policy episodes, such as the Kennedy tax cut or the Nixon wage-price controls. Other cases present empirical work to underline points of theory, for example, studies of the sources of U.S. economic growth, of the effects of wage and price controls, or of the history of income and consumption.

If such illustrative material is to do its job, it must not interrupt proper concept flow. For that reason, the cases are short, to the point, and placed directly in the text just at the point they are needed. They thus appear not as digressions or interruptions, but as an integral part of the learning process.

Teaching and Learning Aids

This is a book from which students can and will learn. Some students come to college equipped with the study skills they would need to learn their economics by reading Marshall and Keynes in the original. Others, as we all know, come less well equipped. This book takes the realistic attitude that we must teach our students as they come to us and must help them develop good study skills as they go along.

Readability

For one thing, this book has a fully controlled reading level. It is designed to match the actual reading abilities of today's university freshmen and junior college students. Sad to say, the reading skills of many of them fall one, two, or even three years below established college standards. That puts the major competitive textbooks out of the reach of too many of the students who are asked to use them. This book, however, is designed to be fully readable for all of today's students. This combination of an accessible style of writing with sophisticated, up-to-date content makes the book unusually easy to teach and learn from.

As a further step toward readability, it should be added, this book discards the "alphabet soup" approach to teaching economics. When we talk about the marginal propensity to save or consume, those are the very words we use, not MPS or MPC. It does not cost much in paper or ink to spell the words out in full. It does save students the unnecessary step of memorizing a whole bagful of abbreviations before they can even get down to learning economic principles.

Vocabulary

That brings us to another point—vocabulary. For many students, vocabulary is one of the big stumbling blocks in learning economics. This book uses a unique three-level reinforcement technique to handle the problem. First, each new term is printed in boldface at the point it is first used and defined. Next, the term and its definition are repeated on the same page in a marginal vocabulary note. Finally, there is a complete alphabetical glossary of all terms at the end of the book.

Working with Graphs

Another big obstacle for many students is working with graphs. For that reason, we have an appendix on working with graphs at the end of Chapter 1. This appendix does more than just explain techniques. It also addresses the most common student problems of working with graphs. One of these problems is the tendency to memorize graphs as meaningless pictures, with no understanding of their content. Another is the inability to draw original graphs when needed in note taking or on examinations. Our appendix carefully warns of the pitfalls and explains how they can be avoided.

Other Learning Aids

Other learning aids are provided for the student as well. A very important item is the Study Guide, a companion volume written by Thomas Anderson of Eastern Michigan University. In the textbook itself, students are provided with chapter previews and summaries, profiles of well-known economists, discussion questions, review suggestions, suggestions for further reading, and a complete index.

Teaching Aids

This book is also accompanied by a complete set of teaching aids for you, the instructor. First and foremost, there is an Instructor's Manual. This contains learning objectives, lecture notes, and answers to the end-of-chapter questions in the text. It also contains a section for each chapter entitled "What's Different Here, and Why." This section provides the information you need to convert your course to using this book from using whichever major competing textbook you had adopted in the past. A complete test bank and a set of transparency masters are also available to instructors, printed separately from the Instructor's Manual.

The Newsletter

As a final feature to help both you and your students, a twice-yearly newsletter is available to all instructors adopting this textbook. This newsletter serves a number of purposes. First, it contains fresh case studies of the same format as those included in the text. These can either be used as lecture material or be duplicated and distributed to students. Second, the newsletter updates the suggestions for further reading with mini-reviews of new books suitable for use in the principles course. Finally, the newsletter updates the most important statistical series used in the text.

Appendixes

Appendixes are used here and there in this book to cover those "can't please everyone" topics that some instructors like to include and others do not. Two of these in particular deserve special comment. The appendixes to Chapters 10 and 13 present simple algebraic versions of the income determination model expounded verbally in the text. The text itself uses no algebra at all, and this approach will best serve the needs of most students and instructors. Even though a majority of students may never use them, however, the algebraic appendixes are valuable for two reasons.

First, almost every university economics class contains a few students who are very good at mathematics and who can actually catch on faster to a set of equations than to a whole chapter of verbal exposition. Such students can read the appendixes on their own. Second, at schools that emphasize a technical curriculum, nearly all students may be well trained in mathematics. The appendixes can then be used as a regular part of the course.

Planning Your Course

This book and its companion, *Microeconomics: Understanding Prices and Markets,* are designed to give you maximum flexibility whatever the academic calendar employed by your particular school. You may either begin with the introductory chapters in Part 1, or, if your students have completed the micro course first, you may begin directly with the core macro material in Chapters 5–17.

Part 3, "The Economics of Life on a Small Planet," is suitable for use as applied material in either the micro or macro course, so these chapters appear in both paperback volumes. Chapter 21, which covers the pure theory of international trade, also appears in the micro paperback, but Chapter 22, which requires some macro background, appears only here.

For your use in course planning, here is a table of contents of the companion micro paperback. Chapters that appear in both texts are shown in color.

Chapter Outline:
Microeconomics: Understanding Prices and Markets

[1]Includes an appendix on elasticity of supply and demand.

A Word or Two of Thanks

I have been extremely fortunate in getting help of many kinds from many quarters while writing this book. It is a pleasure to acknowledge this help here.

I owe the greatest thanks to my collaborating author, David E. Lindsey. David, my longtime friend and professional colleague, provided the theoretical inspiration and technical details for the basic macroeconomics model presented in Part 2. The approach is one he developed over many years of teaching at Ohio State University and Macalester College. Although the heavy commitments he has now as a senior research economist at the Federal Reserve Board of Governors prevented him from participating actively in the actual writing of this book, Part 2 is really as much his as mine. Of course, it must be made clear that the contributions he has made are his personally, and can in no way be construed as representing the official views of the Federal Reserve System on matters either of theory or of policy. It ought also to be added that any errors or shortcomings in Part 2 of this book are, just as much as elsewhere, entirely my own responsibility, not his.

Second, I would like to thank two people who helped me prepare the ancillary materials for this text. Tom Anderson, already mentioned as author of the Study Guide, did an excellent job. Bill Rushing of Georgia State University also made a valuable contribution in the form of items for our test bank.

Next, I must thank the many reviewers who commented on various drafts of the text and suggested countless improvements. I was very fortunate in having an especially astute critic and reader as my neighbor in Vermont, Herbert Goertz of Royalton College. Professor Goertz did his job so diligently that at times his written comments and suggestions seemed longer than my draft chapters! I find it hard to imagine how I could have gotten the job done without his help.

Of course, I do not by any means wish to belittle the contributions of all the other people who read and commented on all or part of the manuscript. My thanks, in this regard, to

Dr. Thomas Anderson
Eastern Michigan University

Charles Britton
University of Arkansas

Steven G. Dworsky
Hudson Valley Community College

Dr. Upton Henderson
Central State University

John Gilliam
Texas Technical University

William Holahan
University of Wisconsin

David R. Kamerschen
University of Georgia

Randolph C. Martin
University of South Carolina

Kent W. Olson
Oklahoma State University

John Pisciotta
University of Southern Colorado

Robert Pollard
University of Texas

Francis W. Rushing
Georgia State University

Courtenay Stone
California State University—Northridge

Carl B. Turner
North Carolina State University—Raleigh

Raymond F. Turner
Anne Arundel Community College

Royce J. Watts
West Virginia University

Travis Wilson
DeKalb College—Central Campus

At one critical point in writing the text I was able to find specialized research help when I needed it. Chris Tame of the Institute for Economic Affairs in London researched the profiles of leading economists for me. As always, of course, the credit is his and the blame for any errors is mine.

Last but not least I would like to recognize three very efficient and long-suffering typists: Maureen Bayman and Norma Scott of Belvedere, Kent, in England and Ellen Blanchard of Gaysville, Vermont. Among the three of them they produced literally thousands of pages, working most of the time under the pressure of overly tight deadlines.

Dozens of other people who go unnamed here—publishers, editors, consultants, and staff—have worked hard to make this book what it is. Remember, though, that all we have done is only half the job. The rest is up to you, the instructor.

South Royalton, Vermont
June, 1977

Edwin G. Dolan

Contents
in Brief

Detailed Contents

CHAPTER 4
The Role of Government in the Economy   53

PART TWO
National Income, Inflation, and Unemployment   69

A. National Income—Concepts, Measurement, and Growth

CHAPTER 5
The Circular Flow of Income and Product   71

CHAPTER 6
Measuring National Income and Product   85

C.   Second Lesson in Macroeconomics—The Role of Money

CHAPTER 11
The Banking System and the Supply of Money 167

CHAPTER 12
The Demand for Money and the Money Market 185

CHAPTER 13
The Interaction of Money and the Multiplier 195

D. Third Lesson in Macroeconomics—Unemployment
and Inflation

CHAPTER 14
Unemployment and Inflation: The Problem and Some Traditional Answers 217

CHAPTER 15
A Closer Look at Unemployment 235

PART ONE
An Overview of the Market Economy

Economics, as it is usually taught in the United States, is largely a study of how markets work. Economic activity is not entirely a matter of buying and selling things, but buying and selling are of central importance. In this part we shall learn that the buying and selling activities taking place in markets accomplish two important functions. The first function is to move goods and services around, passing them from people who value them less to people who value them more. The desire to move goods and services around is the main intended consequence of market activity. When people buy and sell, however, they also fulfill a second, unintended function; that is generating information that can be used in economic decision making. This information takes the form of market prices.

In Chapters 2 and 3, we shall look in some detail at how markets perform these two functions. First we shall take a general view, in order to learn how markets function as a mechanism for utilizing knowledge. After that, we shall develop some elementary theoretical tools for analyzing markets. These tools of supply and demand analysis will be put to work in every subsequent chapter of the book.

Although economics is largely the study of markets, markets are not the only mechanism used for moving resources around in our economy. Government also plays a major role. Government does some buying and selling just as private individuals do, but that is not all that government does. In addition, government has the power to move resources by nonvoluntary means. It can take a part of people's incomes through taxation. It can, to a limited extent, order people to perform specific economic tasks. And it can regulate much private economic activity.

In the United States, government is large, but not too large to prevent us from thinking of our economy as primarily a market economy. We thus study markets first, and then look at how the presence of government modifies the way they operate. Chapter 4 will introduce the role of government in the economy, and provide background for looking at particular problems of economic policy in later chapters.

CHAPTER 1
What Economics Is All About

What You Will Learn in This Chapter
Understanding economics means learning the economic way of thinking. Key ideas in the economic way of thinking are scarcity, choice, and division of labor. To make these abstract ideas easy to visualize, economists sometimes use diagrams such as the *production possibility frontier.* Economic science can contribute to the evaluation of economic policy, but economic policy decisions also require value judgments. Science and value judgments must stand in the proper relationship to one another if valid policy evaluations are to be made.

Understanding economics means learning how to think like an economist. So what is the economic way of thinking? Sometimes people call economics "the science of common sense," a definition that gives us a good start. To say that economics is common sense means that economists do not have some mysterious special logic all their own. There is no theory or concept in all of economics that cannot be expressed in a straightforward English sentence. Economists frequently draw pictures in the margins of their books in order to put their ideas across more vividly, but the pictures themselves are not economics. They are just learning aids. At other times (especially when exchanging ideas among themselves) economists write mathematical equations as a sort of shorthand, but that does not mean that economics is a branch of mathematics. You can read right through the main parts of this book without coming across a single algebraic equation, and besides, mathematicians tell us that their science is just common sense too.

If the economic way of thinking is not a special kind of logic, or graphs, or mathematics, then what is it? The key to the economic way of thinking lies not in the *way* economists think, but in the things they think *about.* Learning the economic way of thinking means developing a certain alertness or sensitivity to certain features of ordinary, everyday situations. The same can be said of other social sciences. When psychologists look at what is going on in the world around them, they are likely to be sensitive to how people's motivations and personalities shape their behavior toward one another. Political scientists might be alert to clues that signal certain kinds of power relationships. Economists have their own list of what to look for.

The purpose of this chapter will be to introduce a few signals that economists look for, as a sort of sensitivity training. This will give a big head start on understanding the economic way of thinking.

Scarcity and Opportunity Cost

Scarcity

Scarcity As used in economics, not having enough to fill all subjective wants.

The most basic concept of economics is **scarcity.** In economics, scarcity means not having as much of some thing as we want. Economic scarcity is not measured by any objective physical standard. A geologist might say that tin ore is scarce relative to iron ore, but an economist would say that both are scarce because we do not have as much of either one as we want. Because scarcity is subjective—part of the human condition—we cannot escape from it. **Ascetics** may try to escape from scarcity by limiting their desires, but even when they go out to look for twigs to build a fire to cook a bowl of rice, they come up against the fact that twigs are scarce. They have to take time off from meditation in order to gather them; so they would carefully build the fire in such a way as to boil the water with the least possible amount of fuel.

Ascetic A person who tries to achieve happiness by purposely limiting desires.

Choice

Because things are scarce, we must make choices. What is more, in economic life we are almost always closely constrained in the range of alternatives among which we must choose. We shall be talking a lot about constraints and choice in this book. We shall examine the choices that a shopper makes among items in a supermarket, when constrained by a weekly food budget. We shall look at the way a business firm chooses what to produce and what inputs to use when constrained by the actions of its competitors and its own past decisions. We shall look at economic policy decisions that governments make, at how political constraints affect their choices, and at how those choices, in turn, affect all of us.

Opportunity Cost

Opportunity Cost The cost of doing something as measured by the loss of the opportunity to do the next best thing instead with the same amount of time or resources.

Because economists are so sensitive to choice and scarcity, they are very much concerned with costs. The most important kind of cost in economics is what is called **opportunity cost.** The opportunity cost of doing something is the loss of the opportunity of doing the next best thing instead with the same time or resources.

Opportunity cost is everywhere, so we do not have to look far to find illustrations. In fact, we have already given one illustration without noticing it. For the ascetics of whom we just spoke, the opportunity cost of a bundle of twigs was the loss of an hour's meditation. The following case study provides an illustration somewhat closer to home.

CASE 1.1
The Opportunity Cost of a College Education
Susan, an average student, is enrolled at National Average University. If you ask her how much it is costing her to go to college, she will refer you to a little budget she has drawn up for her four years at NAU. It is shown in

EXHIBIT 1.1

The cost of a college education

Part *a* of this exhibit shows the out-of-pocket costs of a four-year college education for a typical student. Each entry in that table represents an actual cash payment that the student must make. Part *b* shows the opportunity cost of an education at the same college. Each entry there represents a sacrifice that the student must make in order to obtain an education. Note that room and board (Part *a*) is only an out-of-pocket cost, while foregone income (Part *b*) is only an opportunity cost.

a. Budget of out-of-pocket costs	
Tuition and fees	$12,000
Books, transportation to and from home, etc.	2,000
Room and board	10,000
Total out-of-pocket costs	$24,000
b. Budget in terms of opportunity costs	
Tuition and fees	$12,000
Books, transportation, etc.	2,000
Foregone income	32,000
Total opportunity cost	$46,000

Exhibit 1.1*a*. This budget bears the heading "out-of-pocket costs" because it includes all the items, and only those items, for which Susan actually makes a cash payment.

Your own out-of-pocket costs for a college education may be considerably higher or lower than these national average figures, but chances are that the items in this budget are the same ones that would come to your mind if you were asked about the matter. As soon as you start to learn the economic way of thinking, though, a different set of items will come to mind. Which of the items in Exhibit 1.1*a* represent opportunities foregone in order to go to college? Are there any foregone opportunities that are missing from the table? To see the answers, look at Exhibit 1.1*b,* which is an opportunity cost budget for Susan, our average student.

The first two items in the out-of-pocket budget show up again in the opportunity cost budget. In order to spend $14,000 on tuition, fees, books, and transportation, Susan has to give up the opportunity to consume an equivalent quantity of other goods, say, to buy a car, make a down payment on a house, or travel to Europe. Not so with the third item in the out-of-pocket budget. By spending $10,000 on room and board while she is in college, this student is not really giving up an opportunity to do something different than she could otherwise have done. Whether she went to college or not, she would have to eat something and live somewhere. Room and board is a cost that she would have to meet in any case and is not a specific opportunity cost of college.

Thinking about what Susan would have done had she not gone to college suggests an item that must be added to the opportunity cost account but that does not show up on the out-of-pocket account. Had she not gone to college, she very likely would have taken a job and begun earning money right after leaving school. Suppose that she had taken a job as, say, a clerk in a local shoe factory and earned $8,000 annually. This potential income—$32,000 over a four-year period—is something that she must give up to attend college. It is part of the opportunity cost of a college education.

Trade-offs[1]

Our discussion of opportunity cost gives us a good chance to show how economists use diagrams to put their ideas across more vividly. In the example we just looked at, we saw that a college education involves certain opportunity costs. That means that for the economy as a whole, there is a trade-off between producing education and producing other goods that people also desire. Let us see how a simple diagram can give us a visual image of what that trade-off is like. Look at Exhibit 1.2. The horizontal

[1]Readers who want a quick brush-up on how to work with graphs may wish to look at the appendix to this chapter (pp. 18–24) before proceeding.

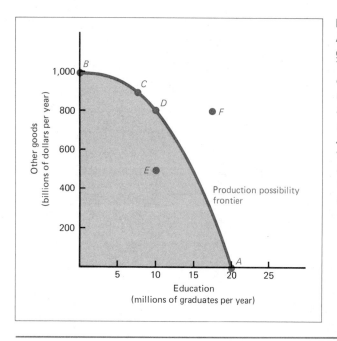

EXHIBIT 1.2
A production possibility frontier for education and other goods.
This diagram shows a production possibility frontier for education and other goods. Point A represents the maximum production of education if no other goods are produced, and point B represents the maximum production of other goods if no education is produced. A, B, C, D, and all other points along the frontier, as well as points such as E in the shaded area under it, are possible. Points such as F, outside the frontier, are not possible given the quantity and quality of factors of production available.

axis of the figure measures the quantity of education produced in terms of the number of college graduates produced per year. The vertical axis measures the production of all other goods in billions of dollars per year. Any combination of education and other goods that were produced in the economy in some year can be shown as a point in the space between the two axes. For example, the production of 10 million college graduates and $500 billion worth of other goods would be represented by point E in Exhibit 1.2.

Production Possibility Frontier

Even if we all devoted all our time and all our resources to producing education, there would be a limit to the quantity of education that could be produced each year. For the sake of illustration, let us suppose this limit to be 20 million graduates per year. This extreme possibility of producing 20 million graduates and nothing else is shown by point A in Exhibit 1.2. Point B in the exhibit shows the maximum rate of output of other goods if no resources at all were put into education and $1,000 billion of other goods were produced. Between these two extreme cases, there is a whole range of possibilities for producing education and other goods in combination. Those intermediate possibilities are represented by points such as C and D, which fall along the curve drawn in the diagram. Such a curve is called a **production possibility frontier.**

This curve is called a *frontier* because it is a boundary between those combinations of education and other goods that can be produced, and those that cannot possibly be produced. Points A, B, C, and D, which lie right on the curve, represent combinations of education and other goods that can be produced. A combination such as that represented by point E in the shaded area under the production possibility frontier can be produced without even making the maximum effort, or even if some resources are used wastefully. In contrast, a combination of education and other goods such

Production Possibility Frontier
A curve showing the possible combinations of goods that can be produced by an economy, given the quantity and quality of factors of production available.

as that represented by point *F* cannot possibly all be produced in one year. All the points outside the shaded area are impossible.

At any point along the production possibility frontier, there is a trade-off between education and other goods. More of one cannot be produced without giving up some of the other. For example, suppose that we began at point *C*, where 8 million students were graduating from college each year and $900 billion of other goods were being produced. If we wanted to increase the output of graduates to 10 million per year, we would have to give up some other goods and use those resources to build classrooms, print books, and staff lecture halls instead. That would move us to point *D*, which represents 10 million graduates and only $800 billion of other goods.

Now we can see how the production possibility curve allows us to visualize the concept of opportunity cost. In moving from *C* to *D* on the production possibility frontier, 2 million extra graduates are obtained at the opportunity cost of $100 billion in other goods. Putting this on a per student basis, we can say that the opportunity cost of college education (in the range between *C* and *D*) is approximately $50,000 per additional graduate. In geometric terms, we can say that the opportunity cost of education, in terms of other goods, is given by the slope of the production possibility frontier.

Factors of Production

It is important to point out that the limits on our range of choice imposed by the production possibility frontier apply only so long as available quantities of **factors of production** do not change. Factors of production are the basic inputs we use in the production of all goods. They include (1) **natural resources**—land with its original fertility and mineral deposits, (2) **labor**—the productive contributions made by people working with their minds and their muscles, and (3) **capital**—all manufactured productive resources, such as tools, industrial equipment, structures, and artificial improvements to land. As time passes and the available quantities of factors of production expand, the production possibility frontier expands too, as shown in Exhibit 1.3.

Improvements in the quality of factors also permit the expansion of production possibilities. The quality of labor done by a given population improves as people become healthier and better educated. The quality of capital increases dramatically as technological change improves equipment and brings new methods of production. Only natural resources do not undergo qualitative improvements; in fact, many actually decline in quality as they are depleted by use. So far, the increases in quantity and quality of other factors has more than made up for the depletion of natural resources. Whether this will continue to be possible is a matter we shall discuss in Chapters 7, 19, and 20 of this book.

Factors of Production The basic inputs of natural resources, labor, and capital used in the production of all goods.

Natural Resources As a factor of production, land with its original fertility and mineral deposits.

Labor As a factor of production, the contributions to production made by people working with their minds and their muscles.

Capital As a factor of production, all manufactured productive resources such as tools, industrial equipment, structures, and artificial improvements to land.

Specialization and the Margin

Specialization

You may have wondered why the production possibility frontier is a curve rather than a straight line. If it were a straight line, that would mean

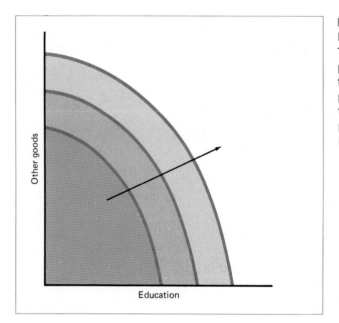

Education

Other goods

EXHIBIT 1.3
Expanding production possibility frontier.
The position of the production possibility frontier at any point in time depends on the quantity and quality of the factors of production available. As time goes by, population grows, new capital is accumulated, and technological change takes place, permitting the production possibility frontier to shift outward, as indicated by the arrow in this diagram.

Homogeneous Having the property that every unit is just like every other unit.

that the opportunity cost of educating an additional college graduate, in terms of other goods, would be the same no matter how people chose to divide their efforts and resources between the two possibilities of production. Why should this not be so?

The answer concerns specialization. Factors of production are not **homogeneous;** that is, the individual units of labor, capital, and natural resources that we have available are different from one another. Individual units of labor—individual people—are the most diverse of all. It is easy to see what this implies.

Imagine that starting today we wanted to increase the output of college graduates. The first thing we would need would be more teachers. The opportunity cost of getting the first few teachers would be low. We could call on professors who had just retired, or on their spouses who might be qualified but not currently working, or on graduate students who could combine teaching with learning. Few other goods would be lost by engaging these people. Next we might turn to industry, and hire chemists, engineers, or economists working there to staff additional classrooms. These people might make very productive teachers, but they would be sorely missed by the firms that had employed them, and there would be a noticeable drop in the output of other goods. The opportunity cost of education would rise, and the production possibility curve would begin to bend as we moved along it. Pretty soon we would have to start calling in people who were not even well qualified to be teachers, even though they might be doing a good job at something else. These people would not add much at all to the output of education, but a lot would be lost elsewhere. The production possibility frontier would bend still more sharply. In short, we see that differences of ability and specialization among people (and also differences among units of other factors) can be counted on to give the production possibility frontier its typical bowed-out shape.

The Division of Labor

People are not interchangeable parts, so we must pay careful attention to the division of labor if we are to do well in our struggle with the pervasive problem of scarcity. Once again let us use our handy tool, the production possibility frontier, to show why. Suppose that for some reason or other we chose to devote half the nation's labor power to producing education and half to producing other goods, but that we used the wrong half in each place. Skilled production workers would awkwardly mumble their way through lecture notes on Greek history, while professors got their thumbs jammed in delicate factory machinery. What would happen is that we would not produce as much as possible of either education or other goods. The economy would drop right off the production possibility frontier and end up at some interior point, such as point *A* in Exhibit 1.4. Just by using the proper division of labor, we could produce the output combination indicated by point *B* instead, and have more of both goods.

More than 200 years ago, Adam Smith began the most famous economics book of all time with an example emphasizing the importance of the division of labor. Smith had visited a pin factory and had seen how when one man specialized in putting heads on the pins, another in sharpening the points, another in placing them on cards, and so forth, they all together could produce 100 times more than could the same number of men working separately. Smith went on to show how free markets and private enterprise solve the problem of the division of labor. We shall spend many chapters doing the same ourselves (beginning with Chapter 2) and have time left over for a look at how governments sometimes try to improve on the market by substituting their own judgments concerning the division of labor.

EXHIBIT 1.4
Effects of a poorly organized division of labor.
Poor organization of the division of labor can cause the economy to drop off the production possibility frontier and end up at an interior point such as *A* in this diagram. Just by getting the division of labor right, more of both goods could be produced, as at point *B*.

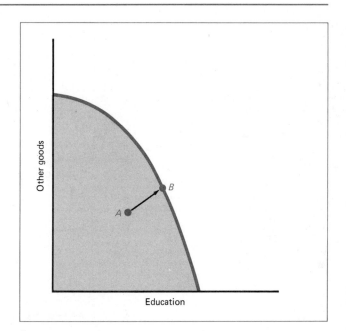

Adam Smith (1723–1790)

Adam Smith was born in Kirkaldy, on the east coast of Scotland. He studied first at Glasgow University, and then at Oxford. In those days, the universities of Scotland were greater centers of learning than those of England, so Smith returned to the north after finishing his studies at Oxford, and obtained a chair at Glasgow. It was not, of course, a chair in economics. Economics had not yet been invented as a distinct discipline, and besides, it was not yet Smith's major interest. His specialty was moral philosophy.

During his long career, Smith wrote just two books. It was his good fortune, however, to have both bring him immediate fame. Smith's first book was *The Theory of Moral Sentiments,* published in 1759. His second, *The Wealth of Nations,* appeared seventeen years later, in 1776. David Hume, a friend of Smith's, commented that "the reading of it necessarily requires so much attention, and the public is disposed to give so little, that I shall still doubt for some time of its being at first very popular." Hume, however, was wrong. The book sold well from the start.

The task Smith sets himself first of all is to explain the workings of the economic system, that is, the sources of the "wealth of nations." The greatest source, he discovers, is the division of labor. Chapter 1 opens with the observation that "the greatest improvement in the productive powers of labor, and the greater part of the skill, dexterity, and judgment with which it is anywhere directed, or applied, seem to have been the effects of the division of labor." He then goes on to give his famous pin factory example.

It is not enough for Smith to just describe the division of labor, however. He wants to explain how the division of labor comes about. His explanation is highly characteristic. "This division of labor, from which so many advantages are derived, is not originally the effect of any human wisdom, which foresees and intends that general opulence to which it gives occasion. It is the necessary, though very slow and gradual consequence of a certain propensity in human nature which has in view no such extensive utility; the propensity to truck, barter, and exchange one thing for another." Here, for the first time in the book, Smith emphasizes the importance of the unintended consequences of human action. Each person acting in the marketplace has only his narrow ends in mind, but the joint result of the actions of everyone is a general benefit that none intended.

As the *Wealth of Nations* progresses, Smith adds another theme, that of the benefits of economic liberty. The free, spontaneous interaction of people in the marketplace is not just one way to bring about the general benefit of mankind—it is the best way. Government attempts to guide or regulate the market end up doing more harm than good. Smith especially attacks the privileges of legally protected monopolies, the Poor Laws (which he saw as inhibiting the mobility of labor), and the apprenticeship system (which worked against free entry into occupations). All such restraints on the market tended to force trade into "unnatural" and less beneficial channels.

Smith's book has meant various things to various people. To some it has been a handbook of laissez-faire liberalism. To others, it has been the fountainhead of economic science. Still others have found it, not without reason, to be unoriginal and crammed with errors. Whatever its faults, it is a book that continues to be read and debated. In 1976, its bicentennial brought leading economists from all over the world to Glasgow to pay tribute to the absent-minded professor of moral philosophy who had lectured there so long before.

The Margin

Next we come to an element of the economic way of thinking that was not around in Adam Smith's day but that has become very important since.

That is the idea of the **margin.** Whenever economists talk about the margin or use the adjective "marginal," they are talking about the effects of making a small increase or decrease in some economic activity. "Margin" is an idea that is hard to define abstractly but easy to illustrate. When we talk about "the marginal cost" of producing cars at General Motors, we are referring to the added cost of producing one more car beyond the limit of the number currently being produced. When we speak of the "marginal benefit" of sewage treatment in a certain river basin, we mean the benefit of making a small increase in the effort put into sewage treatment in the area. These particular terms and quite a few more will be defined more precisely when we come to them in later chapters. For now, though, let us look at just one example that will give us a general idea of why thinking in terms of the margin is important.

Margin, Marginal Terms referring to the effects of making a small increase in any economic activity. See specific glossary entries under *marginal cost, marginal product,* etc.

CASE 1.2
The Marginal Cost of Oil

Ever since the oil crisis of 1974, we have all become very much concerned about the cost of oil. But what is "the" cost of producing oil? That depends on where you extract it. There are fields in the Middle East and in Texas and Oklahoma where getting oil out of the ground costs practically nothing. There are medium-cost fields, such as those where such secondary recovery methods as pumping live steam down the wells to make the oil more liquid are used. And there are high-cost fields, such as those in Alaska or under the North Sea, where oil is very expensive to extract, especially when the necessary environmental safeguards are taken. To repeat, then, of all this range of figures, what is "the" cost of oil?

The economist's answer to this question is that the cost that counts is the *marginal cost* of oil. The marginal cost of oil means the cost per barrel of getting a few additional tons of oil, given the efforts that are already being made. Because easy fields are usually exploited to capacity before the hard ones are tapped, the marginal cost of oil means the cost of getting it where it is hardest to get, say, in Alaska or the North Sea.

In the United States today, special price control laws keep the market price of oil below its marginal cost and close to its cost of production as averaged over good fields and bad fields alike. When important decisions are to be made, though, thinking in terms of the artificially low controlled price can lead to mistakes. Suppose, for instance, that a government economist were trying to decide whether to increase spending on solar energy research. Solar energy costs more than energy from the oil that is pumped from average fields, but with just a little more research and development, it is likely to cost less than energy from the most expensive Alaskan or North Sea oil. If the solar energy decision were made on the basis of the low, controlled price, solar power research might seem uneconomical, but that is wrong. Each extra barrel of oil burned has to be replaced not from average fields—those that are already running at capacity—but from the most difficult fields. As long as there is a hope that additional research can bring the cost of solar energy down to or below the *marginal* cost of oil, that research is worthwhile.

Economic Science and Economic Policy

A great part of what one reads about economics in the newspapers or hears about economics on television is focused on specific problems of economic policy. Should the federal government spend more money and run a larger budget deficit? Should price controls on oil be lifted in the hope of increasing production and decreasing consumption? Should the government encourage or discourage exports of American agricultural products? If we are to learn the economic way of thinking, we must learn how economists think about policy issues as well as how they think about pure theory.

The mention of economic policies such as price controls or budget deficits tends to set little lights labeled "hurrah" or "ugh" flashing in our minds. Sometimes our mental circuits work so fast that we do not notice that between the mention of the policy and the flashing of the lights, a chain of thinking somewhat like the following must occur:

1. If policy X is followed, outcome Y will result.
2. Outcome Y is a good (or a bad) thing.
3. Therefore, hurrah! (or ugh!) for policy X.

In order to understand the contents of this book and how to put what you learn to work as a citizen or in public life, it is very important to understand the logic of this three-step chain of thinking. Let us go through it one step at a time.

Positive Economics

Economic science cannot foretell the future, but it can offer predictions of the limited, "if . . . , then . . ." form: "If A occurs, then B will occur, other things being equal." An economist might, then, make the assertion: "If government spending were increased, then unemployment would decline, as long as no other changes in economic conditions occur in the meantime." Such a statement is sometimes called a **scientific prediction.** It is a statement of cause and effect, but one that is valid only under specified conditions. In making scientific predictions of the "If A, then B, other things being equal" form, economists rarely attempt to foretell whether or not A will actually occur or whether other things will actually remain constant.

When economists limit their attention to statements that are pure scientific predictions, they are said to be practicing **positive economics.** All sound analysis of economic policy must begin with positive economics as step number one.

Resolving Disagreements

Of course, economists sometimes disagree on whether a certain scientific prediction is valid. In fact, a great deal of the day-to-day work in which economists engage is directed toward resolving disagreements on matters of positive economics. Some scientific disagreements among economists concern matters of pure theory and are much like the disagreements among mathematicians concerning whether some unproved theorem is true or false. These disputes can, in time, be resolved by a process in which each party tries to state as carefully as possible the reasoning that seems to lead to a certain conclusion, while others try to verify the reasoning or to detect logical errors.

Very frequently, economists try to resolve disputes over matters of positive economics by looking carefully at past experience. Much of this work is done by specialists in the statistical analysis of economic data who are

Scientific Prediction A conditional prediction having the form "if A, then B, other things being equal."

Positive Economics That part of economics limited to making scientific predictions and purely descriptive statements.

called **econometricians.** Suppose that the scientific prediction in dispute were one that said: "If government spending were to increase, then unemployment would decline, other things being equal." An econometrician might enter the debate with the announcement that according to a study of postwar data taken from the American economy, an increase in government expenditure has, in fact, been consistently associated with a decline in unemployment, taking into account the probable influence of other factors. Or the econometrician might, instead, assert that the data reveal no systematic association at all between government spending and unemployment when advanced statistical techniques are used to eliminate the influence of other changes in economic conditions. Questions of this sort are not usually resolved by a single econometric study, but repeated studies and the gradual accumulation of evidence serve to narrow areas of disagreement and contribute to scientific progress in economics.

Econometrician An expert in the statistical analysis of economic data.

Normative Economics

A positive economic statement of the type "if policy X, then outcome Y" cannot by itself resolve the issue of whether policy X is desirable. To come to a conclusion on the desirability of the policy, one must decide whether the outcome Y is good or bad. When economists make statements of the type "outcome Y is good," they are engaging in **normative economics.**

Most economists do not consider themselves experts in ethical theory, and few economists would be prepared to defend their normative statements with the same rigor and clarity as they would use to defend their positive economic analysis. Nonetheless, economists who wish to speak persuasively on the subject of economic policy should be able at least to point to some general ethical principles on which their normative conclusions might plausibly be based. Economists who base their liking or disliking of a particular policy on arbitrary whims are less likely to be listened to than are economists who speak in terms of consistent and well-thought-out values. With this in mind, let us look at a few basic ideas that frequently arise in discussions of normative economics.

Normative Economics That part of economics devoted to making value judgments about what economic policies or conditions are good or bad.

The Efficiency Standard

The standard of **efficiency** occupies a prominent place among those by which economists judge the performance of the systems they observe. In its most general sense, the word "efficiency" means the property of producing or acting with a minimum of expense, waste, and effort. We gave a good economic example of the difference between efficiency and inefficiency in Exhibit 1.4. That diagram showed how a badly organized division of labor could cause the economy to drop off the production possibility frontier and end up at an *inefficient* interior point. A better division of labor would have permitted the production of more output with the same quantities of inputs and thus would have been more efficient.

Efficiency The property of producing or acting with a minimum of expense, waste, and effort.

Efficiency and Equity

Most economists think that efficiency is, in itself, a good thing. This does not mean, however, that any economic policy that promotes efficiency is automatically a good policy. Other norms and values must be introduced into policy analysis to supplement the efficiency standard. Among the most important of these supplementary standards are those to which we refer in everyday speech as equity, merit, and justice.

The standard of equity has two roles to play in relation to that of efficiency. First, it may be used to supplement the efficiency standard in cases where the choice to be made is between policies that are equally efficient. Efficiency alone does not define a single, unique pattern of economic life but only a range of possible patterns. Different but equally efficient patterns often involve different distributions of welfare among specific individuals. In one efficient state of the world, Jones may be rich and Smith poor; in another, Smith may be rich and Jones poor; and in a third, Jones and Smith may be equally well off. When such alternatives confront us, we may be led to reason like this:

1. Policies X and Y produce equally efficient outcomes but imply different distributions of individual welfare.
2. The distributional outcome of policy X is more equitable.
3. Therefore, let us undertake policy X.

A second possible use for the criterion of equity is to override that of efficiency. For many people, efficiency is not a goal that should be pursued at the expense of equity but rather should, if needed, be sacrificed to the pursuit of equity. In such cases, our logic might run as follows:

1. Policy X would be bad for efficiency but would help achieve greater equity.
2. The loss of efficiency is unfortunate, but the gain in equity outweighs it.
3. Therefore, in the absence of a policy that will serve both goals at once, let us go ahead with policy X.

A Difficulty

Whichever way it is used, the concept of equity plays an important role in policy analysis. Using it involves a difficulty, however, that did not bother us in the case of efficiency. The difficulty is that equity has no universally agreed-upon meaning. It means different things to different people, depending on the values they hold and the ideologies they profess. Few things are more harmful to intelligent debate on questions of economic policy than for two parties to a discussion to use the same word to mean different things. The word "equity," and the associated terms "merit" and "justice," are possibly the cause of more misunderstanding than are any other terms in economics.

In the interest of avoiding such misunderstanding, we might wish to establish beyond doubt that one particular meaning of the term "equity" is the right one. But to attempt this would take us deep into details of philosophy and far from the main subject of this book. Instead we shall, more modestly, simply suggest two alternative meanings of the equity concept (or, rather, two classes of meanings within which there are many minor variations) without authoritatively choosing between them.

Equity as Distributive Justice

The first meaning of "equity" makes equity equivalent to **distributive justice.** The popular phrase, "from each according to his abilities, to each

Distributive Justice The principle of distribution according to innate merit or, roughly, the principle of "from each according to his abilities, to each according to his needs."

according to his needs," gives us a rough idea of what the principle of distributive justice means. The concept of distributive justice is based on the idea of innate merit; that is, all people are presumed, solely by virtue of their birth, their existence, and their common humanity, to merit some share of the total stream of goods and services turned out by the economic system. We could improve the popular phrase by making it read "to each according to his innate merits."

Just what each person's innate merits are is a point that gives rise to many variations on the idea of distributive justice. For example, some people believe that all economic goods should be distributed equally among all members of society. This view is known as **egalitarianism.** Others think that a person's innate claims on economic goods ought to be limited to some minimum standard of living and would be willing to see any surplus above this minimum distributed according to other principles. Still others conceive of innate merits as being limited to certain specific types of goods. Each person might have, for example, an innate claim to a share of food, shelter, medical care, and education, but no such claim to even a minimum share of tobacco, imported wine, or manicuring services.

Egalitarianism The principle that economic goods should be distributed equally among all members of society.

Equity as Market Justice

The second meaning of the concept of equity makes equity equivalent to what we can call **market justice.** The justice of the marketplace is *value for value.* Market justice is based on the idea of acquired merit. Individuals have no innate claims to a share in the total economic output but merit only whatever share they acquire through production, exchange, or voluntary donation.

Market Justice The principle of distribution according to acquired merit. The observance of property rights and the honoring of contracts. Roughly, the principle of "value for value."

The idea of market justice gives a special significance to the concepts of property and contract. Suppose that the entire mass of economic goods is divided up as the properties of specific individuals (or voluntary associations of individuals), so that for every loaf of bread, some person stands ready to say "this bread is mine—my property to use and to exclude others from the use of." Then the central meaning of "market justice" becomes the movement of property from hand to hand only by fair contract (except for voluntary gifts). By "fair contract," we mean that each party must be satisfied that the value to him of the property he receives is at least as great as the value of the property he gives. Market justice may be summed up as the observance of property rights and the honoring of contracts.

Economic Ideology

Each person carries out the job of policy analysis, whether in a systematic or a casual way, within a personal framework of thought that, for lack of a better term, we might call an **economic ideology.** An economic ideology includes a person's judgments concerning the relative priority (and exact interpretation) of distributive justice and market justice and attitudes toward the relative importance of equity and efficiency as goals of economic policy. An economic ideology often also includes a set of prejudices and more or less rationally founded beliefs concerning matters of positive economics. Liberalism, Marxism, libertarianism, conservatism—these and many other "isms" are the labels we use to refer to economic ideologies.

Economic Ideology A set of judgments and beliefs concerning efficiency, market justice, and distributive justice as goals of economic policy, together with a set of prejudices or beliefs concerning matters of positive economics.

To deal with every policy issue from all possible ideological points of view would be too much for us to attempt in this book. Instead, we shall, for the most part, content ourselves with pointing out the implications of various policies in terms of the standards of efficiency and equity we have just discussed. Readers will have to reach their own conclusions on the ideological level.

Why Distinguish?

When policy analysis is broken down into a three-step process, in which positive and normative elements are clearly separated, orderly debate on important economic issues is made easier in several ways.

First, the breakdown of policy analysis into positive and normative components makes it clear that disagreements on policy questions can arise from two different sources. If you and I disagree as to whether policy X is good or bad, it may be either because we disagree on the positive issue of whether X will, in fact, result in outcome Y, or because we disagree on the normative issue of whether Y is good or bad. Our analysis also indicates that a particular sort of spurious agreement could arise between us: You might think that X will cause Y and that Y is good, whereas I think Y is bad but that X will not cause it! This sort of thing occurs surprisingly often. In any event, it is clear that intelligent policy analysis requires careful thinking.

Second, if a positive statement is associated with an unpopular normative position, it is less likely to gain acceptance. Critics must be persuaded that both are valid. We are less likely to pay serious attention to the claim that fluoridation of water harms our bodies when its opponents also claim that fluoridation is an evil communist plot. A positive statement divorced from any normative view is not disadvantaged in this way.

Third, when a positive statement is associated with a very popular normative position, it may be accepted too uncritically. Why? It is because reactions to value judgments are much more pronounced than are reactions to positive statements, so that value judgments surreptitiously tend to dominate our thought. We are all too likely to accept a "what is" statement from someone who agrees with us about "what ought to be." This natural reaction helps, for example, to explain the inability of economists to persuade politicians that increases in the legal minimum wage have worsened the employment opportunities of poor people.[2] Politicians say they want to help the poor and resent being informed that a method they support has not worked. Perhaps they even suspect that economists critical of minimum wages do not share their values. They mistakenly believe that minimum wage laws help the poor simply because they believe that the poor ought to be helped.

Conclusions

In a once-over fashion, we have tried to give some idea of the kinds of things to which economists are sensitive when they look at the world around them.

---

[2]Minimum wage laws are discussed in Chapter 15.

We have learned that economists think in terms of scarcity, choice, and trade-offs. We have seen some simple examples of how economists use diagrams to make it easier to visualize abstract concepts in a concrete form. We have seen how to distinguish between positive and normative economics and why that distinction is important. What can we say now to sum it all up?

If there is one single feature of overriding importance about the economic way of thinking, it is this: *Economics is about people.* Individual people are the units of analysis in all economic theory. Every economic principle that we develop in this book must be a statement about the way that individuals make choices, struggle with the problem of scarcity, and respond to changes in their environment. And all economic policies must be judged in terms of their impact on the welfare of individual people.

This does not mean that economists are all "rugged individualists," in the sense that they do not care about social issues, or that they are political know-nothings who do not care about the national interest. What it does mean is that economic science (and all valid social science, for that matter) is based on the recognition that "society" and "the nation" have no existence and no importance apart from the individual people of which they are composed. "Society" is not a super-being, and "the nation" is not a sentient creature capable of feeling pain when a pin is stuck in the national thumb. They are only the names of groups of which you, I, and all the rest of us are equally members. *We* are what economics is all about.

SUMMARY

1. The economic way of thinking is less a matter of the way economists think than a matter of the things they think about. In looking at ordinary situations in the world about them, economists are sensitive to the ways in which such considerations as scarcity and opportunity cost influence the ways in which people relate to one another.
2. The production possibility frontier shows which combinations of goods can be produced and which cannot. The slope of the production possibility frontier shows the opportunity cost of the good measured on the horizontal axis in terms of the good measured on the vertical axis. The position of the production possibility frontier depends on the quantity and quality of factors of production available to an economy. Over time, the production possibility frontier may expand and the economy may grow. If the division of labor is not organized efficiently, the economy may drop off the production possibility frontier and end up at an interior point.
3. Positive economics cannot foretell the future, but it can offer scientific predictions in the form "if A occurs, then B will occur, other things being equal." Disputes in positive economics can, in principle, be resolved by reasoned discussion or by the examination of statistical data.
4. Normative economics is concerned with statements about what ought to be. Most economists think that efficiency is, in itself, a worthy goal of economic policy. The efficiency standard must, however, be supplemented by considerations of equity when policy decisions are to be made. There is no universal agreement on what equity means. Some economists maintain that equity is primarily a matter of distributive justice. Others emphasize market justice. Partly because of such disagreements on the meaning of equity, economists try to distinguish carefully between their positive statements and their normative statements.

5. Economics is about people. All economic principles must be framed in terms of the way individuals make choices and respond to changes in their environment, and all economic policies must be judged in terms of their impact on the welfare of individual people.

DISCUSSION QUESTIONS

1. Suppose that you want to get as high a grade-point average as you can this term, yet your time and abilities are limited. Would it be possible to look at the way you spend your time as an economic problem? What is the opportunity cost of getting higher grades?
2. Suppose that you won a lottery prize of $20 million. Would this solve all of your personal economic problems? Explain.
3. Can you give some real-world examples of how the economy, a firm, or even an individual might be operating on the interior of its respective production possibilities curve?
4. Do you think it is possible to achieve both efficiency and equity in the real world? Or is this another economic problem in which it is necessary to sacrifice one for the other? Explain.
5. Could we say that economics is about money, or about goods and services, rather than about people? Explain.
6. Do the animals in a forest face an economic problem? What are their objectives, constraints, and alternatives? What has happened to their economic problems as people have impinged on their habitat? Is economics about nonpeople too?
7. Should we all be entitled to our fair share of the earth's produce? Would this question be better stated if we replaced the phrase, "the earth's produce," with "the goods and services that Smith and Jones and Jansen and M'Boye and Li Ha Ching and . . . (listing all the earth's 4 billion people by name) produce"? To make it still easier, suppose that Smith and Jones are the only two people on earth. Is Smith entitled to a fair share of what Jones produces and vice versa?
8. List several problems that you think you will be better able to analyze after reading this book.

Appendix
Working with Graphs

How Economists Use Graphs

At one of our country's well-known colleges, the students have their own names for all the courses. They call the astronomy course "stars," the geology course "rocks," and the biology course "frogs." Their name for the economics course is "graphs and laughs." This choice of names indicates two things. First, it says that the students think the professor has a noteworthy sense of humor. Second, it shows that in the minds of students, economics is a matter of "learning about graphs" in the same sense that astronomy is a matter of learning about stars, or geology a matter of learning about rocks.

Let us begin, then, by saying that economics is not "about" graphs. Economics is about people. It is about the way that people make choices, use resources, and cooperate with one another in an effort to overcome the universal problem of scarcity. Economics is a social science, not an offshoot of analytic geometry.

Well, the skeptical reader may say, "If economics is not about graphs, why are there so many of them in this book?" The answer is that economists use graphs to illustrate the theories they develop about people's economic behavior in order to make them vivid, eye-catching, and easy to remember. Everything that can be said in the form of a graph can also be said in words, but saying something twice in two different ways is a proven aid to learning. The purpose of this appendix is to help you to be able to make maximum use of an important learning aid by explaining how to work with graphs.

Pairs of Numbers and Points

The first thing to learn is how to use points on a graph to represent pairs of numbers. Consider Exhibit 1.5. The small table in that exhibit presents six pairs of numbers. The two columns in the table are labeled x and y. The first number in each pair is called the x value, and the second is called the y value. Each *pair* of numbers is labeled with a capital letter A through E. Pair A has an x value of 2 and a y value of 3; pair B has an x value of 4 and a y value of 4, and so forth.

Next to the table in Exhibit 1.5 is a diagram. First look at the lines placed at right angles to one another along the bottom and the left-hand side of the diagram. These are called *coordinate axes*. The horizontal axis is marked off into units and is used for measuring the x value, while the vertical axis is marked off into units for measuring the y value. In the space between these axes, we can represent each lettered pair of numbers from the table as a lettered point. For example, to put point A in place we go two units to the right along the horizontal axis to represent the x value of 2, and then three units straight up, parallel to the vertical axis, to represent the y value of 3. The other points are placed the same way.

Very often the visual effect of a graph is improved by connecting the points we have located by a smooth line or curve. When this is done (as shown in the diagram) we can see at a glance that as the x value increases, the y value also tends to increase.

EXHIBIT 1.5

Pairs of numbers and points

Each lettered pair of numbers in the table corresponds to a lettered point on the graph. The x value of each point corresponds to the horizontal distance of the point from the vertical axis, and the y value to the vertical distance from the horizontal axis.

	x	y
A	2	3
B	4	4
C	6	5
D	8	6
E	10	7

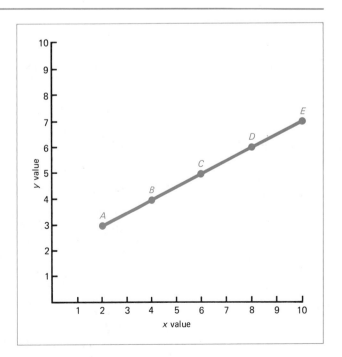

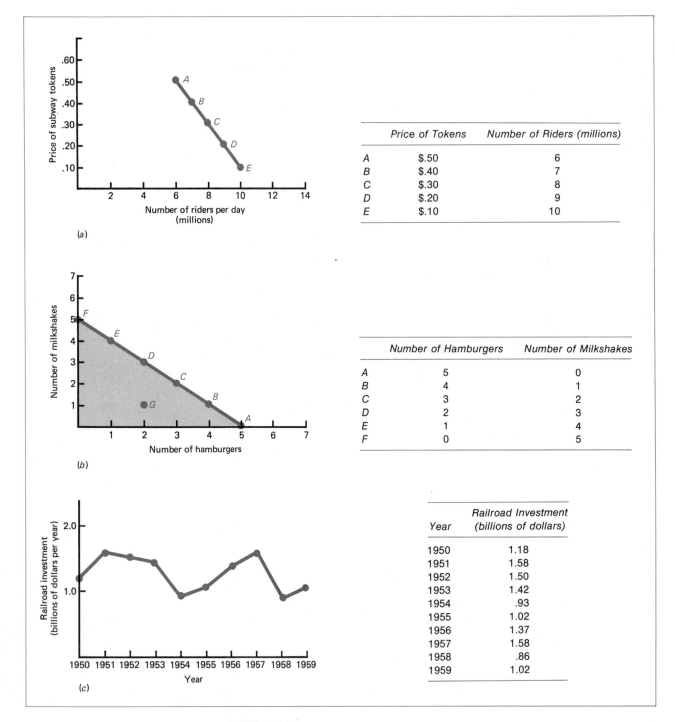

	Price of Tokens	Number of Riders (millions)
A	$.50	6
B	$.40	7
C	$.30	8
D	$.20	9
E	$.10	10

	Number of Hamburgers	Number of Milkshakes
A	5	0
B	4	1
C	3	2
D	2	3
E	1	4
F	0	5

Year	Railroad Investment (billions of dollars)
1950	1.18
1951	1.58
1952	1.50
1953	1.42
1954	.93
1955	1.02
1956	1.37
1957	1.58
1958	.86
1959	1.02

EXHIBIT 1.6
Three typical economic graphs.
This exhibit shows three graphs typical of those used in economics. Part *a* shows the relationship between the price of tokens and the number of riders per day on a certain city subway system. When a graph shows the relationship between a price and a quantity, it is conventional to put the price on the vertical axis. Part *b* shows the possible choices open to a person who has $1 to spend on lunch, and can buy hamburgers at $.20 each or milkshakes at $.20 each. Part *c* shows how a graph can be used to represent change over time.

Source: (c) Economic Report of the President, 1976, Table B-38.

Common Economic Graphs

In economics, we are not interested in abstract relationships between x's and y's but, rather, in relationships concerning people and the things they do under various conditions. This means that graphs in economics are labeled in terms of the ideas used in putting together economic theories. Exhibit 1.6 shows three very common ways of labeling coordinate axes. Each of these will be encountered many times in this book.

In Exhibit 1.6a, we have represented the relationship between the price of subway tokens in some city and the number of people who would choose to ride the subway each day at any given price. The table shows that as the price of tokens goes up, fewer people choose to ride the subway. The graph shows the same thing. As a matter of tradition in economics, whenever we draw a graph where both money values and quantity units are involved, we use the vertical axis to measure the money values (in this case, the price of subway tokens) and the horizontal axis to measure the quantity units (in this case, the number of riders per day).

Exhibit 1.6b uses quantity units on both axes. Here our problem is to represent the various combinations of milkshakes and hamburgers that a student can buy at the local carry-out when milkshakes cost $.20 each, hamburgers cost $.20 each, and the student has exactly $1 to spend on her lunch. The table shows that she can buy five burgers and no shakes, four burgers and one shake, three burgers and two shakes, and so forth.

The graph gives us a visual picture of the "menu" the student has available to choose from, given the limited money she has to spend. The points from the table are drawn in and labeled. Our student can choose any of these. A diagonal line has been sketched in to connect these points, and if we allow the purchase of parts of hamburgers and milkshakes, the student can choose from among all the points along this line. (For example, she could buy 2½ burgers and 2½ shakes.) If she wanted to have some money left over, she could buy a lunch represented by a point within the shaded area, such as point G. (Point G stands for two hamburgers and one shake, and costs only $.60.) But unless she gets some more money, our student cannot choose from points outside the shaded area.

Exhibit 1.6c shows still another kind of graph frequently used in economics. Here we are interested in how some economic magnitude changes over time. The table gives data on railroad investment over a series of ten years. The graph is drawn using time on the horizontal axis and billions of dollars per year on the vertical axis to give a visual representation of the ups and downs of railroad investment.

Slopes

When we are talking about graphs, it is frequently convenient to describe lines or curves in terms of their *slopes*. The slope of a straight line drawn between two points is defined as the ratio of the change in the y value to the change in the x value between two points. In Exhibit 1.7, for example, the slope of the line drawn between points A and B is 2. The y value changes by six units between these two points, while the x value changes by only three units. The slope is the ratio $6/3 = 2$. When a line slants downward like the line between points C and D in Exhibit 1.7, the x value and the y value change in opposite directions. As we go from point C to point D, the y value changes by -2 (that is, it decreases by two units), while the x value changes by $+4$ (that is, it increases by four units). The slope of this line is the ratio $-2/4 = -1/2$. This type of a line is said to have a negative slope.

We can also speak of the slope of a curved line, but we must remember that the slope of a curved line varies from point to point. The slope of a curve at any given point is defined as the slope of a straight line drawn tangent to the curve at that point. (A tangent line is one just touching the curve without crossing it.) Consider the curve in Exhibit 1.8. Applying our definition, we see that the slope of this line at point A is 1, and its slope at point B is -2.

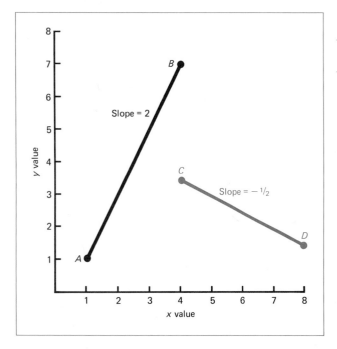

EXHIBIT 1.7
Slopes of lines.
The slope of a straight line drawn between two points is defined as the ratio of the change in the *y* value to the change in the *x* value between the two points. For example, the line drawn between points *A* and *B* in this exhibit has a slope of +2, whereas the line drawn between points *C* and *D* has a slope of −½.

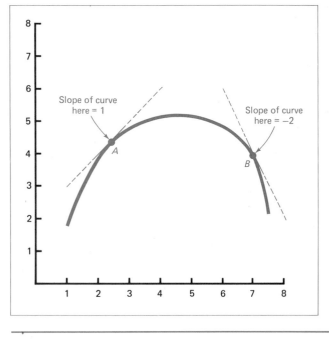

EXHIBIT 1.8
Slopes of curves.
The slope of a curve at any given point is defined as the slope of a straight line drawn tangent to the curve at that point. A tangent line is one that just touches the curve without crossing it. In this exhibit, the slope of the curve at point *A* is 1, and the slope of the curve at point *B* is −2.

Abstract Graphs

In all our examples so far, we have had specific numbers to work with for the *x* and *y* values. Sometimes, though, we only know the general nature of the relationship between two economic magnitudes without knowing specific numbers. For example, we might know that when people's incomes rise, they tend to increase their consumption of meat rapidly at first, but then as very high incomes are reached, their meat consumption levels off. If we want to represent a relationship like this without getting specific about the numbers involved, we draw a graph

EXHIBIT 1.9

An abstract graph.

When we know the general form of an economic relationship but do not know the exact numbers involved, we can draw an abstract graph. Here we know that as people's income rises, their consumption of meat increases rapidly at first, and then levels off. Because we do not know the exact numbers for meat consumption or income, we have not marked any units on the axes.

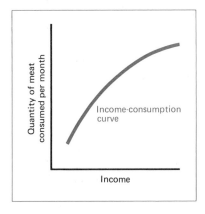

like that shown in Exhibit 1.9. The vertical axis is just labeled "income" without any units, and the horizontal axis "meat" without any units. The curve, which rises rapidly at first and then levels off, tells us the general nature of the relationship between income and meat consumption. We shall use abstract graphs like this one very frequently in this book. Abstract graphs are used to express general principles, whereas graphs with numbers on the axes are used to summarize specific known information.

Study Hints for Graphs

When you come to a chapter in this book that is full of graphs, how should you study it? The first and most important rule is *do not ever memorize graphs*. I have never taught economics without having at least one student come to me after failing an exam and say, "But I learned every one of those graphs! What happened?" I always tell those students that they should have learned the economics instead of learning the graphs, or else that they should have taken analytical geometry instead.

Here are some specific study hints for working with graphs. After you have read carefully through a chapter that uses graphs frequently, go back through the graphs one at a time. Put your hand over the explanatory note that appears beside each graph and try putting what the graph says into words. If you cannot say at least as much in words about the graph as the explanatory note says, read the text over again.

If you do all right going from graphs to words, half the battle is won. Next, try covering up the graph and, using the explanatory note as a guide, sketch the graph on a piece of scratch paper. If you understand what the words mean and can comfortably go back and forth between the words and the graphs, you will find out that the two together are much easier to remember and apply than either would be separately. If you "learn the graphs" as meaningless patterns of lines, you are lost.

Constructing Your Own Graphs

For some students, the hardest kind of question to answer on an exam is the kind that requires construction of an original graph as part of an essay answer. Here are some hints for constructing your own graphs.

1. Put down in words the answer to the question. If you cannot do that, you might as well skip on to the next question without wasting time on the graph. Try underlining the most important quantities in what you have written. The result might be something like: "The larger the *number of students* who attend a university, the lower the *cost per student* of providing them with an education."

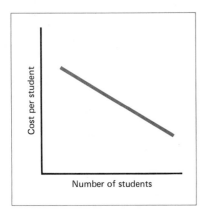

EXHIBIT 1.10
Constructing a graph.
To construct a graph, first put down in words what you want to say: "The larger the *number of students* at a university, the lower the *cost per student* of providing them with an education." Next, label the coordinate axes. Then, if you have exact numbers to work with, construct a table. Here we have no exact numbers, so we draw an abstract graph that slopes downward to show that cost goes down as numbers go up. For graphs with more than one curve, repeat these steps.

2. Decide how you are going to label the coordinate axes of your graph. In our example, because it is conventional to put money values on the vertical axis, we shall label the vertical axis "cost per student" and the horizontal axis "number of students."

3. Do you have exact numbers to work with? If you do, your next step should be to make a table showing what you know and then to use that to sketch your graph. If you do not have numbers, you will be drawing an abstract graph. In this case, all you know is that costs per student go down when the number of students goes up. Sketch in any convenient downward-sloping line (as in Exhibit 1.10), and you will have done as well as can be done.

4. If your graph involves more than one relationship between pairs of economic quantities, repeat steps 1–3 for each relationship that you want to represent by a line or curve. When sketching graphs with more than one curve, pay particular attention to points where you think two curves ought to intersect (which will happen whenever both the x and y values of the two relationships are equal) and to points where you think they ought to be tangent (which will happen whenever the slopes of two curves are equal).

5. After your graph is completed, try translating it back into words. Does it really say what you wanted it to say?

Conclusion

That is about all we can say about graphs in general. As you work through this book and are introduced to various specific kinds of graphs, turn back to this appendix now and then. Do not commit the fatal error of memorizing graphs as meaningless pictures. Do remember that if you can go back and forth between graphs and words, the underlying theory that both are trying to express will stay with you more vividly than if you rely on either graphs or words alone. Do remember that economics is about *people,* not graphs.

CHAPTER 2
The Price System and the Market Economy

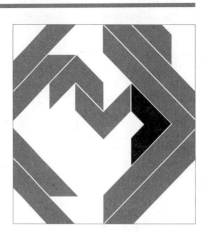

What You Will Learn in This Chapter
Resource allocation means determining what will be produced, how it will be produced, who will produce it, and for whom it will be produced. In the American economy, most resource allocation decisions are made in markets. Markets perform three major functions. They act as mechanisms for utilizing knowledge, as sources of incentives, and as windows on the future.

When economists speak of the **allocation of resources,** they mean the determination of *what* will be produced, *how* it will be produced, *who* will produce it, and *for whom* it will be produced. Millions of people are involved in finding the answers to these questions, and the interaction of all that they do determines, in turn, the whole course of economic life.

In the American economy, most resource allocation decisions are made by people acting in **markets.** By "markets" we mean all of the various arrangements that people have for trading with one another. Markets may be very elaborately organized, like the New York Stock Exchange, with its computers and ticker-tape machines, or very informal, like the word-of-mouth network that puts teenage babysitters in touch with the people who need them.

However markets are organized, they play an important role in determining *what, how, who,* and *for whom.* Businesspeople look to markets for clues as to *what* can be sold and, accordingly, *what* to produce. They look at the markets where factors of production can be bought and decide *how* to make their products at the least cost, given the prices of those factors. The question of *who* is to produce what is decided by millions of working men and women who search on the job market for the opportunities best suited to their interests and abilities. And as to the matter of *for whom* it is all produced, the answer, for the most part, is for whoever is willing and able to buy things at the price for which they are put up for sale.

Because so many important economic decisions are made in the marketplace, it is a wise custom among writers of economic textbooks to devote a few early chapters to a general overview of the theory of prices and markets before proceeding to more specialized topics. We shall follow that custom here, in this chapter and the next.

Allocation The distribution or assignment of things to specific uses. In economics, the term *resource allocation* means determining what will be produced, how it will be produced, who will produce it, and for whom it will be produced.

Markets A general term referring to all of the various arrangements that people have for trading with one another.

Markets as Mechanisms
for Utilizing Knowledge

The insight that markets are, first and foremost, *mechanisms for utilizing knowledge* comes to us from Friedrich von Hayek. Hayek saw that if any one person, or a small group of people, could possess *complete knowledge* of the economy, the economic problems of *what, how, who,* and *for whom* would be comparatively easy to solve. With *given* knowledge of resources available, *given* knowledge of production techniques, and *given* knowledge of the relative importance of various economic goals, all economic problems would be problems of pure logic. A computer (although it would take a rather large one) could be programmed to give the answers that would best satisfy human needs, given the available resources.

Time and Place

What puts the idea of a computer-controlled economy in the realm of fantasy is not any shortcoming of electronic technology. Instead, it is the fact that complete economic knowledge is not, and by its nature cannot be, possessed by any one or a few individuals. To be sure, some types of economic knowledge could be collected and sent to a single central point. We could compile a census of labor and natural resources. We could put together a library of the techniques of modern production engineering. We could conduct opinion surveys of consumer preferences. But when we had collected all this information, and expressed it in the form of general rules, trends, and regularities, it would not represent the totality of economic knowledge. There would still remain a vast amount of vital knowledge that, by its very nature, is always fragmented and widely spread among large numbers of individuals. That is the knowledge of *particular circumstances of time and place.*

The importance of the knowledge of particular circumstances of time and place can be clearly understood if we consider the extent to which day-to-day business decision making depends on it. A young management trainee straight out of business school earns less and contributes less to the firm for which he works than he will later on. In time, he will have supplemented his theoretical knowledge with a knowledge of the strengths and weaknesses of the particular individuals with whom he works, knowledge of the likes and dislikes of particular customers, and in general, knowledge of all the things that make his firm just a little different from its competitors. In addition to knowing that, as a general principle, a certain component part of his firm's product can be made out of either steel or plastic, he also will learn to be alert to any pending shortage of steel and know which particular supplier will be able most rapidly to fill his order for the plastic replacement.

The difference between success and bankruptcy for a firm hinges on how well such detailed, localized knowledge is utilized. So does the difference between a prosperous and a stagnant economy for a nation as a whole.

Centralization Not Possible

Because so many economic decisions depend on detailed knowledge of time and place, it is not possible to handle most economic problems by first communicating information to a central point, making decisions there, and then sending instructions back to someone at a particular spot. Yet leaving decisions up to someone on the spot does not in itself guarantee the effective use of economic knowledge. The person on the spot may know the ins and outs of the particular business, but also needs information about variations in general business conditions, about technological changes in other, different industries, perhaps even about shortages developing somewhere on the other side of the globe. The market plays a vital role as a mechanism for transmitting knowledge of such distant changes to the person who actually makes decisions on the spot. Here is an example that Hayek uses to make this point:

CASE 2.1
Knowledge and the Price System[1]

"Assume that somewhere in the world a new opportunity for the use of some raw material, say tin, has arisen, or that one of the sources of supply of tin has been eliminated. It does not matter for our purpose—and it is very significant that it does not matter—which of these two causes has made tin more scarce. All that the users of tin need to know is that some of the tin they used to consume is now more profitably employed elsewhere, and that in consequence they must economize tin. There is no need for the great majority of them even to know where the more urgent need has arisen, or in favor of what other needs they ought to husband the supply. If only some of them know directly of the new demand, and switch resources over to it, and if the people who are aware of the new gap thus created in turn fill it from still other sources, the effect will rapidly spread throughout the whole economic system and influence not only the uses of tin, but also those of its substitutes and the substitutes of these substitutes, the supply of all the things made of tin, and their substitutes, and so on; and all this without the great majority of those instrumental in bringing about these substitutions knowing anything at all about the original cause of these changes. The whole acts as one market, not because any of its members survey the whole field, but because their limited individual fields of vision sufficiently overlap so that through many intermediaries the relevant information is communicated to all."

[1]F. A. Hayek, "The Use of Knowledge in Society" *American Economic Review*, vol. XXXV, no. 4. (Sept. 1945), pp. 519–530.

The most remarkable thing about all this is how little each participant in the whole chain of events needs to know in order to play his part. The person on the spot needs only one scrap of information, namely, that the price of tin has risen. All the rest—shipping schedules, Bolivian politics, techniques of nonferrous metallurgy—need be known only by a few other people at other points in the chain. In short, prices are the market's telegraph signals—cryptic, abbreviated bits of information that allow general knowledge to be combined with particular knowledge of time and place and to be put to work when and where it is needed.

Markets as Sources of Economic Incentives

Markets transmit to economic decision makers the knowledge they need to put the resources they control to good use. At the same time, markets are

Friedrich August von Hayek
(1899–)

In 1944, a slim volume entitled *The Road to Serfdom* burst onto the world's best-seller list. This book warned that an enthusiasm for economic planning and strong central government was leading Western democracies down a path that, if not checked, could end in Soviet- or Nazi-style totalitarianism. The author of the book was as surprised as anyone to find it a best seller. He was Friedrich von Hayek, then a Professor at the London School of Economics.

Hayek, born and educated in Vienna, by 1944 already had a first-class international reputation as an economic theorist. He had written widely on monetary theory and on the subject we now know as macroeconomics. In contrast to many of his contemporaries, he did not believe that the Great Depression of the 1930s signaled the final failure of the market economy. The market would and could work, he held, if it were freed of the distortions introduced by ill-advised government policies. Most of all, what the economies of the world did not need as a cure for their troubles was comprehensive economic planning. Planning could never replace the market as a method for utilizing knowledge and guiding the division of labor. The attempt to make it do so would lead only to a loss of political freedom, not greater economic prosperity.

In 1950, Hayek left London for the University of Chicago, where he taught for twelve years as professor of social and moral science. Much of his time he now spent writing on broad issues of law and social philosophy. His major work of the University of Chicago period was *The Constitution of Liberty*. In this book, he defended the classical liberal ideal of the limited state based on a free market economy and a written constitution.

In 1962, Hayek saw that the University of Chicago's mandatory retirement age was fast approaching. Retirement seemed such an impossible idea to him that he returned to Europe, where professors could serve for a lifetime. He is now Visiting Professor at the University of Salzburg in Austria, and Professor Emeritus of the University of Freiburg in Germany. In 1974, the name Friedrich von Hayek was back in the international headlines once again. The Swedish Academy of Science had awarded him the Nobel Memorial Prize in Economics—the highest professional distinction there is. A fitting time to retire from a distinguished career? Not for Hayek. The first volume of his new work, *Law, Legislation, and Liberty,* had just appeared the year before, and there were two more volumes to complete. Asked recently what he would do when that job had been finished, Hayek indicated that he would then, after a detour of many years, be ready to get back to some unfinished problems of economic theory.

---

also the sources of the incentives necessary to encourage decision makers to carry out the actions that are known to be the correct ones.

Profits

Every businessperson watches the market for one thing: an opportunity to buy low and sell high. To take a prosaic example, suppose that Smith is a used car dealer. He learns that a certain Ms. Jones owns a used VW microbus for which she will accept any offer over $300. From his experience, Smith judges that if he buys the car and puts it on his lot, some third party will come along who will be willing to pay $600 for the vehicle. It is clear how Smith can put his knowledge to work and earn a **profit** by buying low and selling high. It is also clear that the result of his action will be the right result: The car will be moved from Ms. Jones, who values it less, to the third party, who values it more.

Profit Income earned by buying low and selling high. Includes the case in which an entrepreneur buys factors of production and uses them to make something that can then be sold for more than the cost of obtaining the factor inputs.

In the example just given, the trading process involved one buyer, one seller, one commodity, and one middleman. This served to illustrate the general principles involved in the transaction, but simpler and more complex arrangements are also possible.

Trade takes a simpler form if the middleman is left out and the original owner sells directly to the final user. In that case, the gains from trade are split just two ways, so the share of the gains for each party can be larger. This being the case, we might wonder why trade would ever involve a middleman. The reason is that the middleman plays the role of a "communications specialist" in the economic system. The ultimate buyer and seller may be miles apart and totally unacquainted with each other's needs and resources. The middleman, in contrast, makes it his business to be well informed of the bidding and asking prices everywhere, and to initiate transactions that would never be noticed or carried out by the original owners and final users.

It is important to notice that the presence of a middleman in a transaction is not in any way wasteful or inefficient. The total gains from trade are the same whether he is there or not. If buyer and seller can get together directly and eliminate the middleman, that is fine for them, but it does nothing to improve resource allocation in general. On the other hand, if, for lack of a middleman, they fail to get together to do business, then efficiency suffers.

The Entrepreneur

Trade takes a more complex form when middlemen sell things in a form different from the one in which they buy them. When middlemen buy factors of production and organize them for the production of new goods before selling, they are called **entrepreneurs.** They still make their profits by buying inputs low and selling output high, but their role as "communication specialists" is more important than ever. Entrepreneurs must make it their business not only to keep informed of all bidding and asking prices of their customers and suppliers, but also to be aware of technical information about production processes as well. Their reward lies in the fact that if they know their business well, they can offer prices to their suppliers that are sufficiently high to induce them to sell, and prices to their customers that are sufficiently low to induce them to buy, and still have a margin of profit left over for themselves.

Entrepreneur In general, anyone who is alert to opportunities for buying low and selling high in order to make a profit. More particularly, someone who undertakes to buy factors of production and organizes them for the production of useful goods or services in the hope that those goods or services can be sold at a profit.

Other Incentives

Profits are not the only incentives that markets offer. There are particular kinds of incentives to encourage every economic decision maker to seek out and make the best use of the information that the price system provides. Consumers who shop the sales and pay careful attention to the way product prices vary from place to place and time to time find themselves rewarded by the satisfaction of more needs with a limited budget. Workers who know their way around the job market earn better wages and salaries by working where their productivity is highest. Markets for rental housing help match tenants to landlords in a mutually satisfactory way. In every case, the person who first learns a new bit of economic knowledge has an economic incentive to put that knowledge to work and not just to file it away.

Markets as Windows on the Future

There are many kinds of knowledge that can be turned to profit in the marketplace, but the most profitable of all to possess would be true knowledge of the future. To know next week's stock market quotations, or whether a drought that threatens Russia's wheat crop will be broken, or whether the Japanese will tighten their restrictions on textile imports, and to know these things with certainty, would be worth millions. Sadly, true knowledge of the future is beyond human reach.

Nonetheless, intelligent economic decisions cannot be made without taking the future into account. Everyone has to do some guessing and take some chances. In a market economy, this guessing is not completely random or undirected. It turns out that market prices provide a *window on the future* because they reflect, in summary form, the guesses of all the people whose business leads them to trade in any particular market. Let us see how this works in a variety of cases.

Commodity (1) In a general sense, any good or service produced to be sold in any market; (2) in a more particular sense, any of a number of basic industrial raw materials and agricultural products, such as gold, silver, wheat, corn, cattle, or hogs, that are traded in organized future markets.

Future Markets A market in which buyers and sellers agree to deliver or take delivery of some commodity at a specified future date and at a price currently agreed on.

Commodity Future Markets

For many basic **commodities,** the necessary window is provided by special markets called **future markets.** In future markets, people meet and agree to deliver or take delivery of some commodity at some specified *future* date, and at a price *currently* agreed on. The agreed future prices are published in the business pages of most major daily newspapers. For example, if you had read *The New York Times* of July 16, 1976, you would have found the table reproduced here in Exhibit 2.1. Reading down that table to the line we have marked, we can see that at the opening of that trading day, you could have placed an order for 5,000 bushels of wheat to be delivered the next March and found someone to agree to sell it for a payment of $4.03 per bushel on the day of delivery. Reading across the line, we see that the price at which such a contract could have been made fluctuated during the day, touching the high of $4.03 at opening, reaching a low of $3.90 at one point, and ending up at $3.95 per bushel when the market closed in the afternoon. If you had been interested in placing an order for wheat to be delivered in December, May, July, or September, other lines of the table would have told you what you needed to know. Traders in gold, orange juice, soybeans, or hogs would have looked at still other parts of the table.

Clearly, the kind of information future markets provide is very useful. Suppose that you were a farmer who was planning to plant wheat to be harvested in July. You could agree to a selling price before you even planted, and then spend the next eight months worrying about the technical details of farming rather than about the ups and downs of market prices. Or if you were a manufacturer planning a production run of 50,000

Listing of Prices of Commodity Futures

Thursday, July 15, 1976

WHEAT

	Open	High	Low	Close	Prev
Jul	3.71	3.71	3.58	3.61½	3.73
Sep	3.75	3.76	3.63	3.67	3.79
Dec	3.92	3.92	3.77½	3.81½	3.92
Mar	4.03	4.03	3.90	3.95	4.05
May	4.08	4.08	3.96	3.99½	4.11
Jul	4.10	4.11	4.00	4.02	4.13

CORN

Jul	3.06	3.10	3.01	3.05¾	3.09
Sep	3.06	3.06	2.96¾	3.00	3.06¾
Dec	2.91	2.94¾	2.85	2.90	2.95
Mar	3.00	3.03¼	2.94	2.99	3.04
May	3.05	3.09	2.99	3.03	3.08
Jul	3.08	3.12	3.03½	3.08	3.13

OATS

Jul	1.96	1.96½	1.91	1.91	1.96¾
Sep	1.89	1.90½	1.84	1.85	1.90
Dec	1.88	1.89½	1.83½	1.84½	1.89¼
Mar	1.87½	1.88½	1.82½	1.82¾	1.88½
May	1.85½	1.86	1.80½	1.80½	1.86

SOYBEANS

Jul	7.43	7.43	7.13½	7.13½	7.33½
Aug	7.46	7.46	7.14	7.14	7.34
Sep	7.49	7.52	7.18	7.18	7.38
Nov	7.58	7.58	7.27	7.27	7.47
Jan	7.60	7.65	7.32	7.32	7.52
Mar	7.68	7.68	7.36½	7.36½	7.56½
May	7.66	7.67	7.36½	7.36½	7.56½
Jul	7.65	7.65	7.35½	7.35½	7.55½

SOYBEAN OIL

Jul	24.00	24.00	22.30	22.70	22.75
Aug	24.00	24.05	22.48	22.60	23.48
Sep	24.15	24.30	22.60	22.70	23.60
Oct	24.45	24.55	22.70	2.80	.70323
Oct	24.45	24.55	22.70	22.80	23.70
Dec	24.50	24.60	22.95	23.00	23.95
Jan	24.50	24.55	23.00	23.05	24.00
Mar	24.55	24.60	22.98	23.05	23.98
May	24.65	24.65	23.10	23.15	24.10
Jul	24.65	24.65	23.10	23.20	24.10

SOYBEAN MEAL

Jul	214.00	214.00	199.50	20.000	212.50
Aug	215.00	21)00	203.20	203.20	213.00
Sep	214.00	215.00	204.00	204.00	214.00
Oct	216.00	216.00	204.80	204.80	214.50
Dec	216.00	217.00	206.20	206.20	216.00
Jan	217.00	217.00	207.00	207.00	217.00
Mar	217.00	218.00	208.20	208.20	218.00
May	217.00	218.50	208.00	210.00	218.00
Jul	220.00	220.00	211.00	213.00	221.00

KANSAS CITY WHEAT

July	3.75	3.77	3.67½	3.68½	3.80
Sept.	3.87	3.87	3.73¾	3.75½	3.88
Dec.	3.95	3.96	3.84½	3.86¾	3.98½
Mar.	4.06	4.06¼	3.96	3.97½	4.08
May	4.10	4.10	4.03	4.03	4.12½

SUGAR

Contract No. 12

Raw sugar spot 14.65 nominal.

Contract No. 11

Sep	14.00	14.00	13.10	13.20	14.04
Oct	14.32	14.35	13.60	13.65	14.45
Jan	14.70	14.70	13.75	13.75	14.75
Mar	14.80	14.86	14.18	14.20	14.87
May	14.72	14.78	14.10	14.20	14.77
Jul	14.70	14.70	14.05	14.05	14.65
Sep	14.45	14.45	13.85	13.85	n14.49
Oct	14.35	14.35	13.70	13.75	n14.42

Sales 8,429.
n-nominal

COCOA

	Open	High	Low	Close	Prev.
	Open	High	Low	Close	Prev.
Jul	94.35	94,35	94.25	93.85s	95.35
Sep	94.50	94.75	91.00	91.75s	92.65
Dec	91.25	91.25	88.00	88.85s	89.35
Mar	87.69	87.75	84.40	85.40s	86.05
May	84.75	84.80	81.40	82.65s	83.55
Jul	82.25	82.25	78.95	80.00s	81.25
Sep	79.50	79.50	79.25	77.40s	78.50
Dec	75.50	75.50	72.50	73.65s	74.75

Sales: 1,941.
Spot Accra 106½.
s-Settling.

EGGS (Shell)

Chicago Mercantile Exchange

Jul	57.50	57.50	57.15	a57.15	57.50
Aug	57.30	57.35	56.75	57.35	57.20
Sep	60.55	60.85	59.50	59.50	60.45

Oct	58.00	58.00	58.00	58.00	57.75
Nov	61.75	61.90	60.90	61.00	a61.50
Dec	63.80	63.95	62.50	62.50	63.30

Sales: Jul 7; Aug 12; Sep 324; Oct 1; Nov 16; Dec 164.
Open interest: Jul 47; Aug 120; Sep 1494; Oct 12; Nov 458; Dec 1012.

FROZEN PORK BELLIES

Jul	67.70	68.80	67.25	68.10	67.70
Aug	65.50	66.75	65.05	66.00	65.60
Feb	61.60	62.95	61.60	62.80	61.60
Mar	61.52	62.85	61.52	b62.65	61.70
May	62.25	63.30	62.10	a63.05	62.10
Jul	63.05	63.05	62.50	a62.50	a62.00

Sales: July 337; Aug 4074; Feb 924; March 38; May 8; July 5.
Open interest: July 1007; Aug 5050; Feb 2484; March 754; May 278; July 26.
b—Bid; a—Asked; n—Nominal

POTATOES

N.Y. Mercantile Exchange

	Open	High	Low	Close	Prev.
Nov	5.55	5.63	5.47	5.47	b5.50
Mar	6.80	6.88	6.64	6.70	6.74
Apr	7.72	7.85	7.60	7.64	6.72
May	8.40	8.40	8.40	a8.35	8.25

Sales 815.
a-asked

PLATINUM

New York Mercantile Exchange

Oct.	182.0	182.70	179.20	179.30	183.00
Jan.	185.90	186.10	182.50	182.50	186.50
Apr.	189.50	189.50	186.10	186.10	189.50
July	192.70	193.20	191.50	191.50	190.20
Oct.	197.00	197.00	197.00	197.00	190.20

Sales, 798 contracts.

PALLADIUM

New York Mercantile Exchange

Sept.	61.50	61.70	61.10	61.70	61.90
Dec.	63.00	63.20	61.70	62.85	62.70
Mar.	63.00	63.25	62.80	63.20	63.20

Sales, 62 contracts.

U.S. SILVER COINS (In Dollars)

New York Mercantile Exchange

Oct.	3,507	3,507	3,415	3,415	3,505
Jan.	3,500	3,500	3,460	3,460	3,587
Apr.	3,575	3,575	3,575	3,575	3,625
July	....	....	....	3,575b	....
Oct.	....	....	....	3,635b	3,737

CSales, 12 contracts.

COPPER

New York Commodity Exchange

	Open	High	Low	Close	Prev.
Jul	76.70	76.70	74.90	74.90s	76.30
Sep	77.50	77.70	75.40	75.70s	77.30
Dec	79.40	79.80	77.40	77.60s	79.20
Jan	79.90	80.20	78.10	78.10s	79.70
Mar	81.00	81.40	79.30	79.30s	80.80
May	81.90	82.20	80.20	80.20s	81.70
Jul	82.50	83.00	81.00	81.00s	82.40

Sales: estimated 6,500.
s-settling.

GOLD

New York Commodity Exchange
100 troy ounce contracts

	Open	High	Low	Close	Prev.
Aug	122.10	122.20	120.10	117.50s	123.10
Sep	122.40	122.40	120.10	118.10s	123.70
Oct	123.50	123.50	121.60	118.70s	124.40
Dec	124.50	124.70	121.00	120.00s	125.70
Feb	126.80	126.80	124.20	121.50s	127.20
Apr	128.00	128.00	125.30	123.00s	128.70
Jun	130.00	130.00	127.60	124.50s	130.20
Aug	131.50	131.50	128.80	126.00s	131.70
Oct	133.00	133.10	132.40	127.60s	133.20

Sales 1,651.
s-settling

N.Y. SILVER (5,000 troy oz.)

	Open	High	Low	Close	Prev.
Jul	501.00	501.00	493.50	483.80s	500.00
Sep	504.50	505.90	487.00	487.50s	503.60
Dec	511.00	511.10	491.00	492.80s	509.00
Jan	512.50	512.50	494.50	494.50s	511.20
Mar	517.50	517.50	499.00	499.40s	515.70
May	521.50	522.00	505.00	504.10s	520.40
Jul	526.50	526.50	510.00	508.80s	525.10
Sep	527.50	527.50	514.00	513.50s	529.80

Sales estimated 10,035.
s-settling

ORANGE JUICE (Frozen Concentrated)

Jul	54.80	54.85	54.50	b54.30	54.75
Sep	54.70	54.70	54.10	b54.10	54.60
Nov	56.20	56.20	55.30	b5.30	5.06
Jan	57.10	57.10	56.40	b56.40	56.90
Mar	57.90	57.90	57.90	b57.50	b57.85
May	58.70	58.70	58.70	b58.60	b58.90

Sales 150.
b-bid

WOOL

Open	High	Low	Close	Prev.

No trades.

COFFEE

	Open	High	Low	Close	Prev.
Jul	131.00	131.50	128.50	128.50	n133.90
Sep	132.30	131.00	129.35	a129.35	132.15
Dec	130.50	131.00	127.15	a127.15	130.15
Mar	128.20	128.30	124.30	124.30	127.10
May	128.50	128.50	124.05	a124.05	b127.05
Jul	127.80	127.80	124.00	a124.00	127.00

Sales: 603.
Parana spot 1.43.
a-Asked. n-Nominal.

LIVE BEEF CATTLE

Aug	40.25	40.82	40.05	40.45	40.45
Oct	43.85	44.40	43.85	44.00	43.97
Dec	45.60	46.00	45.55	45.70	45.55
Feb	45.30	45.95	45.30	b45.70	45.45
Apr	45.30	45.80	45.30	45.65	b45.40
Jun	46.35	46.75	46.35	b46.60	46.40
Aug	—	—	—	b45.60	n46.15

Sales: Aug 4540; Oct 2366; Dec 1926; Feb 225; April 15; June 16; Aug 0.
Open interest: Aug 14619; Oct 9223; Dec 5792; Feb 3090; April 666; June 267; Aug 42.

FEEDER CATTLE

Aug	39.67	40.22	39.65	40.05	39.65
Sep	40.25	40.50	40.25	40.50	a40.35
Oct	39.80	40.65	39.80	40.55	40.05
Nov	40.15	40.70	40.15	40.50	40.30
Mar	—	—	—	n43.25	43.25
Apr	—	—	—	n43.10	a43.10
May	42.75	42.75	42.75	42.75	43.10

Sales: Aug 48; Sep 4; Oct 71; Nov 11; March 0; April 0; May 1; .
Open interest: Aug 371; Sep 148; Oct 1421; Nov 331; March 43; April 21; May 55; .

LIVE HOGS

Jul	49.10	49.30	48.75	48.82	48.95
Jul	48.85	49.00	48.35	48.62	48.82
Aug	45.50	45.52	44.90	45.15	45.15
Oct	41.50	41.97	41.30	41.60	41.50
Dec	41.50	41.90	41.25	41.50	41.10
Feb	41.55	42.05	41.55	41.82	41.60
Apr	40.60	40.75	40.52	a40.60	40.50
Jun	41.65	41.90	41.65	b41.90	41.90
Jul	42.00	42.20	41.55	42.00	41.90
Aug	41.10	41.10	40.60	40.90	40.70

Sales: July 844; Aug 1860; Oct 714; Dec 287; Feb 86; April 21; June 18; July 1; Aug 1.
Open interest: July 1434; Aug 4260; Oct 2245; Dec 1489; Feb 756; April 403; June 143; July 100; Aug 3.

ICED BROILERS

Chicago Board of Trade

Jul	42.40	42.40	42.20	42.35	42.45
Aug	41.75	41.80	41.37	41.50	41.70
Sep	40.65	40.65	40.45	40.55	40.75
Nov	40.10	40.20	39.60	39.60	40.00
Jan	41.50	41.57	41.15	41.30	41.45

b-Bid; a-Asked; n-Nominal.

LUMBER

Chicago Mercantile Exchange

Jul	152.10	154.30	151.10	152.90	152.10
Sep	151.80	153.90	151.10	151.50	152.00
Nov	153.50	155.20	152.00	152.40	154.00
Jan	160.00	160.90	158.00	158.00	160.00
Mar	165.90	166.00	163.50	163.50	166.00

Sales: July 192; Sep 978; Nov 325; Jan 155; March 33.
Open interest: July 251; Sep 2278; Nov 1462; J an930; March 181.

PLYWOOD

Chicago Board of Trade

Jul	147.00	14.700	144.50	144.60	147.00
Sep	147.80	148.20	145.20	146.20	147.80
Nov	150.50	151.00	148.00	149.00	150.20
Jan	152.50	152.80	150.00	151.00	152.30
Mar	154.00	154.30	153.00	153.00	154.00
May	155.20	156.0	0154.50	155.00	155.00
Jul	157.00	157.00	155.50	155.50	156.90

EXHIBIT 2.1

Future market prices for selected commodities.

Future markets allow people to meet and agree to deliver or take delivery of some commodity at some specified future date, and at a price currently agreed on. This daily table of commodity future prices was published in *The New York Times* on July 16, 1976. The table shows, for example, that on June 15, at the opening of the trading day, an agreement could have been made to buy or sell wheat at $4.03 per bushel in March 1977.

Source: The New York Times, July 16, 1976. © 1976 by The New York Times Company. Reprinted by permission.

gold-plated cigarette lighters next February, you could place a firm order for the gold now, and not have to worry that a change in the price of gold would upset your cost calculations in the meantime.

Other Windows

Not all goods and services have organized future markets, but there are also other ways in which people's judgments and guesses about the future are conveyed to us by the price system. For one thing, the stock market serves to transmit much information about what people think future business conditions will be like. If people think that the automobile industry will be hard-hit by the energy crisis, the stocks of automobile firms will fall in price. At the same time, the stocks of firms that have invested in, say, solar power technology are likely to rise. These stock price movements give investors a clue to which kinds of businesses are worth expanding and which others will not need to grow as much.

Real estate prices also reflect people's judgments about the future. Today's prices for land just outside the boundaries of a city reflect not just the value that the land has in its present use, but also the value the land is likely to have in the future, based on guesses of how fast the city will grow. Present prices of Vermont woodland are based not just on the value of the timber now standing on it, but also on guesses about whether Vermont will retain its popularity among New Yorkers as a site for weekend cottages.

Speculation

How can we be sure that the information that prices give us about the future is a summary of the *best* guesses people are capable of making? Why is it not just as likely to be true that the market will give us false signals, based on the guesses of the ignorant or of people with chronically bad judgment? A large part of the answer has to do with the incentives that the market provides and, especially, on the incentives that it provides to **speculators.**

Speculator A person who buys something now at a low price, hoping to be able to sell it later at a high price.

A speculator is a person who buys something now at a low price, hoping to be able to sell it later at a high price. To make money, a speculator must be able to make better guesses about the future than the average of other traders in the market. Suppose, for instance, that you have the ability to make shrewd guesses about future residential patterns. You buy land in places that you think people will be moving into. Later, you will sell it at a great profit. (Meanwhile, although it is no part of your intention, your speculative buying will signal other people that land values are changing in that area, and they can plan accordingly. For example, farmers will know that the area you are buying in will not be a good one for them to move into.) The market thus gives you an incentive to put your ability to make shrewd guesses to work and not just keep the information to yourself.

Survivorship

Survivorship Principle The principle that business decisions are more often made by people with good judgment than by people with bad judgment, because those with good judgment make profits and survive, while the incompetents soon lose their decision-making positions.

There is a further guarantee that prices will reflect the guesses of those best able to judge the future and not the guesses of incompetents. This guarantee is provided by what economists call the **survivorship principle.** This principle simply tells us that people with consistently good business judgment survive and prosper and achieve positions of great influence in the market economy, while people with chronically bad judgment or faulty sources of information lose money and eventually go out of business. It follows that, on the average, the people who have the most money at their disposal (and, hence, have the greatest impact on market prices when they decide to buy or sell) are the survivors, whose judgment has been tested and found reliable. Those whose judgment is faulty do cause the price system to send out false signals for a while, but not for long, because they soon go bankrupt.

Conclusions

In a modern economy, efficient resource allocation requires a very complex division of labor. Millions of different people are involved every day in the crucial decisions of *what, how, who,* and *for whom.* Somehow, their activities must all be coordinated. In a market economy, the price system is the most important coordinating force. The price system makes information about what is happening far away available to the person on the spot, so that the information can be combined with that person's own special knowledge of time and place. The price system provides an incentive for people to put their knowledge to work earning profits, and although that is not their intention, their buying and selling activities send useful signals to others. The price system even provides information about the future, because prices reflect the guesses that everyone makes about future patterns of resource use. Having said this much in general about *what* markets do, let us turn to a more detailed analysis of *how* they work. That will require a separate chapter.

SUMMARY

1. Resource allocation means determining *what* will be produced, *how* it will be produced, *who* will produce it, and *for whom* it will be produced. In the American economy, most resource allocation decisions are made in markets.
2. Markets play an important role as mechanisms for utilizing knowledge. They transmit general information in the form of prices from distant sources to the people on the spot. These individuals in turn combine the general information with their own particular knowledge of time and place and make decisions that utilize both kinds of information.
3. Markets also are a source of incentives. Entrepreneurs earn profits by buying low and selling high. Often this means buying factors of production and combining them to make goods and services that have a higher market value than the factors themselves did when purchased separately. Consumers and workers also have an incentive to make use of the information with which market prices provide them.
4. Finally, markets act as windows on the future. For some commodities, there are specially organized future markets to serve this purpose. For other goods, present prices reflect not only the uses to which the goods can now be put, but also people's judgments and guesses about what the future will bring. The incentives offered by the market to speculators, combined with the survivorship principle, guarantee that market prices reflect a summary of the *best* guesses that people make about the future.

DISCUSSION QUESTIONS

1. In your opinion, do the salaries and employment possibilities of different occupations have a very strong influence on people's decisions as to whether to go to college and what to major in? Justify your position. Explain how this is another example of the market system operating to determine *what, how, who,* and *for whom.*

2. If you were the manager of a division of a major automobile manufacturer and you noticed that the price of steel had been going up relative to the prices of other materials used in the manufacturing of automobiles, how would you react? What would you do and have others do to make adjustments? How would you expect your competitors to react? Explain.

3. Is it possible to have a market system without money? How important is money in the efficient operation of the market system? What advantages and disadvantages does it have over barter?

4. Often you can get more for something (say, a home or a car) if you sell it yourself rather than selling it through a dealer. Why is it, then, that everyone doesn't sell everything themselves, in view of the fact that dealers charge commissions? What is the dealer providing? Is it logical for the individual to settle for less money?

5. When you purchase something, are you improving your economic situation or not? Under what circumstances would you be being exploited? If you think someone is exploiting you whenever you buy something, are you also exploiting someone whenever you sell something?

6. There have been times when the government has stepped in and prevented the market system from functioning fully, as during wars, the oil embargo of the early 1970s, or the wage-price controls period of the Nixon administration. Why doesn't the government let the price system function all of the time? What are the advantages and disadvantages (the benefits and costs) of this government interference?

7. Is it possible that the market might give business firms the wrong signal as to what will happen in the future? Explain.

CHAPTER 3
Supply and Demand— The Basics

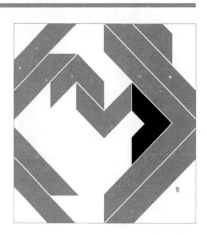

What You Will Learn in This Chapter
People tend to be more eager to buy when prices are low and more eager to sell when prices are high. That is the basis of supply and demand analysis. This useful tool of economics explains how shortages and surpluses of goods are related to changes in market prices and under what conditions markets can be in equilibrium. Thinking in terms of supply and demand also gives additional insight into the role of markets as mechanisms for utilizing knowledge.

For Review
Here are some important terms and concepts that will be put to use in this chapter. Be certain that you understand them, or review them before proceeding.
Opportunity cost (Chapter 1)
Working with graphs (Appendix to Chapter 1)

The number of markets in our economy is as large as the number of different kinds of goods and services produced—and that is very large. These markets differ enormously from one another in all sorts of details. Despite the great diversity of markets, though, there are some economic principles so powerful that they are useful in understanding all of them. The principles of supply and demand fall in this category.

The fundamental ideas of supply and demand have been known to merchants and traders of all ages. As long as there have been markets, sellers have realized that one way to encourage people to buy more of their product is to offer it at a lower price, and buyers have known that one way to get more of the goods they want is to offer to pay more for them. It is really only about 100 years, though, since economists began to make systematic use of the principles of supply and demand as a central basis of their science. In the English-speaking world, Alfred Marshall deserves much of the credit for showing how widely useful the ideas of supply and demand can be. This chapter—and the corresponding chapters in all modern textbooks—is little more than a rewrite of the principles as he taught them in his own famous *Principles of Economics*.

Alfred Marshall (1842–1924)

Alfred Marshall was born in London in 1842, the son of a Bank of England cashier. His father hoped that he would enter the ministry, but young Marshall had other ideas. He turned down a theological scholarship at Oxford to study mathematics instead. He received an M.A. in mathematics from Cambridge in 1865.

While at Cambridge, he joined a philosophical discussion group. There, he became interested in promoting the wide development of the human mind. He was soon told, however, that harsh economic reality would prevent his ideas from being carried out. Britain's productive resources, it was said, could never allow the mass of the people sufficient leisure for education. This disillusioning episode appears to have first turned Marshall's attention to economics.

At the time, British economics was dominated by the so-called classical school. Marshall had great respect for the classical writers. Initially, he saw his own work as simply one of using his mathematical training to strengthen and systematize the classical system. It was not long, however, before he was breaking new ground and developing a system of his own. By 1890, when he brought out his famous *Principles of Economics,* he had laid the foundation of what we now call the *neoclassical* school.

Attempting to explain the essence of his approach, Marshall included this passage in the second edition of his *Principles:*

> In spite of a great variety in detail, nearly all the chief problems of economics agree in that they have a kernel of the same kind. This kernel is an inquiry as to the balancing of two opposed classes of motives, the one consisting of desires to acquire certain new goods, and thus satisfy wants; while the other consists of desires to avoid certain efforts or retain certain immediate enjoyment . . . in other words, it is an inquiry into the balancing of the forces of demand and supply.

Marshall's influence on economics, at least in the English-speaking world, was enormous. His *Principles* was the leading text for decades, and the modern student can still learn much from reading it. As a professor at Cambridge, he taught a great many of the next generation of leading economists. Today the neoclassical school he founded continues to dominate the profession. It has received many challenges, but so far, has weathered them all.

The Law of Demand

Law of Demand The quantity of a good demanded by buyers tends to increase as the price of the good decreases, and tends to decrease as the price increases, others things being equal.

Our analysis begins with the **law of demand.** The law of demand says simply that in the market for any good, the quantity of that good demanded by buyers tends to increase as the price of the good decreases and tends to decrease as the price increases, other things being equal. This law corresponds so closely to what common sense tells us about the way markets work that we might, perhaps, simply state it without further elaboration. To make sure that it is properly understood, though, we shall add a few explanatory comments.

Effective Demand

Effective Demand The quantity of a good that purchasers are willing and able to buy at a particular price.

First, what do we mean by quantity demanded? It is important to understand that by the quantity demanded at a given price we mean **effective demand,** that is, the quantity that purchasers are *willing and able* to buy at that price. The effective demand at a particular price may be different than the quantity that consumers *want* or *need*. I may *want* a new Rolls Royce, but given my limited financial resources, I am not willing actually to offer to buy such a car at its current price of $30,000. My want does not count as part of the quantity demanded in the market for Rolls

Royces. Similarly, a poor man might *need* corrective dental surgery to avoid premature loss of his teeth, but if he is unable to pay, and no other person or agency is willing to pay, his need it not counted as part of the quantity demanded in the market for dental services.

Other Things Equal

Second, why do we attach the phrase "other things being equal" to the law of demand? The reason is that a change in the price of a product is not the only thing that will affect the quantity of that product demanded. If people's incomes go up, they are likely to increase the quantities they demand of a great many goods, even if prices do not change. If the price of beef rises, the effective demand for soy-protein meat substitute is likely to rise, even if the price of soy-protein does not change. And if people *expect* the price of sugar to rise soon, they are likely to increase the quantity of sugar they demand even before the price actually changes. When we state the law of demand, which says that the quantity of a good demanded changes when its price changes, we place incomes, prices of other goods, and expectations about future price changes in a box labeled "other things being equal" simply in order to be able to study one thing at a time. In a moment, we shall come back to the effects of changes in some of these "other things."

Why?

Now that we have made the meaning of the law of demand clear, we may ask why it works. Three particular explanations are worth considering.

First, when the price of a good falls while the prices of other goods remain unchanged, it is likely that we shall *substitute* some of that good for other things. For example, if the price of fish falls while the price of meat remains the same, we are likely to put fish into our menu a few days a month where we would have put meat had the price of fish not changed.

Second, when the price of a good changes, other things being equal, our effective purchasing power changes even though our income, measured in money terms, does not. For example, if the price of clothing rises while nothing else changes, we shall feel poorer, very much as if a few dollars a year had been trimmed from our paycheck or allowance. Feeling poorer, it is likely that we shall buy a bit less of many things, including clothing.

Third—and this reason is not quite distinct from the other two—when the price of a good falls, new buyers who did not use a product at all before are drawn into a market. There was a time, for example, when tape recorders were playthings for the rich, or technical tools for business uses only. Now tape recorders can be bought very cheaply. Rich people do not now buy ten or twenty tape recorders, but sales have gone up ten- or twentyfold because many people now buy them who never entered that market at all before.

Exceptions to the Law

Are there exceptions to the law of demand? Are there cases in which an increase in the price of a good causes us to use more of it? Theoretically, such exceptions are possible, although in practice they are quite rare. One possible kind of exception can occur if the change in the price of a good has such a strong impact on effective purchasing power that it causes a radical change in people's whole pattern of consumption. Imagine a family that lives in Minnesota, and habitually spends January each year vacationing in Florida. One year the price of home heating fuel jumps dramatically. The family reacts by turning down their thermostat a little, but their fuel bills for September through December still go up so much that they cannot afford to take their Florida vacation in January. Yet staying at home, even though it is cheaper than going to Florida, requires them to burn more fuel than during previous winters, when they left the house unheated for that month. The total effect of the rise in fuel price is thus to cause an *increase* in their consumption of the product.

Perhaps other rare kinds of exceptions to the law of demand are also possible. The point is, though, that we have to think so hard to come up with examples that we end up being more convinced than ever of the widespread validity of the law.

Demand Schedules and Curves

The law of demand, like so many other economic ideas, can usefully be illustrated with numerical tables and graphs. Suppose, for example, that we wished to study the operation of the law of demand in the market for widgets.[1] One way to express the relationship between the price of widgets and the quantity of widgets demanded by all buyers in the market is in the form of a table like that given in Exhibit 3.1.

First reading column (1) of this table, we learn that when the price of widgets is $1.50, the quantity demanded will be 200,000 units per year. Reading further, we find that as the price decreases, the quantity demanded increases. At $1.40 per widget, buyers would be willing and able to purchase 240,000 units per year; at $1.30 it would be 280,000 units, and so forth. This complete table is called the **demand schedule** for widgets.

Demand Schedule A table showing the quantity of a good demanded at various prices.

The information given by the demand schedule can be expressed just as easily in graphical form. This is also done in Exhibit 3.1. The diagonal line drawn in the graph is called the **demand curve** for widgets. Suppose that we want to use the demand curve to determine what the quantity demanded will be when the price is $1.20 per unit. Beginning at $1.20 on the vertical axis, we follow across as shown by the arrow until we reach the demand curve, and then down from that point to the horizontal axis, where we read off the answer. This answer, 320,000 widgets per year, is, of course, the same one given in the tabular demand schedule.

Demand Curve A graphical representation of the relationship between the price of a good and the quantity of that good demanded.

Shifts in the Curve

At the risk of being overly repetitive, let us say again that the demand curve shows how the quantity demanded changes in response to price changes, *other things being equal*. When a change in the quantity of widgets demanded occurs as a result of a change in the price of widgets acting

---

[1]Why widgets, and not some real product, such as wheat or haircuts? Our reason for using widgets is to emphasize that we are studying the workings of supply and demand under *idealized* conditions. No real-world market quite corresponds to the theoretical ideal. We shall say more on this point as we go along.

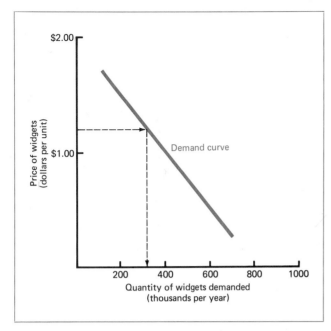

Demand Schedule	
(1) *Price of Widgets* *(dollars)*	*(2)* *Quantity of Widgets Demanded* *(thousands of units per year)*
1.50	200
1.40	240
1.30	280
1.20	320
1.10	360
1.00	400
.90	440
.80	480
.70	520
.60	560
.50	600
.40	640

EXHIBIT 3.1

The demand curve and demand schedule for widgets.

Both the demand schedule and the demand curve show the quantity of widgets demanded at various possible prices. Either the demand curve or demand schedule tell us, for example, that when the price is $1.20 per unit, the quantity demanded will be 320,000 units per year.

alone, that change is represented graphically as a *movement along* the demand curve for widgets. If the quantity demanded changes for some reason other than price, the graphical representation of the change is different.

Consider Exhibit 3.2. The demand curve labeled D_1 in that figure is the same as that shown in Exhibit 3.1. It is drawn on certain assumptions about household income, the prices of other goods, and buyers' expectations about future changes in price. Given those assumptions, the quantity demanded at a price of $1.00 per unit would be 400,000 units per year, as at point A on the demand curve D_1. A fall in the price from $1.00 per unit to $.50 per unit, other things being equal, would cause the quantity demanded to increase to 600,000 units per year. This change in price would be represented by a movement along the demand curve D_1 from point A to point B.

Return now to point A. Suppose that the price does not change, but that something else changes—say, household income rises. A sufficiently large increase in household income could cause the quantity of widgets demanded to increase by 200,000 units per year, even without a change in the price of widgets. This change would be represented by a movement from point A to point C in the diagram, a movement *off* the demand curve D_1 rather than along it. With household income established at its new, higher level, changes in *price* would now cause movements up or down along the new demand curve D_2, which passes through point C, and lies

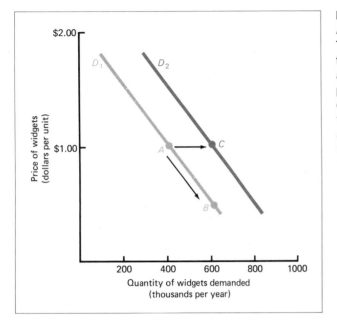

EXHIBIT 3.2
A shift in the demand curve for widgets.
The effect of a change in the price of widgets, other things being equal, is represented by a movement along the demand curve for widgets, as from point *A* to point *B* along the demand curve D_1. When the quantity of widgets demanded changes for some reason other than a change in the price of widgets (say, because of a change in household income), the change must be represented by a shift in the entire demand curve, as from the position D_1 to the position D_2.

everywhere to the right of the old demand curve D_1. The new demand curve indicates that whatever the price of widgets, the quantity demanded, given the new, higher level of household income, will be larger than it would have been at the same price, given the old level of income.

We could have told a similar story if it had been the prices of other goods or buyers' expectations that had changed rather than income. The general point we wish to establish is this: When the quantity of some good demanded changes for a reason *other* than a change in the price of that product itself, the change is represented graphically by a *shift* in the entire demand curve to a new position.

Normal and Inferior Goods

Economists have some special terms that are used in discussing the sources of shifts in demand curves. Changes in income are one source of such shifts. When a rise in buyers' income causes the demand curve for a good to shift to the right (as happened in Exhibit 3.2) the good is called a **normal good.** People tend to reduce their consumption of some goods when their incomes go up. Such goods are called **inferior goods.** Inferior goods are those for which there are more desirable, but more costly substitutes. Hamburger and intercity bus travel are often cited as examples. An increase in buyers' income causes the demand curve for an inferior good to shift to the left.

Normal Good   A good for which an increase in the income of buyers causes a rightward shift in the demand curve.

Inferior Good   A good for which an increase in the income of buyers causes a leftward shift in the demand curve.

Substitutes and Complements

The position of the demand curve for a good may also be affected by changes in the prices of other, closely related goods. For example, salads can be made either from lettuce or from cabbage. As a result, an increase in the price of lettuce is likely to cause not only a decrease in the quantity of lettuce demanded (represented graphically by a movement up and to the left along the lettuce demand curve) but also an increase in the quantity of cabbage demanded (represented graphically by a shift to the right in the entire cabbage demand curve). When an increase in the price of one good causes an increase in the quantity demanded of another good, those two goods are said to be **substitutes** for one another. Other goods, such as photographic film and flashbulbs, tend to be used together. If the price of film were to rise, we would expect not only a decrease in the quantity of film sold, but a decrease in the quantity of flashbulbs sold also. The effect of the change in the price of film would be represented graphically as a movement along the film demand curve, but as a leftward shift in the flashbulb demand curve. When an increase in the price of one good causes a decrease in the quantity demanded of another good, the two goods are said to be **complements.**

Substitutes A pair of goods for which an increase in the price of one good causes an increase in the quantity demanded of the other, other things being equal.

Complements A pair of goods for which an increase in the price of one good causes a decrease in the quantity demanded of the other, other things being equal.

Supply

The next step in our analysis of markets will be to examine the relationship between the price of a good and the quantity of that good that suppliers are willing and able to provide for sale. The relationship between product price and quantity supplied does not conform quite so closely to one simple rule as does the relationship between price and quantity demanded. We shall not state any general "law of supply." Instead, we shall simply look at some important cases.

The Upward-Sloping Supply Curve

Among the possible variations of the relationship between product price and the quantity supplied, there is a very important class of cases for which increases in the quantity supplied are associated with increases in price. In particular, this will be true when the cost per unit of producing some good or service increases as the quantity supplied increases. Then, producers will usually be willing to increase the quantity supplied to the market only if offered a sufficient increase in price at least to cover the increased cost of producing the additional units. Imagine that the production of widgets takes place under these conditions. We would then expect the **supply schedule** and **supply curve** for widgets to look something like those shown in Exhibit 3.3. Unless there is some special reason to think that the supply curve for a product has some different shape, economists usually draw supply curves with an upward slope, like the one in Exhibit 3.3.

Supply Schedule A table showing the quantity of a good supplied at various prices.

Supply Curve A graphical representation of the relationship between the price of a good and the quantity of that good supplied.

Other Supply Curves

Sometimes special conditions are encountered, and the supply curve loses its upward slope. Other possible shapes of supply curves are shown in Exhibit 3.4.

The supply of some goods cannot be increased at all, at any cost. Original drawings by Picasso are an example, so the supply curve for Picasso drawings is a vertical line, as shown in Exhibit 3.4a. The total number of such drawings in existence corresponds to the point on the horizontal axis

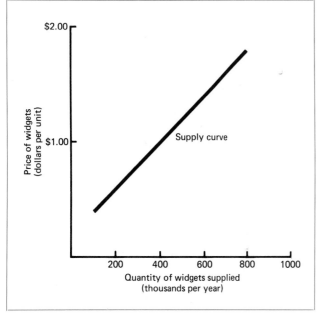

Supply Schedule	
Price of Widgets (dollars per unit)	Quantity Supplied (thousands of units per year)
1.50	650
1.40	600
1.30	550
1.20	500
1.10	450
1.00	400
.90	350
.80	300
.70	250
.60	200
.50	150
.40	100

EXHIBIT 3.3

The supply curve and supply schedule for widgets.

Upward sloping supply curves are produced when the cost per unit of making some good increases as the quantity supplied increases. In that case, producers will be willing to increase the quantity supplied to the market only if offered a sufficient increase in price at least to cover the increased cost of producing additional units. Unless there is some special reason to do otherwise, economists usually draw supply curves with upward slopes like this one.

from which the supply curve begins. This number stays the same regardless of the price that owners of such drawings might be offered by enthusiastic buyers.

There are some markets in which producers can be persuaded to increase the quantity supplied without requiring an increase in price. The local market for Campbell's cream of tomato soup in Ithaca, New York, might provide an example. Within any reasonable range, whatever quantity Ithaca's consumers desire can be supplied at no more and no less than $.21 per can. The shape of the supply curve in a market like this is a horizontal line, as shown in Exhibit 3.4b.

Finally, there are some products for which the cost of production decreases as the quantity of the product produced increases. Automobiles are often cited as an example. The more cars of a given model a plant produces, the more it can take advantage of mass-production techniques to reduce the cost per unit. The result can be a downward-sloping supply curve like that shown in Exhibit 3.4c.

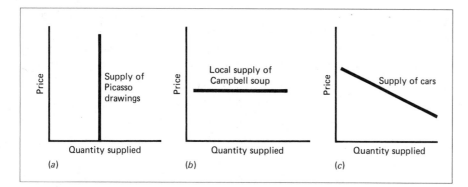

EXHIBIT 3.4
Other possible supply curves.

Supply curves do not always have upward slopes. Part *a* of this exhibit shows the vertical supply curve for a good, such as original Picasso drawings, which cannot be increased in supply at any price. Part *b* shows a horizontal supply curve, typical of the local market for a widely distributed good such as Campbell's soup. Part *c* shows that the supply curve for a mass-produced product such as automobiles can have a downward slope.

Shifts in Supply Curves

Supply curves, like demand curves, are drawn on the basis of an "other things being equal" assumption. Other things being equal, changes in the price of a good are reflected in movements up or down along a given supply curve. When underlying conditions change, supply curves may shift their position.

The most important of the conditions underlying the position of the supply curve for a good is the cost of producing it. Any change in the price of the factors of production used in making a good, or any change in technology that affects the quantity of inputs used per unit of output, will cause the supply curve of the good to shift. A reduction in cost will cause a downward or rightward shift, and an increase in cost will cause an upward or leftward shift. Some examples of shifting supply curves will be given later in this chapter.

Supply and Demand

Market Equilibrium

In Chapter 2 we saw how the market transmits information in the form of prices to the people who are potential buyers and sellers of any good. Taking the price of the good into account, together with the other knowledge that they possess, these buyers and sellers form plans. Each one decides to enter the market and buy or sell a certain number of units of the good.

Commonly, large numbers of buyers and sellers formulate their market plans independently of one another. When buyers and sellers of some particular good actually meet and engage in the process of exchange, some of them may find it impossible to carry out their plans. Perhaps the total quantity of planned purchases will exceed the total quantity of planned sales at the expected price. Some of the would-be buyers will find their plans frustrated, and will have to modify them. Perhaps, instead, it is planned sales that exceed planned purchases. Then some would-be sellers will be unable to sell all they had expected to, and will have to change their plans.

Sometimes no one will be disappointed, and, given the information that market prices have conveyed, the total quantity of the good that buyers plan to purchase will exactly equal the quantity that suppliers plan to sell. The separately formulated plans of all market participants turn out to mesh exactly when tested in the marketplace, and no one has frustrated expectations or is forced to modify plans. When this happens, the market is said to be in **equilibrium.**

Market Equilibrium A condition in which the separately formulated plans of buyers and sellers of some good exactly mesh when tested in the marketplace, so that the quantity supplied is exactly equal to the quantity demanded at the prevailing price.

If we have supply and demand schedules for a market, we can describe more exactly the conditions under which that market will be in equilibrium. Let us take the market for widgets as an example. In Exhibit 3.5, columns (1)–(3) give the supply and demand schedules. Reading down column (2), we see how many widgets producers will plan to sell at each price. Reading down column (3), we see how many widgets buyers will plan to purchase at each price. Comparing the two, it does not take long to dis-

EXHIBIT 3.5

Supply and demand in the market for widgets

When the quantity demanded of a product exceeds the quantity supplied, there is an excess quantity demanded, or shortage, of the product. A shortage puts upward pressure on the price of the product. When the quantity supplied exceeds the quantity demanded, there is an excess quantity supplied, or surplus of the product. A surplus puts downward pressure on the price. Only when the price of this product is $1.00 is their no shortage or surplus, and no upward or downward pressure on price. At that price, the market is in equilibrium.

(1) Price	(2) Quantity Supplied	(3) Quantity Demanded	(4) Shortage	(5) Surplus	(6) Direction of Pressure on Price
$1.50	650	200	. . .	450	Downward
1.40	600	240	. . .	360	Downward
1.30	550	280	. . .	270	Downward
1.20	500	320	. . .	180	Downward
1.10	450	360	. . .	90	Downward
1.00	400	400	. . .	. . .	Equilibrium
.90	350	440	90	. . .	Upward
.80	300	480	180	. . .	Upward
.70	250	520	270	. . .	Upward
.60	200	560	360	. . .	Upward
.50	150	600	450	. . .	Upward
.40	100	640	540	. . .	Upward

cover that only when the price is $1.00 do the separately formulated plans of buyers and sellers exactly mesh. The price for which this market is in equilibrium is $1.00 per unit. If both buyers and sellers make their market plans in the expectation that the price will be $1.00, none of them will be disappointed, and none of them will have to change their plans.

Shortages

What if, for some reason, buyers and sellers expect the market price to be something different than $1.00? Suppose, for example, that a price of $.50 per unit somehow became established in the market. Column (2) of Exhibit 3.5 tells us that at this price, producers would plan to supply widgets to the market at a rate of 150,000 per year. Column (3) tells us that buyers would plan to purchase at a rate of 600,000 per year. When the quantity demanded exceeds the quantity supplied, the difference between the two is called an **excess quantity demanded** or, more simply, a **shortage**.[2] In the case of widgets, the shortage [shown in Column (4) of the exhibit] is 450,000 units per year when the price is $.50 per unit.

When there is a shortage, some buyers will be disappointed. Suppliers will run out of the product before all buyers are able to make their planned purchases. What happens next may vary in detail from one market to another. Perhaps some producers will take advantage of the shortage to raise their price, hoping for greater profits. Perhaps buyers will take the initiative, and offer a premium price in order to get at least some of the good. Whatever happens, one generalization can be made fairly safely: A shortage puts upward pressure on the product price.

As the price of the product rises, producers begin to plan to sell more, and buyers begin to plan to purchase less. The higher the price, the smaller the shortage. When the price reaches $1.00 per unit, shortage is entirely eliminated. With the elimination of the shortage, there is no further upward pressure on prices. The market is in equilibrium.

Surpluses

Suppose now that, for some reason, the price of widgets were to become established at a price higher than the equilibrium price, say at $1.50. At this price, Exhibit 3.5 tells us, producers would plan to sell 650,000 units per year, but buyers would plan to purchase only 200,000. When the quantity supplied exceeds the quantity demanded, we say that there is an **excess quantity supplied** or a **surplus.** As column (5) of the exhibit shows, the surplus of widgets is 450,000 units per year when the price is $1.50.

When there is a surplus of the product, some producers will be disappointed and not be able actually to make all their planned sales at the expected price. Although again the details may vary from market to market, the generalization can be made that a surplus puts downward pressure

Excess Quantity Demanded The amount by which the quantity demanded of a good exceeds the quantity supplied when the price of the good is below the equilibrium level.

Shortage In technical economic terminology, an excess quantity demanded.

Excess Quantity Supplied The amount by which the quantity supplied of a good exceeds the quantity demanded when the price of the good is above the equilibrium level.

Surplus In technical economic terminology, an excess quantity supplied.

---

[2]We introduced two equivalent terms, "shortage" and "excess quantity demanded," in order to make it clear that economists use the term shortage in a different and somewhat narrower sense than it is used in everyday speech. In this book we shall use the word "shortage" most of the time, when it is clear that the economic meaning is intended, but sometimes, to avoid possible ambiguity, we shall use the more precise term "excess quantity demanded" instead. The same considerations apply to the terms "surplus" and "excess quantity supplied" defined below.

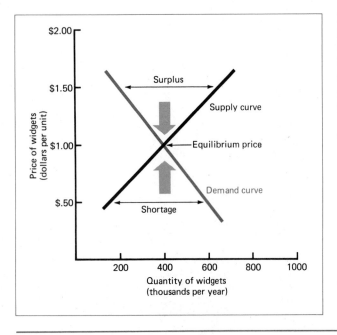

EXHIBIT 3.6

Supply and demand in the market for widgets.

In this diagram, a surplus or shortage is indicated by the horizontal distance between the supply and demand curves. A surplus puts downward pressure on price, and a shortage upward pressure, as indicated by the large arrows. The market is in equilibrium at the price where the supply and demand curves intersect. Compare this diagram with the table in Exhibit 3.5.

on the product price. The table shows that as the price falls, the quantity supplied decreases and the quantity demanded increases. Gradually, the surplus is eliminated, until, when the price reaches $1.00 per unit, the market returns to equilibrium.

Graphical Presentation

It is so important to understand the principles of supply, demand, and market equilibrium clearly that we shall go back again over the ground we have just covered, this time making a graphical presentation. Look at Exhibit 3.6. In the diagram presented there, we have drawn both the demand curve for widgets (taken from Exhibit 3.1) and the supply curve for widgets (taken from Exhibit 3.3). With both curves on the same diagram, we can directly compare the quantity demanded and the quantity supplied at any price. The distance from the vertical axis to the demand curve measures the quantity demanded, and the distance from the vertical axis to the supply curve measures the quantity supplied. It follows that the horizontal gap between the two curves measures the surplus or shortage at any price. The surplus at a price of $1.50 and the shortage at a price of $.50 are indicated in the exhibit.

As we saw when working through our numerical example for this market, a surplus tends to put downward pressure on the price, and a shortage tends to put upward pressure on it. These "pressures" result from the actions of frustrated buyers and sellers, who must change their plans when they find that they cannot buy or sell the quantities they had intended at the price they had expected. The pressures are indicated by large arrows in the diagram.

There is only one price where neither upward nor downward pressure is in force. That is the price of $1.00 per unit, where the supply and demand curves intersect. There is neither shortage nor surplus at that point. The quantity that buyers plan to purchase exactly equals the quantity that suppliers plan to sell. Everyone can carry out his or her plans exactly as intended, and the market is in equilibrium.

Changing Economic Conditions

When underlying economic conditions change, supply and demand curves can shift to new positions. These shifts upset the plans of buyers and sellers who may have adjusted to some previous market equilibrium, and they bring about changes in prices and quantities. The following example describes an episode that is typical of the way that markets work every day. In reading through the example, pay particular attention to the distinction between the kinds of changes that cause shifts in supply or demand curves and the kinds of changes that cause movements along curves.

CASE 3.1
Supply and Demand in the Soybean Market[3]

In the second quarter of 1976, the market for soybeans experienced a virtual explosion of prices. Between April and July, the price shot up from less than $5 a bushel to more than $7. Writing for *The New York Times*, market analyst H. J. Mainenberg attributed the price rise directly to supply and demand factors.

On the demand side, a major factor in the price rise was the appearance of the Soviet Union as a big buyer of soybeans. Previously, the Soviet Union had not been active in the international soybean market, relying on other sources of edible oils and high-protein livestock feed. Now they were forced to change this policy. Bad Soviet harvests the previous year had created a serious shortage of livestock feed of all kinds. What is more, in July 1976, Peru announced a ban on the export of fishmeal and fish oil. The disappearance of these substitutes from the international market further increased the Soviet demand for soybeans.

Exhibit 3.7a gives a graphical interpretation of the Soviet entry into the soybean market. The immediate result is shown as a rightward shift in the demand curve, from its initial position D_1 to a new position D_2. Before this shift occurred, the market equilibrium price would have been p_1. After the shift, there would be a shortage of soybeans as long as the price remained at its previous level. The shortage would cause the market price to be bid up. As the price rose, suppliers would move up and to the right along the supply curve S_1. When the price had risen to p_2, the shortage would be eliminated, and if no further changes in economic conditions occurred, p_2 would be the new equilibrium price.

Other economic conditions did not remain unchanged, however. At the same time the demand shift occurred, conditions were also changing on the supply side of the market. Soybeans, it seems, are favored as an alternate crop by cotton growers. If the weather is poor for cotton, or the cotton price is low, these farmers grow lots of soybeans. In 1976, though, the weather favored cotton and cotton prices were quite high. As a result, farmers shifted from soybeans to cotton, cutting the bean crop from 1.5 million bushels in 1975 to an estimated 1.3 million in 1976. We can represent the effect of these supply-side changes as an upward shift of the supply curve, from its original position S_1 to a new position S_2, as shown in Exhibit 3.7b. With the supply

[3]Based on H. J. Mainenberg, "Why Prices of Soybeans Are Soaring," *The New York Times,* July 13, 1976, p. 47.

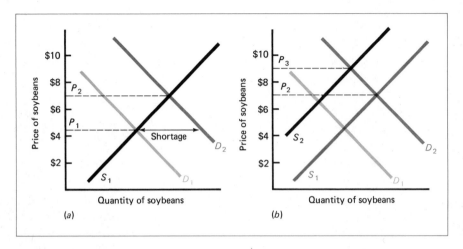

EXHIBIT 3.7
The effects of changing economic conditions of the price of soybeans
Part *a* shows the effects of a demand shift resulting from the entry of the Soviet Union
into the soybean market as a new major buyer. The demand curve is shifted to the
right, from D_1 to D_2. The resulting shortage of soybeans drives the price up from
p_1 to p_2. Part *b* shows the effects of a reduction in soybean supply, as farmers shifted
partially from soybeans to cotton. Now the supply curve shifts too, from S_1 to S_2.
Together, the shift of both curves requires an increase in price to p_3 in order to restore
equilibrium.

curve shifting at the same time as the demand curve shifted, a rise in price
from p_1 to p_2 would no longer be sufficient to eliminate the entire shortage
of soybeans. Instead, the price would have to rise all the way to p_3. In comparison to the equilibrium shown in part *a* of the exhibit, we can see that the
shift in the supply curve requires a movement of consumers along their new
demand curve D_2, until equilibrium is finally reached at the point where S_2
and D_2 intersect. The simultaneous shifts in the supply and demand curves
reinforced one another and caused the rise in the price of soybeans to
be much sharper than it would have been had only one of the changes
occurred.

Markets in Disequilibrium

We have seen that when a market is not in equilibrium, an excess quantity demanded or excess quantity supplied will put upward or downward
pressure on the price. If the price is free to respond to this pressure, a new
equilibrium will be established at a higher or lower price. Sometimes,
though, market prices are not free to fluctuate. The forces of supply and
demand must then work themselves out in some other way, as the following
example shows.

CASE 3.2
The Gasoline Shortage of 1974

In the winter of 1974, a significant gasoline shortage struck the United States.
Arab countries, trying to gain political advantage in the Middle East conflict,
drastically cut the supply of imported oil. Because there was no immediate

EXHIBIT 3.8

The gasoline shortage of 1974

During the gasoline shortage of 1974, government price controls prevented gasoline prices from rising to the equilibrium level, here estimated as $1.00 per gallon. Instead of causing the price to rise, the shortage of gasoline caused long lines to form at gas stations, until the opportunity cost of waiting in line became great enough roughly to fill the gap between the official ceiling price and the true equilibrium price.

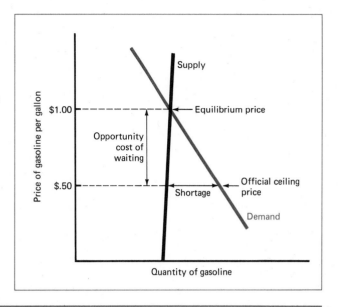

alternative source to which to turn, the supply curve for gasoline could be considered almost vertical, as shown in Exhibit 3.8.

This exhibit shows that a sufficiently high price ($1.00 per gallon as the graph is drawn, but this is only a guess) would have put the gasoline market in equilibrium. However, government price controls in force at the time kept the price from rising much above $.50 per gallon. There was a substantial excess quantity demanded that, instead of making itself visible in terms of rising prices, made itself visible in the form of long lines at gas stations.

People who waited in line for gasoline had lots of time to think, and anyone who had studied a little economics could have figured out that the forces of supply and demand were still at work in a roundabout way. There were opportunity costs of waiting in line. Some people actually missed work. Others sacrificed valuable leisure hours. As the lines grew, the opportunity cost of waiting in them grew also, until at some point the *total* cost of gasoline—the money cost plus the opportunity cost of waiting—was at least roughly equal to the price of $1.00 to which gasoline would have risen without controls. At that point, the lines stopped growing longer, and a sort of rough-and-ready equilibrium was established.

Who benefited from the fact that long lines, rather than high prices, were used to ration scarce gas among users? Who was harmed? Consumers in general did not gain, because what they saved in money, they lost in time. But some consumers—those for whom the opportunity cost of time spent in line was low—were hurt less severely than they would have been by a price rise, whereas those for whom time was particularly precious were hurt more.

Conclusions

This completes our presentation of the basics of supply and demand analysis. To conclude the chapter, we shall make a few remarks relating supply and demand to the role of markets as a mechanism for utilizing knowledge, and a few remarks also concerning the scope of applicability of supply and demand analysis.

Knowledge and Equilibrium

There is a simple connection between the idea of equilibrium and the idea of the market as a mechanism for utilizing knowledge. The connection is found in the fact that the market can be in equilibrium when, and only when, it has entirely completed its job of distributing knowledge among buyers and sellers.

It is easy to see why this is true. First, if buyers and sellers have incomplete knowledge of prices, and of other economic conditions, it is very unlikely that their separately formulated market plans will exactly mesh. It may be that both buyers and sellers expect the price tomorrow to be higher (or lower) than it actually will be. It may be that buyers have one idea about what price will be, and sellers another. Whatever the case, someone is bound to be disappointed, and disappointed plans are the stuff of which disequilibrium is made.

On the other hand, if both buyers and sellers had complete and accurate knowledge of both present and future prices and market conditions, how could their plans fail to mesh? No one would plan to buy at a certain price knowing that there would be no one willing to sell, or plan to sell knowing that there would be no one to buy. With perfect knowledge, people would formulate only such market plans as they knew could be carried out on the expected terms, and that is what we mean by equilibrium.

Saying that markets are in equilibrium only when all buyers and sellers have perfect knowledge leads us to a conclusion that perhaps seems strange. The conclusion is that in the real world, we can hardly ever expect to find a market that is in equilibrium! To paraphrase a famous saying, all people know something all of the time, and some people may know a great deal all of the time, but everybody does not know everything all of the time. In real markets, prices are always being pushed this way or that by changes in underlying economic conditions. Some people learn of these changes right away, and the buying and selling they do telegraphs that information, via the price system, to others. But the market telegraph does not work with the speed of light. Before everyone who is directly or indirectly interested in what goes on in a particular market learns of some change, other changes have occurred. The whirling stream of human knowledge never quite catches up with an even more fluid reality.

Applicability

The fact that markets are never really in equilibrium is, in a sense, a limitation on the applicability of supply and demand analysis. There are other limitations too. Supply and demand analysis applies in its pure form only to markets where the numbers of buyers and sellers are very large, and where the products offered by one seller differ very little from those offered by another. Our imaginary market for widgets perfectly fitted these conditions—that is why we made it up. Some real-world markets fit the conditions fairly well. The markets for agricultural products are an example. But the markets for many other products do not look exactly like the idealized markets of economic theory.

For now, though, we do not need to be overly concerned with differences between the real and the ideal. The theory of supply and demand may not *exactly* fit any market at any particular moment in time, yet in a general sense, thinking in terms of supply and demand can give us extremely useful insights into the way that almost all markets work. The usefulness of these tools will be proved in application as we work through this book. Fine points can be left for more advanced courses.

SUMMARY

1. The law of demand tells us that the quantity of a good demanded by buyers tends to change in a direction opposite to any change in price, other things being equal. By quantity demanded, economists mean effective demand, as distinguished from wants or needs not backed up by willingness and ability to buy. By other things being equal, we have in mind such things as buyer's incomes, the prices of other goods, and buyers' expectations concerning future price changes.

2. When the quantity demanded of a good changes solely because of a change in the price of that good, the change is represented graphically as a movement along a demand curve. When the quantity demanded of a good changes because something other than its price changes (for example, buyer's incomes, the prices of substitutes or complements, or buyers' expectations), the change is represented graphically as a shift in the entire demand curve.

3. A supply curve shows us the relationship between the price of a good and the quantity of that good supplied, other things being equal. Unless there is some particular reason to do otherwise, economists usually draw supply curves with upward slopes. Exceptions to the rule of upward-sloping supply curves are much more common, though, than are exceptions to the rule of downward-sloping demand curves. It is easy to find illustrations of vertical, horizontal, or downward-sloping supply curves.

4. A change in the quantity of some good supplied caused solely by a change in the price of that good is represented graphically as a movement along the supply curve. A change in the quantity supplied brought about by some other cause—for example, by a change in the cost of production—is represented by a shift in the supply curve.

5. Market equilibrium is a condition in which the separately formulated plans of buyers and sellers exactly mesh, so that the quantity supplied is equal to the quantity demanded. If the price of a product is too high for equilibrium, there will be a surplus of the good, which, in turn, will tend to push the price down. If the price is below the equilibrium level, there will be a shortage, which will tend to drive the price up. Equilibrium is possible only when the market has completely carried out its job of distributing information among buyers and sellers.

DISCUSSION QUESTIONS

1. The text notes that the "law" of demand states that there is an inverse relationship between the price of a good and the quantity that people will be willing and able to pay for. How is this "law" like the law of gravity? How is it different? Explain.

2. Illustrate the supply of McDonald's hamburgers to an individual consumer. What is the slope of the supply curve?

3. Suppose that there were a drought in the Midwest, where much of the nation's wheat is grown. What would be the impact of the drought on the demand and supply of wheat? What would happen to the price of wheat? Why? How would this be likely to affect the individual consumers of products containing wheat?

4. If you drop a marble in a bowl it will eventually come to rest at the bottom. We could say the marble is at equilibrium at the bottom of the bowl. What is

meant by equilibrium? In what ways is equilibrium in a market similar and in what ways is it different from the equilibrium of the marble?

5. If you were a wholesaler and you could see sooner than your competitors when a market was going to be in disequilibrium, how could you use this advance knowledge to make money? Would you be benefiting anyone besides yourself in getting rid of the disequilibrium? Explain.

6. Suppose that you read the following news item in the daily paper: "Frost in Brazil has caused a severe shortage of coffee, which has driven the price well above normal levels. The shortage is expected to persist for several years until new coffee bushes can be planted and reach maturity." Do you think the newswriter is using the word "shortage" in the same sense as we have used it in this chapter?

7. Suppose that the opportunity cost of time spent waiting in line to buy gasoline were uniformly $5 per hour for all consumers. Would imposing price controls on gasoline to deal with a sudden decrease in supply then benefit anyone at all? Would it make anyone worse off than if the price were simply allowed to rise to a higher equilibrium level? Should the owners of gas stations and oil companies be counted as "anyone" in answering this question?

CHAPTER 4
The Role of Government in the Economy

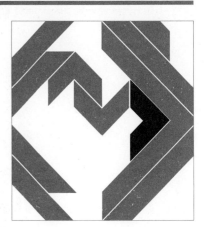

What You Will Learn in This Chapter
Although markets are the most important mechanisms for allocating resources in the American economy, government is too large to be ignored. Just how big is government in the United States, both in absolute terms and in comparison to the governments of other countries? How does decision making in government differ from decision making in the private sector? What economic functions does government perform, and who pays the bill? It is important to know answers to all of these questions as background for later topics taken up in this book.

For Review
Here are some important terms and concepts that will be put to use in this chapter. Be certain that you understand them, or review them before proceeding.
   Resource allocation (Chapter 2)
   Supply and demand (Chapter 3)

Understanding markets gives the most important single key to the way the basic questions of *what, how, who,* and *for whom* are answered in the American economy. The forces of supply and demand, acting through markets, affect every economic decision of significance. Still, ours is not a pure market economy. There are other economic forces at work as well that affect resource allocation. By far the most important of these nonmarket forces is that of government.

How Big Is Government in the United States?

Before getting into a discussion of how government works, it is important to get some idea of just how big government is in economic terms. Exhibit 4.1 gives three alternative measures of the size of government in the United States.

EXHIBIT 4.1

The size of government in the United States (1974 figures)

This table provides three different measures of the size of government in the United States. The first item tells how big government is as a buyer in all markets. The second item shows what share of Gross National Product passes through government hands in the form of taxes. The third shows government as a source of income for individuals.

1. Government purchases of goods and services as a percent of gross national product	Federal	8.4%
	State and local	13.7%
	Total	22.1%
2. Taxes as a percent of gross national product	Federal	20.8%
	State and local	14.8%
	Total	35.6%
3. Government-derived and private income as a percent of all personal income	Wages and salaries of government employees, including military	13.7%
	Transfer payments to individuals by all levels of government	11.8%
	Total government-derived, income	25.5%
	Wages, salaries, and other labor income paid in private sector	56.0%
	Property income of private individuals	18.5%
	Total personal income	100.0%

Government Purchases

The first group of figures in Exhibit 4.1 tells us how large government is as a buyer of goods and services from private individuals and business firms. The term **government purchases of goods and services** (or just *government purchases,* for short) includes all the finished products purchased by government (everything from submarines to typewriter ribbons) plus the cost of hiring the services of all government employees (everyone from the President right down to the courthouse janitor). Government purchases are compared with gross national product (GNP), a measure of the economy's total output of goods and services.[1] We see that in 1974, 22.1 percent of all goods and services produced by the American economy were purchased by federal state, and local governments.

Taxes and Transfers

Government purchases, although a useful measure of the size of government, do not tell the whole story. Looking at government purchases alone somewhat understates the size of the public sector, because governments do more than just buy things. They give money away, too. More precisely, a large portion of the money that governments at all levels take in as taxes are distributed to individuals in the form of **transfer payments.** Transfers are all payments made to individuals that are not made in return

Government Purchases of Goods and Services (government purchases) Expenditures made by federal, state, and local governments to purchase goods from private firms and to hire the services of government employees.

Transfer Payments All payments made by government to individuals that are not made in return for goods or factor services currently supplied. Social security benefits, welfare payments, and unemployment compensation are major forms of transfers.

[1]Gross national product will be given a precise definition in Chapter 6.

for goods or factor services currently supplied. They include such things as social security benefits, welfare payments, and unemployment compensation. The second item in Exhibit 4.1, which shows total taxes as a percentage of gross national product, reflects the size of transfer payments as well as purchases of goods and services. We see that in 1974 approximately $.36 in taxes were paid for every dollar's worth of goods and services produced in the economy.

Government-Derived Income

A third way to gauge the size of government in the economy is to look at the extent to which individuals depend on government for their income. The third item in Exhibit 4.1 shows how total personal income can be broken down into income derived from government, wages and salaries paid in the private sector, and property income (rents, interest, dividends, and so forth) earned in the private sector. It shows that somewhat more than a quarter of all personal income arrives in the form of a check from some agency of federal, state, or local government.

Growth of Government

These figures can be put in perspective by looking at what has happened to the size of government over time. Exhibit 4.2 shows the growth of government purchases as a percentage of GNP from 1909 to the present. In the early part of the century, government expenditures amounted to less

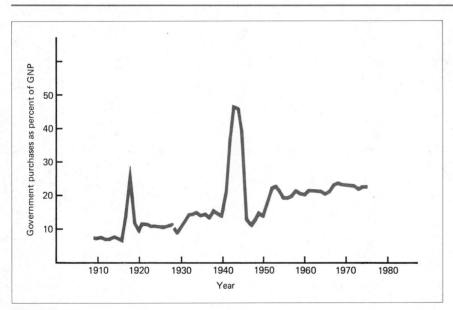

EXHIBIT 4.2

Growth of government purchases in the United States

The percentage of total government purchases in GNP has grown substantially over time. In the early years of the century, government purchases averaged less than 10 percent of GNP. Except for peaks during the war years, this figure did not grow very much until the 1950s. Government purchases now average over 20 percent of GNP, and they may still be growing.

Source: Data from Bureau of the Census, *Historical Statistics of the United States: Colonial Times to 1970* (Washington, D.C.: U.S. Government Printing Office, 1975).

than 10 percent of GNP, and grew only very slowly, except for brief peaks during World War I and World War II. After World War II, government purchases dropped back to their prewar levels, falling to 11 percent of GNP by 1947. The 1950s saw a steady growth of this figure, and by 1959, a level of 20 percent was reached. Since then, the figure has fluctuated from year to year, averaging around 20 percent. It is too early to tell whether the new highs reached in the mid 1970s represent the start of a new upward trend.

International Comparisons

Some international comparisons can give us additional perspective on the size of government in the United States. Using government purchases as our measure, the public sector of the American economy is neither remarkably large nor remarkably small by Western standards. In the early 1970s, countries like Sweden and Denmark spent 2 or 3 percent more of their GNP on government purchases than did the United States. France and Switzerland, on the other hand, had substantially smaller public sectors, with government purchases taking only about 12 percent of their GNP.[2]

Still another way to get a perspective on the size of the American government is to ask how large the public sector of an economy could possibly get. There is no purely theoretical way to answer this question, but again, some international comparisons can help. Perhaps unexpectedly, the largest public sectors among developed economies are not to be found in the communist countries. It is true that in those countries, the government plays a much larger role in directing industry than does the American government, but if a comparison is made in terms of government purchases and transfers, the governments of communist countries are only three or four percentage points larger than that of the United States.[3] A better indication of where the economic limits to the size of government lie is provided by the example of Britain, as the following account shows.

CASE 4.1
The Growth of Government Expenditure in Britain

During the 1970s, the British economy has experienced a virtual explosion in the size of the public sector. In the early 1960s, total government expenditures, including both purchases of goods and services and transfer payments, averaged about 43 percent of GNP. By 1975, as we see from Exhibit 4.3, this figure had reached a remarkable 65 percent.

It appears that this figure of 65 percent marks the limit, or even exceeds the limit, of the size a government can attain without severe economic disruption. In order to channel two-thirds of GNP through the public sector, taxes must be raised so high that work incentives are seriously distorted. This is true not just for the wealthy classes, who have long borne a very heavy burden of taxation in Britain, but also now for the average worker, and even

[2]These comparisons are based on data given in the UN Statistical Yearbook, 1974, Table 182.

[3]F. L. Pryor has done some very careful work adjusting U.S. and Soviet data on public expenditure to make them as closely comparable as possible. He calculates that "adjusted budget expenditure" in 1962 was 23 percent of GNP for the United States, and 27 percent for the Soviet Union. With defense excluded, the figures were 15 percent and 18 percent, respectively. See F. L. Pryor, *Public Expenditures in Communist and Capitalist Nations* (London: Allen & Unwin, 1968).

EXHIBIT 4.3

The growth of public expenditure in Britain, 1960–1975
Since the early 1960s, total public expenditure in Britain has grown from approximately 43 percent of GNP to approximately 65 percent. The data on which this chart is based include both government purchases of goods and services and transfer payments.

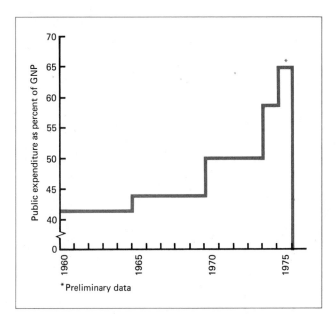

* Preliminary data

Source: Official figures as reported in the London *Times,* February 16, 1976.

the poor. In fact, the British now speak of a "poverty trap" produced by high taxation—a person who gets a low-paying job and leaves the welfare roles is immediately hit with such high rates of income taxes that he may be worse off working than he was while on public assistance.

Because taxes just cannot be raised high enough to pay for all that expenditure, the British government has had to borrow enormous sums of money from the public. This huge government borrowing robs industry of investment funds needed for expansion and modernization, and this deepens the general economic crisis.

There is a sobering lesson to be learned from the British experience. This lesson lies in the fact that the growth of the British public sector does not seem to have resulted from conscious policy decisions by any government. Expenditures grew both under Labour Party and Conservative administrations. In every year, expenditures grew faster than policy makers intended them to grow. Among the major sources of unplanned expenditure growth were (1) increased subsidies to nationalized industries, which were supposed to pay their own way but in fact ran increasing losses; (2) rising levels of transfer payments, including unemployment compensation, brought about by business recession; (3) poor cost-control practices, especially in local government; and (4) a tendency to use public service jobs as a buffer against unemployment in periods of business downturn.

It appears that in a country with a democratic political system, government expenditure tends to grow to its natural maximum even if political authorities do not actively encourage that growth. Instead, active political effort seems to be required simply to prevent expenditures from spontaneously running out of control.

Government and the Market

Clearly, however we measure it, government is too big to be ignored in any thorough discussion of what goes on in the American economy. The public sector requires special treatment in economic analysis because governments play the game of *what, how, who,* and *for whom* according to one set of rules, while the private individuals and firms who make up the market sector play according to another. Three characteristics in particular distinguish the economic behavior of government from that of most private persons and firms.

Distinguishing Characteristics of Governments

First, governments at all levels engage in the systematic and legitimate use of force in economic affairs. In the private sector, firms and households are limited by law and custom to peaceable means of production and exchange requiring the voluntary consent of everyone involved. Governments, on the other hand, are able to employ force, coercion, and involuntary expropriation in pursuit of their economic goals. When the government taxes incomes, regulates prices, drafts soldiers, or outlaws gambling it does not require the immediate, explicit consent of the individuals thus taxed, regulated, conscripted, or outlawed. Although in a democracy these uses of government power are supposed to rest, at least indirectly, on the consent of a majority of voters, they are binding on minorities and nonvoters as well. Without the use or threat of force, government could do very few of the things it does.

A second characteristic setting governments apart from other economic agents is the fact that the great bulk of goods and services that governments produce are provided to users without charge. In most cases, people do not have to pay for the defense services, highway use, education, or police protection that they receive. Instead, they pay for these things indirectly, through taxes. Only in a few cases do the taxes paid vary according to the quantity of public service consumed. The fact that governments do not charge users for most of their services has important implications for measuring the total contribution of government to the national product, and for the degree of efficiency with which government services are utilized. More on this in later chapters.

A third way governments differ from other economic agents is in the methods by which they arrive at economic decisions. The system of voting and bargaining by which public decisions are made is very much more complex and hard to analyze than the decision processes of private business firms and consumers. As a result, economists have not gotten as far in formulating simple rules or theories to explain resource allocation in the public sector. In the past, economists have traditionally treated government decisions as "givens" for purposes of economic analysis, and not tried to explain why one governmental decision rather than another is made at a particular time. In recent years, though, some progress has been made in formulating an economic theory of "public choice" to parallel the theory of private choice with which economists have traditionally worked.

Market Influences on Government

Despite the peculiarities of government, market forces of supply and demand do make themselves felt to a degree even within the public sector of the economy. The principal reason is that governments have to purchase most of the inputs they require on the open market. The U.S. Department of Justice cannot hire a new clerk unless it pays the wage determined by supply and demand for workers with that particular skill. The city of Chicago cannot buy police cars unless it pays something pretty close to what private individuals would pay for the same vehicles. The necessity of purchasing inputs at market prices makes government aware of the relative cost of various programs and helps constrain total public spending.

Of course, sometimes particular government agencies ignore the messages the market sends to them via the price system. Corrupt bidding practices sometimes result in government purchases from politically favored firms at higher than market prices. Sometimes devices such as eminent domain or the draft are used to obtain resources without paying their full market value. In such instances, the degree of market influence on government is less than usual.

The Economic Functions of Government

We have talked about how large government is, and how governments differ from households and private firms. Next we turn to the subject of what governments do with our money once they have collected it as taxes. First we shall analyze government programs in terms of five general economic functions. Then, in the next section, we shall look at government spending in terms of specific programs and agencies.

Public Goods

The first function of government is to provide what economists call **public goods.** Public goods are goods or services having the two properties that (1) they cannot be provided to one citizen without being supplied also to his neighbors, and (2) once provided for one citizen, the cost of providing them to others is zero. Perhaps the best example of a public good is national defense. One citizen cannot very well be protected against foreign invasion or atomic attack without having the protection "spill over" on his neighbors. Also, it costs no more to protect a single resident of a given area from invasion or nuclear holocaust than to protect an entire city.

Public goods are traditionally provided by government because their special properties make it hard for private business to market them profitably. Imagine what would happen if someone tried to set up a commercially operated ballistic missile defense system. If my neighbor subscribed, I would have no reason to subscribe too, but would instead play the "free rider," relying on the spillover effect for my protection. But he would not subscribe, hoping that I would, so that he could be the free rider. The missile defense company would soon go bankrupt.

The Transfer Function

The second function of government consists of making transfers of income and wealth from one citizen to another. Income or wealth is usually taken from citizens by means of taxation but sometimes, as in the case of the military draft or jury duty, it is taken by conscription of services. Benefits are distributed either in the form of direct cash payments or in the form

Public Goods Goods or services having the two properties that (1) they cannot be provided to one citizen without being supplied also to his neighbors, and (2) once they are provided for one citizen, the cost of providing them to others is zero.

of the free or below-cost provision of goods and services. Among the more familiar types of cash transfers are social security payments, welfare benefits, and unemployment compensation. Goods and services used for transfers include public education, public housing, fire protection, and subsidized mass-transit systems. These are provided at low or zero cost on the basis of political decisons rather than at market prices on the basis of ability to pay.

From the viewpoint of economic theory, the subsidized services that serve as vehicles for income transfers are different from the true public goods discussed above. They are consumed individually by selected citizens, and do not share the two special properties of public goods. It sometimes happens, though, that services provided primarily as transfers may be public goods in part. For example, consider the fraction of fire protection devoted to preventing general conflagration as opposed to putting out fires in individual private buildings, or the fraction of public health services devoted to controlling epidemic diseases as opposed to treating individual patients. We shall discuss a variety of transfer programs in detail in our chapter on the problem of poverty.

Stabilization

Economic stabilization is a third major economic function of government. By economic stabilization policies we mean all those aimed at controlling unemployment, inflation, and economic growth. The Employment Act of 1946 defines the federal government's responsibility for economic stabilization in these terms:

> The Congress hereby declares that it is the continuing policy and responsibility of the federal government to use all practicable means consistent with its needs and obligations and other essential considerations of national policy, with assitance, and co-operation of industry, agriculture, labor and state and local governments, to coordinate and utilize all its plans, functions, and resources for the purpose of creating and maintaining, in a manner calculated to foster and promote free competitive enterprise and the general welfare, conditions under which will be afforded useful employment opportunities, including self-employment, for those able, willing and seeking to work and to promote maximum employment, production and purchasing power.

We shall spend almost all of Part Two of this book talking about economic stabilization policy and developing the economic theory necessary to understand that policy.

Regulation

A fourth major function of government is the regulation of private business. Regulatory control is exercised through a network of dozens of specialized agencies. Regulation takes a variety of specific forms. Some agencies, such as the Federal Power Commission, set maximum prices at which certain products can be sold, whereas others, such as the Civil Aeronautics Board, set minimum prices. The Food and Drug Administration and the Federal Communications Commission exercise considerable control over *what* can be produced by the firms they regulate. Agencies such as the Occupational Health and Safety Administration and the Environmental

Protection Agency regulate *how* things are produced. Finally, the Equal Employment Opportunity Commission exercises a major say over *who* shall produce which goods.

Over the years, the federal regulatory establishment has grown into a virtual "fourth branch of government," alongside the legislative, executive, and judicial branches set up by the Constitution. Regulation is a subject of widespread research and controversy.

Administration of Justice

The fifth major economic function of government is the administration of justice. Usually we do not think of the police and courts as part of the *economic* branch of government, but their activities do, in fact, have important economic consequences.

Consider what happens, for example, when a judge makes a decision in a case involving an unsafe product, a breach of contract, or an automobile accident. The decision will have an immediate effect on resource allocation in the particular case, because one party will have to pay damages to the other, or make some other form of compensation. More importantly, other people will observe the outcome of the decision, and may change the way they do things as a result. If the courts say that buyers can collect damages from the makers of unsafe products, firms are likely to design their products differently. If certain standards are set for liability in automobile accidents, car makers, road builders, and insurance companies will take notice.

In recent years, an entire field of research has opened up in the "law and economics" area. Unfortunately, space will not permit us to say much about this field in this book, but readers interested in practical applications of economic thinking may wish to pursue this area on their own or in advanced courses.[4]

One further area of economic policy combines the judicial and regulatory functions of government. That is the field of antitrust policy and the control of monopoly.

Overlapping Functions

This five-way classification of government activities by functions helps give us a theoretical understanding of the role of governments in the economy, but it does not correspond very well to any breakdown of government activities by program or agency. Particular programs and agencies often perform a number of different functions at the same time. For example, the main business of the Defense Department would appear to be the provision of a public good, national defense, but it performs other functions as well. In wartime it performs a transfer function by shifting part of the cost of wars from the general taxpayer to young lower-class males via the draft. In peacetime it provides an instrument of economic stabilization through the way its huge budget for the purchase of goods and services is administered.

[4]A good place to start is with Richard Posner, *The Economics of Law* (Boston: Little, Brown, 1972).

To get a full picture of the role of government, then, we should look not only at a breakdown of its activities by function, but also a breakdown by levels of government, agencies, and programs. We shall do this in the next section.

The Composition of Government Budgets

Federal Receipts and Outlays

Exhibit 4.4 shows the percentage distribution of receipts and outlays of the federal government for 1975. Total federal outlays in that year were $313 billion, and total receipts were $279 billion.

Looking first at outlays, we see that the biggest single category was income security. This category includes the social security program, unemployment compensation, public assistance (welfare), and federal employee retirement and disability benefits   Income security began to take the largest share of the federal budget only in 1974. Before that, defense had been the largest category. Throughout the 1960s, defense spending consistently took over 40 percent of the budget, peaking at 45 percent in 1968, at the height of the Vietnam war. The other items on the outlay side of the budget are largely self-explanatory.

The biggest single source of receipts for the federal government was the individual income tax. This accounted for some 42 percent of all federal revenues in 1975. Next in line were social insurance taxes and contributions, with 31 percent of the total. This item has been growing rapidly in recent years. In third place were corporate income taxes. These used to be the second biggest revenue source, but are now much less significant than formerly. A number of smaller items make up the balance. All these revenues together were sufficient to pay for only 89 percent of all federal expenditure in 1975. The remainder, some $35 billion, was made up by government borrowing.

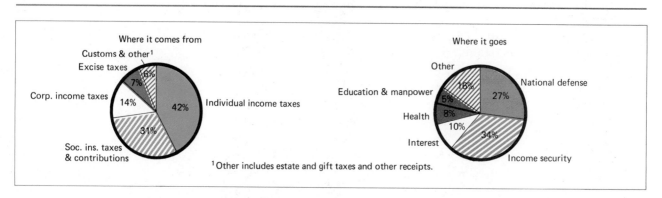

EXHIBIT 4.4

The federal budget, 1975

Source: Chart prepared by U.S. Bureau of the Census. Data from U.S. Office of Management and Budget.

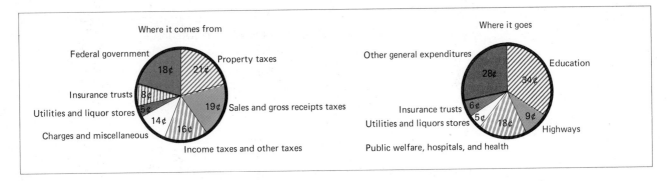

EXHIBIT 4.5
The state and local government dollar, 1973
Source: U.S. Bureau of the Census.

State and Local Receipts and Outlays

Exhibit 4.5 shows how the receipts and outlays of state and local government were distributed in 1973. Total state and local expenditures in that year were $205 billion. Of this amount, local government took about two-thirds, and state government one-third. State and local government spending together made up just over 47 percent of all government spending. State and local government have both grown more rapidly than the federal government in recent years. Twenty years ago, state and local spending accounted only for 37 percent of the total.

The biggest single item in state and local expenditure was education. A little more than three-quarters of this figure went for elementary and secondary education, and a little less than a quarter for higher education. Public welfare, hospitals, and health (18 percent), and highways (9 percent) were the other really large categories. The item "other general expenditures" includes a large number of things, including police and fire protection, sanitation, parks and recreation, and housing, which do not amount to very much separately.

The revenue side of the state and local government budget is quite different from that of the federal budget. State and local income taxes bring in only 16 percent of total revenue, and a few states do not use the income tax at all. Instead, the major sources of revenue are property taxes and sales taxes. Property taxes are used more by local government, and sales taxes by state governments. The federal government provides some 18 percent of all state and local revenues, and a variety of smaller sources make up the balance.

Who Pays the Taxes?

Tax Incidence

Exhibits 4.4 and 4.5 tell us what kinds of taxes are paid to support federal, state, and local governments, but not who pays them. Economists refer to the question of who bears the burden of taxation as the problem of **tax incidence.**

Tax Incidence The matter of who bears the economic burden of taxation.

The problem of tax incidence is not at all an easy one to solve. It is not enough just to look up the tax records of federal, state, and local governments. That would reveal only who had actually handed over the tax money to the authorities, not who actually bore the economic burden of the taxes. What makes tax incidence a difficult problem is the fact that the party who is obligated by law to pay the tax can often shift the burden of the tax to someone else.

For a simple example, suppose that a law is passed that asks all retailers to turn over a tax payment of $.10 to the government for each pack of cigarettes they sell. Who will bear the economic burden of this tax? We can use simple supply and demand analysis to find an answer.

Look at the supply and demand curves drawn in Exhibit 4.6. We see that without the tax, the equilibrium price of cigarettes would be $.20 per pack and 200 million packs per day would be sold. Next we have to figure out how the equilibrium price and quantity will change when the tax is imposed. We know that in the new, aftertax equilibrium, two things must be true. First, the price paid by buyers, including the tax, must be $.10 greater than the price received by sellers, net of the tax. Second, at the new equilibrium price, there must be neither an excess quantity of cigarettes

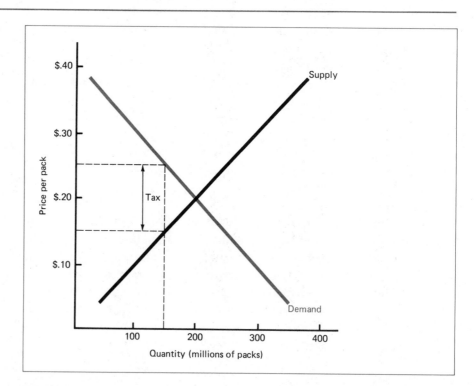

EXHIBIT 4.6

Effects of a sales tax on cigarettes

Before imposition of a tax of $.10 per pack, the market equilibrium price is $.20 per pack, and the quantity sold is 200 million packs. After imposition of the tax, a new equilibrium will be established in which buyers pay $.25 per pack, sellers receive $.15 per pack, and $.10 per pack goes to the government. The burden of the tax is divided equally between buyers and sellers.

supplied nor an excess quantity demanded. From the diagram we see that there is only one position at which *both* of these things are true. This is an output of 150 million packs, which corresponds to the place where the vertical gap between the supply and demand curves is exactly $.10. In this new equilibrium, consumers must pay $.25 per pack, and sellers receive only $.15 per pack after tax.

Comparing the before-tax with the after-tax equilibrium, we see that although retailers must hand over $.10 to the government for each pack they sell, half of the burden of this tax is shifted to buyers. Sellers actually end up receiving only $.05 less per pack than before ($.15 instead of $.20), while buyers must pay $.05 more ($.25 instead of $.20). We can say that, in this case, the *incidence* of the cigarette tax falls half on buyers and half on sellers.

In our example, the economic burden of the tax was divided equally between buyers and sellers, but the division need not always work out that way. If the demand curve we drew had happened to be a little steeper and the supply curve a little flatter, the major share of the burden would have fallen on buyers. If the supply curve had been steeper than the demand curve, sellers would have borne the bigger part of the incidence of the tax. A large part of solving the puzzle of tax incidence, then, is determining just what the shapes of supply and demand curves really are for the important goods and services on which taxes are placed.

The Incidence of Major Taxes

This is not the place to treat each kind of tax in detail, but we ought to take a moment to compare some of the major kinds of taxes in terms of their incidence. Economists usually assume that the burden of the personal income tax is not shifted, and remains to be borne by the taxpayers themselves. Sales taxes, in contrast, are believed to be shifted to consumers to a very substantial degree. Property taxes are more difficult to analyze. Probably property taxes on owner-occupied houses are largely borne by the owner-occupant, while property taxes on rental housing seem to be shifted, at least in part, to tenants.

Sometimes the analysis of tax incidence can have important implications for economic policy. A few pages back, we noted the growing importance of social insurance contributions as a source of federal revenue. By law, employees pay a tax of 5.2 percent on their wages to support social insurance programs, while employers contribute an additional 5.2 percent. Analysis of the incidence of payroll taxes shows, however, that the economic burden of both the employer and employee share rests entirely on the employee. Because of the legal fiction of having half the tax paid by employers, wage earners do not always realize how burdensome the tax is. Many economists now believe that social insurance taxes are inequitable, and that less reliance should be placed on them as a source of federal revenue.

In some cases, it is not possible to come to any firm conclusion about the incidence of a tax. The most puzzling case of all is the corporate income tax. The most obvious conclusion would be that the owners of corporations bear the burden. A closer look, however, seems to indicate that part of the burden of the corporate income tax may be shifted to owners of noncorporate businesses. Some of the corporate income tax may also be shifted to consumers through higher prices, but there is wide disagreement about how much is shifted in this way.

Overall Tax Incidence

Taxes can be classified, in terms of their incidence, as **progressive** or **regressive.** A progressive tax takes a larger percentage of income from people whose incomes are high, and a regressive tax takes a larger percentage of income from people whose incomes are low. One of the most interesting questions in the economics of taxation is whether the overall effect of federal, state, and local taxes are progressive, regressive, or somewhere between.

In a recent study, Joseph Pechman and Benjamin Okner of the Brookings Institution tried to bring together all of the available evidence in order to answer this question. They came up with a range of estimates differing according to the exact assumptions made about the incidence of various taxes. Exhibit 4.7 summarizes their results in terms of two variants. The

Progressive Tax One that takes a larger percentage of income from people whose incomes are high.

Regressive Tax One that takes a larger percentage of income from people whose income is low.

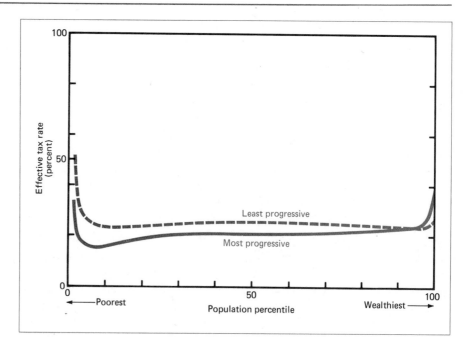

EXHIBIT 4.7
Effective rates of federal, state, and local taxes under the most and least progressive incidence variants, by population percentile, 1966
Pechman and Okner's study of tax incidence shows that the U.S. tax system is neither notably progressive nor notably regressive. To the extent that it accomplishes any redistribution at all, it seems to take from both extremes, thus easing the burden on middle-income groups.

Source: Joseph A. Pechman and Benjamin Okner, *Who Bears the Tax Burden?*, (Washington, D.C.: Brookings Institution. 1974), Fig. 1–2, p. 5. © 1974 by the Brookings Institution, Washington, D.C.

"most progressive" variant assumes in all cases of doubt that the rich are unable to shift taxes to the poor (for example, that landlords cannot shift the property tax to tenants, and that corporations cannot shift the corporate income tax to consumers of their products). The "least progressive" variant decides all cases in doubt as if the rich *could* shift the tax burden to the poor.

Two things are particularly interesting about the results shown in the exhibit. First, whichever variant is considered, the broad middle range of the population, excluding only the richest 5 percent and the lowest quarter, all pay very nearly the same portion of their total income in taxes. Second, the *very* rich and the *very* poor *both* pay much more of their income in taxes than do those in the middle. The tax systems of federal, state, and local government do not, taken all together, accomplish very much by way of redistribution of income. They are neither notably progressive nor notably regressive. To the extent that taxes redistribute income at all, they seem to take from both extremes and make things easy for those in the middle.

Conclusions

We have learned now that government plays a very big role in allocating resources in the American economy. Nearly a quarter of all goods and services produced are purchased by government and over a third of all income passes through the government budget in the form of taxes. If we take the regulatory function of government into account, its role appears even bigger.

One major question that we have not asked is *how well* all this vast machinery of government does its job. This is an important question and involves both normative and positive economics. The normative element comes in deciding what goals the government ought to pursue, and the positive element in measuring how closely it comes to meeting those goals. This question of *how well* is one to which we shall return repeatedly throughout the book.

Part Two of this book will begin to explain about the analytical tools needed to determine how well the government performs its function of economic stabilization. This is one of the most important applications of economics, and in some respects one of the most controversial. The high rates of inflation and unemployment that the American economy has experienced in the 1970s have given rise to some important new theories, and also to some important new doubts about how well the government has been doing its job. In the last two parts of the book, more questions of the *how well* variety will be raised. They will deal with the problems of pollution, economic growth, and international trade.

Until we get to all these later chapters we shall at least have the preliminary conclusion that government is there, and that it is important. In our theorizing, we may often speak of how markets work, as if the public sector were not there, but we shall always come back to questions of government policy.

SUMMARY

1. The American economy has a large and important government sector. Government purchases are nearly a quarter of gross national product, and taxes take over a third of GNP. The American government is neither remarkably large nor remarkably small by world standards, but it appears to have a tendency to grow.

2. Government differs from private households and firms in several ways. Government can use force in pursuit of its economic goals, while private individuals cannot. Government gives away most of the services it produces without charge. Also, political decision making processes differ substantially from those of the private sector. Still, because government must go to markets to buy most of what it needs, market forces do exercise some influence over the public sector.

3. Five major economic functions of government are the provision of public goods, the carrying out of transfers, the stabilization of the economy, the regulation of the private sector, and the administration of justice.

4. The determination of the incidence of various kinds of taxes is a difficult problem of applied economics. The burden of many taxes can be shifted from those who bear the legal obligation of paying the tax to other parties. When all kinds of shifting are taken into account, it appears that the combined federal, state, and local tax systems are neither progressive nor regressive overall. Instead, the burden of taxes is shifted to some degree from middle-income groups to both the very rich and the very poor.

DISCUSSION QUESTIONS

1. What would happen to our society if we completely did away with the federal government? Could state and local governments fill in? In which cases could they or could they not?

2. List the major goods and services that are provided by the government at different levels. Then determine the extent to which these goods are public goods. Which level of government tends to supply relatively more "public" goods? Which one the least? Can you determine which?

3. How can a government respond to changes in the relative prices of the goods and services that it buys and provides for its constituents? How is it subject to the same forces as a business? How not?

4. Transfer payments obviously affect the question of *for whom*. Do you think government tax and transfer programs also affect the economy's *who, what,* and *how?*

5. Would you prefer living where income taxes are very progressive or regressive? Why?

6. When a tax is imposed on cigarettes, the price paid by consumers goes up and the price received by sellers goes down. The government benefits by the amount of the difference on each pack sold. There is also a second effect of the tax. Fewer packs are sold. Who benefits and who is hurt by the fact that fewer packs are sold? Does the fact that cigarettes are harmful to people influence your answer? What if they were good for people?

PART TWO
National Income, Inflation, and Unemployment

Economic science is traditionally divided into two branches, called *macroeconomics* and *microeconomics.* The prefix *macro* comes from a Greek word meaning *big,* and *micro* from a Greek word meaning *small.* Macroeconomics deals primarily with issues relating to the operation of the economy as a whole, and microeconomics with issues relating to individual people, firms, and markets.

For example, the study of inflation (by which we mean a rise in the average price of all goods and services) is a part of macroeconomics, whereas the study of relative prices (by which we mean the study of such things as why a pair of socks costs the same as a dozen eggs, but only a third as much as a haircut) is a part of microeconomics. Likewise, the study of rising and falling levels of unemployment, measured as a percentage of the national labor force, is part of macroeconomics, and the study of the reasons why there are more unemployed engineers than unemployed lawyers is a part of microeconomics.

In this book we are concerned primarily with macroeconomics. However, many of the most important microeconomic principles have been sketched in Chapters 2, 3, and 4; and others will be introduced as they are needed in the next several chapters. In Chapters 5, 6, and 7 we will discuss the concepts, measurement, and growth of national income. Chapters 8, 9, and 10 will deal with multiplier theory. Chapters 11, 12, and 13 will be concerned with the role of money. Chapters 14 to 17 will encompass a discussion of unemployment and inflation.

CHAPTER 5
The Circular Flow of Income and Product

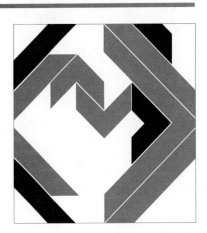

What You Will Learn in This Chapter

The circular flow of income and product sends goods moving from firms to households, and factor services moving from households to firms. At the same time, payments for these goods and services flow in the other direction through the economy. The idea of the circular flow serves two purposes in economic analysis. First, it provides a framework for a set of important definitions and equalities. Second, it shows how the concepts of supply, demand, and equilibrium can be applied in a macroeconomic context.

For Review

Here are some important terms and concepts that will be put to use in this chapter. Be certain that you understand them, or review them before proceeding.

Factors of production (Chapter 1)
Equilibrium (Chapter 3)
Government purchases and transfers (Chapter 4)

The Structure of the Circular Flow

With this chapter, we begin to put together a theory that will explain unemployment, inflation, and economic growth, and that will give us a framework for thinking about the major issues of economic stabilization policy. Because it will take several chapters to complete this theory, it will help to have a clear idea of the lay of the land before we start. The best way to get an overview of the economic system we shall be discussing is to represent it in terms of a **circular flow of income and product.**

The idea of the circular flow is based on two simple principles. First, each time anything is bought or sold in any market, the payment received by the seller must equal the amount paid out by the buyer. Second, every market transaction takes the form of money passing in one direction while goods or services pass in the other.

A Simple Economy

To see the circular flow in its most basic form, we shall begin by imagining an economy made up only of households and firms—an economy with no public sector at all. To make things simpler still, we shall suppose that

Circular Flow of Income and Product The flow of goods from firms to households and factor services from households to firms, counterbalanced by the flow of expenditures from households to firms and factor payments from firms to households.

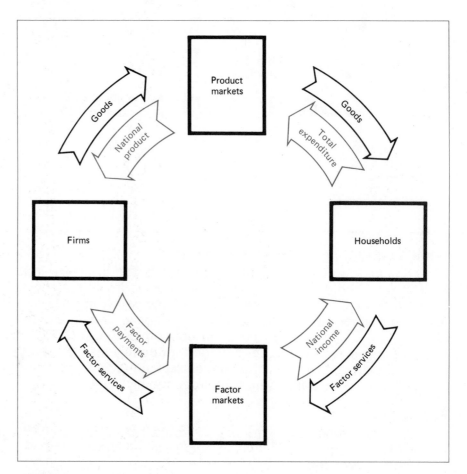

EXHIBIT 5.1

The circular flow in a simple economy

In this simple economy, households spend all their income on consumer goods as soon as they receive it, and firms sell all their output to households as soon as they produce it. Physical goods and factor services flow clockwise, while corresponding money payments flow counterclockwise.

our households live entirely from hand to mouth, spending all of their income on consumer goods as soon as that income is received, while firms sell their entire output to consumers as soon as it is produced.

The circular flow of income and product for this ultrasimple economy is shown in Exhibit 5.1. In the diagram, physical goods and services flow clockwise. Goods are produced by firms and sold to households through product markets. Factor services provided by people who work for the firms (or who supply them with capital and natural resources) flow from households to firms through factor markets. This clockwise flow of goods and services generates a corresponding counterclockwise flow of money payments. At the top of the diagram, we see the stream of money payments made by households to firms in exchange for the consumer goods they buy in product markets. At the bottom, we see a stream of money payments made by firms to households in exchange for the productive inputs that firms buy in factor markets.

Stocks and Flows

Having said this much, we should pause for a moment to comment on a word we have been using in almost every sentence. Economists call all of the things shown in Exhibit 5.1 **flows** because they are processes that occur continuously through time. Flows are measured in units per time period, for example, in dollars per year, gallons per minute, or tons per month. Measurements of flows are measurements of rates at which things are happening. In the technical language of economics we always distinguish carefully between flows and **stocks.** A stock is an accumulated quantity of something existing at a particular time. (The word stock in this general sense has nothing to do with the stockmarket kind of stocks that are bought and sold on Wall Street.)

For a homely example of the difference between stocks and flows, think of a bathtub filling. When we talk about how fast the water is running, we are talking about a *flow,* measured in gallons per minute, and when we talk about how much water there is in the tub at a given moment, we are talking about a *stock* measured just in gallons. Similarly, in the world of economics, we might talk about the rate of housing construction in Buffalo, New York, in terms of new units per month (a *flow*) as distinct from the housing *stock* in Buffalo as of January 1, 1977, meaning the actual number of houses standing on that date.

National Income and Product

Two of the flows in Exhibit 5.1 deserve special attention and have special names. The first is **national income,** which is the total of all wages, rents, interest payments, and profits received by households. National income is shown in our diagram as an arrow passing into the box representing households. The second important flow is **national product,** which is a measure of the total value of the goods and services supplied. In the diagram, national product is shown as an arrow passing from the box representing firms into the product markets.

In this simple economy, national income and national product are equal, simply because of the way that they are defined.[1] We can verify this equality in either of two ways. First, consider household expenditures as a link between national income and national product. Households are assumed to spend *all* of their income on consumer goods as soon as they receive them, and firms are assumed to sell *all* of their output to consumers as soon as it is produced. The payments made by buyers must equal the payments received by sellers, so national product must equal national income.

Alternatively, consider factor payments as a link between national income and national product. When firms receive money for the goods they sell, they use part of it to pay the workers, natural resource owners, and others who contributed factors of production to make the goods. Anything

Flows Processes occurring continuously through time, measured in units per time period.

Stocks Accumulated quantities existing at a particular time, measured in terms of simple units.

National Income The total of all incomes, including wages, rents, interest payments, and profits, received by households.

National Product The total value of all goods and services supplied in the economy.

---

[1]In Chapter 6 we shall see that the equality between national income and product does not hold precisely as these concepts are actually measured by the official statisticians of the U.S. government. It would be pointless, though, to let this statistical detail complicate all our theoretical discussions. Everywhere in this chapter, and everywhere from Chapter 7 onward, we make the necessary simplifying assumption so that national income and product *are* equal.

left over is profit. Factor payments, including profits,[2] account for all the money received by firms, so total factor payments must be equal to national product. Factor payments also account for all of the income received by households, so total factor payments must be equal to national income. It again follows that national income and national product must be equal.

Saving and Investment

The circular flow shown in Exhibit 5.1 is so simple that there is not really very much of interest to be said about it. To build a theory that will be useful for understanding the real-world economy, we have to introduce a few complications.

Our first change will be to drop the requirement that households immediately spend all of their income to purchase consumer goods, and instead permit them to save part of what they earn. The rate of saving by households, under this assumption, is simply the difference between national income and household consumption expenditures.

The second change we shall make is to drop the requirement that firms immediately sell all of their product to consumers. Instead, we shall now allow them to sell some products to other firms, and let some accumulate in inventory before they are sold to anyone. When firms buy newly produced capital goods (for example, production machinery, newly built structures, or office equipment) from other firms, they are said to engage in **fixed investment.** When firms increase the stock of finished products or raw materials that they keep on hand, they are said to engage in **inventory investment.** The rate of inventory investment can be less than zero in periods when firms are decreasing their stocks of goods or raw materials goods on hand. The sum of fixed investment and inventory investment will be called simply **investment.**

Circular Flow with Saving and Investment

Exhibit 5.2 shows how the circular flow of income and expenditure looks when saving and investment are added. (The clockwise arrows showing the flows of goods and services have been omitted to simplify the diagram.) There are now two pathways along which expenditures can travel on their way from households to product markets. Some household income is used for consumption expenditure, reaching product markets directly. Other household income is diverted to saving, which supplies a source of funds for firms to use in making investment expenditure, thus reaching product markets indirectly.

On the way from households to firms, the flow of saving passes through a set of markets called **credit markets.** These markets are made up of a great variety of financial institutions, including commercial banks, savings and loan associations, the stock and bond markets, insurance companies, and others that act as intermediaries between households which save and

Fixed Investment Purchases by firms of newly produced capital goods, such as production machinery, newly built structures, office equipment, and so forth.

Inventory Investment Changes in the stocks of finished products and raw materials firms keep on hand. If stocks are increasing, inventory investment is positive; if they are decreasing, it is negative.

Investment The sum of fixed investment and inventory investment.

Credit Markets A general term for the complex of financial institutions, including commerical banks, savings and loan associations, the stock and bond markets, insurance companies, and others that act as intermediaries between households which save and firms which invest.

---

[2]In macroeconomic theory, it is traditional to consider profits to be a part of factor payments, along with the wages, interest payments, and rentals received by workers and the owners of capital and natural resources. In contrast, microeconomic theory traditionally draws a distinction betwween profits on the one hand and factor payments on the other. Throughout Part Two we shall use factor payments in the macroeconomic sense, that is, including profits.

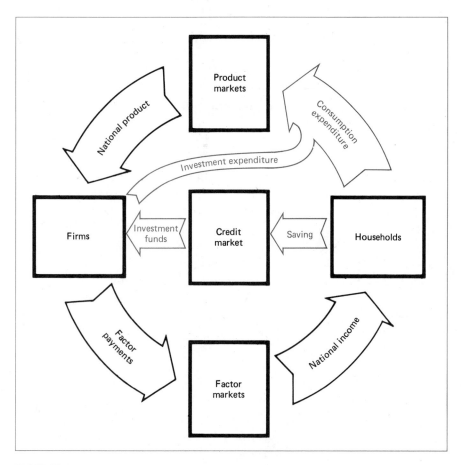

EXHIBIT 5.2
The circular flow with saving and investment
When saving and investment are added to the circular flow, there are two pathways by which expenditures can travel on their way from households to product markets. Some income is spent directly on consumer goods. The rest is saved, and passes to firms via credit markets. The firms then use the investment funds to make investment expenditures in the product markets.

firms which make investment expenditures. Households supply funds to the credit markets (for example, by depositing money in their bank accounts). Firms can then borrow from credit markets to obtain the funds they need to make investment expenditures.

Equilibrium and Disequilibrium in the Circular Flow

Adding saving and investment to the circular flow raises an entirely new issue. The issue is, can we still count on total expenditure to provide an equalizing link between national income and national product? We now have two entirely different sets of people making expenditure decisions. Households decide how much to spend on consumption, and firms decide how much to spend on investment. How can we be sure that when these two kinds of expenditure are added together, the total will just equal the total value of all goods produced? A new way of applying supply and demand analysis will help us find the answers we need.

Aggregate Supply and Demand

Economists use the term **aggregate** to describe any quantity that is a grand total for the entire economy. **Aggregate supply,** then, means the grand total of all goods supplied by all firms in the entire economy. We already have another term for the same thing: national product. Aggregate supply and national product are just two different names for the total value of goods and services supplied by all firms. Following the same terminology, we can use the term **aggregate demand** to mean the grand total of all goods demanded for the whole economy. In defining aggregate demand this way, though, we have to be very careful just what we mean by "demand." The precise way of defining aggregate demand is to say that it means the total *planned* expenditures of all buyers in the economy.

In discussing ordinary markets (such as the market for wheat, or cars, or widgets), our next step after defining the terms supply and demand was to explain what we meant by equilibrium. Let us do the same now, and show how aggregate supply and aggregate demand can be used to explain the ideas of equilibrium and disequilibrium in the circular flow.

A Numerical Example

We shall use a numerical example to make our point. Imagine an economy in which only three goods are produced: apples, milling machines, and widgets. Looking at this economy, we find that various firms have plans to produce apples at a rate of $30,000 worth per year, milling machines at a rate of $40,000 worth per year, and widgets at a rate of $30,000 worth per year. All firms are busy carrying out their plans. The result is a flow of output at a rate of $100,000 per year. This output flow, which we can call either national product or aggregate supply, is detailed in lines 1–4 of Exhibit 5.3.

While producers are busy carrying out their plans, various buyers make plans too. Consumers plan to buy apples at a rate of $25,000 worth per year and to buy widgets at a rate of $30,000 worth per year. Also, the firms that make widgets are planning to buy milling machines at a rate of $30,000 worth per year, in order to increase their widget-producing capacity for the future. No one is planning either to increase or to decrease the stocks of finished products that are held in inventory, so planned inventory investment is zero. All these buying plans are expressed in lines 5–11 of Exhibit 5.3. The total of all planned expenditures (consumption plus planned investment) is listed in line 11 with the label *aggregate demand.*

Comparing line 1 with line 11, we see that the plans of producers and the plans of buyers do not mesh. Aggregate supply is not equal to aggregate demand. There is nothing very surprising about that. After all, there were no direct consultations between the various buyers and sellers when plans were being made. Each acted on the basis of what knowledge was available from the price system, plus private judgments about future trends or changes. What happens is just that things do not always work out for

---

Aggregate An adjective used in economics to describe any quantity that is a grand total for the whole economy.

Aggregate Supply The total value of all goods and services supplied in the economy; identical to national product.

Aggregate Demand The total value of all planned expenditures of all buyers in the economy.

EXHIBIT 5.3

A numerical example of the circular flow for a simple economy

National product must always be equal to total expenditure even when the circular flow is not in equilibrium. In the example shown here, national product (aggregate supply) exceeds total planned expenditure (aggregate demand), so unplanned inventory investment makes up the difference.

Output resulting from producers' plans			
1 Total national product (aggregate supply):			100
2 Apples	30		
3 Widgets	30		
4 Milling machines	40		
Expenditures resulting from buyers' plans			
5 Total consumption expenditure:		55	
6 Apples	25		
7 Widgets	30		
8 Total planned investment expenditure:		35	
9 Fixed investment	35		
10 Planned inventory investment	0		
11 Total planned expenditure (aggregate demand)			90
Other expenditure			
12 Total unplanned inventory investment:			10
13 Unsold apples	5		
14 Unsold milling machines	5		
Summary			
15 Total national product			100
16 Total national expenditure:			100
17 Planned	90		
18 Unplanned	10		

everyone according to plan. The apples, widgets, and milling machines are all produced, but not all of them are sold. After buyers have bought all they planned to, $5,000 worth of apples are left over and so are $5,000 worth of milling machines. These products cannot simply vanish into thin air. The firms that made them put them into inventory, even though they had not planned to, and hope to sell them at some time in the future. The result is unplanned inventory investment of $10,000, as shown in lines 12-14 of Exhibit 5.3.

An Important Equality

Because aggregate buying plans do not mesh with aggregate production plans, we say that the circular flow is in disequilibrium. Aggregate supply and aggregate demand are not equal. National product and total planned expenditure are not equal. One crucial equality still *does* hold, though. National product is still equal to total expenditure *when both planned and unplanned expenditure are taken into account.* The reason is that goods that are produced and not sold *must* be added to inventories, whether firms planned to put them there or not. To repeat, they cannot simply vanish into thin air. As long as we count unplanned inventory investment as a part of total expenditure—and we do—total expenditure is by definition equal to national product. In equation form, we can write

$$\text{National Product} = \text{Total Planned Expenditure} + \text{Unplanned Inventory Investment} = \text{Total Expenditure}$$

Another way to write exactly the same thing is

$$\text{Aggregate Supply} = \text{Aggregate Demand} + \text{Unplanned Inventory Investment}$$

Reactions to Disequilibrium

In our numerical example, outlined in Exhibit 5.3, aggregate demand fell short of aggregate supply. Because buyers' and sellers' plans failed to mesh, there was an unplanned accumulation of inventories. Firms would not want this unplanned rise in inventories to go on and on. In order to stop it, they would reduce their rate of output, or lower prices in order to stimulate sales, or both. These reactions would amount to a reduction in aggregate supply. The size of the circular flow would begin to shrink as the number of dollars received by firms for their products and the number of dollars paid out to workers fell.

It might be that at another time, aggregate demand would exceed aggregate supply. With total planned expenditures greater than national product, unplanned inventory depletion would take place. Firms would react in a way opposite to their reaction to an excess of aggregate supply over aggregate demand. Either they would increase output to rebuild inventories, or they would take advantage of the high level of demand to raise prices, or both. Whichever they did, the size of the circular flow would grow as incomes and expenditures rose.

Finally, it is entirely possible that when the plans of buyers and sellers were tested in the market, they would turn out just to mesh. In that case, with production and planned expenditure equal, no unplanned inventory investment would occur, and no corrections would be necessary. The circular flow would be in equilibrium.

Income and Expenditure

We have not yet said anything about national income. Let us go back for a moment to the situation shown in Exhibit 5.3. Firms are shown to be producing $100,000 worth of goods a year. To produce those goods requires them to make factor payments (including profits, if any) of $100,000 to households, which means that national income is $100,000 too. The households receiving this income planned to buy consumer goods at a rate of $55,000 per year, which meant that they planned to save at a rate of $45,000 per year. (Remember that saving plus consumption exhaust income in this simple economy.)

Now, household saving plans do not mesh with firms' investment plans, as shown in line 8 of Exhibit 5.3. As things actually turned out, though, firms invested more than they had planned to. The actual total of investment, including unplanned inventory investment, *was* exactly equal to saving. It had to be. Once again, goods cannot vanish into thin air once produced, and unplanned inventory investment acts as the balancing item.

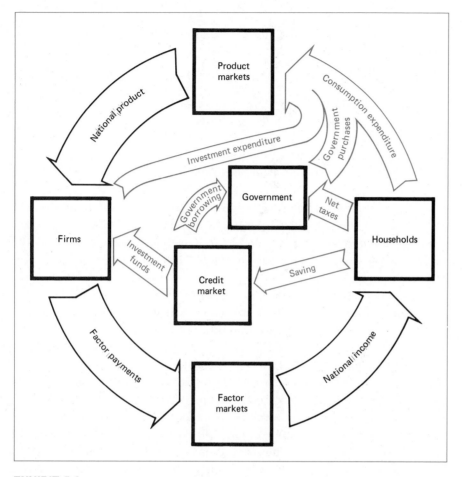

EXHIBIT 5.4

The circular flow with government included

With government added to the circular flow of income and product, there are two new channels along which funds can flow from households to product markets. Some income is diverted to government in the form of net taxes, and then used to finance government purchases. Alternatively, if the government runs a budget deficit, it may borrow from the public via credit markets and use the borrowed funds to finance its expenditures. If the government runs a budget surplus, the flow of funds along this pathway may be reversed, in which case the arrow from government to the credit market would point in the opposite direction from that shown.

The Place of Government
in the Circular Flow

When government enters the circular flow of income, expenditure, and product, things become slightly more complicated. Exhibit 5.4 shows how the circular flow looks when government is added. Two new pathways are opened up along which expenditures can flow from households to the product markets.

First, governments take in money from taxes that they levy on households. Some of that money, as we saw in Chapter 4, is immediately returned to households in the form of transfer payments. The difference between

Net Taxes Total tax revenues collected by government at all levels minus total transfer payments disbursed.

Deficit (of the government budget) An excess of government purchases over net taxes.

Surplus (of the government budget) An excess of net taxes over government purchases.

what governments take in as tax revenue and what they pay out in the form of transfer payments is called **net taxes.** Funds thus flow from households to government as net taxes and then from government to product markets as government purchases.

Second, if government purchases of goods and services exceed net taxes, the government may need to borrow money from the public through credit markets. In this case, the government budget is said to be in **deficit.** When the government runs a deficit, funds flow from households to the credit market as savings, then from credit markets to the government as government borrowing, and finally from government to the product markets as government purchases.

Sometimes the government budget is in **surplus** rather than in deficit. In that case, government borrowing from the public is less than its repayment of past debts. The net flow of funds between government and the credit market would be the reverse of what is shown in Exhibit 5.4.

Numerical Example with Government

Another numerical example will show that a government surplus or deficit does not disturb the basic equalities of the circular flow of income, expenditure, and product. Exhibit 5.5 shows an economy in which firms are again producing output at a rate of $100,000 per year, so national product is $100,000. Total expenditure is made up of consumer purchases at a rate of $60,000 per year, investment (planned and unplanned) at a rate of $25,000 per year, and government purchases of goods and services at a rate of $15,000 per year. Total expenditure is, as always, equal to national product because it includes unplanned inventory investment as a balancing item in case the planned expenditures of households, firms, and government do not exactly add up to current production.

Production of the national product of $100,000 per year generates a national income flow of the same amount. Households are making consumption expenditures out of this at a rate of $60,000 per year, as already noted. Part of the rest, $10,000 per year to be exact, is taken by government in net taxes. What is not spent or taxed away is saved, at a rate of $30,000 per year.

The government in this example has not balanced its budget. It is running a deficit of $5,000 per year. This does not disturb the equality of national income and total expenditure, however, because there is an offsetting surplus of saving over investment of $5,000 per year. The government can use this excess saving to finance its deficit by borrowing it from households via the credit market.

It is not just chance, of course, that the difference between saving and investment is exactly equal to the government deficit. The equality is maintained exactly because investment includes unplanned inventory investment. Suppose that the government suddenly reduced its expenditures by $1,000 per year, without giving time for any planned adjustments on the part of firms or households. The result would be that firms that produced the type of goods the government usually bought would find their inventories unexpectedly increasing at a rate $1,000 per year faster than previously. Now total investment would be $26,000 rather than $25,000, and the difference between saving and investment, now $4,000, will automatically have adjusted to the reduced size of the budget deficit.

EXHIBIT 5.5

A numerical example of the circular flow with government

When government is added to the circular flow, national product, total expenditure, and national income must still all be equal. If government purchases are not equal to net taxes, the difference will be offset by an equal difference between saving and investment. Another way to put this is to say that saving plus taxes must equal government purchases plus investment. As always, unplanned inventory investment acts as a balancing item, so that these equalities hold whether the circular flow is in equilibrium or not.

1	National product		100
2	Total expenditure:		100
3	Consumption	60	
4	Investment	25	
5	Government purchases	15	
6	National income allocated to:		100
7	Consumption	60	
8	Net taxes	10	
9	Saving	30	

We can put what we have learned from this example into an important new equality. If the difference between saving and investment is always equal to the goverment deficit (or surplus), then it must also be true that

$$\text{Saving} + \text{Net Taxes} = \text{Investment} + \text{Government Purchases}$$

Conclusions

Key Equalities

We have put some very big ideas into this short chapter. For one thing, we have used the circular flow to show how various parts of the economy fit together. First we established that national product must be equal to total expenditure, and that total expenditure, in turn, is made up of consumption plus investment plus government expenditure. In equation form,

$$\text{National Product} = \text{Total Expenditure}$$
$$= \text{Consumption} + \text{Investment} + \text{Government Purchases}$$

We then saw that national income can be broken down into three components representing the three different things people can do with their money: spend it, save it, or pay taxes. In equation form, this means that

$$\text{National Income} = \text{Consumption} + \text{Saving} + \text{Net Taxes}$$

Finally, we discovered that saving plus taxes must always equal investment plus government purchases, with the difference between saving and investment exactly offsetting any government deficit or surplus. This crucial relationship provides a link between the two equations we have just written. Our final conclusion, summarized in Exhibit 5.6, is that national income is equal to national product.

The conclusion that national product and national income are equal was trivial and obvious for the simplified economy shown in Exhibit 5.1. With saving, investment, taxes, and government purchases added, it is not so trivial or obvious, but it is no less true.

Equilibrium

Up to that point in this chapter we used the circular flow simply as a descriptive device, a set of pegs on which to hang some important definitions. At the same time as we were establishing these definitions and equal-

EXHIBIT 5.6
Key equalities in the circular flow

Three key equalities

National Product = Total Expenditure = Consumption + Investment + Government Purchases (1)

National Income = Consumption + Saving + Net Taxes (2)

Saving + Net Taxes = Investment + Government Purchases (3)

Fit together to make a fourth equality

$$\text{National Income} = \text{Consumption} + \text{Saving} + \text{Net Taxes} = \text{Investment} + \text{Government Purchases} + \text{Consumption} = \text{National Product} \quad (4)$$

ities, though, we used the circular flow in a different way. As soon as we introduced the terms aggregate supply and aggregate demand, the circular flow was no longer just dollars chasing goods around in a circle. Instead, it became a living, active market economy in which buyers met and tested their plans and encountered success or disappointment.

We saw that the idea of equilibrium could be applied to the circular flow to describe a situation in which the plans of buyers and sellers exactly meshed. More than that, we saw what happens when plans do not mesh, so that the circular flow is not in equilibrium. If buyers do not demand as much as firms supply, the excess products go on the shelf, whether firms had planned to put them in inventory or not. To correct the unplanned inventory accumulation, firms must cut output or reduce prices to boost sales. Either action causes the circular flow to shrink, when this flow is measured in terms of dollars spent on products or earned in incomes. If buyers demand more than firms currently produce, goods come off the shelf, even if firms had not planned to run their inventories down. This unplanned inventory depletion causes firms to raise prices or increase output, either of which causes the volume of the circular flow to grow.

If you have mastered this chapter, do not put down the book thinking that you know everything there is to know about macroeconomic theory. Still, you have made a pretty good start.

SUMMARY

1. Two of the most important elements of the circular flow are national income and national product. These two elements are linked on one side by factor payments and on the other by total expenditures. National income and national product are equal.
2. Saving and investment can be added to the circular flow without disturbing the equality between national product and total expenditure. If total *planned* expenditure is not exactly equal to national product, unplanned inventory investment (positive or negative) will make up the difference between the two.
3. Aggregate supply is another term for national product, and aggregate demand another term for total planned expenditure. When aggregate supply is equal to aggregate demand, unplanned inventory investment must be zero, and the circular flow is said to be in equilibrium. When aggregate supply and demand are not equal, unplanned inventory investment (positive or negative) must take place. The circular flow is then said to be in disequilibrium.

4. Adding government to the economy does not disturb the basic equalities of national product, total expenditure, and national income. If government purchases are not equal to net taxes, the surplus or deficit will be offset by the difference between saving and investment, with unplanned inventory investment acting as a balancing item if necessary. It follows that saving plus net taxes must be equal to investment plus government purchases.

DISCUSSION QUESTIONS

1. Contrast the flow of money you put into your bank account each payday with the stock of money indicated by the balance in your passbook. How are the flow and stock related? Why is one referred to as a flow and the other as a stock?

2. In the real world, who are the savers and who are the investors? Are they the same people all of the time? Some of the time? Can you provide examples of when a person can be both the saver and the investor? Give examples where someone is a saver but not an investor; an investor but not a saver.

3. In what sense is the owner of a grocery store chain "investing" when his inventories increase? How is this similar to investment in new display freezers for his stores? How is it different?

4. Because savers and investors are not always the same people, why is it that after the fact savings must always equal investment? Or must they? Is this relationship true in the real world or only under certain restrictive assumptions? What assumptions?

5. Suppose that you bought a dollar's worth of gasoline. Trace through the route this dollar might take, in fact several different ways it might take, to go through the whole circular flow.

6. Use the circular flow diagram to analyze each of the following:
   (a) The interest rate falls and businesses borrow more money and do more investing.
   (b) People decide to work less; they prefer more time off to watch ball games or some other leisure activity.
   (c) Governments in the economy raise their taxes.
   (d) Firms decide to lower their inventories, so they lay off 10 percent of their work force.
   (e) The government increases its flow of both taxes and government spending.

7. How would the circular flow model change if there were no money in the system, that is, if all exchanges had to be barter exchanges?

8. How do unemployed or unproductive workers fit into the circular flow diagram? What flows are connected to them?

CHAPTER 6
Measuring National Income and Product

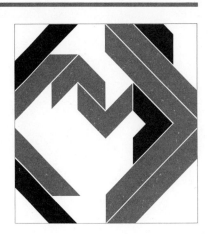

What You Will Learn in This Chapter

National income accounting means attaching numbers to the elements of the circular flow of income and product. By providing a statistical record of what has happened in the economy in the past, national income accountants help economists to refine and develop their theories, and help give decision makers in business and government a basis on which to formulate plans for the future. National income accounting is not an exact science, and published measurements of saving, investment, expenditure, income, and output are always estimates or approximations that fall short of the theoretical ideal. But despite their imperfections, these measures are so widely publicized and so frequently mentioned in economic discussions that it is important to learn how the basic national accounts are put together, and how to read them.

For Review

Here is an important concept that will be put to use in this chapter. Be certain that you know it, or review it before proceeding.

Basic equalities of the circular flow (Chapter 5)

Introduction

Measurement Problems

In Chapter 5 we cut the circular flow of income and product into convenient pieces, and gave them names like "national income," "investment," "saving," and so forth. These are the concepts on which much economic theory is based. Because they are so central to our theory, it is useful to be able to measure them, in order to see how well our theory fits the real world.

Unfortunately, measurement is not a completely straightforward job. National income, investment, and saving do not run around out there with labels tied around their necks. At least three important measurement problems face national income accountants.

First, there are problems of fitting concepts to reality. Things that are distinct in economic theory turn out to be mixed up in the real world. Consider factor payments as an example. When the owner-operator of a one-man gas station earns a net income of $8,000 per year, how can anyone tell what part of that money is wages he deserves for manning the pumps, what part is rent he deserves as owner of the corner lot where the station stands, and what part is interest he earns as the man who put up the capital to get the business started? Not only are we unable to identify things our theory says should be out there in the real world, we keep running into things that theoreticians wish would just go away. Sales taxes and business property taxes are good examples of complications in the national accounts that, for the sake of theory, we would like to ignore.

Second, measuring national income and product gets us into problems with recording and sampling. Statisticians cannot take the time to check up on what everyone does, so they sample the economic activities of some households and firms and hope that these more or less represent the rest. There is also the problem that when things like tax returns are used as a source of data, people may have turned in false information.

Nominal and Real Values

Third, and this is perhaps the greatest single problem of national income accounting, we have to worry about changing prices. Changing prices make it necessary to keep two entirely separate sets of accounts, one in **nominal** terms and one in **real** terms. Nominal measurements are those made in terms of actual market prices at which goods are sold. Real measurements are those that include adjustments for changes in prices from one year to another. Nominal measurements are fine for some purposes. If we wished to compare the incomes of white workers in Los Angeles in 1975 with the incomes of nonwhite workers in the same city during the same year, a nominal measurement would be appropriate. In other cases, though, nominal measurements can be highly misleading. If we said that the nominal starting salary for economics professors at Dartmouth College had gone up by $1,000 between 1970 and 1975, we would be drawing attention away from the fact that the cost of living had risen so much that the 1975 salary actually bought less than the 1970 salary did. Comparisons over time require real measurements.

Nominal Values Measurements of economic values made in terms of actual market prices at which goods are sold.

Real Values Measurements of economic values that include adjustments for changes in prices between one year and another.

Personal consumption expenditure		973.2
Durable goods	131.7	
Nondurable goods	409.1	
Services	432.4	
Plus: Gross private domestic investment		183.7
Producers durable equipment	96.4	
New construction	101.8	
Change in business inventories	−14.6	
Plus: Government purchases of goods and services		339.0
Federal	124.4	
State and local	214.5	
Plus: Net exports of goods and services		20.5
Exports	148.1	
Less imports	−127.6	
Equals: Gross national product (GNP)		1,516.4
Less: Capital consumption allowance	−161.4	
Equals: Net national product (NNP)		1,355.0

EXHIBIT 6.1

Nominal gross national product by type of expenditure, 1975

Gross national product is officially estimated by the expenditure approach. This means adding together the values of expenditures on newly produced goods and services made by all economic units to get a measure of aggregate economic activity. Net national product is derived from gross national product by excluding the value of investment expenditures that merely replace worn out or obsolete capital equipment.

The national income accountants who keep the country's official economic statistics deserve a lot of credit for doing their very best to overcome all these difficulties. National income accounting is a relatively young branch of economics. Forty-five years ago, when the Great Depression was hitting the country, national economic statistics were very bad. So bad, in fact, that policy makers in Washington literally did not know what was going on. By comparison, today's still far from perfect statistics make life much easier for policy makers and economic theorists alike.

In the remainder of this chapter we shall take a brief tour through some of the mechanics of national income accounting. We shall start with nominal measures, then turn to the problem of prices and real measures, and finally end with an evaluation of the validity of national income statistics as a whole.

Measuring Nominal Income and Product

Gross National Product

Of all economic statistics, perhaps the most widely publicized is the measure of an economy's level of total production called the **gross national product,** or GNP. This statistic represents the dollar value at current market prices (that is, the nominal value) of all final goods and services produced annually by the nation's economy.

In principle, gross national product could be measured directly, by constructing a table showing the quantity of each final good and service produced—massages, apples, submarines, housing units, and all the rest—multiplying these quantities by the prices at which they were sold, and adding the resulting column of figures. That is not, of course, what national income accountants actually do. Instead, they take a shortcut based on the equality of national product and total expenditure. In practice, then, GNP is measured by summing the nominal expenditure of all economic units on domestically produced final goods and services. This way of measuring aggregate economic activity is known as the **expenditure approach.** Exhibit 6.1 provides an illustration of how it works, using actual 1975 data.

Consumption

Consumption expenditures by households and unattached persons fall into three categories: durable goods, nondurable goods, and services. In principle, goods that do not wear out entirely in one year, such as automobiles, furniture, or household appliances, are considered durable, and goods that are used up in less than a year, such as soap, food, or gasoline, are considered nondurable. (In practice, the classifications actually used are often arbitrary. All clothing, for example, is considered nondurable, whether it is a pair of stockings, which wears out in a matter of weeks, or a woolen overcoat, which may be used for a decade.) The remaining item, services, includes things such as haircuts, legal advice, or education, which are not embodied in any physical object when sold. No distinction is made between services that are durable and nondurable in their effects.

Both the goods and the services components of consumption contain items that are produced but do not actually pass through the marketplace

Gross National Product (GNP) The dollar value at current market prices of all final goods and services produced annually by the nation's economy.

Expenditure Approach A method of estimating aggregate economic activity by adding together the nominal expenditure of all economic units on newly produced final goods and services.

on their way to consumers. One of these is an estimate of the food produced and directly consumed on farms. Another is an estimate of the rental value of owner-occupied homes. Rental payments on tenant-occupied housing are included automatically.

Investment

The item called gross private domestic investment is the sum of all firms' purchases of newly produced capital goods—fixed investment—plus changes in business inventories. Fixed investment, in turn, is broken down into the durable equipment of producers (such as machine tools, trucks, and office equipment) and new construction (including both business structures and residential housing).

When thinking about investment, keep in mind the phrase "newly produced capital goods." The businessperson who buys a used machine is not engaging in an investment expenditure according to the national income accountants' definition. The machine was already counted in some previous year. Also, anyone who says that he just made an "investment" of $2,000 when he means he paid that much for a plot of land or a corporate bond is not using the word "investment" in the national income accountants' sense. Real estate or securities are not capital goods. In fact, they are not even part of the more general category, goods and services, with which the measure GNP is concerned.

Government Purchases and Net Exports

Government purchases of goods and services are the next item to be added in. Transfer payments are not included in GNP because they do not represent expenditures made to purchase newly produced products.

Net Exports The value of all domestically produced goods and services sold to foreigners less the value of all goods and services bought from foreigners; exports minus imports.

The final item in GNP is **net exports.** This is the difference between the nominal value of goods and services exported to foreigners and the nominal value of goods and services imported from abroad. Exported goods must be added in because they are products produced in the United States, even though they are bought by foreigners. Imports are subtracted because some of the expenditures on consumer goods, investment goods, and government purchases, which we have already added in, were purchases of goods made abroad, and we do not want to count these as part of *national* product. When we add *net* exports into GNP, then, what we are doing is first adding all expenditures by Americans on goods and services regardless of where they were produced, then adding the total of American goods purchased by foreigners, and finally deducting purchases by Americans of goods made abroad.

Net National Product

What makes gross national product "gross"? It is the fact that gross private domestic investment is not a measure of the actual change in capital assets and business inventories for a particular year. In the process of production, existing buildings and equipment and other capital assets wear out. Other capital goods do not wear out, but lose their value through obsolescence. Accountants say that this part of the nation's capital stock existing at the beginning of the year *depreciates* by the year's end. It follows, then, that the actual increase in the stocks of capital goods and business inventories each year, which we call net private domestic investment, differs from gross private domestic investment by an allowance for the capital assets that depreciate each year. This allowance is called the capital consumption allowance.

Investment that merely replaces plant and equipment that has worn out during the year does not move the economy ahead, but only keeps it standing in the same place. Gross national product is thus, in a sense, an overstatement of how much we are getting out of the economy. To arrive at a measure of national product that includes only the actual net increase in capital goods and business inventories, the capital consumption allowance is subtracted from GNP. The resulting figure is called **net national product** (NNP). All told, net national product is the sum of personal consumption expenditure, net private domestic investment, government purchases of goods and services, and net exports of goods and services.

Income Approach

So much for gross national product, as measured by the expenditure approach. Let us turn now to a rather different way of measuring what goes on in the circular flow: the **income approach** to national accounting.

As the name implies, the income approach measures the overall nominal rate of the circular flow by adding up all the different kinds of income earned by households. This is done as shown in Exhibit 6.2. The categories of income used by national income accountants differ somewhat from the theoretical classification of incomes into wages, rent, interest, and profit, and deserve some explanation.

Compensation of employees includes not only wages and salaries, but two other items as well. One is employer contributions for social insurance. In Chapter 4 we argued that the economic burden of these taxes was borne by employees even though employers actually made the payments. The second is "other labor income," which includes various fringe benefits received by employees.

Rental income of persons includes all income in the form of rent and royalties received by owners of property. Net interest includes only interest payments from firms to households or government, on the grounds that interest payments made by consumers or government do not represent part of the cost of producing current output.

Net National Product (NNP) A measure of national product adjusted to exclude the value of investment expenditures that merely replace worn out or obsolete capital goods. Officially, NNP equals GNP minus the capital consumption allowance.

Income Approach A method of estimating aggregate economic activity by adding together the incomes earned by all households.

EXHIBIT 6.2

Nominal national income, 1975

National income is officially estimated by the income approach. This means adding together the values of all income earned by households. Note that some items of income, such as the portion of corporate profits that go to pay corporate profits taxes, are counted as "earned" by households even though households never actually receive the income.

Compensation of employees		928.8
Wages and salaries	806.7	
Employer contributions for social insurance	59.7	
Other labor income	62.5	
Rental income of persons		22.4
Net interest		74.6
Corporate profits		91.6
Dividends	32.1	
Corporate profits taxes	49.2	
Undistributed corporate profits	10.3	
Proprietors income		90.2
National income		1,207.6

Corporate profits include all income earned by the owners (that is, the stockholders) of corporations, whether the owners actually receive that income or not. Dividends are the part of that income that the owners actually receive. Another part goes to pay corporate profits taxes, and a third part, "undistributed corporate profits," is retained by the corporations to use for investment purposes.

The final component of national income, proprietors' income, is a sort of grab-bag including all income earned by owners of unincorporated businesses and self-employed professionals. National income accountants make no attempt to sort out what parts of this income ought theoretically to be classified as wages, rent, interest, or profit.

National Income and GNP

In our theoretical circular flow of Chapter 6, national income and national product were defined in such a way that they were exactly equal. In the real world, things do not work out quite so neatly. Some adjustments must be made to make national income, as measured by the income approach, fit GNP, as measured by the expenditure approach. These adjustments are shown in Exhibit 6.3.

For one thing, in the real world we must distinguish between net and gross national product, a difference we ignore in elementary theoretical discussions. The investment expenditures made to replace worn-out or obsolete equipment are counted as part of the business expenses of firms, so that they do not show up either in corporate profits or in proprietors' income. The first step in going from GNP to national income, then, is to subtract the capital consumption allowance, leaving us with net national product.

Next an adjustment must be made to reflect the fact that some of the money that firms receive from sales of their product is not "earned" by owners of the firms. Instead, it is taken directly by government in payment of indirect business taxes. These include sales taxes, excise taxes, and business property taxes paid to federal, state, and local governments. These taxes are treated differently from the corporate income tax, which is considered to be earned by owners, and then taken by government out of corporate profits. Indirect business taxes are included in the prices of goods and services, so they count as part of net national product, but they are not

Gross national product	1,516.4
Less: Capital consumption allowance	−161.4
Equals: Net national product	1,355.0
Less: Indirect business taxes*	−143.0
Less: Statistical discrepancy	−4.4
Equals: National income	1,207.6

*Includes minor adjustments for business transfer payments and net subsidies to government enterprises.

EXHIBIT 6.3
Relation of national income to GNP, 1975
In the simple world of elementary economic theory, national product and national income are equal by definition. In the real world, certain adjustments must be made to get GNP and national income to "fit." First the capital consumption allowance is subtracted from GNP to get NNP. Then indirect business taxes and the statistical discrepancy are subtracted from NNP to get national income.

included in income, so they must be subtracted when going from NNP to national income, as shown in Exhibit 6.3.

In principle, subtracting the capital consumption allowance and indirect business taxes from GNP ought to give us national income, but in practice there is one further difficulty. GNP is estimated by the expenditure approach, using one set of data, and national income is measured by the income approach, using an entirely different set of data. Inevitably, no matter how carefully the work is done, there are some errors and omissions so that the two sets of figures do not quite fit. The difference between NNP less indirect business taxes, on the one hand, and national income, on the other, is called the statistical discrepancy. It has no theoretical significance; it is simply a "fudge factor" that makes things balance.

Personal Income

National income, as we have mentioned several times, is a measure of income earned by households, whether those households ever actually get their hands on the income or not. For some purposes, it is more important to measure what households actually receive, instead of what they earn. The total of income actually received by households is called **personal income.**

Exhibit 6.4 shows the steps required to translate national income into personal income. First we subtract three items that are earned by households but not received by them. These are contributions for social insurance (both employer and employee), corporate profits taxes, and undistributed corporate profits. Next we add transfer payments, which represent money received by households although it is not earned by them. The result is personal income.

One further income measure is shown at the bottom of Exhibit 6.4. This is **disposable personal income** (or just **disposable income,** for short). Disposable income is what households have left of their personal income after they pay personal income taxes.

This completes our discussion of the nominal side of national income accounting. In the next section, we turn to the problem of making adjustments for changing prices.

Personal Income The total of all income, including transfer payments, actually received by households before payment of personal income taxes.

Disposable Personal Income (disposable income) Personal income minus personal income taxes.

EXHIBIT 6.4

National income and personal income, 1975

National income is a measure of all income earned by households, while personal income is a measure of the income they actually receive. To go from national income to personal income, we subtract payroll taxes, corporate profits taxes, and undistributed corporate profits, and then add transfer payments. If we subtract personal income taxes from this, we get disposable personal income.

National Income		1,207.6
Less: Contributions for social insurance		−109.6
Employer contributions	59.7	
Employee contributions	50.0	
Less: Corporate profits taxes		−49.2
Less: Undistributed corporate profits		−10.3
Plus: Transfer payments*		211.2
Equals: Personal income		1,249.7
Less: Personal income taxes		−168.8
Equals: Disposable personal income		1,080.9

*Includes government and consumer interest payments and business transfer payments.

Measuring Real Income and Prices

A Simple Economy

Let us begin our investigation of real income and prices by looking at an economy much simpler than that of the United States. This will permit us to present the essentials in the clearest possible way, before getting into practical details.

Exhibit 6.5 shows nominal GNP accounts for two years in a simple economy where only three goods are produced: movies, apples, and shirts. The tables show us that nominal GNP grew from $400 in 1972 to $1,000 in 1977. But how are we to interpret these figures? Do they mean that people really had more of the things they wanted in 1977 than in 1972? More exactly, do the figures mean that they had 2½ times as much? We need to take a closer look.

A line-by-line comparison of the two tables in Exhibit 6.5 shows that the figures on nominal income do not tell the whole story. The problem is that prices went up sharply between 1972 and 1977. Movies cost twice what they used to, apples three times as much, and shirts half again as much. So how much more was *really* produced in the second year than in the first?

We could try looking directly at the quantities of individual goods and services produced, but if we do so, we get conflicting indications. We see that twice as many movies and shirts were produced in 1977 as in 1972 but only half as many apples. Instead, it might occur to us to approach the matter in another way, by asking how much the total value of output would have changed from 1972 to 1977 if prices had not changed.

This approach to the problem gives us the results shown in Exhibit 6.6. There, we see that the 1977 output of 100 movies, 500 apples, and 20 shirts, which had a value of $1,000 in terms of the prices at which the goods and services were actually sold, would have had a value of only $500 in terms of the prices that prevailed in 1972. This figure of $500, which eliminates the effect of changing prices, is the one we should compare with the 1972 GNP of $400 if we want to know what really happened to physical production in the economy between the two years. Much of the apparent growth of the economy appears to have been due to higher prices. It seems that instead of having 250 percent more in 1977 than in 1972, the people in our simple economy had only about 25 percent more.

	Quantity	Price	Value
		1972	
Movies	50	$ 2.00	$ 100
Apples	1,000	.20	200
Shirts	10	10.00	100
1972 nominal GNP			$ 400
		1977	
Movies	100	$ 4.00	$ 400
Apples	500	.60	300
Shirts	20	15.00	300
1977 nominal GNP			$1,000

EXHIBIT 6.5

Nominal GNP in selected years for a simple economy
In this simple economy, where only three goods are produced, nominal national income grew from $400 in 1972 to $1,000 in 1977. Prices also went up between the two years, though, so people did not really have two and a half times as much of the things they wanted in 1977.

EXHIBIT 6.6

Nominal and real GNP in 1977 for a simple economy

This exhibit shows how the numbers from Exhibit 6.5 can be adjusted to take changing prices into account. The 1977 quantities are multiplied by 1972 prices, to get the value of 1977 GNP as it would have been had prices not changed. The total of 1977 quantities valued at 1972 prices is called the real GNP for 1977.

	1977 Quantity	1977 Price	Value at 1977 Price	1972 Price	Value of 1977 Output at 1972 Prices
Movies	100	$ 4.00	$ 400	$ 2.00	$200
Apples	500	.60	300	.20	100
Shirts	20	15.00	300	10.00	200
Totals		1977 nominal GNP = $1,000		1977 real GNP = $500	

Real GNP and the Price Index

Let us put the ideas we have gotten from this example into a convenient definition. When we make a comparison of GNP between a given current year and some other year (called the **base year**), we shall use the term **real GNP** to mean the total value of current-year quantities of final output evaluated in terms of base-year prices.

This definition of real GNP immediately suggests a simple way of measuring the change in prices between the base year and the current year. Look once again at the example summarized in Exhibits 6.5 and 6.6. We saw that nominal GNP grew from $400 to $1,000 from 1972 (the base year in our example) to 1977 (the current year). Real GNP, in contrast, rose only from $400 to $500. The difference between the nominal and real GNP figures for 1977 is attributable to rising prices. As a measure of the change in prices between the two years, then, it seems natural to use the ratio of nominal to real GNP in the current year. To make another definition, we say that the **price index** for any current year, measured in relation to any given base year, is given by the formula

$$\text{Price Index} = \frac{\text{Current-Year Nominal GNP}}{\text{Current-Year Real GNP}} = \frac{P_1 Q_1}{P_0 Q_1}$$

or, alternatively,

$$\text{Price Index} = \frac{\text{Current-Year Quantities Evaluated in Terms of Current-Year Prices}}{\text{Current-Year Quantities Evaluated in Terms of Base-Year Prices}}$$

If we use the data from our example to compute the price index for 1977 in terms of the 1972 base year, we get

$$\text{Price Index} = \frac{\$1,000}{\$500} = 2.0$$

We can think of this figure as meaning that, on the average, goods and services were twice as expensive in 1977 as in 1972. Alternatively, we could interpret the price index as indicating a decline in the purchasing power of our simple economy's dollar. We could say that the 1977 dollar was worth only half as much as the 1972 dollar.

Base Year For measurement of real GNP, the year from which prices are used in evaluating both base-year and current-year outputs.

Real GNP A measure of aggregate economic activity obtained by evaluating current-year quantities in terms of the prices of some base year.

Price Index In the most general sense, the ratio of current-year nominal GNP to current-year real GNP. See also *consumer* and *wholesale price indexes.*

Price Indexes in the American Economy

Official government statisticians calculate not just one, but several price indexes for the American economy. The underlying principle is the same for all these indexes, but because first one and then another may come to our attention in the news, it is useful to understand how they differ.

The broadest measure of price changes is an index called the implicit price deflator of the GNP. It is exactly the kind of index defined above, and can be interpreted as showing the "average" or "general" price level of all final goods and services. It is called "deflator" because dividing (deflating) nominal GNP by this price index gives real GNP. The U.S. Department of Commerce currently uses 1972 as the base year for its GNP deflator.

Two other important measures of prices are the **consumer price index** (CPI) and the **wholesale price index** (WPI), which differ from the implicit deflator both in the products that are included in calculating them and in the way they are constructed. The consumer price index measures the average prices of all major categories of goods and services purchased by urban wage earners and clerical workers. A "representative market basket" has been chosen from studies of actual expenditures by such individuals. The prices of approximately 400 different goods and services are currently included in this index. The wholesale price index, in contrast, excludes prices paid by household consumers, and measures the average prices of commodities purchased in large quantities in transactions between firms. Currently, the constituent price quotations are obtained on a sample of about 2,500 items from manufacturers or other producers; no services are included in the wholesale price index. At the time this book is being written, the CPI and WPI are using 1967 as their base year. The U.S. Bureau of Labor Statistics, which constructs these indexes, changes the base year once a decade or so.

Both the consumer price index and the wholesale price index are constructed using base-year quantities rather than current-year quantities. They are found by the formula

$$\text{Price Index} = \frac{\substack{\text{Value of Base-Year Quantities} \\ \text{at Current-Year Prices}}}{\substack{\text{Value of Base-Year Quantities} \\ \text{at Base-Year Prices}}} \qquad \frac{P_1 \, Q_0}{P_0 \, Q_0}$$

Using base-year rather than current-year quantities provides an important practical advantage. It means that in order to recalculate the index it is necessary to collect new data only on prices, which are easily available, and not on quantities, which are not quite so readily measured. Consequently, the Bureau of Labor Statistics is able to issue up-to-date computations of the consumer price index and the wholesale price index every month, before data on the implicit deflator of the GNP are issued.

Exhibit 6.7 shows how the wholesale price index and the consumer price index have moved over the last decade. As everyone knows, having studied economics or not, the price levels have risen sharply over this period. Later, in Chapters 14–17, we shall discuss the causes of these price increases at some length. Now, though, we need to add a few cautionary words about interpreting the indexes.

Consumer Price Index A price index based on a "representative market basket" of about 400 goods and services purchased by urban wage earners and clerical workers. This index is calculated using base-year quantities.

Wholesale Price Index A price index based on a sample of about 2,500 goods purchased in large quantities in transactions between firms. This index is calculated using base-year quantities.

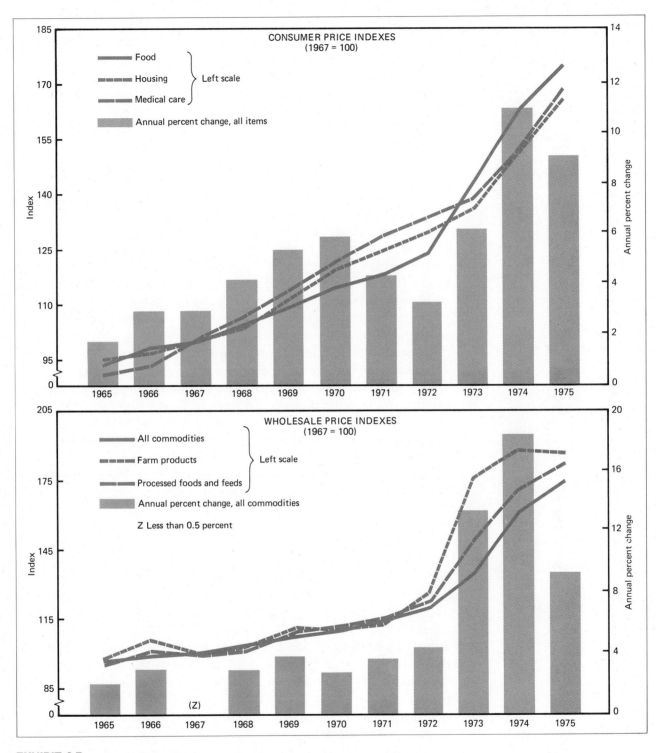

EXHIBIT 6.7

Prices indexes, 1965–1975

The CPI is based on a "representative market basket" of goods and services purchased by urban wage earners. The WPI is based on a sample of about 2,500 items purchased in large quantities in transactions between firms. Both indexes have risen sharply in recent years.

Source: Charts prepared by U.S. Bureau of the Census; data from U.S. Bureau of Labor Statistics. 1975 data from *Economic Report of the President,* 1976.

Biases in Price Indexes

Two important problems affect the accuracy of price indexes as measures of price change. One stems from buyers' reactions to price changes and the other from quality improvements and new products.

In the simple three-good economy which we looked at earlier, the prices of movies and apples rose relative to the price of shirts between 1972 and 1977. The law of demand would lead us to expect buyers to react to these changes by stepping up their purchases of the relatively lower-priced shirts. By using the 1977 quantities, the implicit price deflator places too much weight on the relatively lower-priced shirts and too little weight on the relatively higher-priced movies and apples in comparison to the quantities actually bought in 1972. For this reason it understates the amount of inflation, or as we say, it has a downward bias.

The consumer and wholesale price indexes, on the other hand, use base-year quantities. In so doing, they put too little weight on lower-priced goods, which are now purchased in greater quantities, and too much weight on higher-priced ones, which are now purchased less. For this reason, the consumer and wholesale price indexes tend to overstate the amount of inflation, or to have an upward bias.

A second problem imparts an upward bias to all three indexes and probably outweighs the first in importance. Economists would not want to attribute to "inflation" those price increases that arise solely from improvements in the quality of goods and services. Government statisticians attempt to hold "quality" constant in constructing the price indexes. They also attempt to substitute new products for obsolete ones in making up the price indexes. But careful studies indicate that quality improvements and new products are not adequately accounted for. Unfortunately, the actual magnitude of this upward bias cannot be determined very accurately.

Conclusions

We have now looked at length at the ways nominal and real GNP are measured. In most cases, we have given the benefit of the doubt to the national income accountants who put our official statistics together. They do, in fact, do quite a competent job, given the imperfect nature of the materials with which they have to work. Still, we would not want to give more credit than is due, and above all, we would not want to leave the reader thinking that national income statistics have more significance than they really have. We shall conclude this chapter, then, by listing all the things that GNP is not.

GNP and Output

Gross national product tries only to be a measure of the value of all goods and services produced in the economy. A number of technical difficulties keep it from doing even this in a very satisfactory way. We have already discussed some of these technical difficulties. One is the problem that GNP statistics are only estimates of actual economic activity, based on an incomplete sample of the activities of firms and individuals. Another is the problem that when nominal GNP figures are converted into real terms, they pick up a further source of error from the biases inherent in price indexes.

GNP does not measure perfectly the things it tries to measure, and there are some things that it does not measure at all. Nonmarket goods are one example of omitted items. Two kinds of nonmarket goods are included in GNP (the rental value of owner-occupied housing and the food produced and consumeed on farms), but many others are left out. All do-it-yourself activities are left out, and these include such very large items as the domestic services of housewives. The man who marries his former housekeeper causes a decline in GNP by the amount of her former salary even though her workload and productive services stay the same (or even rise).

Not only are many nonmarket goods left out, but a great many goods and services that *are* bought and sold in market transactions do not show up in GNP. The most important are those arising from illegal activities. Prostitution, bootlegging, narcotics, and gambling are industries whose multibillion-dollar sales go unreported, despite the fact that producers engaged in these lines yield real services to their customers. Some legal economic activity also goes unreported for purposes of income tax evasion, such as part of the cash income of professionals.

GNP Not a Measure of Welfare

Even if real GNP did measure output accurately, a measure of output is not the same thing as a measure of welfare or human satisfaction. There are a number of factors that affect human satisfaction but are not reflected in the real GNP measure. These factors can change, and would alter welfare even if real GNP remains constant.

First, the size of the population may affect the satisfaction derived from a given level of real GNP. The adjustment of real GNP to a per capita figure by dividing by population is a crude allowance for this factor.

Second, the way income is distributed may affect the level of satisfaction. The level of real GNP per capita does not directly reflect the number of families in poverty or the relative income status of upper- and lower-income groups. This situation is as it must be, because positive economics as a science cannot compare the relative satisfactions of different people. It cannot say what effect a redistribution of income has on "total" satisfaction. Do the recipients of government transfers gain more welfare than the taxpayers lose? There is no scientific way to tell.

Third, fewer and fewer labor-hours per worker are devoted to producing real GNP as the years go by. It seems plausible to think that more leisure would cause satisfaction to rise. Leisure is evidently a scarce economic good valued by workers. However, the substantial increase in the leisure of the American worker in this century is not explicitly reflected in GNP calculations.

Fourth, real GNP is a measure only of currently produced goods and services. Satisfaction is also provided by durable consumer goods produced in the past that are still providing services. Surely, the larger the present stock of consumer durables, the higher is satisfaction.

Fifth, the market prices at which goods are sold do not reflect costs or benefits affecting third parties not directly involved in the exchange. For example, environmental pollution caused by productive activities detracts from welfare. Pollution adversely affects people who are neither buyers nor sellers of the goods whose production created it. Like several of the nonmarketed goods discussed above that affect satisfaction, pollution is not entered into GNP calculations. Unlike those goods, though, pollution is a "bad"—a kind of output with a negative value. Annual additions to the amount of pollution should, in principle, be subtracted from GNP, but practical problems make this adjustment impossible.

Sixth on the list, an increase in output would not necessarily imply an increase in welfare, even if none of the problems yet mentioned were there. An unseasonably cold winter, for example, or an epidemic of infectious disease could cause the purchases of heating fuel or medical services to rise dramatically. Yet the resulting increases in real GNP would hardly represent an increase in satisfaction! Wartime defense expenditures provide another example of the lack of direct correspondence between output and welfare. We could argue that in principle these kinds of expenditures are for the maintenance of the stock of human beings, and should be treated just like investment expenditures that offset depreciation of the capital stock; that is, they should be subtracted from real GNP to get real NNP. Putting this idea into practice, however, would be quite difficult.

Finally, it should be pointed out that many aspects of human welfare are not related at all to the flow of economic goods and services or to the economic satisfaction obtained from them. Everyone would agree that people do not live by bread alone, although obtaining agreement about exactly what personal and social attributes are important, and how much each contributes, would not be easy. How important are unspoiled natural areas, unalienating work, loving human contact, space exploration, social justice, income equality, economic growth, or freedom? These are normative questions that each person may answer individually. The positive economist could never hope to lump these social and economic conditions into an objective measure of social welfare.

For all these reasons, then, real GNP should never be interpreted as a measure of social welfare. Still, it is not completely worthless. Real GNP provides a roughly accurate picture of the economy's annual production of final goods and services, which, of course, is all that it was ever intended to do. As we shall see, it is valuable for several purposes even given its limitations.

SUMMARY

1. Official measurements of national product are made using the expenditure approach. Gross national product is obtained by adding together the values of all expenditures on newly produced goods and services. Net national product is derived from gross national product by excluding the value of investment expenditures that merely replace worn-out or obsolete capital equipment.
2. National income is officially estimated by the income approach. This means adding together the values of all income earned by households. In the real world, certain adjustments must be made to get GNP and national income to fit, even though for elementary theoretical purposes, we consider the two to be equal. The difference between GNP and national income is equal to the capital consumption allowance plus indirect business taxes plus the statistical discrepancy.
3. National income measures all income earned by households, while personal income measures all the income they actually receive. To go from national income to personal income, we subtract payroll taxes, corporate profits taxes, and

undistributed corporate profits, and then add transfer payments. If we subtract personal income taxes from personal income, we get disposable personal income.

4. Measurements of aggregate economic activity can be made in real terms in order to adjust for changes in prices. Real GNP means the total value of current-year quantities of output evaluated in terms of the prices of some base year. The price index (GNP deflator) is defined as the ratio of current-year nominal GNP to current-year real GNP.

5. Real GNP does not attempt to be a measure of welfare or satisfaction, but only a measure of the output of goods and services. It does not do even that job perfectly because of sampling error, omitted items, and biases in price indexes. It is important to remember that a great many things contribute to overall human welfare that are not in any way measured by GNP.

DISCUSSION QUESTIONS

1. During this past year I received a raise of 5 percent, but the cost of living (the prices of all the goods and services I buy) went up 10 percent. Explain what happened to my nominal and real income.

2. If all mothers in the United States traded off housework with their neighbors, received a wage for doing their neighbor's work, and hence did none of their own housework, what would happen to GNP as measured by national income accountants? Would society be better off with a situation where everyone got paid? Explain.

3. Do you think transfer payments should be included in the measure of GNP? Justify your answer.

4. Is it possible that net private domestic investment could be negative? Show how this could happen by providing an example.

5. A firm gets rid of its inventory of $10,000 worth of shoes by having a sale to the public. What happens to GNP in this case? What happens to each of its components?

6. If the government increased the social security payroll deduction from 6 to 10 percent, what would happen to GNP, national income, and personal income?

7. Determine whether each of the following expenditures of my own earnings is consumption, saving, investment, or something else:
   (a) Purchase of a new home
   (b) Purchase of an automobile for cash
   (c) Payment of a monthly installment on a loan
   (d) Purchase of an item of $4.00 plus $.20 sales tax
   (e) Purchase of common stock
   (f) Giving my children a weekly allowance
   (g) Payment of tuition for additional education
   (h) A tip at a restaurant

8. What would happen to GNP and national income if an attorney married her secretary and she no longer paid him a wage? Has real production or the economic well-being of the nation changed as a result?

CHAPTER 7
Economic Growth and Living Standards

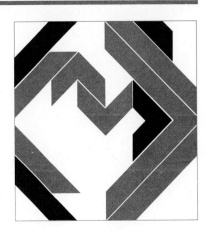

What You Will Learn in This Chapter
The high American standard of living is built on a long record of past economic growth. The American economy is still growing at a respectable rate, although some other industrialized countries are catching up through even more rapid growth. In the short run, the rate of growth can vary substantially from year to year because of changes in the share of available resources that are actually employed. In the long run, growth of output depends on advances in knowledge, education, increases in the amount of work done, and the accumulation of capital. In recent years, many people have begun to doubt that further economic growth is possible or desirable. These doubts are not groundless, but extreme pessimism does not seem to be justified.

For Review
Here are some important terms and concepts that will be put to use in this chapter. Be certain that you understand them, or review them before proceeding.

Production possibility frontier (Chapter 1)
Real GNP (Chapter 6)
GNP not a measure of welfare (Chapter 6)

American Economic Growth
Economic growth means the growth of opportunities to satisfy economic wants. At any one time, economic opportunities are limited. Labor, natural resources, and capital are scarce. Their scarcity, together with the state of our technological knowledge, limit production possibilities. Not all the useful goods and services we want can be produced at once.

As time passes, though, the range of possibilities among which we may choose expands. Capital accumulates and new resources are found. New methods of production make it possible to get more output from each unit of input. We still will not be able to have everything at once, but we can have more things at once than before.

The Growth Record
Economic growth is commonly measured in terms of real gross national product. Although real GNP is not a perfect measure of our ability to satisfy wants, or even of output, it is the best measure we have. Exhibit 7.1

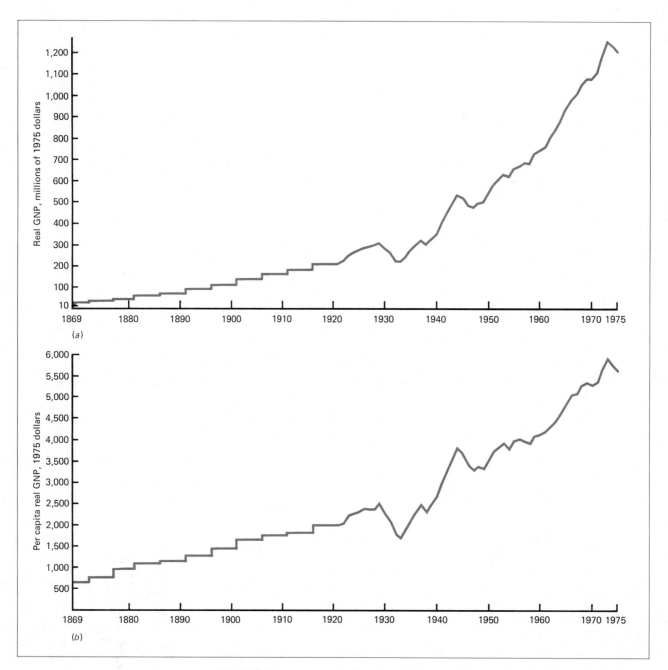

EXHIBIT 7.1

The American economy has a long record of economic growth At the time of the Civil War, per capita GNP appears to have been roughly what it is in Brazil today. Since then per capita GNP has increased by nearly a factor of ten. The growth of total real GNP has been even more impressive. Aided by population growth, it is nearly forty times higher now than a century ago.

Source: 1869–1946, Historical Statistics of the United States. 1946–1975, Economic Report of the President, 1976.

shows what has happened to real GNP in the United States from 1869 to the present, both in total and per capita terms. The per capita figures give us a better idea of how individual economic welfare has changed. The total

EXHIBIT 7.2

Economic growth in selected developed and less developed countries during the 1960s

This table shows the growth rate for a selection of countries during the 1960s, about half of which grew faster than the United States in per capita terms, and half more slowly. U.S. growth was a little on the low side by Western standards. Per capita growth in many less developed countries was seriously reduced by rapid population growth. This is shown by big differences between total and per capita growth rates for those countries.

Country	Total Growth Rate of GNP	Per Capita Growth Rate of GNP
Developed Countries		
Japan	10.5	9.3
Italy	5.3	4.8
France	5.7	4.6
Canada	5.6	3.7
West Germany	4.6	3.5
Sweden	4.2	3.5
Australia	5.4	3.4
United States	4.6	3.3
United Kingdom	2.8	2.1
Switzerland	3.2	2.0
Less Developed Countries		
South Korea	8.9	6.3
Thailand	8.3	5.0
Turkey	6.0	3.5
Kenya	6.9	3.3
Sudan	6.3	3.0
Guatemala	5.6	2.5
Pakistan	5.4	1.9
Peru	4.8	1.7
Indonesia	3.0	0.4
Haiti	0.7	−1.3

Source: U.N. Statistical Yearbook.

figures, on the other hand, tell us more about the growth of national economic power or military power.

International Comparisons

American economic growth has been respectable but not really outstanding compared with that of other nations. Exhibit 7.2 shows average annual growth rates for a selected group of countries during the 1960s. About half of these are countries that did better than the United States in per capita terms, and half are countries that did worse.

The champion of the growth league, as the table shows, is Japan. Not only did it benefit from a high absolute rate of growth, but also from a fairly stable population, so that per capita growth was high too. Some less developed countries, such as Thailand and South Korea, had absolute growth rates nearly as high as Japan. However, their populations grew rapidly so that per capita income did not grow as fast.

Among the fully industrialized countries on our list, the United States ranks a bit lower than most in terms of the growth of per capita GNP. The differences in growth rates were sufficient to bring living standards in most of these countries gradually closer to those in the United States.

The range of growth rates is much wider among the less developed countries than among the industrialized countries. Some of the poor nations did quite respectably in the decade covered by the table, but most dropped farther behind the rich. In every country on the list, population growth was more rapid than in the developed countries. This shows up in the dif-

Country	Per Capita Income in Terms of Purchasing Power, Percent of U.S. Level, 1970
Kenya	5.7
India	7.1
Colombia	15.9
Hungary	40.3
Italy	45.8
Great Britain	60.3
Japan	61.5
West Germany	74.7
France	75.0
United States	100.00

Source: Irving B. Kravis et al., *A System of International Comparisons of Gross Product and Purchasing Power* (Baltimore: Johns Hopkins, 1975). Published for the World Bank by The Johns Hopkins University Press, © 1975.

EXHIBIT 7.3

International comparisons of living standards
Direct comparisons of per capita GNP show living standards in many Western countries and Japan to be very close to those in the United States. This set of figures attempts to correct GNP comparisons by taking the actual purchasing power of income in various countries into account. In terms of real purchasing power, the United States still appeared to have a lead over other wealthy countries in 1970.

ference between the good absolute rates of growth and the disappointing per capita rates. We shall discuss the special problems of economic growth in the less developed countries in Chapter 20 of this book.

Comparing Living Standards

Americans are used to thinking of themselves as the richest people in the world. Is this still the case, even though other nations have been growing faster in recent years? One set of figures suggests that the American lead in living standards has greatly diminished, if not disappeared completely. Direct comparisons of GNP per capita show West Germany at 94 percent of the United States, France at 81 percent, and Japan at 64 percent (an increase from just 40 percent five years earlier).

The trouble with figures like this is that GNP is not a very accurate guide to living standards. Recently, a group of economists at the University of Pennsylvania did a study comparing living standards in terms of the things people really consume.[1] They used a "market basket" of goods rather like that used in drawing up the consumer price index as a basis for their comparisons. The results are shown in Exhibit 7.3.

The University of Pennsylvania study contained a few surprises for people who were used to thinking in terms of GNP. For one thing, the study shows living standards in the most advanced Western European countries, such as France and West Germany, to still be much below those in the United States. For another, the new figures appear to put living standards in Japan equal to or even a little ahead of those in Great Britain. (As recently as 1950, they were something like a fourth of the British level.) Finally, the new figures make the poorest countries shown in Exhibit 7.3, Kenya and India, look a little less poor than do straight GNP comparisons. On a GNP basis, 1970 living standards in Kenya would have been only 3.2 percent of those in the United States instead of 5.7 percent. Those in India would have been only 2.3 percent instead of 7.1 percent.

[1]Irving B. Kravis et al., *A System of International Comparisons of Gross Product and Purchasing Power* (Baltimore: Johns Hopkins, 1975).

EXHIBIT 7.4

The process of economic growth

Economic growth can be represented as an outward expansion of the production possibilities frontier. In any one year, getting more "guns" means giving up some "butter," as in a movement from B to A. Over time, however, growth could give us more of both "guns" and "butter," as in a movement from A to C, D, and E.

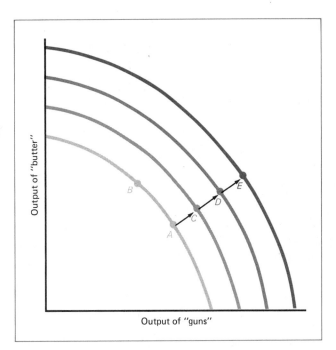

Output of "butter"

Output of "guns"

Actual and Potential Growth

Growth and Production Possibilities

The production possibilities frontier can give us some important insights into economic growth. Resources and technology limit production possibilities at any one time. Once this year's production possibilities are fully exploited, we must give up some of one thing to get more of another. Over time, though, resources and technology change. The frontier expands and we can have a little more of everything if we wish.

Exhibit 7.4 shows how the process of economic growth looks in these terms. We imagine an economy in which only two goods are produced: "guns" and "butter." In any one year, more of one good can be produced only at the opportunity cost of producing less of the other. Economic choice is limited to movements along the frontier, as from point A to point B. Over time, though, economic growth moves the frontier outward. New technology and new productive resources provide the opportunity to produce more of one good while also expanding output of the other. As growth proceeds, we might move, if we wished, from point A to C, and eventually to D and E and beyond.

Actual and Potential Output

There is just one hitch. In order actually to be on the production possibilities frontier in any year, all available resources must be fully used. If some go to waste, output will be less than it could be. The economy will fall below the frontier.

This creates a problem for measuring the rate of economic growth. It turns out that we have two reasons why real GNP could change from one year to the next. One reason is that the production possibilities frontier

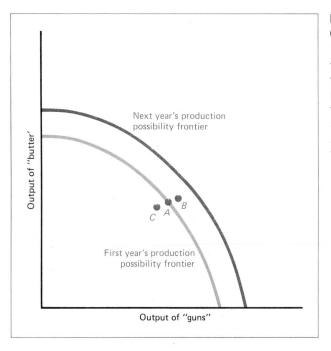

EXHIBIT 7.5
Growth and resource utilization

In order actually to be on the production possibility frontier in any year, all available resources must be put to efficient use. This figure shows that growth of potential output (represented by the outward shift of the frontier) need not bring an equivalent growth of actual output. The economy could move from *A* only to *B,* or even to *C* as the frontier expanded if at the same time the proportion of resources actually employed fell.

Potential Output (potential real GNP) The level of output that the economy could in principle achieve if it were operating on the production possibilities frontier. Potential output can be estimated from actual real output using Okun's law.

Okun's Law A rule of thumb that says that for each percentage point by which the unemployment rate rises above the ''full employment'' benchmark (traditionally taken to be 4 percent measured unemployment), actual output will fall below potential output by about 3 percent.

Output Gap The difference between actual real GNP and potential real GNP in any year.

could expand. The other is that the proportion of available resources that are put to efficient use could change.

Consider Exhibit 7.5. In one year, the economy might be at point *A*, with all production possibilities fully utilized. In the next year, investment, new technology, or new resource discoveries might shift the production possibilities frontier outward as shown, but at the same time, actual use of resources might decline. With many resources idle, the economy could end up at point *B*, with only a little real growth, or even at point *C*, with a fall in real output.

Economists call the level of output that the economy would achieve if it were on its production possibility frontier **potential output** to distinguish it from the actual level of real output as measured in the national income accounts. As Exhibit 7.5 shows, potential output can grow faster than actual output. Potential and actual output can even move in opposite directions. In the long run, changes in potential output determine the rate of economic growth, but this need not be true in the short run.

Okun's Law

We learned how actual real output was measured in Chapter 6. For many purposes, it is useful to be able to measure potential output too. The standard way of measuring potential output is to use a simple rule of thumb called **Okun's law.** Okun's law tells us that the difference between actual and potential output in any year depends on how fully the economy's labor resources are employed. If labor is not fully employed, there is said to be an **output gap** between actual and potential GNP. In numerical terms, Okun's law says that for each percentage point by which the unemployment rate differs from full employment, there will be an output gap of 3.2 percent.

Arthur Okun is one of the best known of a generation of "new economists" who dominated economic policy making during the Kennedy and Johnson administrations of the 1960s. In 1961, the young Associate Professor left Yale to join the "New Frontier" as a staff economist on the President's Council of Economic Advisors. In 1964, he became a full member of the Council, and eventually, in 1968–9, was its chairman. When Johnson left office, Okun stayed in Washington as a Senior Fellow of the Brookings Institution, a position that permitted him to combine research with active public affairs involvement.

Okun's name is perhaps most widely heard in connection with his famous "law" relating changes in unemployment to changes in real national product. This noteworthy empirical generalization was first formulated in a paper, "Potential GNP, Its Measurement and Significance," written for the American Statistical Association in 1962. In this paper, Okun tried to answer the question of how much output the economy could produce under conditions of full employment. Because of his concern for "the enormous social cost of idle resources," he found this question a central one for economic policy.

At the time Okun was on the Council of Economic Advisors, "growthmanship" was at its height in the economics profession. Okun saw rapid economic growth as crucial to avoiding the "waste and extravagance" of unemployment. "The economy loses ground if it stands still," he wrote. "Unless the growth of output keeps pace with our ever-expanding potential, the unemployment rate tends to rise. The nation needs continually to set new records in production and sales. Its economy needs to grow bigger and better than ever before—because its labor force, capital stock, technology, and managerial and organizational resources are always getting bigger and better."

Are Okun's words the echo of a naively optimistic era now past, or do they represent a lesson yet to be learned? The issue is far from settled, and Okun himself is still vigorously involved in the debate.

Arthur Okun (1928–)

The original formulation of Okun's law used a measured unemployment rate of 4 percent as its "full employment" benchmark. That means that for an unemployment rate of 5 percent, actual output would be 3.2 percent below its potential, for an unemployment rate of 6 percent it would be 6.4 percent below potential, and so forth. Knowing actual real GNP and the unemployment rate for any year, then, we can calculate potential GNP. Exhibit 7.6 shows actual GNP, potential GNP, and the output gap for the American economy from 1950 to 1975.

There are some difficulties in using 4 percent unemployment as the "full employment" benchmark. On the one hand, it seems more logical for zero unemployment to be the benchmark. That would avoid the awkward matter of having actual GNP being higher than potential GNP in years when unemployment is less than 4 percent, so that the output gap is negative. On the other hand, many economists now argue that 4 percent is too low a level to use as a benchmark. For various reasons, it is said, unemployment tends to be around 5 percent even when the economy is functioning as well as we can normally expect it to. The whole issue of just what "full employment" means will be taken up in some detail in Chapter 15. For now, we can stick with Okun's original 4 percent benchmark, for the sake of tradition if nothing else.

One peculiarity of Okun's law needs additional explanation. Why is it that output is so sensitive to unemployment? If 1 percent more people go to work, why should output rise by more than 1 percent?

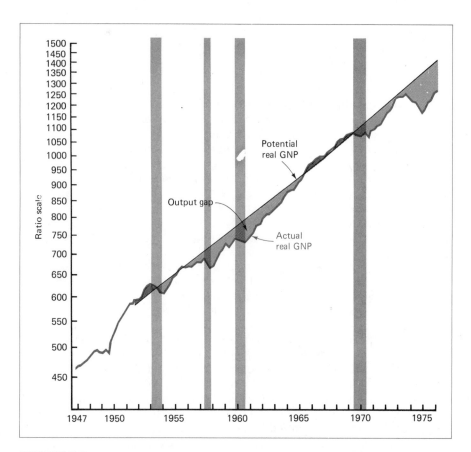

EXHIBIT 7.6
Growth of actual and potential GNP in the American economy
According to Okun's law, there is an output gap between actual and potential real GNP whenever the unemployment rate is above its "full employment" benchmark. In drawing this figure, full employment is considered to mean 4 percent measured unemployment. In some years unemployment was below 4 percent, so the output gap was negative.

The easy answer is that that is just the way it happens. Okun's law is not based on any deep economic theory. It is just a rule of thumb based on what has usually been seen to happen in the past.

A slightly closer look, though, shows us a little of what lies behind the high-powered effect of a change in unemployment. For one thing, the unemployment rate is measured as a percentage of people who are "in the labor force." Roughly speaking, the labor force means those people who have a job or who are looking for one.[2] When times are bad, some people do not even bother to look. They withdraw from the labor force. When things begin to look up, then, we find not only that the employed percentage of the labor force grows, but that the labor force itself grows as formerly discouraged workers reenter the market. The number of employed persons thus grows faster than the measured unemployment rate falls.

A further reason for the high-powered effect of changes in unemployment is "labor hoarding." When business turns down, firms do not always

[2]See Chapter 15 for a full discussion of how unemployment and the labor force are measured.

lay off every nonessential worker. Instead, they cut back overtime work, or let workers double up on jobs, or keep them on to do odd bits of work that do not have very high priority. That way, the firms know that when business turns up again, the workers they need will be right at hand. Output can be expanded without new hiring just by putting the existing labor force back to work more productively. Because productivity per worker rises during an upturn, output expands more than in proportion to the expansion of number of people at work.

Sources of Potential Economic Growth

Actual economic growth from year to year, we have seen, need not reflect changes in real economic potential. Over the long run, though, it is growth of potential that counts. Putting year-to-year changes in employment aside, then, what are the sources of the long-run growth of potential output?

Population and Productivity

As a start, we can identify two major sources of long-run economic growth. These are growth of the working population and growth of output per worker.

If we want to talk about the growth of per capita income, it is growth of output per worker that really counts. Some per capita gains can be realized by putting a higher percentage of the population to work, but sooner or later this reaches a limit. Normally, increasing the absolute size of the population without changing the proportion of people who work will not improve per capita income. In fact, many less developed countries of the world are so short on capital and natural resources that population growth actually detracts from the growth of per capita income. Let us put population growth aside, then, and look at the sources of the growth of output per worker.

Growth of Knowledge

The growth of knowledge is the greatest source of economic growth in the long run. We often tend to think of whole periods of growth in terms of one or two key inventions. When we think of the Industrial Revolution in England, we think of the steam engine. When we think of growth in nineteenth-century America, the railroad comes to mind. In the twentieth century, first the automobile and then the computer have led the way.

New technology is not the only important form of new knowledge. Changes in business organization also play a big role. The modern corporation and the assembly line are cases in point. Future growth will very likely see still more organizational changes, for example, the spread of worker participation in business decisions.

Capital Accumulation

Another leading source of economic growth is capital accumulation. More tools and equipment enable each worker to produce more per hour. Drainage and fencing allow farmers to grow more on each acre of land. What is more, most new knowledge needs to be embodied in new capital goods before it can be put to work.

Growth by capital accumulation involves a trade-off between present and future living standards. We know that gross national product is composed of consumption, investment, and government purchases. To raise the rate of capital accumulation, we must save and invest more. That means that there will be less left over for private consumption and government purchases. In return for giving those things up now, though, the added investment will make output grow faster. In the future, we can have more consumption and government purchases than we could have if we saved less now.

We can be grateful to our ancestors that they saved and invested as much as they did. The high living standards we enjoy today are built in large part on the capital they piled up for us. Does this mean that we should make an effort now to save more than we do for the sake of future generations? That is not an easy question to answer. Some economists point out that Americans invest only a very small part of national product compared with other advanced countries. This is one reason for our slightly slower rate of growth. Others argue, though, that building more machines and factories just means that we shall run out of natural resources sooner, and have more future pollution. According to this view, we should create less new capital, not more. We shall return to this complex issue later in the chapter.

Human Capital

Output also grows when education and job training raise the quality of the labor force. Economists refer to this source of growth as the accumulation of **human capital.** In what way is education or job training like building new tools or factories? The main point of similarity is that education and job training involve the same sort of trade-off between the present and the future as does investment in physical capital. People who stay off the job market in the present to finish school or learn new job skills give up earning power or consumption in the present. In return, they hope to earn more and have a higher standard of living in the future.

Human Capital A name for the productive potential of an individual person. The term calls attention to the fact that this productive potential can be increased by "investing" in education or job training.

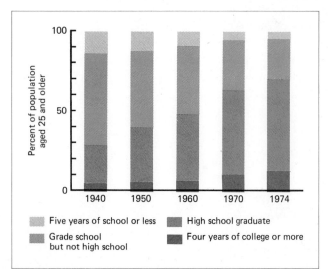

EXHIBIT 7.7
Education as an indicator of the growth of human capital in the American economy.
Formal education is a very important part of investment in human capital. Since 1940, the average education level attained in the United States has increased very substantially. The proportion of the population with a high school education or better has increased two-and-a-half-fold, and the proportion with four years of college or more has tripled.

Source: Statistical Abstract of the United States, 1975.

The amount of investment in human capital in the American economy has been enormous. Exhibit 7.7 gives an idea of what has been achieved since 1940.

Relative Importance of Sources of Growth

With so many sources of economic growth available, there is more than one way to grow. In some countries, growth has been built largely on the discovery of new natural resources and the cultivation of new land. Other countries have grown by the sheer effort of investing an enormous proportion of current output. The following case study gives an idea of the relative importance of various sources of growth for our own economy.

CASE 7.1
Sources of U.S. Economic Growth[3]

The best-known attempt to measure the sources of U.S. economic growth is that of Edward F. Denison. His study covers the period 1929 to 1969. The American economy grew at an average annual rate of 3.3 percent during these years. In the second half of the period, 1948–1969, the rate of growth was a bit faster, at 3.85 percent per year. Exhibit 7.8 presents Denison's estimates of the relative importance of various sources of economic growth for the time span his study covered.

The most important source of growth throughout the period was the growth of knowledge. Denison was not able to measure this item directly. He made direct measurements of the other sources of growth and assumed that all growth that could not otherwise be explained came from advances in knowledge.

The first of the items that could be measured directly is what Denison calls "more work done." This includes the effects of population growth, changes in hours worked per week, and changes in the composition of the work force by age and sex. Next comes the accumulation of capital. Some people find the contribution of new capital to be surprisingly small in view of the importance sometimes given to this source of growth in theoretical discussions. The growth of human capital was almost as important as that of physical capital when the whole forty years are taken into account. Since World War II, though, this item has been less important.

These four items together can be said to have brought about an outward shift of the production possibility frontier. The rest of the economic growth during the period under study came from two sources. One was the more efficient use of available factors of production. A major shift of surplus labor from agriculture to industry played a big role here. The other source of growth from 1929 to 1969 was a small reduction in the unemployment rate.

[3]Based on Edward F. Denison, *Accounting for U.S. Economic Growth, 1929–69* (Washington, D.C.: Brookings Institution, 1974).

EXHIBIT 7.8
Sources of U.S. economic growth
This table shows the relative importance of various souces of economic growth for the American economy. The first four items can be considered to account for the expansion of the production possibility frontier. The remaining part of economic growth comes from fuller and more efficient use of resources, which has moved the economy closer to the frontier.

Source	Percent of Growth Rate 1929–1969	1948–1969
Advances in knowledge	31.1	34.1
More work done	28.7	23.9
Capital accumulation	15.8	21.6
Increased education	14.1	11.9
Other	10.3	8.5
Total	100.0	100.0

Source: Edward F. Denison, *Accounting for U.S. Economic Growth, 1929–69* (Washington, D.C.: Brookings Institution, 1974) © 1974 by the Brookings Institution, Washington, D.C.

Limits to Growth?

For many years, everyone thought economic growth was a good thing. The only debates about growth took place between people who thought that the present pace was good enough and those who wanted government action to increase the growth rate. Now things are different.

Today, the people who are satisfied with our record of growth and those who would like to step up the pace have been forced into a defensive alliance. On the other side are two groups. One is made up of people who think that further economic growth is impossible, or will soon be so. The other is made up of those who think that further growth may be possible, but who do not want it. Of course, some people belong to both groups, thinking that no significant future growth is possible, and also that to keep trying to grow anyway will just make things worse.

The growth debate raises some rather technical issues. Some of these will be discussed later in this book, in the chapters on pollution, resources, and economic development. The matter is important enough, so that it is worth giving at least an outline of the main issues here.

Growth Undesirable

Let us look first at the claim that we ought not to want further economic growth, whether it is possible or not. The heart of this argument is the perfectly valid proposition that GNP is not a measure of human welfare. The trouble, it is said, is that growth of GNP can be offset by a decline in the "quality of life." These fears can be expressed in the form of a parable:

Imagine a peaceful little country with a per capita GNP of $100. All of this is produced by the women, who work the fields in the morning and gossip in the afternoon. The men do nothing at all but sit around and play cards and drink tea all day. Suppose now that an enterprising foreign businessperson sets up a soap factory and puts all of the men to work. Each man can make $40 worth of soap per year. Previously there was no market for soap in this pastoral nation, but now the soap factory belches black coal smoke from its boilers and this soils everyone's curtains. The entire output of the soap factory is sold to local housewives who now spend all of their afternoons at the laundromat.

Question: What has happened to the GNP of this country? As any economist will tell you, it has gone up by 20 percent, to $120 per capita. Farm output has not fallen, and industrial production of $20 per capita has been added. Question: What has happened to the level of well-being of the people of this country? They have no more to eat than before. Their curtains are no cleaner than before. Yet they are working four times as long. They are, let us say, about one-quarter as well off as before.

Many people believe that this parable applies to the American economy. They are worried not only about pollution, but about other values as well that they think tend to be lost as growth continues. Rapid economic growth makes skills, and hence people, obsolete before their working lives are over. Economic growth crowds out green places and covers them with asphalt. It replaces the community life of the town with the anonymity of the city. In all these ways, growth is said to make life less worth living in ways for which more cars and toaster ovens do not fully compensate.

EXHIBIT 7.9
Pollution and economic growth

In any one year, there is a trade-off between cars and clean air. More cars make the air dirtier, whereas having fewer cars makes cleaner air possible. As the production possibility frontier moves outward, we can choose between two kinds of growth. We can make as many dirty new cars as possible, moving from A to B, if that is what we want. Alternatively, we can spend more on each car to make it run cleaner, and move from A to C instead.

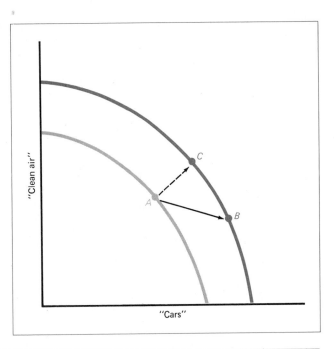

Separating the Issues

How valid is this "quality of life" argument? Are we really becoming worse off year by year, or is that just romanticism? It cannot be denied that economic growth is a *potential* threat to the quality of life. As it stands, though, the argument we have given is misleading because it confuses two issues. One issue has to do with the size of gross national product, and the other with its composition.

In Exhibit 7.9, we have used the production possibility frontier to help separate these two issues. The diagram shows an economy in which the two goods produced are called "clean air" and "cars" rather than "guns" and "butter." In any one year, there is a trade-off between the two goods. More cars make the air less clean. Making fewer cars (or spending more money on each car to make them run cleaner) allows us to have better air.

As technology improves and as we accumulate more capital, the production possibility frontier shifts outward. If the actual growth path of the economy is from point A to point B, people will complain that the quality of life has deteriorated. It is not really economic growth that is to blame though. Instead, the problem is the composition of output that has been chosen. Instead of moving from A to B by producing as many new dirty cars as possible, we could have grown along the path from A to C. That would mean fewer cars, each more carefully built to cause less pollution. Growth *could* bring us more cars *and* more clean air if we chose to go that way.

Pollution is a serious problem. It cannot be brushed aside. Still, it is wrong to blame pollution on economic growth. To stop growth in order to stop pollution would be to throw out the baby with the bath water. Controlling pollution requires policies to encourage the correct composition of national product, not policies to control its size. We shall take a look at a number of such policies in Chapter 18.

Growth Impossible

There is little point in arguing about the direction of growth if growth is impossible. Is it? Exhibit 7.8, which gave us the sources of past growth, can help us to think about future growth too. Turn back to it for a moment.

Let us begin with some optimistic observations. The greatest source of growth in the past has been the growth of knowledge. We can be pretty certain that the growth of knowledge will continue in the future. Now and then, of course, someone denies this. It is said that at the end of the last century, someone suggested that we close the patent office, because all the important inventions seemed by then to have been made.

Next in order of optimism, we turn to human capital. The growth of human capital does not use up any nonrenewable natural resources, and it is hard to see why it should not continue. It may be, though, that further increases in educational levels will not add as much as before to measured economic output. There may always be some jobs that people cannot do any better with a college degree than they can without one. Perhaps we should put more faith in education as a way of improving the quality of life than as a source of future growth of GNP.

For the moment, let us ignore the "more work done" and "other" categories as sources of future economic growth. We cannot be sure that they will continue to contribute to growth, but there is no real reason to think that they pose limits to growth either. We shall assume that they are neutral.

Resource Depletion

Now we come to the strong point of the growth pessimists. This is the depletion of nonrenewable sources of energy and raw materials. Notice that Denison did not list discoveries of new resources as a major source of growth in the past. In the future, say the pessimists, we shall have to start putting a "natural resources" line in the sources-of-growth table. The entry we put on that line will be a big fat minus, and eventually it will be big enough to cancel out all the pluses.

There are two reasons why the depletion of resources is said to limit growth. First, as the best mines and oil fields are exhausted, more and more work, research, and investment is needed to keep a steady supply of raw materials coming out. Second, it is said that resource depletion puts a brake on capital accumulation. There will not be enough of the right metals to build more machines, or enough energy to dig deeper mines, or enough oil to produce plastic substitutes for the metals we run out of. Without the ability to build new capital equipment, it is said, new knowledge cannot be put to use, and the whole growth machine will grind to a halt.

Separating the Issues Again

There is no doubt some truth to the argument that depletion of resources will make problems for future economic growth. The question is whether we shall be able to get around those problems. We cannot come up with a proper answer to that question unless we once again separate the issue of the growth of output from that of the composition of output.

The great weakness in the argument of the growth pessimists is that

EXHIBIT 7.10

Growth and resource depletion

In this diagram, "cars" stand for all goods that use up large amounts of nonrenewable resources, and "watches" stand for goods that pack a lot of value into a small physical package. As the production possibility frontier expands, growth can continue in value terms even though growth measured in tons of output might fall.

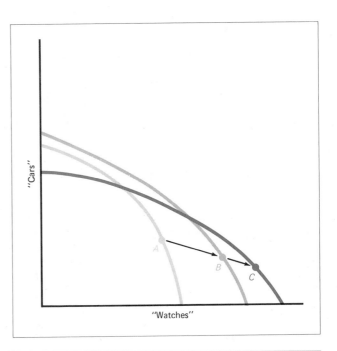

they think of growth in physical rather than economic terms. Resource depletion does place a limit on physical growth. If airplanes are made out of aluminum, and if we run out of aluminum, then we just cannot build any more aluminum airplanes. But economic growth is not measured in tons of aluminum or numbers of airplanes. It is measured in terms of value. The way to beat the physical limits to growth, then, is to switch the composition of output in favor of things that pack a lot of value into small physical packages.

Let us once again use a production possibility frontier to show what we mean. In Exhibit 7.10, we consider an economy with two goods called "cars" and "watches." "Cars" stand for the kind of goods that do face real resource limits. "Watches" stand for goods that face no serious physical resource constraint.

As this car-watch economy expands over the years its production possibility frontier shifts. When the frontier reaches the third position shown, we see that resource depletion actually cuts the maximum potential output of cars. All the time, though, GNP continues to grow as measured in value terms. The economy moves from *A* to *B* to *C,* with the composition of output shifting away from "cars" in favor of "watches."

What is true of consumer goods like cars and watches is also true of capital goods. Resource depletion may at some time stop us from building, say, any new uranium-fueled power stations. In other areas, though, the growth of knowledge shows us how to put more and more capital into smaller and smaller physical packages. The development of electronic computers is a striking case in point. It could well be that, say, putting special computer-controlled thermostats in our houses will make it possible to get along with fewer atomic power stations.

John Stuart Mill (1806–1873)

John Stuart Mill was in every respect one of the most brilliant and remarkable figures of the nineteenth century. Eldest son of the prominent economist and philosopher James Mill, John Stuart lived an extraordinary childhood. He began his study of classical Greek at the age of three. By eight, he was reading Plato's dialogues in the original, and teaching Latin to the younger members of the Mill family. His education in economics began at thirteen, under his father's tutorship, with a study of Adam Smith and the other classics.

This unusual upbringing was bound to produce a strong reaction sooner or later. In his early twenties, young Mill went through a spiritual crisis that led him to reject many of his father's ideas. About that time, he met Mrs. Harriet Taylor and began a long association with her. (Years later, after her husband's death, they were married.) Her ideas on feminism and socialism powerfully influenced Mill's thinking.

John Stuart Mill published his *Principles of Political Economy* in 1848. This work can be seen today as the high-water mark of the classical school, founded by Adam Smith three generations before. As a textbook and authority on economic questions, Mill's *Principles* stood unchallenged until Alfred Marshall transformed "political economy" into "economics" at the end of the century.

Mill's *Principles* is a work by no means limited to the narrowly technical side of economics. Mill always faced the broad social implications of economic theory squarely wherever they arose. For example, like other economists of the classical school, Mill believed there were not-too-distant limits to the process of economic growth. "At the end of the progressive state," he wrote, "lies the stationary state. All progress in wealth is but a postponement of this and all advance is an approach to it." Mill was not content, however, simply to describe the mechanics of growth and the technical properties of the stationary state. He wondered what a world without progress would really be like. His conclusions so clearly address the concerns of our own age that they are worth quoting at length:

> I cannot . . . regard the stationary state of capital and wealth with the unaffected aversion so generally manifested towards it by political economists of the old school. I am inclined to believe that it would be, on the whole, a very considerable improvement on our present condition. I confess I am not charmed with the ideal of life held out by those who think that the normal state of human beings is that of struggling to get on; that the trampling, crushing, elbowing, and treading on each other's heels, which form the existing type of social life, are the most desirable lot of human kind, or anything but the disagreeable symptoms of one of the phases of our industrial progress. . . .
>
> If the earth must lose that great portion of its pleasantries which it owes to things that the unlimited increase of wealth and population would extirpate from it, for the mere purpose of enabling it to support a larger, but not a better or happier population, I sincerely hope, for the sake of posterity, that they will be content to be stationary long before necessity compels them to.

Conclusions

What we have said should not be interpreted as establishing a case for unbounded optimism. Continued growth, we have claimed, is possible *if* the proper shifts in the composition of output are made, and made in time. We may even have to stretch our concept of the "composition of output" to include the way future growth is split between producing more human beings and producing higher living standards for a smaller total population. It is not hard to imagine ways that things *could* go wrong. In fact, the publicity that the prophets of doom get does a great service by calling such possibilities to our attention.

The interlocking issues of economic growth, population, resources, and environment are important ones, and we shall return to them in Part Three. We have said enough for the moment, though, to fit economic growth into our discussion of macroeconomics.

SUMMARY

1. Over the past century, the American economy has grown by nearly a factor of forty in terms of total real GNP, and nearly a factor of ten in terms of per capita GNP. American economic growth is still proceeding at a good rate, although many other economies are growing more rapidly still.
2. If resources are not fully employed, actual output is less than potential output. Okun's law is a simple rule of thumb that lets us put the relationship between unemployment and output more exactly. The law says that for each percentage point by which unemployment rises above its "full employment" benchmark, real GNP will decline by about 3 percent.
3. The major sources of economic growth, in order of their past importance in the American economy, are growth of knowledge, more work done, accumulation of capital, and increases in education. In other countries or at other times, the relative importance of these sources of growth may be quite different.
4. Many people now doubt that further economic growth is either possible or desirable. These growth pessimists base their arguments on some perfectly valid points. Many antigrowth arguments, however, involve a confusion between growth in the size of output and changes in the composition of output. Once these two issues are separated, it is open to us to conclude that further growth can still be a good thing, provided that such growth proceeds in the right direction.

DISCUSSION QUESTIONS

1. Is it possible with increased knowledge and technological know-how for an economy to be better off even if it does not produce any more goods and services? Explain.
2. Suppose that an economy were operating on its production possibilities frontier. What changes could be made to operate inside the frontier and still have full employment? Or is this impossible?
3. In what sense can you say that the education you are getting is an investment in human capital? What is meant by human capital?
4. What has human capital and investment in human capital got to do with the quality of life?
5. How would you go about comparing your standard of living with that of someone in a foreign country? With someone in another state? Can you simply compare incomes?
6. If people are to become better off, is it necessary that they become more productive? Explain.
7. If we were almost out of a particular resource, what would happen to the price of that resource? How might firms and consumers adjust to this increased scarcity?

CHAPTER 8
The Determinants of Planned Expenditure

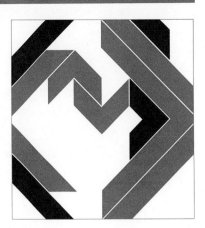

What You Will Learn in This Chapter

The British economist John Maynard Keynes made aggregate demand a key element of his economic theory. Following his approach, our theory building begins by looking at the determinants of each separate component of aggregate demand. Consumption expenditure depends to a substantial extent on the level of national income. Planned investment expenditure depends on the rate of interest and on business expectations concerning the profitability of investment projects. Government purchases and net exports are determined by forces outside the scope of elementary economic theory, so they are treated as "givens" in our analysis.

For Review

Here are some important terms and concepts that will be put to use in this chapter. Be certain that you know them, or review them before proceeding.

Aggregate demand (Chapter 5)
Planned and unplanned investment (Chapter 5)
Relationships among gross national product, national income, personal income, and disposable income (Chapter 6)

In Chapter 5 we introduced the circular flow and the ideas of aggregate supply and demand. In Chapter 6 we saw how national income accountants go about measuring the elements of the circular flow. We discovered how gross national product can be broken down into its separate components of consumption, investment, government purchases, and net exports. In Chapter 7 we saw how all these have grown with time. Now, finally, we are ready to put all these preliminary concepts and definitions to work and begin developing a *theory*. This theory will explain why national income and product are at one level rather than another in any particular year, and why they have their ups and downs over time.

Some Simplifications

In economics, theory building always begins by making some simplifications so that we may concentrate on essentials. One simplification that we shall employ throughout our discussion of macroeconomic theory is the assumption that there are no indirect business taxes, capital consumption allowance, or statistical discrepancy. Getting rid of these elements of the national income accounts greatly simplifies our discussion. Gross national product, net national product, and national income once again become equal by definition, as they were in the simplified circular flow diagrams of Chapter 5.

A second useful simplification that we shall use throughout our discussion is to omit undistributed corporate profits. With neither indirect business taxes nor undistributed corporate profits, personal income will be equal to national income minus net taxes. The term *net taxes,* as in Chapter 5, means all taxes (personal income tax, social insurance contributions, and corporate profits tax) minus all transfer payments.

Nominal and Real Values

Another way in which we shall simplify our theory building is to begin by concentrating our attention on *nominal* values of national income, consumption, and so forth. This is simply a matter of taking one thing at a time. In this chapter and the next five, we shall be trying to understand why nominal national income is, say, $1.5 billion in some year rather than some other value. Then, in Chapters 14–17, we shall turn to the question of why changes in nominal income sometimes take the form of changes in prices rather than changes in real output.

In these early chapters, in which our discussion will be entirely in terms of nominal values, we shall not repeat the term "nominal" every time we mention consumption, investment, income, or whatever. You should keep in mind, though, that we mean nominal values in every case unless we explicitly say something to the contrary.

Keynesian Economics

As we begin our discussion of macroeconomic theory, we are entering the heartland of what is known as Keynesian economics, named after the British economist John Maynard Keynes. It is no exaggeration to say that his writings revolutionized macroeconomic thought. Although many of Keynes' particular conclusions have been challenged by contemporary economists, the fact that these challenges occur within his basic theoretical framework attests to his lasting influence. Keynes' ideas underlie all of modern macroeconomic theory as well as the contents of this book, even in places where we do not pause to acknowledge them specifically.

Keynes made the concept of *aggregate demand* a key element of his theory. He taught that macroeconomic analysis should begin by asking what determines each of the separate types of planned expenditure that make up aggregate demand: consumption, planned investment, government purchases, and net exports. Let us follow his plan by discussing each of these in turn.

Consumption

Consumption and Income

Keynes' theory of consumption expenditure was novel and very simple. Both common sense and experience, he said, suggest that in general and on

John Maynard Keynes was born into economics. His father, John Neville Keynes, was a lecturer in economics and logic at Cambridge University. John Maynard began his own studies at Cambridge with an emphasis on mathematics and philosophy. His abilities soon so impressed Alfred Marshall, however, that the distinguished teacher urged him to concentrate on economics. In 1908, after Keynes had finished his studies and done a brief stint in the civil service, Marshall offered him a lectureship in economics at Cambridge, which he accepted.

Keynes is remembered above all for his *General Theory of Employment, Interest, and Money,* published in 1936, although that was by no means his first important work. Keynes' reputation as the outstanding economist of his generation lay in the departure from classical and neoclassical theory he made there. It is hardly necessary to say much about the substance of Keynes' *General Theory* in these paragraphs, because they are extensively discussed in every modern textbook on economics. It will be enough to say that its major features were a theory boldly drawn in terms of broad macroeconomic aggregates, and a policy position tending toward activism and interventionism.

Keynes was no "narrow" economist. He was an honored member not only of the British academic upper class, but also of Britain's highest financial, political, diplomatic, administrative, and even artistic circles. He was intimately involved with the colorful "Bloomsbury set" of London's literary-Bohemian world. He was a friend of Virginia Woolf, E. M. Forster, and Lytton Strachey, and in 1925, married the ballerina Lydia Lopokovia. He was a dazzling success at whatever he turned his hand to, from mountain climbing to financial speculation. As a speculator, he made an enormous fortune for himself, and as Bursar of Kings College, he turned an endowment of £30,000 into one of £380,000.

In even the briefest discussion of Keynes, it would be unforgivable not to give his most famous quotation. Writing in the *General Theory,* he pronounced that "the ideas of economists and political philosophers, both when they are right and when they are wrong, are more powerful than is commonly understood. Indeed the world is ruled by little else. Practical men, who believe themselves to be quite exempt from any intellectual influences, are usually the slaves of some defunct economist. Madmen in authority, who hear voices in the air, are distilling their frenzy from some academic scribbler of a few years back. . . . There are not many who are influenced by new theories after they are twenty-five or thirty years of age, so that the ideas which civil servants and politicians and even agitators apply to current events are not likely to be the newest."

Was Keynes issuing a warning here? Whether he had any such thing in mind or not, his words, forty years later, have become one of the great ironies of the history of economic ideas.

John Maynard Keynes
(1883–1946)

the average, people increase their consumption as their income increases, but not by as much as the full increase in their income.

A look at the historical record of consumption and income in the United States does in fact reveal this pattern. In Exhibit 8.1, consumption is measured on the vertical axis and disposable income on the horizontal axis. The points on the graph show levels of consumption and disposable income for years from 1929 to 1975. By passing a straight line through as many points as possible, we can see how the level of consumption expenditure varied on average as the level of disposable income varied. Notice that the straight line passes above the points representing war years because rationing and unavailability of certain consumer goods made consumption artificially low.

To make Exhibit 8.1 easier to read, we have drawn in a 45° reference line. The point for any year when consumption and income are equal will

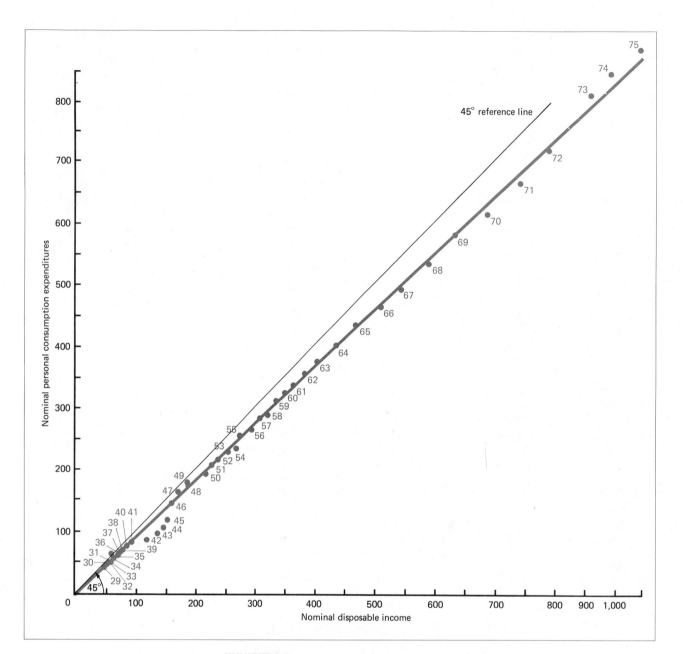

EXHIBIT 8.1
Income and consumption in the United States
The figure shows that since 1929, consumption has increased as disposable income has increased. The 45° reference line helps in interpreting the figure. The points for years when income and consumption were exactly equal fall on the 45° line. In years when the consumption point was below the reference line, the distance between the point and the reference line equals saving.

fall exactly on this line. Since 1939, the points showing actual consumption lie below the reference line. The vertical gap between the reference line and the consumption points is equal to the difference between disposable income and consumption. As we saw in Chapter 5, this difference is saving. In some years in the 1930s the consumption points lie slightly above the 45° reference line. In those years negative saving, or **dissaving,** occurred. Households consumed more than their disposable income either by using up past savings or by borrowing. The illustration shows that since 1929, as disposable income has risen, both consumption and saving have risen.

Consumption Schedule

Keynes suggested that the relationship between income and consumption was deeply rooted in human nature. We shall give the name **consumption schedule** to any table or graph showing the way nominal consumption expenditure varies when nominal income varies, other things being equal.[1] The straight line drawn through the various points in Exhibit 8.1 can be referred to as a historical consumption schedule for the American economy. In our theory building, we shall use a simplified numerical example instead of actual historical data. This simplified consumption schedule is shown in Exhibit 8.2.

Autonomous Consumption

According to Exhibit 8.2, when disposable income is zero, consumption is $150. This indicates that people plan to consume some minimum quantity of goods and services regardless of their disposable income. We shall call this minimum level of planned consumption expenditure ($150 in our example) **autonomous consumption.** In the graphical representation of the consumption schedule, autonomous consumption is equal to the height of the point at which the consumption schedule intersects the vertical axis. Even if people do not have enough current income to finance the autonomous consumption they plan to undertake, they will consume anyway by drawing on past savings or borrowing.

It should be emphasized that autonomous consumption is autonomous only in the sense that it does not depend on the level of disposable income. This does not mean that the level of autonomous consumption is independent of other economic influences. The consumption schedule includes an "other things being equal" clause, and changes in these other things can change autonomous consumption. More on this shortly.

Marginal Propensity to Consume

Look now at columns (3), (4), and (5) in the Exhibit 8.2a. The numbers in these columns show that whenever household income increases, some of the additional income is devoted to additional consumption above and beyond autonomous consumption. The fraction of each added dollar of disposable income that goes to added consumption is called the **marginal propensity to consume.**

We see, for example, that a $100 increase in income, from $500 to $600, raises consumption by $50, from $400 to $450. The ratio 50/100 = 0.5 is the value of the marginal propensity to consume for this numerical example.

In geometric terms, the marginal propensity to consume is equal to the slope of the consumption schedule. In Exhibit 8.2b, a horizontal movement

Dissaving Negative saving; the difference between disposable income and consumption expenditure when consumption exceeds disposable income.

Consumption Schedule A graphical or numerical representation of the way in which nominal consumption expenditure varies as nominal income varies, other things being equal.

Autonomous Consumption The level of consumption shown by a consumption schedule for a zero disposable income level.

Marginal Propensity to Consume The fraction of each added dollar of disposable income that goes to added consumption.

---

[1]The term "consumption function" is also widely used, especially in mathematically oriented writings.

(a)

(1) Nominal Disposable Income	(2) Nominal Consumption Expenditure	(3) Change in Income	(4) Change in Consumption	(5) Marginal Propensity to Consume
$ 0	$150			
		$100	$50	0.5
100	200			
		100	50	0.5
200	250			
		100	50	0.5
300	300			
		100	50	0.5
400	350			
		100	50	0.5
500	400			
		100	50	0.5
600	450			
		100	50	0.5
700	500			
		100	50	0.5
800	550			
		100	50	0.5
900	600			
		100	50	0.5
1,000	650			
		100	50	0.5
1,100	700			
		100	50	0.5
1,200	750			
		100	50	0.5
1,300	800			
		100	50	0.5
1,400	850			

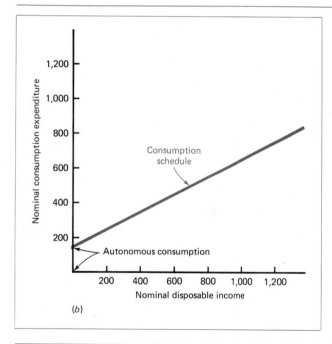

(b)

EXHIBIT 8.2

The consumption schedule (simplified example)
The table and graph both show a simple numerical example of the relationship between disposable income and consumption. The level of autonomous consumption is shown on the graph by the height of the intersection of the consumption schedule with the vertical axis. The slope of the consumption schedule is equal to the marginal propensity to consume.

(a)

(1) Nominal Disposable Income	(2) Nominal Consumption Expenditure	(3) Nominal Saving
$ 0	$150	$ −150
100	200	−100
200	250	− 50
300	300	0
400	350	50
500	400	100
600	450	150
700	500	200
800	550	250
900	600	300
1,000	650	350
1,100	700	400
1,200	750	450
1,300	800	500
1,400	850	550

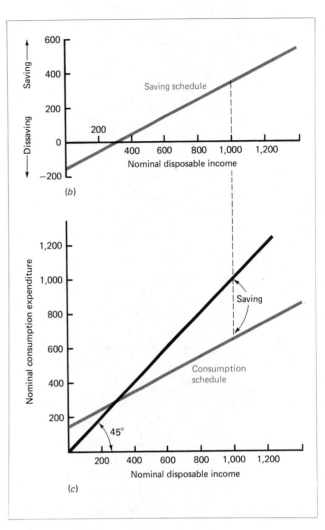

EXHIBIT 8.3

The saving schedule

The saving schedule shows the relationship between saving and income. In the table, saving is found by subtracting consumption from disposable income. In part *b* of the exhibit, the saving schedule is given in graphical form. It could be constructed directly from the numbers in column (3) of the table, or alternatively, from the consumption schedule shown in part *c*.

of $100 in disposable income corresponds to a vertical movement of $50 in planned consumption as we move along the consumption schedule. The slope of the consumption schedule is thus 50/100 = 0.5, the same as the marginal propensity to consume.

Saving Schedule

Once we know the level of consumption corresponding to each level of disposable income, we can easily calculate the level of saving that corresponds to each level of disposable income. The relationship between saving and income is called the **saving schedule.** The saving schedule is given in numerical form in Exhibit 8.3*a*. The numbers in this table are calculated by subtracting consumption from disposable income.

The saving schedule is shown in geometric form in Exhibit 8.3*b*. This figure can be constructed simply by plotting the numbers from column (3) of the table. Alternatively, the saving schedule can be derived directly from the consumption schedule, which is reproduced as Exhibit 8.3*c*. The level

Saving Schedule A graphical or numerical representation of the way in which nominal saving varies as nominal income varies, other things being equal.

of saving corresponding to each level of disposable income is equal to the vertical distance between the consumption schedule and the 45° reference line.

In our numerical example, a dissaving of $150 occurs when disposable income is zero. Saving at zero disposable income is the negative of autonomous consumption. At a $300 level of disposable income there is a "break-even point" at which neither saving nor dissaving occurs. Below that point, consumption exceeds disposable income, and above that point, consumption falls short of disposable income.

Marginal Propensity to Save

Marginal Propensity to Save   The fraction of each added dollar of disposable income that is not consumed.

We use the term **marginal propensity to save** to mean the fraction of each additional dollar of disposable income that is not consumed. Because all disposable income is, by definition, either saved or consumed, it follows that the marginal propensity to save (MPS) is equal to one minus the marginal propensity to consume (MPC):

$$MPS = 1 - MPC$$

In geometric terms, the marginal propensity to save is equal to the slope of the saving schedule.

Long and Short Run

Now let us compare the hypothetical consumption schedule of Exhibit 8.2 with the observed historical record of income and consumption shown in Exhibit 8.1. Both of these diagrams are reproduced in Exhibit 8.4 for easy comparison. In Exhibit 8.4a we have drawn a straight line through most of the consumption points given by United States data. This line has constant slope of about 0.9, indicating that on the average, about 90 percent of each year's increase in disposable income went into consumption. This implies a marginal propensity to consume of about 0.9. Furthermore, we notice that this line passes through the origin of the graph. If income were to fall to zero, it appears that planned consumption would also fall to zero. The historical data do not seem to include any allowance for autonomous consumption.

The relationship between income and consumption indicated by historical data is quite different from the relationship indicated by the hypothetical consumption schedule shown in Exhibit 8.4b. The latter displays a much lower marginal propensity to consume and a substantial positive level of autonomous consumption. Which type of relationship should we use in constructing our theories?

It turns our that one type of relationship is appropriate when dealing with long-run changes in disposable income, and the other when dealing with short-run changes. We have already seen that plotting historical data over a forty-year period creates a steep line passing through the origin. In contrast, if we were to look at data describing consumption behavior over short periods—say changes in consumption within a year, as revealed by quarterly data—we would observe a flatter consumption function and substantial autonomous consumption. (This latter type of relationship is also revealed by so-called *cross-sectional data*, where the level of income of different individual households is measured for a particular year and associated with the level of consumption expenditure of each household.)

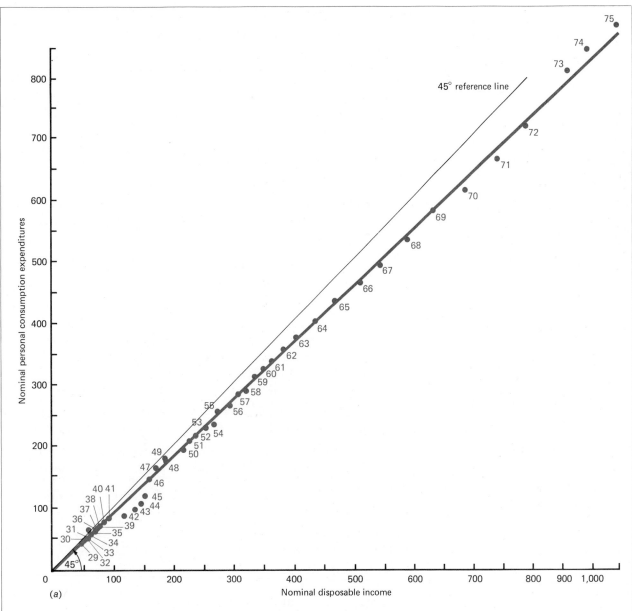

(a)

EXHIBIT 8.4

Long- and short-run consumption schedules

Actual U.S. data on income and consumption expenditures since 1929 indicate a long-run marginal propensity to consume of about .9, as shown in part a of this exhibit. The short-run consumption schedule for the U.S. economy has a lower marginal propensity to consume and a higher level of autonomous consumption, more like the hypothetical consumption schedule of part b, taken from our simplified numerical example.

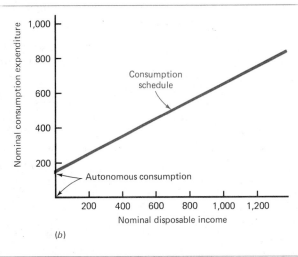

(b)

Permanent Income Hypothesis
A hypothesis that reconciles a high long-run marginal propensity to consume with a low short-run marginal propensity to consume, by saying that people are likely to consume less out of transitory increases in income than out of those increases that they consider to be permanent.

Permanent Income

How can we account for the observed differences in consumption behavior as revealed by long- and short-run data? One ingenious explanation is known as the **permanent income hypothesis.** By *permanent income* we mean the average income that a person expects to receive in the intermediate future. The hypothesis is that people plan to increase their consumption by about $.90 for each $1.00 of additional permanent income they receive. In the short run, though, when people receive additional income they do not always know whether or not to consider the increase permanent. For example, if a person earned $200 more in the first quarter of 1974 than in the fourth quarter of 1973, $100 of that might be regarded as a permanent improvement in earning expectations but the other $100 might be considered a transitory increase in income, which was not likely to be repeated. The permanent income hypothesis assumes that people are not as likely to consume out of transitory increases in income, but instead tend to save all of such income for a "rainy day," when their income may temporarily be lower than their permanent income.

In addition to reconciling the differences between short-run and long-run behavior, the permanent income hypothesis also explains why cross-sectional observations of consumption behavior look more like short-run than long-run observations. Many households with a high measured income in a given year are fortunate in having a high transitory income, and their low consumption expenditure relative to measured income is really based on their lower levels of permanent income. At the same time, the relatively high consumption levels of households with low measured incomes can be explained by the fact that many households with low income in a given year actually have higher permanent income.

Because much of our discussion in later chapters will focus on short-run policies for economic stabilization, we shall use the short-run rather than the long-run consumption schedule in building our theory. There is no magic number that gives "the" proper marginal propensity to consume for all circumstances, but we shall use a value of 0.5 for the short-run marginal propensity to consume in our numerical examples.

Other Factors Affecting Consumption

The consumption schedule shows the relationship between nominal consumption expenditures and nominal income, other things being equal. If any of the "other things" change, the proportion of any given level of income that people devote to consumption can change. Among the other factors of possible importance to consumption are the following:

1. A change in the value of people's accumulated savings or wealth may have an influence on their consumption expenditure. It is thought that, other things being equal, people with a comfortable cushion of accumulated savings may spend more in relation to their current income than people with few financial reserves.

2. The state of consumer expectations can have a strong influence on consumer spending, especially in the short run. If people expect good times, they may spend more freely. If they are pessimistic about the immediate future, they may postpone major spending decisions, and save more than usual.

3. Changes in the price level can affect the level of nominal expenditure associated with a given level of nominal income. Here we must distinguish between long-run and short-run effects. In the long run, a change in the price level will produce a proportional change in the nominal value of autonomous consumption. For example, in 1975 the purchasing power of the dollar was about half what it was in 1945. If people's consumption behavior had called for $150 of nominal autonomous consumption in 1945, they would have had to increase that to $300 in 1975 in order to maintain the real value of that level of autonomous consumption. In graphical terms, the price change would have produced an upward shift in the consumption schedule, so that it would intersect the vertical axis at $300 of nominal expenditure in 1975 if it had intersected at $150 in 1945.

In the short run, the relationship between price changes and consumption expenditure is far less certain. The problem is that inflation, and changes in the rate of inflation, may strongly affect consumer expectations. Inflation can also erode the real value of people's accumulated savings. The uncertain short-run effects of price changes may thus cause the consumption schedule to shift either upward or downward by an unpredictable amount.

With all of these factors at work affecting consumption, we cannot consider the exact shape or position of the consumption schedule to be unchanging. In an elementary discussion like the present one, where we put all the inconvenient features of reality out of sight in an "other things being equal" box, we run the risk of making consumer behavior seem more dependable and predictable than it really is.

Adjusting for Taxes

One more step is needed to get our consumption schedule completely ready for use in theory building. We must make an adjustment for taxes so that the consumption schedule can be expressed in terms of national income rather than in terms of disposable income. Remember that throughout our theoretical discussion, we are assuming that there are no indirect business taxes or undistributed corporate profits. That means that national income is simply equal to disposable personal income plus net taxes.

In adjusting the consumption schedule for taxes, we shall consider two separate cases. In the first case, illustrated by Exhibit 8.5, all taxes and transfers are of the **lump sum** form. That means that they do not change as income changes. Columns (3) and (4) of the table give the familiar consumption schedule in terms of disposable income, while columns (1) and (4) show the relationship between national income and consumption expenditure.

Lump Sum Taxes   Taxes that do not vary as income varies.

In the second case, illustrated in Exhibit 8.6, the government employs a personal income tax. Now the amount of tax collected does change as the level of national income changes. In constructing the table, we have assumed that everyone pays a straight 20 percent income tax, regardless of the amount of earnings. (The actual income tax is much more complicated, of course.) Again, columns (3) and (4) give the consumption schedule in terms of disposable income, and columns (1) and (4) give the consumption schedule in terms of national income.

EXHIBIT 8.5

National income and consumption with lump sum taxes

Lump sum taxes are taxes that do not change when the level of income changes. This table shows how the consumption schedule can be expressed either in terms of disposable income [columns (3) and (4)] or in terms of national income [columns (1) and (4)] for an economy where all taxes are of the lump sum variety. In the simple economy on which the table is based, there are no undistributed corporate profits or indirect business taxes, so that national income is equal to disposable personal income plus net taxes.

(1) Nominal National Income	(2) Nominal Net Taxes	(3) Nominal Disposable Income	(4) Nominal Consumption Expenditure	(5) Nominal Saving
$ 100	$100	$ 0	$150	$ − 150
200	100	100	200	− 100
300	100	200	250	− 50
400	100	300	300	0
500	100	400	350	50
600	100	500	400	100
700	100	600	450	150
800	100	700	500	200
900	100	800	550	250
1,000	100	900	600	300
1,100	100	1,000	650	350
1,200	100	1,100	700	400
1,300	100	1,200	750	450
1,400	100	1,300	800	500

Compare the two cases. With lump sum taxes, an additional dollar of national income results in an additional $.50 of consumption expenditure and an additional $.50 in saving. With an income tax, the additional dollar of national income results in an additional $.40 of consumption, an additional $.40 of saving, and an additional $.20 of net taxes. We might say that in the second case, there are two different marginal propensities to consume. The marginal propensity to consume national income (0.4) is lower than the marginal propensity to consume disposable income (0.5).

The U.S. government does make heavy use of the personal income tax, so the second of the two cases considered here is the more realistic. On the other hand, lump sum taxes simplify our job of theory building. In the chapters that follow, we shall use the simplifying assumption of lump sum taxes whenever possible. When it is important for questions of policy, though, we shall also discuss the effects of an income tax.

Investment Expenditure

Planned Investment and Aggregate Demand

The second major component of aggregate demand is planned investment expenditure. Planned investment, we recall, includes both fixed investment and planned inventory investment. Total investment, as measured in the national income accounts, includes planned investment plus

THE DETERMINANTS OF PLANNED EXPENDITURE

EXHIBIT 8.6

National income and consumption with a 20 percent income tax

With an income tax, net taxes rise as income increases. Each additional dollar of national income results in an additional $.40 of consumption, an additional $.40 of saving, and an additional $.20 of net taxes. Half of each added dollar of disposable income goes to consumption, but only 40 percent of each added dollar of national income goes to consumption.

(1) Nominal National Income	(2) Nominal Net Taxes	(3) Nominal Disposable Income	(4) Nominal Consumption Expenditure	(5) Nominal Saving
$ 100	$ 20	$ 80	$190	$−110
200	40	160	230	−70
300	60	240	270	−30
400	80	320	310	10
500	100	400	350	50
600	120	480	390	90
700	140	560	430	130
800	160	640	470	170
900	180	720	510	210
1,000	200	800	550	250
1,100	220	880	590	290
1,200	240	960	630	330
1,300	260	1,040	670	370
1,400	280	1,120	710	410

unplanned inventory investment. Our immediate interest is to explain what determines aggregate demand, so we ignore unplanned inventory investment for the moment.

Determinants of Planned Investment

The rate of planned investment expenditure depends on two things. First, it depends on the **expected rate of return** on investment. By the expected rate of return we mean the net annual improvement in a firm's cost or revenue that it expects to obtain by making an investment, expressed as a percentage of the sum invested. Second, the rate of planned investment expenditure depends on the rate of interest. By the rate of interest we mean the cost to the firm of borrowing funds from outside sources, or the opportunity cost to the firm of using its own funds. A simple example will show how these two factors enter into the decision to invest.

Suppose that you are the manager of a small factory. You are worried about the rising cost of energy, so you hire a consultant who is a specialist in energy conservation. The consultant tells you that if you insulate the roof of your warehouse, you will save $1,200 per year in heating and cooling costs. The insulation will cost $10,000 to install. How do you decide whether to undertake this investment project?

First, you must calculate the rate of return on the investment. Twelve hundred dollars per year means saving $.12 per year for each dollar invested

Expected Rate of Return The annual net improvement in a firm's cost or revenue that it expects to obtain by making an investment, expressed as a percentage of the sum invested.

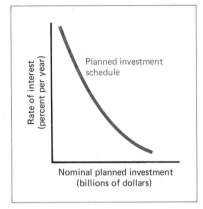

EXHIBIT 8.7
Planned investment schedule
The planned investment schedule shows how the rate of planned investment for the economy as a whole varies as the rate of interest varies, other things being equal. The downward slope of the schedule indicates that decreases in the rate of interest tend to cause increases in the rate of planned investment.

Planned Investment Schedule A graphical representation of the way in which the rate of planned investment for the economy as a whole varies as the rate of interest varies, other things being equal.

Accelerator Effect The tendency of increases in national income to induce new investments, which in turn fuel further increases in national income.

to install the insulation, so the rate of return is 12 percent per year. Next you find out what the rate of interest is. You call your banker, who says that the money is available at 10 percent per year. That means that you will have to pay $1,000 per year in interest charges. Even after paying the interest, you will have $200 in pure profit left out of your $1,200 saving in energy cost. The investment is worthwhile, so you go ahead with it.

Perhaps you do not need to borrow money to make the investment. Instead, your firm has $10,000 or more in uncommitted cash balances left over from last year's profits. In that case, the interest rate you must use for your investment decision is the rate those funds are now earning for you. Let us say that your uncommitted cash is invested in U.S. government bonds, which pay interest of 10 percent per year. Taking $10,000 out of bonds has an opportunity cost to you of $1,000 per year in foregone interest payments, but the $1,200 saving in energy cost will more than make up for that. You still decide to put in the insulation.

This very simple example provides the basis for an important generalization. A firm will find it profitable to undertake an investment project if, and only if, the rate of return on that investment project is higher than the rate of interest. If the rate of return is equal to the rate of interest, the project will just break even, and it is a matter of indifference whether it is undertaken or not. If the rate of interest exceeds the rate of return, the project will involve a loss, and will not be undertaken.

Planned Investment Schedule

Our analysis of the determinants of planned investment suggests a general relationship between the rate of interest and the rate of planned investment for the economy as a whole. The lower the rate of interest, the greater will be the number of profitable investment projects. Other things being equal, then, the rate of planned investment will be higher, the lower the rate of interest. This relationship between interest and planned investment is shown graphically in the form of a **planned investment schedule** in Exhibit 8.7.

Changes in Expectations

The rate of planned investment depends on the rate of interest and the expected rate of return on investment. The planned investment schedule shows the relationship between the first two items, investment and the interest rate, other things being equal. We know, then, that the "other things being equal" box must in this case be filled by all the things that affect the expected rate of return on investment. What are those things? A complete list would go on and on, but here are some of the most important ones.

1. Technological developments may add new items to the list of projects that are expected to be profitable. Major technological developments such as railways or computers can have an economy-wide impact on expected rates of return.
2. Changes in the level of business activity can affect firms' expectations regarding the profitability of investment. The tendency of increases in national income to induce new investments, which in turn fuel further increases in national income, is sometimes known as the **accelerator effect.**

3. Analysis of business trends and forecasts of future trends can strongly affect expected rates of return. Numerous specialized private firms and government agencies feed business decision makers a constant stream of estimates and forecasts concerning consumer demand, inflation, foreign trade developments, and anything else anyone thinks significant. Pessimistic forecasts cause firms to postpone investment decisions; optimistic forecasts induce them to take projects "off the shelf" and get them under way.

4. Changes in government policy, and uncertainty about possible future changes in government policy, can strongly affect expected rates of return. The fear of an adverse change in policy can be as effective as the policy itself in discouraging private investment.

5. Beyond all these more or less tangible influences on expected rates of return, there is an imponderable element of "business psychology." Sometimes optimistic or pessimistic moods having relatively small initial causes can become self-reinforcing and bring about significant changes in investment plans.

Whatever the source of changes in expected rates of return, the effect of such changes can be represented as a shift in the planned investment schedule. Consider Exhibit 8.8, which shows the effects of, say, a government announcement of new tax credits for business firms. The announcement immediately raises the expected aftertax profitability of many investment projects, so the entire planned investment schedule shifts to the right. Whatever the rate of interest, the rate of planned investment will be higher after the announcement than before.

Instability of Investment Expenditure

Because the rate of planned investment depends so heavily on expectations, and because expectations can sometimes change quickly, planned investment expenditure can vary considerably from year to year. As Exhibit 8.9 shows, there have been periods in American economic history when investment has been very unstable, undergoing wide swings over short periods.

Inventory investment is a particularly unstable component of total investment expenditure as Exhibit 8.9*b* shows. Unfortunately, it is impossible to distinguish statistically between year-to-year changes in *planned* inventory investment, and year-to-year changes in *unplanned* inventory investment. As we shall understand more fully when our theory building is complete, changes in planned inventory investment can be considered a *cause* of instability for the economy as a whole, while changes in unplanned inventory investment are a *consequence* of disequilibrium originating elsewhere in the economy. Exhibit 8.9*b* lumps planned and unplanned inventory investment together.

Other Types of Expenditure

Government Purchases

The third major component of aggregate demand, after consumption and planned investment, is government purchases of goods and services. In macroeconomic analysis, the level of government purchases traditionally

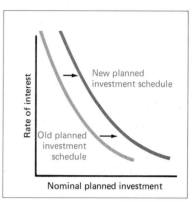

EXHIBIT 8.8
Shift in planned investment schedule

A change in the interest rate, other things being equal, causes a movement along a given planned investment schedule. A change in the expected rate of return on investment causes a shift in the entire planned investment schedule. Here we show the effects of an increase in business optimism caused, say, by a government announcement of new tax credits for private firms.

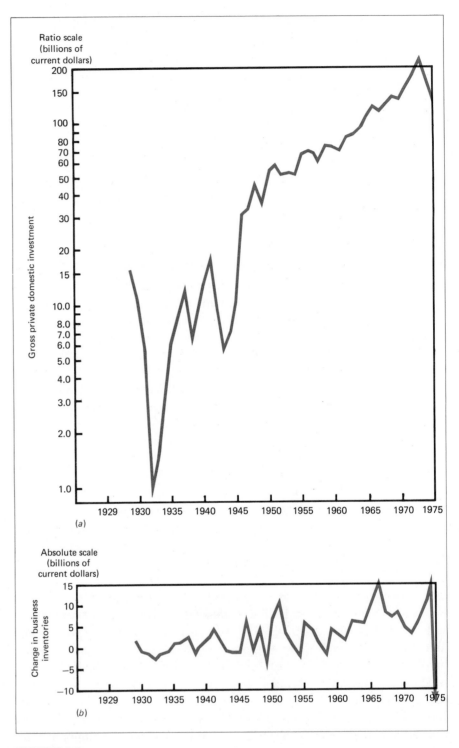

EXHIBIT 8.9

Investment expenditures in the U.S. economy, 1929–1975

Investment expenditure in the American economy has often changed sharply from year to year. The changes shown here were caused partly by changes in interest rates and partly by changes in expected rates of return. The inventory component of total investment expenditure is particularly unstable. The data on inventory investment shown here lump planned and unplanned inventory expenditure together.

is considered to be determined by political decision processes that are "outside" the economic system. In adhering to that tradition here, we do not mean to pretend that the legislators and executives who make spending decisions at various levels of government are wholly uninfluenced by economic considerations, such as the level of national income or the rate of unemployment. It is only that these relationships, whatever they are, are too indirect and complex to put into a simple theory.

Net Exports

Net exports are the fourth and final component of aggregate demand. Much work has been done to develop theories of net export expenditures. However, in the American economy, net exports are a relatively small part of total expenditure. In 1975, net exports were only $20.5 billion, less than 2 percent of a $1,516.3 billion GNP. So, rather than complicate our theory of aggregate demand at this point by taking the small effect of the foreign sector into account, we shall ignore net exports altogether and put off discussion of that part of economic theory until Chapter 22. We shall mention in passing, though, that an increase in nominal income tends to reduce net exports because of its tendency to stimulate spending on imports. This effect can be quite important in the economies of other countries, which depend much more on foreign trade than does the United States.

Conclusions

Aggregate Demand Schedule

Our objective in this chapter has been to look at the determinants of each kind of planned expenditure in order to understand how aggregate demand as a whole is determined. We have discovered that consumption depends on disposable income, that planned investment depends on the interest rate (among other things), that government spending depends on the political process, and that net exports are small enough to be ignored in an introductory discussion. Now we are ready to put together a complete **aggregate demand schedule** for the economy. This will be a schedule that shows what the nominal level of total planned expenditure will be for each possible level of nominal national income. Exhibit 8.10 shows the schedule as both a table and a graph.

To construct the graphical form of the aggregate demand schedule, we first draw a set of axes that shows national income on the horizontal axis and planned expenditure on the vertical axis. We then draw in the consumption schedule, stated in terms of national income using the numbers in columns (1) and (2) of Exhibit 8.10a [based on columns (1) and (4) of Exhibit 8.5]. This schedule is labeled C in Exhibit 8.10b.

Next we add planned investment expenditure. Given the shape and position of the planned investment schedule, and given the rate of interest, planned investment is fixed and does not change as national income changes. We thus draw a line parallel to the consumption schedule, separated from it by a distance equal to the level of planned investment, and label it $C + I$.

Aggregate Demand Schedule A schedule showing what the nominal level of total planned expenditure (aggregate demand) will be at each possible level of nominal national income.

(a)

(1) Nominal National Income	(2) Nominal Consumption Expenditure	(3) Nominal Planned Investment	(4) Nominal Government Purchases	(5) Nominal Total Planned Expenditure (Aggregate Demand)
$ 100	$150	$100	$100	$ 350
200	200	100	100	400
300	250	100	100	450
400	300	100	100	500
500	350	100	100	550
600	400	100	100	600
700	450	100	100	650
800	500	100	100	700
900	550	100	100	750
1,000	600	100	100	800
1,100	650	100	100	850
1,200	700	100	100	900
1,300	750	100	100	950
1,400	800	100	100	1,000

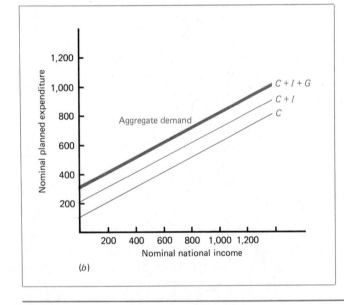

(b)

EXHIBIT 8.10

The aggregate demand schedule

To construct the aggregate demand schedule, we begin by drawing the consumption schedule, adjusted for net taxes. We then add investment, getting the line labeled $C + I$. Finally, layer-cake fashion, we add government purchases. This results in $C + I + G$, the aggregate demand schedule.

Finally, we add government purchases of goods and services in layer-cake fashion. We have assumed that government expenditure does not depend directly on national income, so we draw another line parallel to the first two, and raised above the $C + I$ line by an amount equal to government purchases. This line is labeled $C + I + G$, and is also labeled as the aggregate demand schedule, because it shows the sum of all three components of planned expenditure, as given in column (5) of Exhibit 8.10a.

This completes our discussion of the determinants of planned expenditure and aggregate demand. In the next chapter we shall use what we have learned to carry our theory building one step further.

SUMMARY

1. Following the tradition of Keynesian economics, our theory building begins by looking at what determines each separate component of aggregate demand: consumption, planned investment, government purchases, and net exports.
2. The consumption schedule shows that as income increases, consumption expenditure increases, but not by as much as the increase in income. The fraction of each added dollar of income that is devoted to consumption is called the marginal propensity to consume. That part of disposable income that is not consumed is saved. The marginal propensity to save is equal to one minus the marginal propensity to consume.
3. Planned investment expenditure depends on the rate of interest and the expected rate of return on investment projects. The planned investment schedule represents the way that planned investment varies as the rate of interest varies, other things being equal. Changes in the expected rate of return on investment are represented graphically as shifts in the planned investment schedule.
4. For purposes of elementary theory, we consider government purchases to be determined by forces outside the scope of economic analysis. We also ignore the effect of net exports, because these play a relatively small part in determining aggregate demand in the American economy.
5. The aggregate demand schedule shows the relationship between total planned expenditure and national income. Once we know the determinants of each separate component of aggregate demand, we can put the aggregate demand schedule together like a layer cake.

DISCUSSION QUESTIONS

1. "Marginal" is a term used many times and in many circumstances in economics, yet other terms could be used. What alternative expressions might be used for "marginal propensity to consume" without using the word marginal?
2. Autonomous consumption is the level of consumption that would occur if national income were zero. Because national income will never be zero, why do we talk about autonomous consumption? In other words, what does it really mean? And how does it affect the consumption schedule? What word or expression might you use in place of "autonomous" when talking about autonomous consumption?
3. Because saving and consumption are related, is there an autonomous saving that would be related to autonomous consumption? How would you find "autonomous saving"?
4. What if there were a decrease in the rate of interest and as a result firms planned to invest more. What would happen: Would there be a shift in the investment schedule or a movement along the curve?
5. What if consumers became pessimistic about the future and decided that they had better put more of their money away for a rainy day. What would happen to the consumption and saving schedules?
6. In what sense might the planned expenditure schedule be considered a demand curve? Is demand in this case a function of price, or of some other variable? Explain.
7. If you were a business executive, would you take the rate of interest into account when deciding how large an inventory of your product to keep on hand? How would a change in the rate of interest affect the stock of inventory you keep? How would it affect your flow of inventory investment?

CHAPTER 9
The Multiplier Theory of National Income Determination

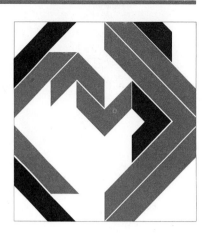

What You Will Learn in This Chapter

Knowing the determinants of planned expenditure allows us to determine the exact level of national income for which the circular flow will be in equilibrium. Any shifts in the components of the aggregate demand schedule—the consumption schedule, planned investment, or government purchases—will result in changes in the equilibrium level of national income. In fact, a $1 shift in the planned expenditure schedule causes equilibrium national income to change by *more* than $1. This is known as the multiplier effect.

For Review

Here is an important concept that will be put to use in this chapter. Be certain that you understand it, or review it before proceeding.
Equilibrium and disequilibrium in the circular flow (Chapter 5)

Determining the Equilibrium Level of National Income

In Chapter 5 we learned that the circular flow could be in equilibrium only when aggregate demand was equal to aggregate supply, that is, only when the total of planned expenditures was equal to total national product. If planned expenditures exceeded national product, the attempt of buyers to purchase more than was currently being produced would lead to unplanned decreases in business inventories. Firms would react to these unplanned decreases in inventories by increasing output or by raising prices, causing the level of the circular flow, as measured in nominal terms, to increase. If planned expenditures fell short of national product, business inventories would accumulate at a rate faster than planned, and firms would react by cutting production or lowering prices, so that the nominal level of the circular flow would drop.

These are the ideas on which the Keynesian theory of national income determination are based. All we need to do now is add a bit more precision by making use of the detailed analysis of planned expenditure that we developed in the last chapter.

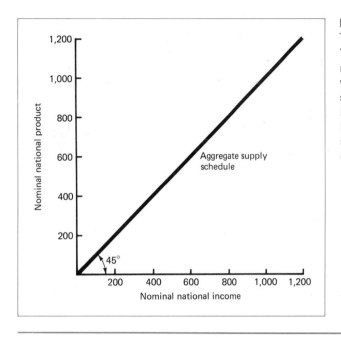

EXHIBIT 9.1
The aggregate supply schedule
The aggregate supply schedule shows the level of nominal national product (aggregate supply) associated with each level of nominal national income. In our simplified economy, national product and national income are equal whatever the level of national income, so the aggregate supply schedule is simply a straight line extending from the origin at an angle of 45°.

The Aggregate Supply Schedule

In Chapter 8 we showed how to draw an aggregate demand schedule. That schedule showed what the nominal level of total planned expenditure would be for each possible level of nominal national income, given certain unchanging assumptions regarding the nonincome factors affecting consumption, investment, and government purchases. As the next step in our theory building, we need an **aggregate supply schedule** to show the level of nominal national product associated with each level of nominal national income.

In the simplified economy we are now using, there are no indirect business taxes, capital consumption allowance, or statistical discrepancy. As a result, there is no distinction between gross and net national product, and national product is equal by definition to national income. That means that our aggregate supply schedule is extremely easy to draw. Because the level of nominal national product associated with any given level of nominal national income is *equal* to that level of nominal national income, the aggregate supply schedule is simply a straight 45° line. Such an aggregate supply schedule is drawn in Exhibit 9.1. The reader can easily check that each point on the schedule is equally far from the horizontal axis (national income) and the vertical axis (national product).

Aggregate Supply Schedule A table or graph showing the level of nominal national product (aggregate supply) associated with each level of nominal national income.

Keynesian Cross

If we draw both the aggregate supply and aggregate demand schedule on one diagram, as in Exhibit 9.2, we get a figure often called the **Keynesian cross.** A diagram much like this was used by Keynes in his *General Theory* to show how the equilibrium level of national income is determined. From Chapter 5, we know that the circular flow will be in equilibrium only when total planned expenditure (aggregate demand) is equal to national

Keynesian Cross A graph that shows how the equilibrium level of nominal national income is determined. The "cross" is formed by the intersection of the aggregate demand and aggregate supply schedules.

EXHIBIT 9.2

The Keynesian cross

In this Keynesian cross diagram, the aggregate demand and aggregate supply schedules are drawn together. The intersection of the two marks the level of national income for which total planned expenditure is equal to national product. That is the equilibrium level of nominal national income, where no unplanned inventory investment occurs.

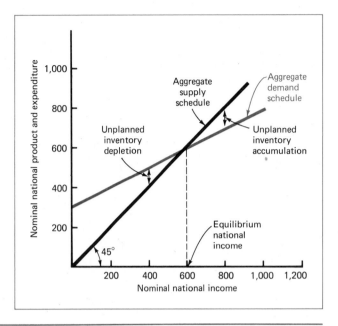

product (aggregate supply). The point of intersection of the two schedules that comprise the Keynesian cross shows us exactly which level of national income permits aggregate supply and demand to be equal. That point, which corresponds to a nominal national income of $600 in Exhibit 9.2, is the equilibrium point.

It is easy to see that no other level of nominal national income can represent equilibrium in the circular flow. If national income were lower than the equilibrium level, say $400, planned expenditure (aggregate demand) would exceed national product (aggregate supply). There would be unplanned depletion of business inventories equal to the vertical distance between the aggregate demand schedule and aggregate supply schedule, as shown in Exhibit 9.2. Firms would try to restore inventories to their planned levels by increasing production and/or prices. That in turn would cause nominal national income to rise until equilibrium were reached.

If, on the other hand, nominal national income were to be higher than the equilibrium level, say $800, then planned expenditures would fall short of national product. The unsold goods would go to unplanned inventory investment equal to the gap between the aggregate demand schedule and the aggregate supply schedule. Firms would react to the unplanned buildup in inventories by cutting production and/or prices. The cutback in production would cause nominal national income to fall until equilibrium was restored.

Numerical Example

The same story is told with numbers in Exhibit 9.3. This table gives numerical values for nominal national income, planned expenditure, and other variables that correspond to the Keynesian cross diagram of Exhibit 9.2. The table confirms that $600 is the only level of national income that

EXHIBIT 9.3

Determination of equilibrium national income

The table gives a numerical example of national income determination corresponding exactly to the Keynesian cross of Exhibit 9.2. If planned expenditure does not equal national product, unplanned inventory change occurs which in turn pushes national income in the direction of equilibrium.

(1) Nominal National Income	(2) Nominal Planned Expenditure* (Aggregate Demand)	(3) Nominal National Product (Aggregate Supply)	(4) Unplanned Inventory Change	(5) Tendency of Change in National Income
$ 100	$350	$ 100	$−250	Increase
200	400	200	−200	Increase
300	450	300	−150	Increase
400	500	400	−100	Increase
500	550	500	−50	Increase
600	600	600	0	Equilibrium
700	650	700	+50	Decrease
800	700	800	+100	Decrease
900	750	900	+150	Decrease
1,000	800	1,000	+200	Decrease
1,100	850	1,100	+250	Decrease
1,200	900	1,200	+300	Decrease

*Planned expenditure based on government purchases of $100, planned investment of $100, autonomous consumption of $150, and marginal propensity to consume of 0.5. See Exhibit 8.10 for details.

allows equilibrium in the circular flow. Column (5) of the table shows that there is a tendency of national income to move toward equilibrium whenever it is at any level other than $600.

Saving Approach

There is an alternative approach to the determination of equilibrium nominal national income that uses the saving schedule rather than the consumption schedule as its starting point. We shall refer to this as the *saving approach* to income determination.

Consider Exhibit 9.4a. Columns (1)–(5) show how national income is divided into net taxes (the lump sum tax assumption is used here), consumption, and saving. In Exhibit 9.4b, we have drawn two diagonal lines to indicate how the part of national income *that is not consumed by households* varies as national income varies. The lower diagonal, labeled S, is the saving schedule, based on column (5) of the table. The diagonal labeled S + T adds the amount of net taxes to saving, and thus shows the total nonconsumed portion of national income.

Columns (6) and (7) of the table show the parts of planned expenditure that are not spent by households, that is, planned investment and government purchases. Neither of these change as national income changes, so they are represented by horizontal lines in the figure. The point in the diagram where the S + T line intersects the I + G line is the level of national income at which the portion of income not spent by households is exactly equal to the planned expenditures made outside the household

(a)

(1) Nominal National	(2) Net Taxes	(3) Disposable Income	(4) Consumption Expenditure	(5) Saving	(6) Planned Investment	(7) Government Purchases
$ 100	$100	$ 0	$150	$ −150	$100	$100
200	100	100	200	−100	100	100
300	100	200	250	−50	100	100
400	100	300	300	0	100	100
500	100	400	350	50	100	100
600	100	500	400	100	100	100
700	100	600	450	150	100	100
800	100	700	500	200	100	100
900	100	800	550	250	100	100
1,000	100	900	600	300	100	100
1,100	100	1,000	650	350	100	100
1,200	100	1,100	700	400	100	100

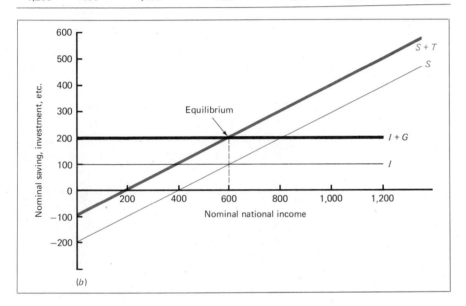

(b)

EXHIBIT 9.4

The saving approach to national income determination

The table and diagram show that the part of national income that consumers do not spend (saving plus net taxes) must equal the planned expenditures of nonconsumers (planned investment plus government purchases) in order for the circular flow to be in equilibrium.

sector of the economy. At this point, and only at this point, total expenditures equal total national income. The saving approach tells us, then, that the circular flow is in equilibrium when, and only when, saving plus net taxes equal planned investment plus government purchases.

A careful comparison of Exhibits 9.4 and 9.2 will reveal that the gap between the $S + T$ and $I + G$ lines at any level of national income is exactly equal to the gap between the aggregate demand and supply schedules at the same level of national income. It is easy to understand why. If the part of national income that consumers do not spend $(S + T)$ is greater than the planned expenditures of nonconsumers $(I + G)$, some goods that were produced will end up in unplanned inventories rather than being sold. The plans of buyers and sellers do not mesh. The part of total output left over after household consumption exceeds the investment demands of firms plus government purchases. On the other hand, if firms and government plan to spend more than consumers set aside in taxes and saving, the difference will have to be made up by unplanned depletion of business inventories. The two approaches are thus entirely equivalent.

Changes in Nominal National Income and the Multiplier Effect

Expenditure Changes

A great many economic factors can affect the level of planned expenditure. When we draw an aggregate demand schedule, we single out the effects of changes in national income on planned expenditure. The effects of changes in national income on planned expenditure are represented by *movements along* a given aggregate demand schedule.

Other factors besides income also influence planned expenditure. Changes in consumer expectations, in wealth, or in prices cause the level of autonomous consumption to change. Changes in the interest rate or in business expectations cause the level of planned investment to change. Changes in policy cause the government purchases component of planned expenditure to change. All of these changes in planned expenditure that arise from reasons other than changes in national income must be represented by shifts in the aggregate demand schedule.

Consider Exhibit 9.5, which shows the effects of a $100 increase in planned expenditure at all levels of income. For the moment, we shall not worry about whether this increase originates in the consumption, invest-

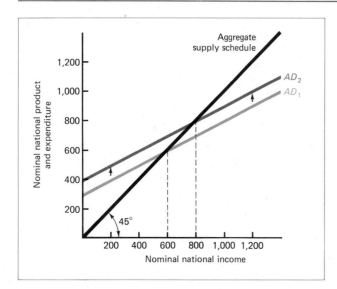

EXHIBIT 9.5

The multiplier effect

If a $100 increase in consumption, planned investment, or government purchases shifts the aggregate demand schedule from AD_1 to AD_2, equilibrium nominal national income will rise from $600 to $800. The ability of a given shift in planned expenditure to induce a larger increase in nominal national income is known as the multiplier effect.

In 1970, the Swedish Academy of Sciences awarded its Nobel Memorial Prize in Economics to MIT Professor Paul Samuelson. In doing so, the Academy announced that "Professor Samuelson's extensive production, covering nearly all areas of economic theory, is characterized by an outstanding ability to derive important new theorems and to find new applications for existing ones. By his contributions, Samuelson has done more than any other contemporary economist to raise the level of scientific analysis in economic theory." The multiplier theory of national income determination is just one of dozens that has been refined, restated, and sharpened by Samuelson's penetrating mind.

Samuelson began his task of raising the level of scientific analysis in economic theory early in his career. His doctoral dissertation at Harvard, written when he was just 26, was boldly entitled *Foundations of Economic Analysis.* (Contrast this with the narrow, ultraspecialized topics of most dissertations!) Published in 1947, the *Foundations* immediately became, and to a great extent remains, the definitive statement in modern mathematical dress of much of neoclassical economics.

In the nineteenth century, leading economists had seen their major theoretical statements go on to become textbooks to future generations. Alas, Samuelson's *Foundations* could not serve that purpose. One must already be well educated in economics and mathematics even to read it! Something had to be done to bring the advances in economic theory made during the 1930s and 1940s into the college classroom. Samuelson solved the problem with his famous *Principles of Economics.* That book was based on the simple assumption that beginning students did not need to be taught a different *kind* of economics than the kind economists wrote in their own professional journals. What they needed was a lucid, step-by-step presentation. The formula was so successful that Samuelson's *Principles* sold millions on millions of copies as it went through a total of ten editions.

On policy issues Samuelson ranks as a liberal and an activist. He derides the laissez-faire market economy as a "system of coercion by dollar votes." Unlike many like-minded colleagues, however, Samuelson did not move to Washington during the Kennedy-Johnson years. He was called on frequently for his opinions and advice, but he resisted service on the Council of Economic Advisors. Although much sought as a lecturer and writer of popular articles, Samuelson remains fundamentally an economist's economist. "In the long run," he has said, "the economic scholar works for the only coin worth having—our own applause."

Paul Anthony Samuelson (1915–   )

---

ment, or government purchases component of aggregate demand. The effect in any case is to shift the aggregate schedule upward by $100, from the position AD_1 to the position AD_2.

The Multiplier Effect

What happens to the equilibrium level of national income when the planned expenditure schedule shifts upward by $100? The immediate effect is that planned expenditures exceed national product, so that inventories start to be depleted at a rate of $100 per year. Firms react to this unplanned inventory depletion by increasing output and/or prices. Nominal national income rises to its new equilibrium level of $800.

Notice what has happened: A $100 upward shift in the aggregate demand schedule has induced a $200 increase in equilibrium nominal income. This ability of a given shift in aggregate demand to create a larger increase

Multiplier Effect The ability of a $1 shift in the aggregate demand schedule to induce more than a $1 change in the equilibrium level of nominal national income.

in equilibrium national income is the famous **multiplier effect,** a central pillar of Keynesian macroeconomics. Let us look closely at the multiplier effect, to see where it comes from.

Round by Round

One way to view the multiplier effect is to imagine the effects of the initial upward shift in aggregate demand percolating down through the economy, "round by round." Suppose that the original shift were caused by a $100 per year increase in the rate of autonomous consumption expenditure. In response to the $100 increase in demand, firms would raise their prices and/or output enough to cause a $100 increase in nominal national product. The increase in national product would result in $100 of additional nominal *income* for some people, in the form of higher profits, wages, rents, or interest payments. Let us call all of what has happened so far the first-round effect of the shift in aggregate demand.

The second round consists in tracing the effects of the $100 in new income generated by the first round. Given an assumed marginal propensity to consume of 0.5, the people who receive this income will spend $50 of it on consumer goods and services. This, in turn, will cause firms to step up output by $50 more and generate $50 in new factor payments and income.

In the third round, half of this $50 is spent, generating $25 more of nominal national product, factor payments, and income. In the fourth round, $12.50 is added, then $6.25 in the fifth round, and so forth until the increments become too small to worry about. When we add together the sum of all the increments to income induced by the original $100 upward shift in the aggregate nominal demand function, we get a total of $100 + $50 + $25 + $12.50 + . . . = $200, just as we expected.

This round-by-round version of the multiplier effect is summarized in Exhibit 9.6.

The Multiplier

Looking at Exhibit 9.6. we see quite clearly that as income increases in response to the original upward shift in the aggregate demand schedule, national income "catches up" with planned expenditure. For each $1 increase in nominal national income, output increases by $1 but expenditure increases by only a fraction of a dollar. The fraction is equal to the marginal propensity to consume. At the new equilibrium, the difference between planned expenditure and national income is eliminated.

Multiplier (Simple) The ratio of an induced change in the equilibrium level of national income to an initial change in planned expenditure. Later known as the simple multiplier, to distinguish it from other specialized terms. The value of the multiplier is given by the formula $M = 1/(1 - \text{MPC})$.

The ratio of the induced increase in national income to the original increase in planned expenditure is called the **multiplier.** The value of the multiplier depends on the fraction of each added dollar of income that goes to added planned expenditure. More precisely, the multiplier M is given by the formula

$$M = \frac{1}{1 - \text{MPC}}$$

where MPC stands for the marginal propensity to consume.

Because we know that the marginal propensity to save is equal to one minus the marginal propensity to consume, we can, alternatively, write the formula for the multiplier as

(a)

Round	Change in Aggregate Demand	Change in Income
First	$100.00	$100.00
Second	50.00	50.00
Third	25.00	25.00
Fourth	12.50	12.50
Fifth	6.25	6.25
. . . . .	. . . . .	. . . . .
All later rounds	6.25	6.25
Totals	$200.00	$200.00

EXHIBIT 9.6
The multiplier effect viewed round by round
A spontaneous $100 increase in planned expenditure (first round) generates $100 in new income. With a marginal propensity to consume of 0.5, half of that is spent, giving a second-round boost of $50 to income. Half of that is spent in the third round, and so forth, until income rises by an eventual total of $200.

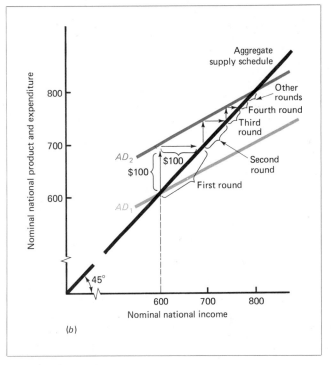

(b)

$$M = \frac{1}{\text{MPS}}$$

where MPS stands for the marginal propensity to save. Whichever way we write the formula, we see that the multiplier is larger the larger the marginal propensity to consume, and smaller the larger the marginal propensity to save.

Conclusions

The multiplier effect plays a central role in Keynesian economic theory and economic policy analysis. The central implication of the multiplier is that even small changes in planned expenditure will have magnified effects on the national economy. Remember how unstable planned investment expenditure can sometimes be. Early Keynesian economists saw the instability of investment, magnified by the multiplier effect, as an explanation of the cycle of boom and bust that had plagued capitalist economies since the nineteenth century. They also saw in the multiplier effect the key to a new policy for economic stabilization. That part of their analysis is important enough for us to devote a separate chapter to it.

SUMMARY

1. *Equilibrium nominal national income.* For a given aggregate demand schedule, the circular flow can be in equilibrium at only one level of nominal national income. The equilibrium condition is that planned expenditure and national product must be equal. If planned expenditure exceeds national product, there will be unplanned depletion of inventories and upward pressure on income.

If national product exceeds planned expenditure, there will be unplanned accumulation of inventories and downward pressure on national income.

2. *Saving approach*. The saving approach to the determination of the equilibrium level of nominal national income shows that equilibrium can occur only when the part of nominal national income that consumers do not spend $(S + T)$ is equal to the planned expenditure of nonconsumers $(I + G)$.

3. *Multiplier effect*. A shift in the aggregate demand schedule changes the equilibrium level of nominal national income. According to the multiplier effect, the induced change in equilibrium nominal national income will be larger than the initial shift in planned expenditure. The ratio of the change in income to the shift in planned expenditure is known as the multiplier.

DISCUSSION QUESTIONS

1. It is possible to analyze the determinants of national income and product with either the circular flow or the Keynesian cross. Which do you prefer? Why? Does each contribute some insights of its own?

2. Explain the "round by round" effect of the multiplier by using the circular flow model.

3. If you expected a depression in the near future, would it be to your advantage to save in order to prepare for it? What would happen if we all tried to save a larger fraction of our income than usual to prepare for an expected depression?

4. If planned saving exceeds planned investment, will gross national product increase or decrease? Suppose you know that the government's budget is exactly in balance. Now can you answer the question?

5. What would be the size of the multiplier if the marginal propensity to consume were 0.5, 0.75, 0.8, 0.9, 0.95?

6. In what ways are the Keynesian cross and the supply and demand diagram of previous chapters similar, and in what ways are they different?

7. What changes in the economy would force a movement along the aggregate demand curve, and what changes would result in a shift of the curve?

8. Suppose that consumers suddenly increase their marginal propensity to consume from 0.5 to 0.75. What effect will this have on the aggregate demand curve? Trace the impact of this change using the Keynesian cross diagram.

CHAPTER 10
Fiscal Policy and the Multiplier Theory

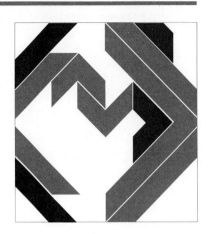

What You Will Learn in This Chapter
Early followers of Keynes believed that the multiplier theory gave them the key to economic stabilization policy. If private investment or consumer spending were not great enough to guarantee full employment of the nation's resources, increased government purchases or tax cuts could be used to fill the gap. When John Kennedy was elected President, he brought economic advisors to Washington who believed that any desired level of national income could be chosen as a target, and any target hit given the political will to apply known policies. Those policies are described here.

For Review
Here are some important terms and concepts that will be put to use in this chapter. Be certain that you understand them, or review them before proceeding.

Potential real gross national product (Chapter 7)
The multiplier theory (Chapter 9)

Early Keynesian economists believed the multiplier theory to have far-reaching significance for economic policy. During the 1930s and 1940s, investment expenditure had been particularly unstable. Now their new theory suggested that year-to-year changes in planned investment would have multiplied effects on national income and product.

What is more, early Keynesians had not distinguished carefully between long- and short-run consumption schedules. If, as they thought, the short-run marginal propensity to consume were close to its long-run level of 0.9, the multiplier would be not 2, as in our examples, but 10. If this were true, a $100 million change in planned investment expenditure would cause a $1 billion change in national income. Their assumption of such a large value for the multiplier reinforced their belief that the instability of investment was the major cause of the historical instability of the economy as a whole.

At the same time that the multiplier theory gave the Keynesians a diagnosis for economic instability, it also suggested a cure. What was needed was a way to manipulate government purchases and consumption spending so that changes in these could be used to offset potentially destabilizing

Fiscal Policy The policies that determine the levels of government purchases and taxes.

changes in planned investment. Government spending could be controlled directly by policy makers, given the political will to do so. Consumption expenditure is not under direct government control, but it can be manipulated indirectly by raising or lowering taxes. Taken together, the policies that determine the levels of government purchases and taxes are known as **fiscal policy.** We shall devote this chapter to explaining the fiscal policy cure for economic instability.

Fiscal Policy and the Target Level of National Income

The Income Target

Target Level of National Income The level of nominal income that policy makers think will permit their main economic goals (full employment, price stability, economic growth, or whatever) to be best realized.

The first step in applying the multiplier theory to fiscal policy is to specify a **target level of national income.** Traditionally, policy makers set a target that they hope will bring about full employment, and that will allow the economy to reach its full potential for real output. We state the income target in nominal terms. It is perfectly possible, of course, for different people to have different ideas about just what target should be chosen, as a result of different ideas about the exact meaning of "full employment" or "potential real gross national product." Considerations of price stability, economic growth, and the balance of payments may also lead to disagreements about where the target should be set. All that is important at the moment, though, is that *some* specific target be chosen that we can use as a reference point.

A Contractionary Gap

The second step in applying the multiplier theory to fiscal policy is to determine the relationship between the *target* level of nominal national income and the *equilibrium* level of nominal national income. Consider Exhibit 10.1. In that figure we have drawn an aggregate demand schedule

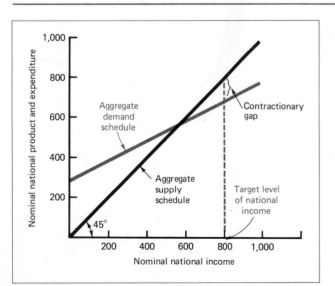

EXHIBIT 10.1
A contractionary gap
A contractionary gap is said to occur whenever planned expenditure (aggregate demand) at the target level of national income is less than national product (aggregate supply) at the target level of national income. Under these conditions, the equilibrium level of nominal national income is below the target level. If national income were at the target level, unplanned inventory accumulation would put downward pressure on the level of income and cause the circular flow to contract.

that gives an equilibrium nominal national income of $600. The underlying data for this schedule are the same as those given in Exhibit 9.3.

Let us suppose that policy makers consider $600 too low a level for nominal income, and set their target instead at $800. With the planned expenditure schedule shown, $800 cannot be the equilibrium level of income, because planned expenditures would fall short of national product by $100. We shall call this crucial $100 a **contractionary gap.** A contractionary gap occurs whenever planned expenditure is less than national product at the target level of income. The size of the gap measures the rate of unplanned inventory accumulation that would take place at the target level of income with the given aggregate demand schedule. The word "contractionary" refers to the fact that unplanned inventory accumulation would put *downward* pressure on the level of nominal national income if income were at the target level.

An Expansionary Gap

Sometimes the equilibrium level of national income can be higher than the target level. Such a case is shown in Exhibit 10.2. In that figure, the aggregate demand schedule yields $200 more expenditure at each level of income than the one shown in Exhibit 10.1. Now planned expenditures would *exceed* national income at the target level of national income. Instead of unplanned inventory accumulation and a contractionary gap at the target income, there is unplanned inventory depletion and an **expansionary gap.**

When there is an expansionary gap, nominal national income will again not be in equilibrium at the target level. If national income were to be at the target level, unplanned inventory depletion would cause the circular flow, measured in nominal terms, to expand. Depending on circumstances, the expansion of nominal income could take the form of an increase in real output, an increase in the price level, or a combination of the two. In later chapters we shall explain just how an expansion in nom-

Contractionary Gap The gap between planned expenditures and national product at the target level of national income when aggregate supply exceeds aggregate demand at that level.

Expansionary Gap The gap between planned expenditures and national product at the target level of national income when aggregate demand exceeds aggregate supply at that level.

EXHIBIT 10.2

An expansionary gap

An expansionary gap is said to occur whenever planned expenditure (aggregate demand) at the target level of national income is greater than national product (aggregate supply) at the target level of national income. Under these conditions, the equilibrium level of nominal national income is above the target level. If national income were at the target level, unplanned inventory depletion would put upward pressure on the level of income and cause the circular flow to expand.

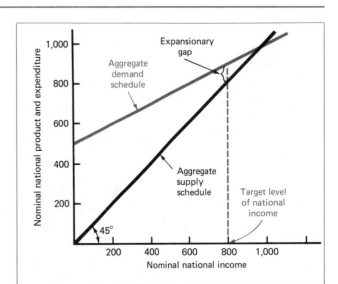

inal national income will be divided between increases in prices and increases in real output. For the moment, though, it does not matter which form a given change in nominal income takes.

Filling the Gap

When there is an expansionary or contractionary gap in the economy, fiscal policy can be used to fill it. In the case of a contractionary gap, consumption plus planned investment plus government purchases are not great enough to add up to national income at the target level. Policy makers can either try to fill the gap directly, by increasing government purchases, or indirectly, by stimulating consumption through reduced taxes. In the case of an expansionary gap, consumption plus planned investment plus government purchases are so great that they exceed national income at the target level. Policy makers then try to eliminate the gap by cutting government purchases or discouraging consumption with a tax increase.

Saving Approach

In Chapter 9 we discussed an alternative approach to national income determination called the saving approach. The saving approach sheds additional light on the process of eliminating expansionary and contractionary gaps. The saving approach tells us that saving plus net taxes must be equal to planned investment plus government purchases in equilibrium. When there is a contractionary gap, households put more income aside in saving and taxes at the target level of income than planned investment and government purchases can soak up. Unless fiscal policy intervenes, the difference will be taken up by unplanned inventory investment, which will then drive nominal income below the target level. Government can step in to buy the goods that would otherwise have gone unsold, or it can reduce taxes to get consumers to buy them. That will keep income at the target level.

When there is an expansionary gap, the saving approach tells us that planned investment plus government purchases exceed saving plus taxes at the target level of income. That means that firms and government are planning to spend more money than households put aside in saving and taxes. Not enough product is left over after household consumption expenditures to meet the planned needs of investment and government purchases. If nothing is done, the planned investment expenditures and government purchases can be carried out only at the expense of an unplanned depletion of business inventories. Fiscal policy can eliminate the gap. It can force consumers to set aside more in taxes, or it can reduce planned government expenditures.

In outline, that is how fiscal policy works, according to the multiplier theory. Now we turn to an examination of details.

Government Purchases Policy

Let us begin with the simplest case: the government fills a contractionary gap by increasing government spending. In Exhibit 10.3, we begin with the state of affairs shown in Exhibit 10.1. The consumption schedule is the same as the one used in Chapter 9 (see Exhibit 9.4). Planned investment is

EXHIBIT 10.3

Filling a contractionary gap with increased government purchases

Increased government purchases can be used to fill a contractionary gap. Initially, government purchases were at the level G_1, putting the aggregate demand schedule at $C + I + G_1$. An additional $100 of government purchases shifted the aggregate demand schedule up to $C + I + G_2$, bringing equilibrium nominal national income up to the target level. Part *b* of the exhibit shows the same process from the point of view of the saving approach to nominal income determination.

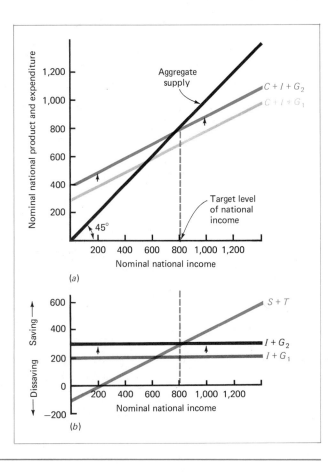

(a)

(b)

$100 and government purchases are $100. The resulting planned expenditure schedule is labeled $C + I + G_1$. This gives an equilibrium level of national income $200 below the target level, with a contractionary gap of $100. (Remember that this gap is always measured vertically at the target level of national income.) The lower part of the diagram shows the same initial situation from the point of view of the saving approach. (Compare this to Exhibit 9.4*b*.)

To bring income up to the target level, the makers of fiscal policy decide to increase government purchases by an amount just equal to the contractionary gap. To be specific, let us suppose that they authorize spending an extra $100 to accelerate the completion of a stretch of interstate highway. If their policy is to work, this added spending *must not* be paid for by increased taxes. Bills for the construction work must be paid either by borrowing from the public or by creating new money. Let us look now at the consequences of this increased spending from three viewpoints.

Round by Round

First, we can take a round-by-round approach. Spending $100 on the highway project creates $100 in new incomes for construction workers. This raises total national income, in the first round, from $600 to $700. Given a propensity to consume of 0.5, the workers save half of this money and spend half of it on, say, clothing. This generates $50 new income for clothing workers and retailers, raising total income to $750 in the second round. In the third round, clothing workers spend half of their new income on something else, adding $25 more to the stream of income and expenditures, so that national total creeps up to $775. As further rounds progress, the target level of $800 national income is approached more and more closely.

Aggregate Supply and Demand Approach

Instead of taking the round-by-round approach, we can refer to Exhibit 10.3a, which shows the effects of the increased government purchases in terms of aggregate supply and demand. The decision to spend $100 on the highway project shifts the aggregate demand schedule upward by $100 to the position labeled $C + I + G_2$. At the initial level of national income ($600), we see that planned expenditures exceed national income, and hence national product, by $100. This tells us that the construction workers' expenditures must initially cause inventories to decline by an unexpected $50. Efforts to replenish these inventories generate $50 in second-round incomes and start national income and product moving upward. The unplanned depletion of inventories will not be eliminated entirely until the new equilibrium level of nominal national income is reached, at the point where the new aggregate demand schedule intersects the aggregate supply schedule. This new equilibrium is, of course, at the target income of $800.

Saving Approach

Finally, let us look at the effects of the increased government purchases in terms of the saving approach. In Exhibit 10.3b, increased government purchases shift the line representing nonhousehold expenditure up by $100 to the position $I + G_2$. Investors and government now spend more at the $600 income level than households set aside in saving and taxes. Inventories are unexpectedly depleted, and income begins to rise as explained above. With a marginal propensity to save of 0.5, $.50 in new saving results from each $1.00 rise in income. By the time national income reaches $800, saving plus taxes have risen enough to cover the total of planned investment plus government purchases.

Notice that in the new equilibrium, planned investment plus government purchases equals saving plus net taxes, as required, but the individual components no longer match up. Saving now exceeds planned investment, and government purchases now exceed net taxes. This *has* to be true, for after all, the whole purpose of the increased government expenditure was to "soak up" the deflationary gap of $100 excess saving that would otherwise have existed at the target level of income.

Multiplier

Whichever approach we use, we come to the same conclusion: *When government purchases are increased while taxes, planned investment, and the consumption schedule remain unchanged, equilibrium nominal national income will change by an amount equal to the change in government purchases times the multiplier.* In this case, where the change in government purchases was $100 and the multiplier was 2, the change in equilibrium income was 2 × $100 = $200.

Politics

The "government policy makers" of textbook economics are able to make decisions and push the appropriate curves and schedules around without worrying about practical politics. Life is not so easy for real policy makers in Washington. Different political interest groups may operate on different assumptions about what economic targets ought to be, and may receive conflicting estimates about how far away from any given target the economy is or will be in the immediate future. Furthermore, policy proposals may be put forward as much with an eye to their effect on the next election as to their effect on national income. The following case study gives a minor, but very typical instance of the kind of political conflict that occurs continually in the actual conduct of fiscal policy.

CASE 10.1
A Job Program Gets a Veto

Throughout most of 1975, President Gerald Ford and the Congress were at odds on the issue of fiscal policy. Looking ahead to 1976, the President and his advisors saw continuing inflationary pressures, and insisted that government purchases should not be allowed to exceed net taxes by more than $60 billion. Congress, on the other hand, was under pressure to spend more federal money to create more jobs, even if the result were a much larger budget deficit.

In May, Congress passed a bill that would have called for spending $5.3 billion of federal money on programs designed to create 900,000 new jobs. The emphasis was on government purchase of services. The bill included money for public service jobs, summer youth jobs, construction and repair of federal buildings, and flood control projects.

The response was a Presidential veto. The bill "would exacerbate budgetary and economic pressures," said President Ford in his veto message. What is more, much of the money would not actually be spent until 1977. By then, according to his advisors' forecasts, the economy's current deflationary gap would already have disappeared without this additional stimulus. The small skirmish in the extended battle over fiscal policy ended this time in victory for the President's point of view.

Tax Policy and the Net Tax Multiplier

Let us go back to the starting point of our previous example, with national income $200 below the target level and a contractionary gap of $100. Suppose now that the fiscal policy authorities decide to stimulate the economy by lowering taxes rather than by raising government spending. To make comparison with the the previous section easier, let us say that they cut net taxes by a lump sum amount of $100. This is a bit extreme, perhaps, because net taxes were only $100 to begin with, but it simplifies the numbers and diagrams and helps clearly establish the principles in which we are interested. Once again, we can look at the effects of this fiscal policy from three points of view.

Round by Round

The $100 tax cut gives households $100 in added disposable income. We cannot add this $100 into the multiplier process directly, though, because it is not *newly generated* income. There has been no increase in production, and no increase in factor payments. All that has happened is that $100 of the original $600 total income has been shifted from government to households.

The multiplier process starts when households spend the money—or more precisely, when they spend half of it, because their marginal propensity to consume is 0.5. Let us say that they spend it on haircuts. That generates $50 of new income for barbers, and national income rises to $650. The first round is complete. When the barbers spend half of their new earnings, they provide the basis for a second-round income increase of $25 in whatever sector they direct their money to. Subsequent rounds add $12.50, $6.25, $3.12½, and so forth until national income has risen to a new equilibrium at $700.

It turns out that although $100 of government purchases caused equilibrium income to rise by $200, a $100 tax cut causes equilibrium income to rise by only $100. Let us check this result.

Aggregate Supply and Demand Approach

Turn now to Exhibit 10.4a, which shows the effect of our tax cut in terms of aggregate supply and demand. The initial position of the aggregate demand schedule is $C_1 + I + G$. When taxes are cut, the consumption schedule shifts *to the left* by $100. The reason for the leftward shift is that disposable income of households is $100 higher at each level of national income than before. Originally, when national income was, say, $600, consumers would have a disposable income of $500 and would have spent accordingly. Now, after the tax cut, consumers would have a disposable income of $500 when national income was only $500. With $100 less tax burden, they would thus spend as much at $500 as they used to at $600, as much at $600 as they used to at $700, and so forth.

The tax cut does not change planned investment or government spending, so when the consumption schedule shifts leftward by $100, it carries the whole aggregate demand schedule with it just the same distance, until it reaches the new position labeled $C_2 + I + G$. Without going through the whole story of what happens after that, we can see that this new aggregate demand schedule intersects the aggregate supply schedule at $700. That will be the new equilibrium level of national income, confirming the result we got by the round-by-round approach.

Saving Approach

Exhibit 10.4b shows how the tax cut works in terms of the saving approach. Here things are very simple indeed, because the tax cut has eliminated the T component of the $S + T$ schedule altogether. Disposable income rises by $100, shifting the saving schedule to its new position S_2. All we have to do to find the new equilibrium is look for the point where the savings schedule S_2 intersects the $I + G$ schedule. That intersection is at the $700 level of national income, just as we expect.

Transfers

Remember that when we talk about net taxes, we mean taxes paid in to the Treasury minus government transfer payments. It might have been, for example, that our original $100 level of lump sum net taxes was com-

EXHIBIT 10.4

Expansionary tax policy

A tax cut has an expansionary effect on the economy. Here, with the aggregate demand schedule at $C_1 + I + G$, there was a $100 contractionary gap. A tax cut of $100 shifted the aggregate demand schedule to $C_2 + I + G$, as consumers received more disposable income. A new equilibrium was reached at $700 nominal income, still below the target but closer than before. Part *b* shows the same events in terms of the saving approach. Because taxes were assumed to be only $100 to begin with, the tax cut entirely eliminated the T component of the $S + T$ schedule.

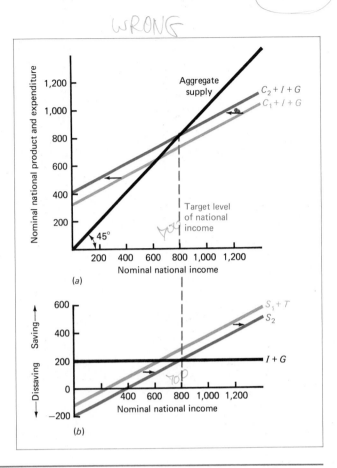

posed of $150 property taxes on homeowners, and $50 in disability benefits to Vietnam veterans. The $100 decrease in net taxes which we have been discussing could have been brought about by cutting property taxes to $50, or by increasing veterans' benefits to $150. Either policy, or a mixture, would bring the level of *net* taxes down from $100 to zero. An increase in transfer payments has, dollar for dollar, the same macroeconomic effects as a cut in the amount of taxes paid into the Treasury.

Net Tax Multiplier

We have seen that the multiplier effect works less powerfully in the case of a tax cut than in the case of an increase in government purchases. Just how much less powerfully depends on the marginal propensity to consume. If the government borrows enough or creates enough new money to add $100 to its budget for purchases of goods and services, it can guarantee that all $100 will be spent. When it adds $100 to household budgets through a cut in net taxes, households will *not* spend all the money directly. They will spend only the portion that their marginal propensity to consume says they will, and they will save the rest.

We now know that a tax cut is less effective than an increase in government purchases exactly in proportion to the marginal propensity to consume. This fact allows us to define a new concept: the **net tax multiplier**. The net tax multiplier is defined by the formula

Net Tax Multiplier A multiplier showing how much equilibrium nominal national income will change in response to a change in net taxes. The formula for the net tax multiplier is $M_T = \text{MPC}/\text{MPS}$.

$$M_T = \frac{\text{MPC}}{\text{MPS}}$$

where M_T stands for the net tax multiplier, MPS for the marginal propensity to save, and MPC for the marginal propensity to consume.

Using this new definition, we can summarize our analysis of tax policy as follows: *When net taxes are changed while government purchases, planned investment, autonomous consumption, and the marginal propensity to consume remain unchanged, equilibrium nominal national income will change in the direction opposite to the change in taxes by an amount equal to the change in net taxes times the net tax multiplier.* In the case we have examined, where the change in net taxes was $100 and the net tax multiplier was 1, the change in equilibrium income was $1 \times \$100 = \$100$.

CASE 10.2
The Kennedy Tax Cut

Probably the most famous episode in the history of fiscal policy was the Kennedy tax cut. John F. Kennedy assumed the office of President in January 1961 in the middle of a business recession. He had been elected on a promise to "get the country moving again," and he brought to Washington a group of economic advisors firmly committed to the active use of fiscal policy.

At first, the emphasis of the new administration was primarily on the spending side of fiscal policy. The President issued orders aimed at stepping up federal expenditures by speeding highway fund allocations and accelerating procurement activities. He also submitted a package of new spending proposals to Congress.

By the next year, the economy seemed to be making considerable progress. Presidential advisors thought that the administration's national income target, aimed high enough to ensure full employment, would be achieved by the end of 1963. But contrary to these forecasts, the expansion slowed. By June 1962, the President decided on more stimulus. On June 7, 1962, he announced that he favored a tax cut of some $10 billion.

Kennedy's tax cut proposal did not get quick treatment from Congress. Long delays resulted from Congressional demands to couple the tax cut to reforms in tax structure and changes in expenditure policy. As it turned out, Kennedy did not live to see his great tax cut enacted. But in February 1964, his successor, President Lyndon Johnson, finally signed the Kennedy tax cut into law. This tax cut is now considered a famous test case of fiscal policy, and we shall return to a consideration of its effectiveness in later chapters.

The Balanced Budget Multiplier

In both of the examples we have looked at so far, fiscal policy makers began with a balanced budget and then tried to plug a contractionary gap by **deficit spending.** That means that they set a policy course under which government purchases would purposely exceed net taxes, the difference being made up by borrowing from the public or creating new money. Now we shall see that deficit spending is not strictly necessary in order for fiscal policy to be effective.

No special diagram or lengthy analysis is required to show this. Suppose simply that we begin again with a contractionary gap of $100 and an equilibrium national income $200 below the target level. As before, government purchases are initially $100 and net taxes also initially $100, so the budget is balanced. Now suppose that fiscal policy makers raise govern-

Deficit Spending A policy of purposely allowing government purchases to exceed net taxes, with the difference being made up by borrowing from the public or creating new money.

ment spending by \$100, and at the same time *raise* net taxes by \$100. What happens?

We know from our first example that the effect of a \$100 increase in government purchases, taken in isolation, is to raise equilibrium national income by \$200. We also know that the effect of a \$100 change in net taxes is a \$100 change in equilibrium national income in the opposite direction of the tax change. The combined policy we have proposed, then, must raise equilibrium national income by \$200 and at the same time lower it by \$100, for a net *upward* effect of \$100. If the fiscal authorities were to raise both government purchases and net taxes by \$200, they could bring equilibrium national income all the way up to the target level without running a deficit at all.

Balanced Budget Multiplier

This example suggests still another kind of multiplier, the **balanced budget multiplier.** The balanced budget multiplier is equal to the simple multiplier *minus* the net tax multiplier. In algebraic terms, we could express the balanced budget multiplier this way:

$$M_B = M - M_T = \frac{1}{\text{MPS}} - \frac{\text{MPC}}{\text{MPS}} = \frac{1 - \text{MPC}}{\text{MPS}}$$

where M_B stands for the balanced budget multiplier, and all other symbols have the same meaning as before. The expression on the extreme right-hand side can be simplified if we remember that $\text{MPC} = 1 - \text{MPS}$. We get

$$M_B = \frac{1 - (1 - \text{MPS})}{\text{MPS}} = \frac{\text{MPS}}{\text{MPS}} = 1$$

It turns out that the value of the balanced budget multiplier is just 1, no matter what is the value of the marginal propensity to consume or save. In short, *an increase in government spending, accompanied by an equal increase in net taxes, with planned investment, autonomous consumption, and the marginal propensity to consume unchanged, produces a dollar-for-dollar increase in equilibrium nominal national income.*

Balanced Budget Multiplier A multiplier showing how much equilibrium nominal national income will change in response to a change in government purchases matched dollar for dollar by an offsetting change in net taxes. The value of the balanced budget multiplier is always exactly 1.

CASE 10.3
Ford's Balanced Budget Proposal of 1975

After skirmishing for a year with Congress over details of fiscal policy, President Gerald Ford undertook an offensive. On October 6, 1975, he went on national television with a major speech on economic policy.

The country, he said, was at a crossroads. The decision before the nation was whether or not to continue in the direction of recent years toward higher taxes, and higher spending by "a massive, overzealous bureaucracy which has become too involved in trying to run too much of your daily life." To put a halt to what he saw as this excessive growth of government, he proposed to cut \$28 billion from projected federal spending in the next year. This spending cut was to be matched by a \$28 billion reduction in taxes. "For every dollar that we return to the American taxpayer, we must also cut our projected spending by the same amount."

As several commentators on the President's proposals pointed out, this policy, if enacted, would have provided a textbook illustration of the balanced budget multiplier in action. Although equal amounts would have been cut from taxes and spending, the commentators feared that the net effect would be contractionary. As a result, the proposal found little favor with Congress, which still believed that the economy would need more, not less stimulus from fiscal policy in the coming year.

The Multipliers Compared

We now have three multipliers, corresponding to three types of fiscal policy. These are the simple multiplier, the net tax multiplier, and the balanced budget multiplier. The simple multiplier is always larger than the net tax multiplier, and the balanced budget multiplier is always equal to 1.

In the cases we have looked at, the balanced budget multiplier and the net tax multiplier were equal, but that was just a coincidence arising from the fact that we used 0.5 for the value of the marginal propensity to consume. If the value of the marginal propensity to consume is between 0.5 and 1.0, the net tax multiplier is between the balanced budget multiplier and the simple multiplier. For example, if the marginal propensity to consume were 0.75, we would get these values for our three multipliers:

$$M = 4.0 \qquad M_T = 3.0 \qquad M_B = 1.0$$

We should caution against an unwarranted interpretation of these multipliers. A change in government spending is the "most powerful" tool of fiscal policy, in the sense that it takes advantage of the full value of the simple multiplier. That does not mean, though, that a change in government spending is necessarily the *best* way to eliminate an expansionary or contractionary gap.

Any one of the three policies is equally good from a macroeconomic point of view, so long as a big enough change in taxes or the balanced budget is used. The important differences between the policies are of a microeconomic nature.

In particular, the policies differ in terms of the proportion of national income devoted to government purchases in the new equilibrium. Let us go back to our example where the initial level of income was $600, the target level $800, and the initial level of both taxes and government purchases $100. If the contractionary gap were filled by only raising government purchases, the new equilibrium level of government purchases would be $200. If the gap were filled entirely by reducing net taxes, the target income could be reached without increasing government purchases at all. (This would require cutting net taxes to *minus* $100; that is, it would require government transfer payments to be $100 greater than tax collections in the new equilibrium.) Finally, if the gap were filled while maintaining a balanced budget, the new equilibrium level of government purchases would have to be $300.

Which is better, a level of government purchases of $100, $200, or $300? It depends on whether the actual government expenditure projects undertaken are judged to be worthwhile *on their own merits,* without looking at their macroeconomic effects. To take an extreme case, suppose that all the government can think of to spend money on is putting men to work digging holes and then filling the holes back in again. If this were the case, filling a contractionary gap with added government purchases would be silly, and a balanced budget policy would be doubly silly. It would be better to cut taxes, even if they had to be cut a lot, and put the men to work producing something that consumers found worthwhile to spend their money on. On the other hand, if the government has a big backlog of projects that give taxpayers more for their money, in terms of real benefits, than they get from the money they spend in the consumer sector, then raising government spending makes sense.

Educated at Harvard, James Tobin has spent most of his professional career at Yale. Tobin is widely recognized for his work in macroeconomic theory. In particular, he has made fundamental contributions to the "portfolio balance" theory of the demand for money, to be discussed in Chapter 12 of this book. He has received many awards and honorary degrees, and in 1971, served as President of the American Economic Association.

Together with his great accomplishments as a theorist, Tobin has long had a very active interest in economic policy. This interest took him to Washington in 1961 as a member of President Kennedy's Council of Economic Advisors. His views at that time appear to have been typical of the economics profession in the Kennedy era. It was an era when economists were confident of their theories and Presidents confident of the power of government to solve social problems.

Writing for the *New Republic* in 1960, just before going to Washington, Tobin summarized his views in these terms: "If the overwhelming problem of democratic capitalism in the 30's and even the 50's was to bring the business cycle under social control, the challenge of the 60's is to bring under public decision the broad allocation of national output. Fortunately, the means are at hand. They are techniques well within the peacetime scope of government. We can do the job without the direct controls of wartime—priorities, rationing, price and wage controls. . . . The means are at hand; to use them we will need to muster more wisdom, maturity, leadership, and sense of national purpose than we displayed in the 1950's."

James Tobin (1918–   )

Tobin stayed on the Council of Economic Advisors only briefly, but by no means lost his active interest in public policy. When George McGovern campaigned for the Presidency in 1972, Tobin was on hand as his most influential economic advisor.

Tobin's most recent book, *The New Economics One Decade Older* (1974), looks back on the policy experiences of the 1960s. His earlier confidence in the infallibility of economic theory plus government power as a means to overcome social injustice is perhaps a bit tempered now, but only a bit. Despite mistakes that may have been made, it is clear that Tobin continues to believe that the means are at hand to solve economic problems, and all that is needed is the political will to use them.

We can put this in terms of a provisional guideline: *Set the level of government purchases by looking at the actual economic merit of spending projects, without considering macroeconomic effects. Then, if the resulting budget does not provide the right amount of macroeconomic stimulus, aim for the target level of national income by adjusting net taxes upward or downward, as required.* This is not an ironclad law that gives the indisputable answer to every problem of fiscal policy. It is just a common sense rule of thumb.

Conclusions

In the decades since Keynes wrote his treatise, thousands of economists and policy makers have seen an exciting picture in the multiplier theory of income determination. Put simply, the Keynesian theory carries the message that *any desired level of national income can be chosen as a target, and any target can be hit given the political will to apply known policies.* The only limits are the physical productive capacity and resource base of the economy.

Does It Work?

Despite the confidence of statements issued from the highest level of the economics profession, you must want to ask, does it work? Do the economic events of the 1970s reflect intelligently chosen targets accurately arrived at by enlightened policy? Were the simultaneous presence of unprecedented peacetime inflation and the highest unemployment since the 1930s the result of careful fine tuning of planned expenditure? From the record, it looks as if either the policies outlined here had not been tried (but we know they have been!) or that there is something more to good economic policy than juggling contractionary and expansionary gaps.

Perhaps the fact that there is more to be learned than we yet know about the intelligent conduct of macroeconomic policy makes economics an even more exciting picture today than a decade ago, when the men at the top thought that they knew all the answers. In this book, too, we have a long way to go, but by the end of seven more chapters we promise that you will at least be in sight of the frontiers of macroeconomic science.

SUMMARY

1. If the equilibrium level of nominal national income is different from the target level, there will be a gap between total planned expenditure and national product measured at the target level of income. If the equilibrium level of income is lower than policy makers want it to be, a contractionary gap is said to exist. If the equilibrium level of nominal income is too high, the gap is said to be expansionary.
2. One way to fill a contractionary gap is by increasing government purchases without increasing net taxes. When government purchases are increased while net taxes, planned investment, and the consumption schedule remain unchanged, equilibrium nominal national income will change by an amount equal to the change in government purchases times the multiplier.
3. A contractionary gap can also be filled by cutting net taxes without changing government purchases. When net taxes are changed while government purchases, planned investment, autonomous consumption, and the marginal propensity to consume remain unchanged, equilibrium nominal national income will change in the direction opposite to the change in taxes by an amount equal to the change in net taxes times the net tax multiplier.
4. An increase in government spending, accompanied by an equal increase in net taxes, with planned investment, autonomous consumption, and the marginal propensity to consume unchanged, produces a dollar-for-dollar increase in equilibrium nominal national income. The balanced budget multiplier is thus equal to 1.
5. A provisional guideline for fiscal policy is to set the level of government purchases by looking at the actual economic merit of spending projects without considering macroeconomic effects. Then, if the resulting budget does not provide the right amount of macroeconomic stimulus, aim for the target level of national income by adjusting net taxes upward or downward as required.
6. Recent experiences tend to cast doubt on the original Keynesian faith that any desired level of national income can be chosen as a target, and that any target can be hit given the political will to apply known policies. There is more to economic policy than juggling expansionary and contractionary gaps.

DISCUSSION QUESTIONS

1. Is the target level of national income always that level of national income at which there will be equilibrium?
2. Do you think that the major tool of fiscal policy should be changes in government spending or changes in taxation? Justify your position.

3. Use the circular flow to trace the effect of government spending in closing a contractionary gap.
4. What importance does the size of the marginal propensity to consume have on the effectiveness of fiscal policy in closing both inflationary and deflationary gaps?
5. Explain why a given change in government spending has a greater impact on the economy than the same change in taxation.
6. If there were a contractionary gap, would there be some advantage to simply paying workers to dig ditches and then fill them in? Under what circumstances would this policy be beneficial?
7. Who pays the cost and who receives the benefits of (a) increased government spending and (b) increased taxes. Does your answer to this question differ now from what it would have been just after you read Chapter 4?
8. Do you think that there is an expansionary gap in the economy right now (as you are taking this course)? A contractionary gap? How can you tell? What is the government doing about the gap if there is one?
9. Do you think the current President and his economic advisors are confident of their ability to make the economy do what they think it ought to? Are you confident of their ability? Why or why not?

Appendix
An Algebraic Approach to Income Determination and the Multiplier

All of the theoretical propositions we have illustrated with graphs and numerical examples in the last three chapters can be expressed equally well in terms of elementary algebraic equations. Let us begin with the consumption schedule. Using **a** to represent autonomous consumption, **b** for the marginal propensity to consume, C for consumption, T for net taxes, and Y for nominal national income, the consumption schedule can be written

$$C = \mathbf{a} + \mathbf{b}(Y - T) \tag{1}$$

Note that the expression $(Y - T)$ that appears in the right-hand side of this equation represents disposable income.

Next we put together the aggregate demand schedule. Using AD for total planned expenditure, I for planned investment, G for government purchases, and other symbols as before, we can write the aggregate demand schedule as

$$AD = C + I + G \tag{2}$$

Substituting for C on the basis of Eq. (1), this becomes

$$AD = \mathbf{a} + \mathbf{b}(Y - T) + I + G \tag{3}$$

Our theory tells us that national income must be equal to planned expenditure in order for the circular flow to be in equilibrium. This equilibrium condition can be written as

$$Y = AD \tag{4}$$

Using Eq. (3) to substitute for AD, the equilibrium condition becomes

$$Y = \mathbf{a} + \mathbf{b}(Y - T) + I + G \tag{5}$$

Solving Eq. (5) for Y gives us this formula for the equilibrium value of nominal national income:

$$Y^* = \frac{1}{1 - \mathbf{b}}(\mathbf{a} - \mathbf{b}T + I + G) \tag{6}$$

The asterisk (*) after the Y in this formula reminds us that the equation holds only for the *equilibrium* value of nominal national income.

Notice that the first term of the right-hand side of Eq. (6), $1/(1 - \mathbf{b})$, gives the value of the simple multiplier.

Let us use this formula to solve some simple problems in the theory of income determination and fiscal policy.

Problem 1: Suppose that $\mathbf{a} = 150$, $\mathbf{b} = 0.5$, $I = 100$, $G = 100$, and $T = 100$. What is the value of equilibrium national income?

Solution: Insert the given values in Eq. (6). This gives

$$Y^* = \frac{1}{1 - 0.5}[150 - 0.5(100) + 100 + 100]$$
$$= 2(300)$$
$$= 600$$

Compare this solution with Exhibits 9.1 and 9.2 in order to see the parallel between the graphical, numerical, and algebraic solutions to this income determination problem.

Problem 2: Suppose that, initially, all variables have the values given in Problem 1, but that the government adopts a target value for nominal national income of $900. Assuming no change in taxes, how much will government purchases have to be in order for the national income target to be reached?

Solution: Insert the known values for $\mathbf{a}$, $\mathbf{b}$, I, and T in Eq. (6). Use the target value of nominal national income, $900, in place of Y^*, and leave G as the unknown. This gives

$$900 = 2[150 - 0.5(100) + 100 + G]$$

Solve this equation for G:

$$900 = 400 + 2G$$
$$2G = 500$$
$$G = 250$$

We see that government purchases must be raised from $100 to $250 in order to raise national income from $600 to $900. This accords with the principle that, other things being equal, the change in equilibrium nominal national income resulting from a given change in government purchases is equal to the simple multiplier times the change in government purchases.

Problem 3: According to the formula given in the text, when the marginal propensity to consume is 0.75, the net tax multiplier must be 3. Confirm this by showing that a $100 tax cut will result in a $300 increase in equilibrium national income if the marginal propensity to consume is 0.75.

Solution: Use Y_0 for the initial equilibrium level of national income, Y_1 for the equilibrium level of national income after the tax cut, T_0 for the initial level of net taxes, a value of 0.75 for $\mathbf{b}$, and the usual letters for the other unknown values. First we get

$$Y_0 = \frac{1}{1 - 0.75}[\mathbf{a} - 0.75(T_0) + I + G]$$

Which simplifies to

$$Y_0 = 4[\mathbf{a} - 0.75(T_0) + I + G]$$

Next find the expression for Y_1 by using $T_0 - 100$ for the new level of net taxes. This gives

$$Y_1 = 4[\mathbf{a} - 0.75(T_0 - 100) + I + G]$$

Which can be rewritten as

$$Y_1 = 4[\mathbf{a} - 0.75(T_0) + I + G] + 300$$

Substituting the expression for Y_0 that we obtained earlier into the right-hand side of this last equation gives

$$Y_1 = Y_0 + 300$$

which is just what we wanted to know. The \$100 tax cut does raise the equilibrium level of national income by \$300, as we expect from application of the net tax multiplier.

CHAPTER 11
The Banking System and the Supply of Money

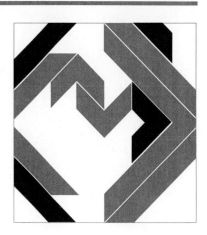

What You Will Learn in This Chapter

Money plays a big role in economic life. We use it every day as a means of payment and a store of value. In the American economy, checking accounts in commercial banks are the most common form of money. The commercial banks that create checking accounts for use as money are closely regulated by the Federal Reserve System. These regulations allow the Federal Reserve to control the total quantity of money supplied in the economy. Later, we shall see that this control of the money supply is a powerful tool of economic stabilization policy.

For Review

Here is an important term that will be put to use in this chapter. Be certain that you understand it, or review it before proceeding.

Opportunity cost (Chapter 1)

There is still a big piece missing from our theory of nominal national income and the multiplier. The missing piece is money. In this chapter and the next two, we fill in what we need to know about money and the banking system. By doing so, we shall add greatly to our understanding of stabilization policy. Once again, our familiar tools of supply and demand will come into use. In the present chapter we shall explain how the banking system controls the supply of money. In Chapter 12 we shall look at the demand for money, and then put supply and demand together. Finally, in Chapter 13 we shall show how the multiplier theory can be modified to take money into account.

The Nature and Functions of Money

Money has three functions. It serves as a unit of account, a medium of exchange, and a store of purchasing power.

Unit of Account

As a unit of account, money serves as a convenient "common denominator" for measuring the value of all goods and services. We have seen how national income accountants use money prices to measure things such as national product and national income. On a smaller scale, we all use money as a unit of account in our day-to-day household budgeting.

Medium of Exchange

In saying that money serves as a medium of exchange, we mean that it is accepted as a means of payment in all market transactions. Without some generally accepted medium of exchange, we would have to trade by barter. Barter sometimes works on a very small scale, as when two farmers swap a ton of hay for a cord of firewood, or on a very large scale, as when the Soviet Union trades a train load of machine tools for a million tons of Polish coal. Most of the time, though, when we go to the grocery store or to our stockbroker it is easier to take along money than a bale of hay or a bag of grain. Needless to say, payment in money is also more likely to be acceptable to grocers and stockbrokers.

Store of Purchasing Power

The third function of money is to act as a temporary store of purchasing power. Money is one of several forms in which we can keep wealth until we need it to make transactions. This function of money is quite important from the point of view of economic theory. It will pay us to look at it in somewhat more detail than the first two functions.

Money is not the only thing that can function as a store of purchasing power. Wealth can be held as real estate, bonds, stocks, consumer durables, precious gems and metals, works of art, and any of a long list of other forms. Why might someone choose money as a store of purchasing power rather than one of these other assets?

Liquidity

Liquidity A property that an asset is said to have if it can be acquired and disposed of quickly and easily without the danger of a loss in nominal value.

Bonds Certificates issued by a borrower that entitle the lender (called the bondholder) to receive fixed periodic payments of interest, plus a larger final payment when the bond "matures" after a set number of years.

The outstanding attraction of money as an asset is **liquidity.** An asset is said to be liquid if it can be acquired and disposed of quickly and easily, without the danger of a loss in nominal value. Compare money in this respect to **bonds,** for example. To buy or sell a bond, you have to visit a broker. This takes time, may be done only during business hours, and means paying a small commission to the broker. Furthermore, there is the danger that when you go to your broker to sell a bond, it may be worth less than when you bought it. If you paid $100 for a bond and its price has gone down to $90, you are in a dilemma. Should you sell it now, suffering a capital loss of $10 on top of paying the brokerage fee? Or should you keep it in the hope that its market price will go back up, even though you really would prefer to change it for some other type of asset? Keeping assets in the form of money makes disposing of them much easier. Almost anyone will take money, night or day. What is more, there is no danger of capital loss on money. The nominal value of a dollar is always a dollar, no more and no less.

Opportunity Costs

There are major opportunity costs to holding money, which must be balanced against the advantage of its liquidity. The biggest opportunity cost is that most forms of money earn no interest return. Stocks and bonds are superior in this respect. Other less liquid assets, such as consumer durables and owner-occupied real estate, do not pay an explicit return, but do provide useful material services to their owners.

Moreover, although holding money avoids the danger of a loss in the nominal value of one's assets, it does involve some risk. The major risk is that of a loss in real purchasing power in the event of inflation. If prices double, all those dollar bills under your mattress will buy only half as many beefsteaks or movie tickets when you pull them out to spend them. In contrast, owning physical assets such as works of art, useful commodities, or real estate gives some protection against inflation, because the prices of these things can be expected to rise in step with other prices. We shall return to a discussion of money as a store of purchasing power in the next chapter.

Types of Money

In modern economies, there are two things that perform all three of the basic functions of money: currency and demand deposits. By **currency** we mean coins and paper money. **Demand deposits** are the accounts in commercial banks that we commonly call checking accounts. By conventional definition, money is held only by households and firms other than banks. No currency or demand deposits that belong to the Treasury, Federal Reserve, or commercial banks are included in the definition of money. When we speak of the economy's stock of money in this book, this is what we mean: the total currency outside banks plus the nonbank public's holdings of demand deposits. This total is called M_1.

Some other assets closely resemble money. Of these, the most important are **time deposits** in commercial banks. By time deposits we mean savings accounts and certificates of deposits. Some economists think that when we total up the economy's money stock we should add these in too. When this is done, the total is called M_2. Exhibit 11.1 shows us the total amount of each component of the money stock for the United States, according to recent data.

Currency outside Banks

Currency is issued by two institutions of the government: the Federal Reserve System and the Treasury. It represents their monetary obligations

Currency Coins and paper money.

Demand Deposits Deposits at commercial banks that permit the depositor to make payments to others by writing a check against the deposit. Demand deposits are what we commonly call checking accounts.

M_1 The money supply defined as currency plus demand deposits.

Time Deposits Interest-paying accounts at commercial banks against which it is not ordinarily possible to write checks. Both passbook savings accounts and certificates of deposits are included, except for certain very large certificates of deposit used by corporate depositors.

M_2 The money supply defined as M_1 plus time deposits at commercial banks.

EXHIBIT 11.1

Components of money and near money, September 1975 (billions of current dollars)

Money takes several forms in the American economy. Currency and demand deposits fully perform all three of the major functions of money. Together they are called M_1. Time deposits in commercial banks act as stores of value, but not as means of payment. M_1 plus time deposits in commercial banks is called M_2.

Type	Amount in Circulation
Currency outside banks*	71.9
Demand deposits†	220.9
Money supply M_1	292.8
Time deposits‡	359.9
Money supply plus time deposits M_2	652.7

*Excludes currency in the vaults of commercial banks, the Federal Reserve banks, and the U.S. Treasury.
†Includes (1) demand deposits at all commercial banks other than those due to domestic commercial banks and the U.S. government, less cash items in process of collection and Federal Reserve float, and (2) foreign demand deposits at Federal Reserve banks.
‡Excludes negotiable time certificates of deposit issued in denominations of $100,000 or more by large banks.

Source: *Federal Reserve Bulletin*, November 1975.

or IOUs to the public. Today, currency consists almost entirely of Federal Reserve notes and Treasury coins.

Paper money and coins are no longer backed by any intrinsically valuable commodity. Neither the Federal Reserve nor the Treasury will now give anything in exchange for a $10 bill or a dime other than another $10 bill or dime—another promise to pay. Up until 1934, the government issued gold coins and paper currency redeemable in gold. Until the mid-1960s one could readily obtain silver coins and "silver certificates" (dollar bills redeemable in silver), but these were gradually phased out. The few remaining silver certificates in circulation can no longer be turned in for metallic silver, and the remaining silver coins are mostly lodged in collections. We now have a currency whose value is based purely on the public's faith in its ability to exchange it for all kinds of goods and services.

Demand Deposits

Demand deposits are bookkeeping entries of commercial banks. They represent obligations of these banks to their depositors. As shown in Exhibit 11.1, demand deposits account for some 75 percent of the money supply, but this figure actually understates their importance. Demand deposits turn out to be used to conduct some 95 percent of the dollar volume of all transactions in the economy. Although demand deposits are issued by private commerical banks, there are limits on the volume of such deposits that banks can create. We shall discuss these limits shortly.

Near Money

Time deposits in commercial banks are also included in Exhibit 11.1. In contrast to demand deposits, time deposits pay interest to depositors. The reason they have not traditionally been considered to be true money is that they could not be used directly as a means of payment. In recent years, though, the distinction between money and near money has begun to blur. A major step in this direction is the introduction of **NOW accounts,** which permit depositors to write checks on interest-bearing savings accounts. Also, recent changes in regulations have made it possible, in some cases, for depositors to transfer money from a savings to a checking account by telephone. That also has the effect of making savings deposits more liquid.

NOW Accounts Accounts that permit checks to be written on interest-bearing time deposits. NOW stands for "negotiable orders of withdrawal."

Although they are not mentioned in Exhibit 11.1, we should note that savings deposits at nonbank financial institutions, such as savings and loan institutions, hardly differ from savings deposits in commercial banks. Securities such as government bonds, commercial paper, and Treasury bills are also very liquid.

The Federal Reserve System[1]

On December 23, 1913, President Woodrow Wilson signed the Federal Reserve Act, which established the **Federal Reserve System,** or **Fed** for

Federal Reserve System (Fed) The central banking system of the United States, which provides banking services to government and commercial banks, and regulates the activities of commercial banks.

[1]This section and the following one give a very concise description of the structure and functioning of the Federal Reserve System and the U.S. commercial banking system. Readers who wish to learn additional details may consult Colin and Rosemary Campbell, *An Introduction to Money and Banking* (New York: Holt, Rinehart and Winston, 1972). For a somewhat more advanced treatment, see Thomas D. Simpson, *Money, Banking, and Economic Analysis* (Englewood Cliffs, N.J.: Prentice-Hall, 1976).

short. The Fed functions as the central bank of the United States. It is the government bank where commercial banks and the Treasury do their banking. It regulates the commercial banking system. It controls the supply of money. By exercising its powers, as we shall see, the Fed can have a major effect on the level of prices of all goods and services, on the level of employment and output in the economy, and on the nation's balance of payments.

By law, the Federal Reserve is an "independent agency" of the federal government, not under the direction of the executive branch. The original intent of making the Fed independent was to prevent the Treasury Department from manipulating monetary conditions for political ends. In practice, the monetary actions of the Fed and the fiscal actions of the Treasury are usually coordinated. The Chairman of the Federal Reserve Board of Governors, the Secretary of the Treasury, and the Chairman of the President's Council of Economic Advisors meet weekly to discuss national policy. It would be more accurate to say that the Fed serves as an equal partner in determining government policy than to say that it acts as an independent agent.

Structure

The overall organizational structure of the Federal Reserve System is shown in Exhibit 11.2. At the heart of the structure are the twelve District Federal Reserve Banks. Ten of these banks have branches, a total of

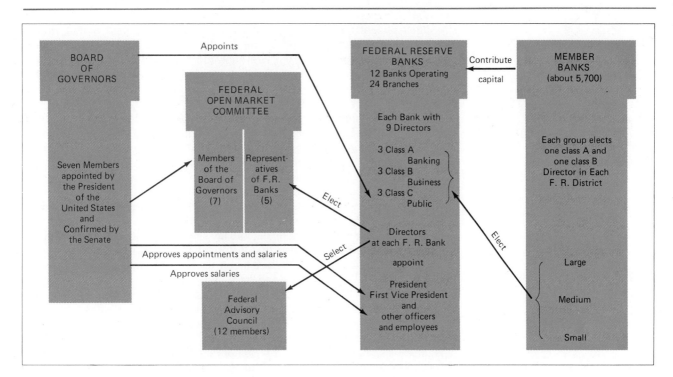

EXHIBIT 11.2
Organization of the Federal Reserve System
The Federal Reserve system, or Fed, acts as the central bank for the United States. It provides banking services to commercial banks and government, and regulates the activities of commercial banks.

twenty-four branches in all. Each of the twelve regional banks is a separate corporation chartered by the federal government and owned by its stockholders, who are the member commercial banks of the district. Although the Federal Reserve banks are owned by their stockholders, they are not typical of privately owned corporations because profit seeking is not one of their goals. Any extra earnings of a Federal Reserve bank over and above operating expenses and the fixed dividends that go to member banks are passed on to the Treasury.

Primary control of each district bank lies with a nine-member board. Of these nine, six are elected by the member bank stockholders, and the remaining three are appointed by the Fed's own Board of Governors. Each board is responsible for the policies of its own bank and for appointing bank officers.

The Federal Reserve banks perform several important functions in the banking system. They carry out policy decisions, examine and supervise the member banks in their district, and provide banking services for the

Arthur Frank Burns (1904–   )

Arthur Burns is among those many distinguished economists born in Austria, but his education and training were entirely American. He moved to America with his parents as a boy, and went on to study at Columbia University, where he earned his doctorate in 1934. During the 1930s and 1940s, Burns taught at Rutgers University and then at Columbia. Early in this period, he began a long association with the National Bureau of Economic Research. His research on business cycles at the Bureau earned him a solid reputation among his professional colleagues. In 1959, they honored him with the Presidency of the American Economic Association.

When Dwight Eisenhower became President of the United States, he appointed Arthur Burns Chairman of his Council of Economic Advisors. Burns served in that capacity until 1956. Perhaps the most important thing he did in those years was to establish a friendship with the ambitious young Vice President, Richard Nixon. He maintained an association with Nixon over the years, advising him in both his 1960 and 1968 Presidential campaigns.

Predictably, when Nixon entered office Burns returned to Washington. Nixon first appointed him to the newly created post of Counselor to the President. Then, in 1970, a job opened up at the Federal Reserve. Members of the Fed's Board of Governors serve 14-year terms, so that by 1970, a majority of the Board had been appointed by Democratic presidents. Nixon naturally wanted his own man as Chairman, and gave Burns the job.

Burns has served as Chairman of the Board of Governors under the most difficult circumstances imaginable. For one thing, the years of his tenure in that post have seen the worst economic instability since the 1930s. Many economists lay the blame for a large share of that instability squarely at the door of the Fed itself. To make matters even more difficult, Burns has served at a time when "monetarist" and "Keynesian" economists have been locked in a furious theoretical debate over the proper conduct of monetary policy. Burns has pursued a cautious middle course that has made no one entirely happy. He has introduced some much-needed changes in the Fed's operating procedures, but these have not gone as far as the monetarists have wanted. At the same time, the Keynesians, many allied politically with the Democrats, have scored Burns for keeping monetary conditions too tight, and thus worsening unemployment.

Publicly, Burns takes all this criticism in stride. He is by nature independent-minded, and did not hesitate even to disagree openly on matters of policy with Nixon. His office is a natural lightning rod for criticism, and that is a role that he seems at times almost to relish.

U.S. Treasury and other governmental agencies. They provide banking services to their member banks, such as clearing checks, handling commercial banks' reserve deposit accounts, making loans to member banks, and providing currency for member banks. In addition, they issue Federal Reserve notes, which form a major part of the stock of currency.

The Board of Governors

The highest policy-making body of the entire Federal Reserve System is its Board of Governors. The board acts as a supervisor of the twelve Federal Reserve banks. The board has seven members who are appointed by the President and confirmed by the Senate. Each governor serves a single fourteen-year term, and devotes full-time service to the business of the Federal Reserve System. One term expires every other year. The present chairman of the board is Arthur F. Burns. Like most recent appointees to the board, he was a professional economist and active in public affairs before his appointment.

The Federal Open Market Committee

A special Fed committee decides when and how open market operations—which, as we shall see, are a powerful instrument of monetary policy—will be used. The Federal Open Market Committee is composed of the seven members of the board of governors, plus five District Reserve bank presidents. It meets every month to decide on changes to be made in the Fed's security holdings. Actual transactions are carried out through the Federal Reserve Bank of New York.

The Commercial Banking System

As of June 30, 1975, there were 14,573 commercial banks in the United States. Among this group of banks, those that have obtained charters from the federal government are called national banks. National banks are required to belong to the Federal Reserve System, which means that they must own stock in the system and be governed by its regulations. In addition to national banks, there are also state-chartered banks, which may choose to join the Federal Reserve System if they wish. Exhibit 11.3 shows the number of each type of bank and their total assets.

Fed Membership

Banks belonging to the Federal Reserve System are entitled to certain privileges of membership. Member banks can acquire loans, currency, and financial advice from their district Federal Reserve bank. They can use the Fed's check-clearing facilities and transfer funds over its teletype wires. They earn a fixed dividend on the stock they are required to own in the system.

There are some disadvantages to membership, though. Member banks are required by the Federal Reserve to keep a larger fraction of their assets in the form of non-interest-bearing reserves than are nonmember banks in most states. They are also subject to more stringent regulations regarding capital, assets, mergers, branches, holding companies, and officers than are nonmember banks.

EXHIBIT 11.3

Number of banks and total assets, June 1975

Commercial banks in the United States may be chartered either by the federal government (national banks) or the individual states. National banks must belong to the Federal Reserve System, but state banks need not be members. Only a minority of all banks are members, but member banks are larger on the average. Member banks hold nearly four-fifths of all bank assets.

	Number of Banks	Percent of Total	Total Assets (in billions of dollars)	Percent of Total
National banks	4,730	32.5	536.8	57.6
State member banks	1,064	7.3	179.7	19.3
Total member banks	5,794		716.5	
Nonmember banks	8,779	60.2	214.4	23.0
Total banks	14,573	100.0	930.7	100.0

Note: Totals may not agree because of rounding.

Source: *Federal Reserve Bulletin*, November 1975.

Nonmember banks use large city banks to provide many of the services that the Federal Reserve system affords member banks.

Balance Sheet

What exactly do commercial banks do? The easiest way to find out is to look at a commercial bank balance sheet. A balance sheet is an accounting statement that describes the financial position of a bank at a particular date in terms of two columns of figures, one describing the bank's assets and the other describing its liabilities and net worth. By assets we mean everything that the bank owns. By liabilities we mean all claims against the bank's assets held by individuals, firms, or institutions other than the bank's owners. A bank's net worth is obtained by subtracting its liabilities from its assets. This figure gives the value of the assets not claimed by outsiders; it is the part of the bank's assets claimed by the bank's owners. Because of the way assets, liabilities, and net worth are defined, the following relationship among balance sheet entries must always hold:

$$\text{Assets} = \text{Liabilities} + \text{Net Worth}$$

Whenever a bank increases its total assets, its liabilities plus its net worth must by definition rise by an equal amount.

Exhibit 11.4 is a consolidated balance sheet for all member banks, with the principal balance sheet items listed as of June 30, 1975. The balance sheet shows that most of the assets held by banks are financial claims against others. These claims are mostly loans granted to individuals and businesses, and securities issued by business and by federal, state, and local governments. On the liability side of the balance sheet, the biggest items are demand and time deposits, which are claims against the bank owned by depositors. The net worth figure represents what would be left to the owners of the bank if they were to sell all their assets and pay off all their liabilities at "book" values.

EXHIBIT 11.4
Consolidated balance sheet of member banks, June 30, 1975
(in billions of dollars)
This table shows the consolidated balance sheet for all member banks of the
Federal Reserve. Listed as assets are everything that the bank owns.
Liabilities are all claims against the bank's assets held by individuals, firms,
or institutions other than the bank's owners. The bank's net worth is obtained
by subtracting liabilities from assets.

Assets			Liabilities and Net Worth	
Total reserves		34.4	Demand deposits	243.2
On deposit with Fed	26.9			
Held as currency	7.5		Time deposits	330.4
Loans		384.2	Borrowings from Fed	.1
Securities		149.7	Other liabilities	85.4
Other assets		182.7	Net worth	57.6
Total		716.6	Total	716.6

Source: *Federal Reserve Bulletin*, November 1975.

Reserves

The **reserves** item on the asset side of the balance sheet deserves some further explanation. Historically, the reason that banks hold some of their assets in the form of reserves is that at any moment depositors may want to withdraw their money from the bank, either by writing a check to someone who will deposit it in another bank, or by walking up to the teller's window and asking for currency. In the U.S. commercial banking system today, the quantity of reserves that banks hold is not left up to the judgment of individual bankers. Instead, the Fed sets certain reserve requirements for member banks. These take the form of fixed percentages of deposits that banks must hold as reserves. These percentages are called **required reserve ratios.** They vary according to the type and size of deposit, as shown in Exhibit 11.5. The Fed permits banks to hold reserves

Reserves (of Commercial Banks) Money held by commercial banks as cash or non-interest-bearing deposits with the Federal Reserve.

Required Reserve Ratios Legally required minimum quantities of reserves, expressed as ratios of reserves to various types of deposits.

EXHIBIT 11.5
Required reserve ratios (October 31, 1975)*
Historically, banks held some of their assets as reserves in order to pay depositors who wanted to withdraw their money. Today reserves still perform that function, but more important, they are a tool of the Fed's regulation of the banking system. Minimum reserves for member banks are set by the Fed. Nonmember banks have reserve requirements set by individual states. These may differ from those shown here.

Demand Deposits					Time Deposits	
0–2	1–10	10–100	100–400	Over 400	Savings	Other Time Deposits†
7.5%	10%	12%	13%	16.5%	3%	1–6%

*Deposit intervals are in millions of dollars. Requirement schedules are graduated, and each deposit interval applies to that part of the deposits of each bank.
†Varies according to maturity date.
Source: *Federal Reserve Bulletin*, November 1975.

either in the form of currency in their own vaults or in the form of non-interest-bearing deposits in the district Federal Reserve bank. As Exhibit 11.4 shows, the latter option is the most heavily used.

Excess Reserves

Excess Reserves Commercial bank reserves in excess of the minimum legally required levels.

The law does not prevent commercial banks from holding more of their assets in the form of reserves than the Fed requires. Any reserves above the required level are referred to as **excess reserves.** However, banks generally try to keep their excess reserves low because reserves earn no interest. They tend to acquire more earning assets, either by making loans or buying securities, whenever they have large excess reserves. As a result, of the $34,706 million total reserves held by member banks on June 25, 1975, fully $34,615 million were required reserves. Excess reserves were only $91 million.

The Supply of Money

Deposits and Reserves

The authority of the Federal Reserve to set required reserve ratios is very important from the point of view of economic theory. That is because a close relationship exists between the level of total reserves and the level of demand deposits, which in turn are the major component of the economy's supply of money. The basic principles of this relationship are quite easy to understand. Let us begin with a numerical example.

For this example, we need to make some simplifications in the banking system. First, we assume that demand deposits are banks' only liabilities, that reserves and loans are their only assets, and that each bank's net worth is zero. Second, we assume that banks always try to keep their level of excess reserves at zero. Third, we assume that the required reserve ratio is a uniform 20 percent for all demand deposits.

EXHIBIT 11.6
Consolidated balance sheet for a simplified banking system, showing the expansion of deposits
In this simplified banking system, demand deposits are banks' only liabilities, reserves and loans their only assets, and net worth is zero. All deposits are subject to a uniform required reserve ratio of 20 percent. An injection of $100 into this system has the effect of increasing the money supply by $500 by the time banks once again reduce their excess reserves to zero.

	Assets				Liabilities and Net Worth		
	Initial Position	Intermediate Position	Final Position		Initial Position	Intermediate Position	Final Position
Total reserves	100	200	200	Demand deposits	500	600	1,000
(Required reserves)	(100)	(120)	(200)				
(Excess reserves)	(0)	(80)	(0)				
Loans	400	400	800				
Total	500	600	1,000	Total	500	600	1,000

Suppose that initially the consolidated balance sheet of this simplified banking system showed total assets of $500, including $100 in total reserves and $400 in loans, and total liabilities of $500, composed entirely of demand deposits. With a required reserve ratio of 20 percent, required reserves are $100 and excess reserves are zero. These figures are shown in the columns labeled "initial position" in Exhibit 11.6.

Now suppose that some depositor comes along with a check, drawn not on one of the commercial banks in our system, but on one of the Federal Reserve banks. When this check is deposited, the commercial bank receiving it credits $100 to the account of the depositor. This appears on the bank's own balance sheet as an addition to liabilities. The bank, in turn, deposits the check in its own account at the district Federal Reserve bank. This action adds $100 in new reserves to the asset side of its balance sheet.

It is important that the original check be drawn on the Federal Reserve System. If it were drawn on another commercial bank, the bank on which it were drawn would lose $100 in reserves when the bank receiving the deposit cashed the check, and the two entries would cancel each other out on the consolidated balance sheet of all commercial banks. Why would the Fed system issue one of its own checks to a private citizen in the first place? Possibly because the citizen presented newly mined gold or foreign currency to a Federal Reserve bank, or possibly, as we shall discuss below, because the citizen sold $100 worth of securities to the Federal Reserve.

Deposit of the Federal Reserve check brings total reserves up to $200. Of this, $120 must now be held as required reserves, because total deposits have risen to $600. This leaves the banking system $80 in excess reserves. The balance sheet of the banking system as it looks at this point is shown in the column of Exhibit 11.6 labeled "intermediate position."

Individual banks are not satisfied with this intermediate position, because they do not like to hold excess reserves. Instead, they want to acquire additional earning assets. They do this by making loans. In exchange for an IOU, a lending bank will credit a borrower's checking account with the amount of the loan. The borrower need not leave the money on deposit, but when he writes checks on his account, those checks will end up in the accounts of other people in other banks. The total level of deposits as shown on the consolidated balance sheet rises by the exact amount of the loan in any event.

How far will the process of deposit expansion go? The limit is determined by the original change in total reserves (which caused the original change in excess reserves) and by the required reserve ratio. Suppose, for example, that banks make $200 worth of new loans on the basis of their $80 in excess reserves. This would raise total assets and demand deposits to $800 and hence raise required reserves to $160. There would still be $40 of excess reserves remaining somewhere in the banking system, and expansion could continue. Not until total deposits reach $1,000 will excess reserves be entirely eliminated. This requires a total of $400 in new loans by the banking system. After this quantity of loans has been made, the consolidated balance sheet looks like the columns labeled "final position" in Exhibit 11.6.

General Principles

Some important general principles can be seen at work in this example. In the banking system we have just looked at, there is a very simple relationship between the total quantity of demand deposits and the level of bank reserves. After the money expansion process is complete and excess reserves have been reduced to zero, the total quantity of demand deposits is equal to total reserves divided by the required reserves ratio.

In the numerical example, the required ratio is 20 percent, so the quantity of demand deposits is five times the quantity of total reserves. An injection into the banking system of $100 in new reserves results in an increase of $500 in the money supply.

Money Multiplier

In the real world, things are a bit more complicated than in our example. For one thing, money includes currency as well as demand deposits. What is more, the ratio of demand deposits to total reserves is not a simple constant. It varies over time, and its variations are not perfectly predictable.

Variations in the ratio of demand deposits to total reserves come from several sources. Partly they result from differing required reserve ratios on different classes of deposits at member banks. Partly they result from different reserve requirements for nonmember banks; these requirements vary considerably from state to state. Finally, the ratio of demand deposits to reserves can be affected by changes in the public's demand for time deposits, and changes in the willingness of banks to hold excess reserves.

Even with all these complications, the general principles of our simplified example carry over at least roughly to the real world. There is still an approximately proportional relationship between the money supply and total reserves. We shall call the ratio of the money supply (M_1) to total reserves the **money multiplier.** It must be remembered, though, that this multiplier is not a constant. Exhibit 11.7 shows that the money multiplier has varied over a range of 7.4 to 8.5 since 1969. About a third of the time, the multiplier has changed by 2 percent or more from one quarter to the next. This variability creates some problems for monetary policy, as the next section will make clear.

Money Multiplier   The ratio of the money supply (M_1) to total reserves.

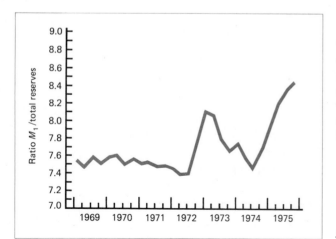

EXHIBIT 11.7
Recent variations in the money multiplier
The money multiplier is subject to significant variations from quarter to quarter. These result from variations in reserve requirements on different types of deposits, changes in the demand for money, and changes in the willingness of banks to hold excess reserves. The data shown here are corrected for statutory changes in required reserve ratios.

Source: Board of Governors, Federal Reserve System, unpublished.

The Instruments of Monetary Policy

Fed's Balance Sheet

We have seen now how the level of total reserves affects the level of demand deposits and the money supply. Next we turn to a discussion of the balance sheet of the Federal Reserve banks, and how the Fed manipulates them to control the level of total reserves.

Exhibit 11.8 is a consolidated balance sheet for the twelve Federal Reserve banks. Looking first at the liabilities side, we see that Federal Reserve notes in circulation are the largest single liability of these banks. The second major type of liability is member banks reserve deposits. Other liabilities include deposits of the Treasury and foreign central banks, and a number of miscellaneous items. The small net worth of the Reserve banks represents member banks' direct ownership claims on the assets of the Federal Reserve System.

On the assets side of the balance sheet, we see that holdings of U.S. government securities are the largest single item. Loans to member banks also appear. These are usually extended on request to help the member banks avoid falling short of their required reserve levels.

Instruments

There are three major instruments by which the Federal Reserve conducts monetary policy. These are **open market operations** (sales and purchases of government securities in the open market), changes in the **discount rate** (the interest rate paid by commercial banks to borrow reserve funds from the Fed), and changes in the *required reserve ratios* for member banks. Let us look at each of these in turn.

Open Market Operations

Open market operations are the Fed's most important policy instrument. The effect of open market operations on monetary conditions is easy to understand now that we have looked at the relationship between commercial bank reserves and the money supply. Once again, let us work through a numerical example.

Open Market Operations Purchases or sales of government securities between the Fed and the public, used as an instrument of monetary policy.

Discount Rate (in the Banking System) The interest rate paid by commercial banks to borrow reserve funds from the Fed.

EXHIBIT 11.8
Consolidated balance sheet of the twelve Federal Reserve Banks, October 31, 1975 (in billions of dollars)
The Federal Reserve banks have liabilities to the general public, in the form of Federal Reserve notes, and to member banks, in the form of reserve deposits. Their main assets are government securities.

Assets		Liabilities and Net Worth	
Securities	87.1	Federal Reserve notes	73.0
Loans to member banks	.1	Member bank reserve deposits	26.3
Other assets	29.6	Other liabilities	15.1
Total	116.8	Total	116.8

Note: Subtotals may not add to totals due to rounding.
Source: Federal Reserve Bulletin, November 1975.

EXHIBIT 11.9

The effects of a $100 open market purchase on the consolidated balance sheets of Federal Reserve banks and commercial banks

If the Fed buys $100 worth of securities on the open market, its assets go up by $100, and its liabilities, in the form of member bank reserve deposits, go up by the same amount. In the commercial banking system, the $100 in new reserves show up on the assets side of the balance sheet. These new assets are initially balanced by new deposits of only $100. The position shown here as "after" is not the final one, for commercial banks now have excess reserves. They will proceed to expand deposits further by making new loans until they reach the required reserve ratio.

Before							
Federal Reserve				Commercial Banks			
Assets		Liabilities		Assets		Liabilities	
Securities	$ 500	Currency	$ 900	Reserves	$100	Deposits	$500
Other assets	$ 500	Reserve deposits	$ 100	Loans	$400		
Total	$1,000	Total	$1,000	Total	$500	Total	$500

After							
Federal Reserve				Commercial Banks			
Assets		Liabilities		Assets		Liabilities	
Securities	$ 600	Currency	$ 900	Reserves	$200	Deposits	$600
Other assets	$ 500	Reserve deposits	$ 200	Loans	$400		
Total	$1,100	Total	$1,100	Total	$600	Total	$600

Exhibit 11.9 illustrates the effects of an open market purchase of $100 in U.S. government securities from a member of the public. The effects are shown as they would occur in the simplified banking system described in our earlier numerical example. In that example, we saw what the effects of such a purchase looked like from the point of view of the commercial banking system. Now we see it from the points of view of both the commercial banking system and the Fed.

The first part of the table shows the consolidated balance sheets of both parts of the banking system before the open market operation. Beginning from there, suppose that the Federal Open Market Committee authorizes the purchase of $100 in government bonds from a private party. It pays with one of its own checks.

This gives the Federal Reserve banks $100 in new assets. The seller of the bond deposits the check in his own commerical bank. That gives the bank $100 in new liabilities, in the form of an increase in the original seller's demand deposits. Finally, the commerical bank deposits the check with its District Federal Reserve Bank, giving the commercial bank $100 in additional assets and the Federal Reserve $100 in additional liabilities, both in the form of increased member bank reserve deposits. The result of all this is shown in the lower portion of Exhibit 11.9. Assets and liabilities are each up $100 for the Federal Reserve banks and each up $100 for the commercial banking system.

This is still not the end of the story. The commercial banking system now has excess reserves. The open market operation is the starting point for a process of deposit expansion of the sort we described earlier. Commercial banks will continue to acquire earning assets until their deposits have risen by the full amount of the money multiplier times the added $100 in reserves.

The Discount Rate

A second policy instrument that the Fed can use is the discount rate. A rise in the discount rate, other things being equal, has the effect of discouraging commercial banks from borrowing to augment their reserves. A decline in the discount rate has the opposite impact.

Changes in the discount rate are initiated by the District banks, but they must be approved by the Board of Governors. The managers of the District banks usually adjust the discount rate to keep it in line with other interest rates charged in the market. If the discount rate were substantially above prevailing market rates, member banks might not borrow at all from the Federal Reserve, finding other sources of funds when necessary. If the discount rate were too far below market rates, commercial banks would be tempted to borrow too readily from the Federal Reserve simply to finance new loans, or to purchase securities with higher interest rates. The discount rate is changed frequently to prevent either circumstance from arising.

The Required Reserve Ratios

The third instrument of monetary policy, changing required reserve ratios, is the most powerful. It is not used as often as other instruments, but recently it has been used more than in the past. Any change in required reserve ratios has a very large impact on total demand deposits because it directly affects the money multiplier. In the simplified case, this multiplier is simply the reciprocal of the required reserve ratio. With total reserves of, say $100 million, an increase in the required reserve ratio from 20 to 25 percent would reduce total demand deposits from $500 million to $400 million. The impact would be the same as the impact of $20 million of open market sales, without a change in the required reserve ratio.

The Board of Governors of the Federal Reserve has sole authority to change required reserve ratios. Such changes are usually made only when very large changes in the money supply are desired. For day-to-day policy purposes, the flexibility of open market operations is preferred. These can be made in any desired magnitude and reversed or adjusted immediately if necessary, without fanfare.

Conclusions

The conclusion to which our analysis of the banking system leads is that the Fed can control at will the quantity of money supplied. It can change total reserves when it wants by using open market operations and the discount rate. It can affect the money multiplier through changes in reserve ratios. Together, these determine the money supply.

In our theoretical discussions in the following chapters, we shall consider the Fed's control over the money supply to be absolute. The quantity of money supplied will be treated as something that changes only in response to changes in policy, and not in response to other economic conditions. In reality, though, the money supply is not under perfect control. We have already seen that the money multiplier can fluctuate sharply even over short periods. Nonmember banks, which hold a fifth of deposits now, are not under the Fed's direct control. As the demand of the public for money changes, people shift from one type of deposit to another, and different types of deposits have different reserve requirements. Finally, banks sometimes choose to hold excess reserves. Even though excess reserves are low on the average, they can sometimes change on short notice.

All of these things complicate the Fed's job of managing the money supply. Federal Reserve Board Chairman Burns takes the position that it would be a mistake even to try to control the money supply too closely. To do so, he believes, would cause many sudden short-term variations in interest rates in the face of short-run, temporary shifts in demand. These would disturb credit markets more seriously than the variability of the money supply does.

Current Fed practice is to announce in each quarter rather broad targets for money supply growth over the next twelve months. As this is written, for example, targets are set at 5 to 7½ percent growth for M_1 and 7½ to 10 percent growth for M_2. Given the political and economic pressures under which it works, the Fed does not always hit even these targets accurately.

All told, the relationships between the Fed's policy, economic conditions, and the money supply are still far from being understood. They are currently the subject of very active economic research by economists both inside and outside the banking system. In sticking with our assumption of a perfectly controlled money supply, then, we are leaving a great many interesting issues to other, more specialized books than this.

SUMMARY

1. Money performs three major functions in our economy. These are the functions of a unit of account, a medium of exchange, and a store of value. Only currency and demand deposits perform all three functions fully. Some other assets are close substitutes for money, notably time deposits at commercial banks.
2. The Federal Reserve System acts as the central bank of the United States. It provides banking services for commercial banks and the government, and also regulates the commercial banking system. Its regulatory powers allow it to control the money supply.
3. Demand deposits, the most common form of money, are created by the commercial banking system. The quantity of demand deposits created is limited by required reserve ratios. These are set by the Fed for member banks, and by the various states for nonmember banks. An injection of new reserves into the banking system causes a multiple expansion of demand deposits and the money supply. Under simplified conditions, the ratio of money to reserves (known as the money multiplier) is just the reciprocal of the required reserve ratio. In reality, the money multiplier is determined by more complex considerations, and it can vary from time to time in an unpredictable way.
4. The Fed has three major instruments of monetary policy. These are open market operations, changes in the discount rate, and changes in required reserve ratios. Open market operations are the most flexible instrument, and the one used for day-to-day policy purposes. For theoretical purposes, we can consider the Fed's control over the money supply to be absolute, but in practice it is imperfect.

DISCUSSION QUESTIONS

1. List the functions that money performs in the economy and illustrate how you have used money for each of these purposes. Then give an example of an occasion on which you have used something other than money for each of these purposes.

2. In what type of bank do you have an account? What type of account? Is the balance in your account part of M_1 or M_2?

3. If a commercial bank is not meeting the reserve requirement, what does it have to do? What changes are possible to make sure it meets its reserve requirement?

4. Over time we have switched from using currency to using demand deposits as money. Why do you think this has occurred?

5. It is possible that with increased use of credit cards we shall eventually do away with currency and demand deposits? Would we then be doing away with money? In what sense "yes" and what sense "no"?

6. Suppose that you put your artistic talents to good use, and print up $10,000 worth of counterfeit $20 bills, which go into circulation and are never detected as counterfeit. Trace the effects of your action through the banking system, and explain what happens to the economy's money supply. Do you think that undetected counterfeiting is a "victimless" crime?

7. Do you think that commercial banks should have required reserves? Would they have reserves if they were not required to do so? Explain.

8. If the Federal Reserve Board wanted to increase the money supply, what are the ways it could go about doing it? How could it decrease the money supply? Is it as easy for it to create money as it is for it to contract the money supply?

CHAPTER 12
The Demand for Money and the Money Market

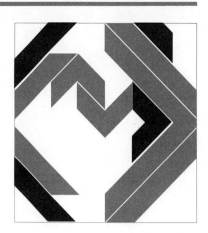

What You Will Learn in This Chapter

The theory of money demand deals with the question of how much money people want under various circumstances. The quantity of money demanded depends on the interest rate and the level of nominal income. The theory of supply and demand and the concept of equilibrium can be applied to the money market in order to show what happens to the interest rate when the quantity of money supplied or the level of nominal income changes.

For Review

Here are some important terms and concepts that will be put to use in this chapter. Be certain that you understand them, or review them before proceeding.

    Supply and demand (Chapter 3)
    Money multiplier (Chapter 11)

In the last chapter we found that, as a general matter, people desire to hold part of their wealth in the form of money because money is highly liquid. Now we are ready to take up the more specific question of just *how much* money people want, and how changing economic conditions affect their need for money. This means developing a theory of the demand for money.

The Demand for Money

Portfolio Balance

Money demand theory is most easily explained in terms of the concept of **portfolio balance.** We say that people hold their wealth in the form of "portfolios" containing a variety of different kinds of assets. For example, moderately well-to-do individuals might include in their portfolios some real estate (their homes), some consumer durables (car, television, and refrigerator), some corporate stocks, some government bonds, and a certain amount of money in the form of currency and demand deposits. They each would have their own particular reasons for owning some of each of these types of assets and for maintaining a certain balance among them.

Portfolio Balance The idea that people try to maintain a balance among the various kinds of assets they own, including money, consumer durables, stocks, and bonds, shifting from one kind of asset to another as economic conditions change.

In order to understand how portfolios are balanced, let us begin by looking at just two types of financial assets, money and bonds. Each of these offers certain advantages that the other does not.

Bonds

Bonds come into existence when business firms or government agencies borrow money and, in exchange, give the lender a certificate representing their promise to pay. The certificate entitles its owner (who is called a bond-holder) to receive an annual interest payment of a fixed number of dollars, plus a larger final payment at the end of a set number of years when the bond "matures." The privilege of receiving the stream of interest payments is, of course, the main reason for holding part of one's wealth in the form of bonds.

A well-defined relationship exists between the rate of return from a bond, expressed as a percentage per year, and the price of the bond. For a very simple example, consider a bond that pays its holder $1 per year, year after year without limit. If investors pay $20 for such a bond, they receive a 5 percent rate of return–$1 per year divided by the $20 purchase price. If they could buy the same bond for $10, they would instead earn a 10 percent rate of return, and so forth. The price of a bond and its rate of return are thus logically linked, and must move in opposite directions.

Exhibit 12.1 gives a short table of the relationship between the rate of interest and the price of a bond paying $1 per year in perpetuity. For bonds that have a fixed maturity date, somewhat more complicated arithmetic is needed to determine the rate of return, given the bond's price. The logic of the relationship is the same for all bonds, though. A high price means a low rate of return, and a low price means a high rate of return.

Money

People who hold part of their wealth in the form of money bear an opportunity cost equal to the interest they could have earned by holding bonds instead. In explaining the reasons that people do hold part of their portfolios in the form of money, despite the opportunity cost of doing so, economists distinguish between the **transactions demand** for money and the **speculative demand** for money.

There is a transactions demand for money because money is acceptable to everyone as a medium of exchange. Holding money makes it easy to

Transactions Demand (for Money) The part of money demand arising from the usefulness of money as a generally acceptable medium of exchange.

Speculative Demand (for Money) The part of money demand arising from the advantages of money as an asset with a fixed nominal value, which offers protection against the danger of capital loss in periods when it is feared that the prices of other assets may fall.

Price	Rate of Return
$100	1%
50	2
20	5
10	10
5	20

EXHIBIT 12.1
Price and rate of return for a bond paying $1 per year in perpetuity

This table shows the relationship between the price and rate of return for a bond paying $1 per year in perpetuity. The rate of return is equal to the annual payment divided by the price. For bonds with a fixed maturity date, the arithmetic of translating a bond's price into its rate of return is somewhat more difficult, but the basic logic is the same. For all bonds, a high price means a low rate of return and a low price a high rate of return.

conduct market transactions—that is, to buy goods and services or financial assets quickly and conveniently, when and where one wants. There is a speculative demand for money because money has a fixed nominal value. Money is an especially attractive store of value in periods when people are afraid that the market price of other assets may fall.

Interest and Portfolio Balance

People balance their portfolios by adjusting the proportion of bonds and money they contain. Just what is a proper balance depends on all the factors that affect the relative attractiveness of different assets.

A major factor affecting the relative attractiveness of bonds and money is the rate of interest. The higher the rate of interest, the more income is earned on each dollar invested in bonds, and consequently, the higher the opportunity cost of holding money. For this reason, the higher the rate of interest, the lower the proportion of their portfolios that people will want to hold in money, other things being equal.

The rate of interest affects the demand for money in a second way, which reinforces the first. If at some particular time the interest rate is high relative to some "normal" rate experienced in the past, bond prices will necessarily be low relative to their "normal" level. If people expect the interest rate to return to normal, they will convert money into bonds in the hope of making a capital gain. When interest rates are "abnormally" low, people are likely to avoid bonds and raise the proportion of their portfolios held in the form of money. They will fear that a return to normal will send bond prices down, causing capital losses. Once again, then, we conclude that the demand for money varies inversely with the interest rate.

Income

An additional major factor affecting the relative demand for money and bonds is the level of nominal income. The higher a person's income, the larger and more frequent the purchases he or she will plan to make. More purchases mean a higher transactions demand for money. Also, over a long period, increases in income are accompanied by increases in wealth. People's portfolios get bigger, so the quantity of money demanded goes up even if they hold the same proportion of their wealth in the form of money.

Money Demand Schedule

The quantity of money demanded increases as the interest rate falls, and increases as nominal income increases. The relationship among the quantity of money demanded, the interest rate, and the level of nominal income that prevails in a given economy in a given period is known as that economy's **money demand schedule.** Exhibit 12.2 shows what the money demand schedule might look like for the kind of economy we have represented in our numerical examples during the last few chapters. The entries in Exhibit 12.2a show the quantity of money demanded when the interest rate is that shown at the left-hand border of the table and the level of nominal national income is that shown at the top of the table. We see, for example, that when the interest rate is 5 percent per year and the level of nominal national income is $600, the quantity of money demanded is $72.

Exhibit 12.2b gives the money demand schedule in graphical form. At

Money Demand Schedule A schedule showing the quantity of money that people desire to hold in their portfolios given various values for the interest rate and the level of nominal income.

(a)

Interest Rate (%)	Level of Nominal National Income					
	200	400	600	800	1,000	1,200
1	120	240	360	480	600	720
2	60	120	180	240	300	360
3	40	80	120	160	200	240
4	30	60	90	120	150	180
5	24	48	72	96	120	144
6	20	40	60	80	100	120
7	17	34	51	68	85	102
8	15	30	45	60	75	90

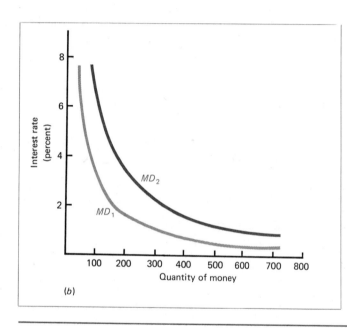

(b)

EXHIBIT 12.2

Money demand schedule for a hypothetical economy
The table and diagram show how money demand
varies as the interest rate and the level of nominal
income vary in a simplified economy like the one we
have used in our numerical examples. The entries in
the body of the table show the quantity of money
demanded at the interest rate corresponding to the
row and the nominal income corresponding to the
column. Each column of the table can be graphed to
get a money demand curve like that shown in part *b*
of the exhibit. The curve MD_1 assumes income to be
fixed at $600. A rise in income to $1,200 would shift
the money demand curve to the position MD_2.

any given level of income, the relationship between the quantity of money
demanded and the interest rate can be shown by a downward-sloping curve,
which looks much like an ordinary demand curve. For example, the curve
labeled MD_1 shows the way money demand varies as the interest rate varies
when income is $600. This curve is drawn from the data in the $600 column
of the table above it. A change in the level of income would produce a shift
in the money demand curve. For example, if income were to increase to
$1,200, the money demand curve would shift to the position labeled MD_2
in the figure. Checking the data given in the last column of the table, we see
that when income doubles, the quantity of money demanded at any particular level of the interest rate doubles.

Proportionality

As Exhibit 12.2 is constructed, the *ratio* of money demanded to income,
at each given interest rate, is constant for all levels of income. When the
interest rate is 3 percent, for example, the quantity of money demanded is
one-fifth of nominal national income at all levels of income. (Check this by
reading across the third row of the table.) Let us check the realism of this
proportionality assumption by using recent U.S. experience as a case study.

CASE 12.1
The Money-to-Income Ratio and Interest Rates in Recent
U.S. Experience

Exhibit 12.3 traces the record of money, income, and interest rates for the postwar American economy. The horizontal axis in this figure measures the ratio of the quantity of money (M_1) to nominal gross national product. The vertical axis measures the corporate Aaa bond rate, that is, the rate of return earned by holders of bonds issued by the most financially sound American corporations. We note that the points representing various years fall rather closely along a curve of the same general shape as the money demand curves drawn for the imaginary economy represented by Exhibit 12.2.

Exhibit 12.3 can be thought of as a crude approximation of the money demand schedule for the American economy. With more sophisticated statistical techniques, we could construct a closer approximation, but even this diagram appears to bear out our two chief assumptions, namely, that the quantity of money demanded is inversely related to the interest rate and directly proportional to the level of nominal income.

It must be emphasized, though, that the relationships among money demand, nominal income, and interest rates are sometimes subject to unpredictable short-run variation. In the last two quarters of 1975, for example, nominal income rose very rapidly while interest rates fell, yet the quantity of money showed virtually no increase. That meant that the point for 1975 in Exhibit 12.3 fell significantly farther to the left than expected. (It should have moved down and slightly to the right compared with the 1974 point.)

In the 1976 Economic Report of the President, the Council of Economic Advisers advanced two possible explanations of the unexpected decline in money demand. Perhaps, they suggested, it was just a temporary deviation from normal, which would soon correct itself. On the other hand, it might indicate the beginning of a permanent shift to the left of the whole money demand schedule. In support of the second interpretation, they noted several

EXHIBIT 12.3

Interest rates and the money/income ratio in the postwar American economy

This exhibit traces the relationship among money, income, and interest rates for the postwar American economy. The horizontal axis measures the ratio of the quantity of money (M_1) to gross national product, and the vertical axis measures the corporate Aaa bond interest rate. In general, the figure bears out the assumptions that the quantity of money demanded is inversely related to the interest rate and directly proportional to the level of nominal income. In some years, however, there have been short-run deviations from the general pattern.

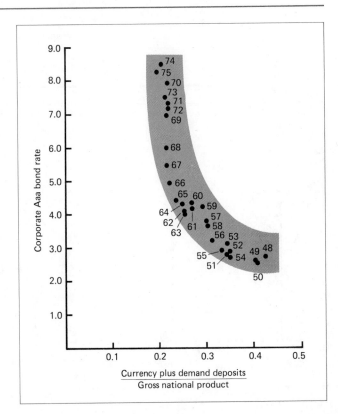

important innovations in banking institutions. These included the increased use of NOW accounts, the recently granted permission to make savings account withdrawals by telephone, and changes in regulations that now permit state and local governments and corporations to hold savings deposits at member banks of the Federal Reserve. It will be at least a year or two before it will be possible to tell if the suspected shift is permanent. Meanwhile, policy makers will find their work complicated by serious uncertainties.

Equilibrium and Disequilibrium in the Money Market

Now we have analyzed both the supply and the demand for money. Our next step will be to put the two together and investigate the nature of equilibrium and disequilibrium in what is called the *money market*. Exhibit 12.4 shows the basic diagram we shall use to do this. It contains a downward-sloping demand curve for money, taken from Exhibit 12.2, using an assumed national income of $1,200. It also contains a money supply curve. This is simply a vertical line, in accordance with our assumption that the money supply is determined solely by Federal Reserve policy and is not directly affected by changes in economic conditions. In this case, the quantity of money supplied is assumed to be $180. It is important to remember that both the demand for money and the supply of money are measured in terms of stocks, not flows. The supply represents the stock in existence at a given time, and the demand represents the stock that people desire to hold in their portfolios under given conditions.

Equilibrium

It is apparent from the diagram that there is only one rate of interest, 4 percent, at which the stock of money that people want to hold is equal to the stock of money supplied by the banking system in accordance with Federal Reserve policy. At any higher rate of interest, there would be an

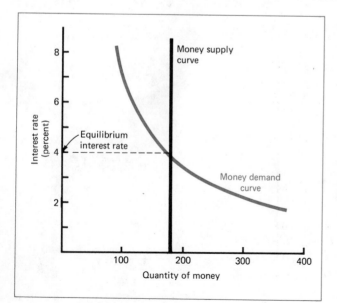

EXHIBIT 12.4
Equilibrium in the money market
The money demand curve in this diagram is based on the data given in Exhibit 12.2, using an assumed nominal national income of $1,200. The money supply curve assumes a quantity of money supplied of $180. The equilibrium interest rate is 4 percent. At any higher interest rate, an excess quantity of money supplied would put downward pressure on the interest rate. If the interest rate were below equilibrium, there would be an excess quantity of money demanded, and upward pressure. Both money supply and demand are measured in stock terms.

excess quantity of money supplied. At an interest rate of 6 percent, for example, the excess quantity supplied would be $60. The excess quantity supplied reflects the fact that people do not want to hold as much money in their portfolios as the Federal Reserve has caused the banking system to put into circulation.

Individual asset holders react to an excess quantity of money supplied by using their excess money to buy other assets. Given the high interest rate, they will be particularly attracted to the idea of replacing some of the money in their portfolios with bonds. However, although some individual asset holders can successfully reduce the quantity of money in their portfolios by buying bonds, not all asset holders can do so at once. Every time someone takes money out of his or her portfolio to buy a bond from someone else, that money ends up in the portfolio of the seller.

No matter how much the money is churned around from portfolio to portfolio in pursuit of bonds, every cent of the fixed stock of money supplied by the banking system always has to be in someone's portfolio at each moment. What occurs as a result of all this churning is not a fall in the money stock, but a rise in the price of bonds. This is just what is needed to restore equilibrium. A rise in the price of bonds means a fall in the percentage rate of interest return on bonds. As the interest rate falls, the excess quantity of money supplied is reduced not because the extra money disappears, but because the amount of money that people desire to keep in their portfolios rises until it catches up with the quantity of money supplied. Soon the interest rate reaches it equilibrium level, and the excess demand is entirely eliminated.

Opposite Process

If the interest rate were for some reason below the equilibrium level, there would be an excess quantity of money demanded and a process opposite to that just described would occur. People would want to sell bonds in order to get the greater quantity of money they would prefer to hold at the low interest rate. This would not increase the total supply of money available in the system, but it would depress the price of bonds. This in turn would raise the interest rate until equilibrium were restored.

This is the nature of equilibrium and disequilibrium in the money market. We can apply what we have learned by seeing how the money market reacts to two important types of disturbances.

Change in Money Supply

First, let us examine the effects of an increase in the money supply resulting from an open market purchase of securities by the Federal Reserve. Suppose that initially the money supply is $180 as shown by the money supply curve MS_1 in Exhibit 12.5. A nominal national income of $1,200 gives the money demand curve MD. The equilibrium interest rate is 4 percent.

Let the money multiplier be 9.0. Now imagine that the Federal Reserve makes an open market purchase of $20 worth of government securities, paying for the purchase with one of its own checks. The immediate effect of this open market purchase is to increase the supply by $20 and to raise bond prices slightly and lower the rate of interest slightly.

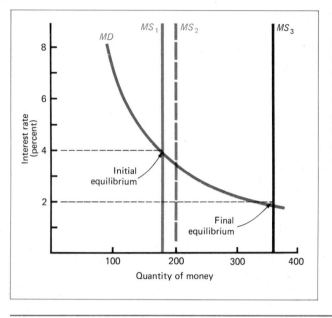

EXHIBIT 12.5
Effects of an increase in the money supply
Initially a money supply of $180 puts the money supply curve in the position MS_1. An open market purchase of $20 by the Federal Reserve has the immediate effect of moving the money supply curve to MS_2. That is not the end of the story, however. With a money multiplier of 9.0, the money supply reaches $360 ($MS_3$) before the deposit expansion process works itself out completely. The new equilibrium interest rate is 2 percent.

If this were the end of the story, it would put the money supply curve in the position indicated as MS_2, and it would put the market in a new equilibrium at the intersection of that curve with the money demand curve. But, of course, this is not the end of the story. As soon as the original Federal Reserve check is deposited in the bondseller's bank, total reserves of the banking system go up by $20. This sets off the process of deposit expansion, which we described in detail earlier, and by the time the reserves-to-money multiplier has worked itself out, the money supply will reach $360. This will shift the money supply curve all the way to the position MS_3.

New Equilibrium

Now there will be a large excess quantity of money supplied. Asset holders will not desire to hold the new money at the old interest rate, and will try to reduce their money holdings. It is likely that some excess money balances will be spent on physical assets, including consumer durables, and it is certain that some will be spent on bonds. As we have seen before, the actions of portfolio holders would bid up bond prices and lower interest rates. When the interest rate falls low enough (to 2 percent as our example is constructed), the demand for money would rise sufficiently to reestablish equilibrium. In the new equilibrium, total money balances outstanding would be larger than initially, and the interest rate would be lower.

Increase in Income

When we looked at the effects of an increase in the money supply on equilibrium in the money market, we assumed that nominal income remained unchanged throughout. Now let us look at the effects of a change in nominal income, assuming the money supply to remain fixed. When we have done this, we shall be ready for the next chapter, where we shall want to consider the two types of changes in combination.

Exhibit 12.6 sets the scene for exploring the effects of a change in nom-

EXHIBIT 12.6

Effects of an increase in national income

Initially, a nominal income of $600 puts the money demand curve at MD_1. The equilibrium interest rate is 2 percent with the money supply at $180. If an increase in nominal income to $1,200 shifts the money demand curve to MD_2, the interest rate will have to rise to 4 percent to restore equilibrium.

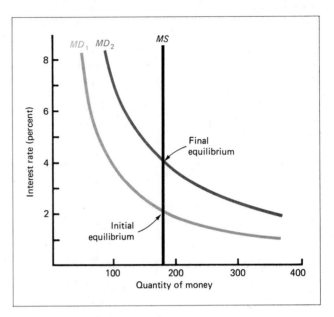

inal income. Suppose that initially the economy is in equilibrium with a money supply of $180 ($MS$), a nominal income of $600 ($MD_1$), and an interest rate of 2 percent. At an interest rate of 2 percent, the desired quantity of money holdings is $180, just equal to the money supply, as of course it must be in equilibrium.

Now let us suppose that for some reason or another, nominal income were to rise to $1,200. The increase in income would cause the money demand curve to shift to the new position MD_2. With the money supply still at $180, this would mean a very substantial excess quantity of money demanded. To meet their increased demand for money, portfolio holders would have to sell some of their earning assets, especially bonds. This would depress the price of bonds and raise the interest rate.

New Equilibrium

As the interest rate rose, the desired ratio of money to income would fall as the higher interest rate raised the implicit cost of holding money balances and weakened the speculative demand for money. When the interest rate rose high enough, the desired quantity of money would fall to $180, entirely eliminating the excess quantity of money demanded. This happens at an interest rate of 4 percent as our example is constructed. Four percent is therefore the new equilibrium rate of interest.

Conclusions

Our theory of the supply and demand for money is now complete. The important next step is to apply this theory to the problem of national income determination. This will be the aim of our next chapter. In it, we shall see that inclusion of the money market in the analysis of national income determination leads to some important modifications of the multiplier theory, and sets the stage for our discussion of inflation and unemployment.

SUMMARY

1. The collection of various assets a person owns (money, real estate, consumer durables, bonds, stocks, or whatever) is called a portfolio. Portfolio holders try to maintain a balance among the various kinds of assets they own, shifting from one to another as economic conditions change. As nominal income rises, people tend to want more money in their portfolios to satisfy their transactions demand. As the rate of interest rises, people tend to want less money in their portfolios, because the opportunity cost of holding money increases, and because their speculative demand for money decreases.

2. To show the money demand schedule in graphical form, we draw a downward-sloping curve showing how the quantity of money demanded changes as the interest rate changes, given some level of nominal income. An increase in the level of nominal income shifts this curve to the right, and a decrease in nominal income shifts it to the left.

3. The money supply curve can be represented by a vertical line, following our assumption that the money supply is fully controlled by Federal Reserve policy. Together the money supply and money demand curves determine the equilibrium rate of interest. With nominal income unchanged, an increase in the money supply causes the equilibrium interest rate to fall. With the money supply unchanged, an increase in nominal income causes the equilibrium interest rate to rise.

DISCUSSION QUESTIONS

1. List the items that you might consider part of your portfolio. Is it basically similar to the portfolio discussed in the text? In what ways is it similar? How is it different?

2. Which is more important in determining your own demand for money: the transactions demand or the speculative demand? Explain.

3. If the interest rate paid on savings deposits were increased, would you change your portfolio? Would you invest more or less in a savings account? Why or why not?

4. What is the average balance in your checkbook (during a typical month)? How much currency do you carry on a typical day? Finding the sum of these two figures gives a quantity of money demanded. In order to get a point on your demand for money schedule, we need a price. What price should we use?

5. Evaluate the following statement: "It is at best a mere metaphor, and at worst seriously misleading to speak of the money 'market.' Money cannot be bought and sold—it is just the means of payment we use in buying and selling everything else. Since it cannot be bought and sold, it cannot have a true market."

6. Do you know what Moody's corporate Aaa bond interest rate is at the time you are reading this chapter? Try to find out.

CHAPTER 13
The Interaction of Money and the Multiplier

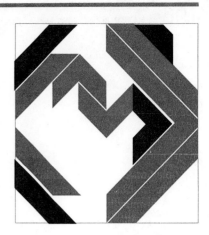

What You Will Learn in This Chapter
To understand the major issues of economic stabilization, we must understand how monetary and fiscal policy interact to determine the equilibrium level of nominal national income. When we take monetary factors into account, we have to make some important modifications in the simple multiplier theory. These modifications give rise to a controversy over how effective fiscal policy really is as a tool of economic stabilization.

For Review
Here are some important terms and concepts that will be put to use in this chapter. Be certain that you understand them, or review them before proceeding.
    Fiscal policy and the multiplier theory (Chapter 10)
    Instruments and effects of monetary policy
       (Chapters 11 and 12)

General Equilibrium and National Income

General Equilibrium

In applying the theory of supply and demand, economists make an important distinction between **partial equilibrium analysis** and **general equilibrium analysis.** The difference between the two lies in the role played by the "other things being equal" assumption. In partial equilibrium analysis, we say "if such-and-such an event occurs, the effect on the market for good X will be so-and-so, *provided that other markets are not disturbed from equilibrium*." In general equilibrium analysis, in contrast, we say "if such-and-such an event occurs, the effect on the market for good X will be so-and-so, *provided that other markets also adjust fully to the event in question*."

So far we have looked at the multiplier theory and the theory of money only from the partial equilibrium point of view. In Chapter 10, for example, we analyzed the effect of a change in fiscal policy on the equilibrium level of the circular flow, without considering the possible effects that the change in fiscal policy might have on the demand for money, the interest rate, or

Partial Equilibrium Analysis An approach to the study of markets in which we say "if such-and-such an event occurs, the effect on the market for good X will be so-and-so, provided that other markets are not disturbed from equilibrium."

General Equilibrium Analysis An approach to the study of markets in which we say "if such-and-such an event occurs, the effect on the market for good X will be so-and-so, provided that other markets also adjust fully to the event in question."

the level of planned investment. Similarly, in Chapter 12 we looked at what effect a change in the money supply would have on the equilibrium interest rate, without considering the possible effect of such an act of monetary policy on the level of nominal national income, or the position of the money demand curve.

Interactions

Our aim in this chapter will be to look again at fiscal and monetary policy, this time using the general equilibrium approach. That means taking into account the interactions between what goes on in the money market and what goes on in the circular flow.

Consider Exhibit 13.1. This figure shows two main channels of interaction between money and the level of nominal national income. The channels are represented by the large arrows. One of these interactions runs from the interest rate, determined in the money market, to the position of the aggregate demand schedule, by way of the effect of the interest rate on the level of planned investment. The other runs from the level of nominal national income, as determined by the intersection of the aggregate supply and demand curves, to the position of the money demand curve.

These interactions mean that we can no longer consider equilibrium of the circular flow and of the money market one at a time. We have to know the equilibrium rate of interest in order to know how much planned investment there will be. Otherwise we cannot put the aggregate demand schedule in its proper position. At the same time, we have to know the equilibrium level of nominal national income in order to put the money demand schedule in its proper position.

Equilibrium Conditions

The money market and the circular flow can both be in equilibrium simultaneously only if a certain pair of values for the interest rate and nominal national income prevail. Let us call the required level of national income Y and the required level of the interest rate r. Then the value of r must be just right to induce the planned investment needed to put equilibrium national income exactly at the level Y, and the value of Y must be just right to put the money demand curve in the position needed to keep the equilibrium interest rate at r.

As Exhibit 13.1 is drawn, an interest rate of 4 percent and a national income of $600 are what we need. The aggregate demand schedule is drawn on the assumptions that autonomous consumption is $150, the marginal propensity to consume is 0.5, government purchases are $100, and net taxes are $100. That means that planned investment must be $100 in order for equilibrium national income to be $600. Checking the planned investment schedule, we see that an interest rate of 4 percent is needed to encourage such an amount of planned investment.

Now turn to the money market, where we have assumed a money supply of $90. We see that for the equilibrium rate of interest to be 4 percent, the money demand curve must be in just the position we have drawn it. This is the position that corresponds to a nominal national income of $600. This verifies that $r = 4$ percent and $Y = \$600$ are an equilibrium pair for the interest rate and national income.

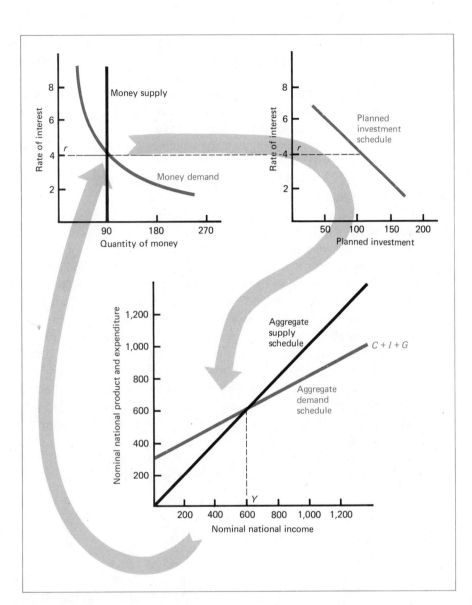

EXHIBIT 13.1

A general equilibrium view of national income determination

The money market and the circular flow can both be in equilibrium at once only if a certain pair of values for the interest rate and nominal income prevail. The large arrows in this figure show how the interest rate and nominal national income interact. The equilibrium interest rate r helps determine the position of the aggregate demand curve via its effect on planned investment spending. The level of nominal national income Y helps determine the interest rate via its effect on the position of the money demand curve.

The Equilibrium Is Unique

For any given set of assumptions about autonomous consumption, the marginal propensity to consume, government purchases, net taxes, the money supply, and the position of the planned investment schedule, there is just one pair of values for the interest rate and nominal national income that permits both the money market and the circular flow to be in equilibrium. We thus say that equilibrium values of nominal national income and the interest rate are *unique*.

To show this, all we have to do is momentarily assume that one of the values is different, and then show that this does not permit both markets to be in equilibrium. Suppose, for example, that the interest rate were only 2 percent, while all the underlying economic conditions were the same as before. The planned expenditure schedule in Exhibit 13.1 shows that a 2 percent interest rate would cause planned investment to rise to $150. With planned expenditure $50 higher than before, equilibrium national income would rise by $100 to $700 under the impact of the multiplier effect. We see, then, that an interest rate of 2 percent requires an equilibrium nominal national income of $700.

Turning to the money market part of Exhibit 13.1, we see that 2 percent cannot be the equilibrium rate of interest when money demand curve is in the position shown and the money supply is $90. The money demand curve would have to shift to the left to make 2 percent the equilibrium rate of interest. But an increase in national income from $600 to $700 would shift the money demand curve not to the left, but to the right. There is no way that 2 percent can be an equilibrium rate of interest when the level of national income is $700, given the assumed money supply. There is also no way that the equilibrium level of nominal national income can be anything but $700 when the rate of interest is 2 percent. Given the underlying economic conditions we have supposed, we are forced to conclude that when the interest rate is 2 percent, there is *no* value of national income that permits *both* the money market and the circular flow to be in equilibrium

The same reasoning could be repeated for any value of *r* other than 4 percent and any value of *Y* other than $600. This pair of equilibrium values for nominal national income and the interest rate is unique.

A Revised Look at the Effects of Fiscal Policy

Government Purchases

In Chapter 10 we studied the effects of three kinds of changes in fiscal policy: changes in government purchases, changes in net taxes, and matched changes in government purchases and taxes under a balanced budget policy. Now let us reconsider the first of these kinds of fiscal policy from the point of view of general equilibrium analysis. For purposes of comparison with what follows, we should recall the conclusion that we reached in Chapter 10 concerning the effects of a change in government purchases: When government purchases are increased while taxes, planned investment, and the consumption schedule remain unchanged, equilibrium national income will change by an amount equal to the change in government purchases times the multiplier.

Initial Effects

First, assume that the economy is in equilibrium with an interest rate *r* and a nominal national income *Y*. Now assume that fiscal policy makers decide that government purchases should be increased by $100, with no accompanying change in taxes. Let us trace the effects of this fiscal policy action as they work their way through the economy. The increase in government purchases shifts the aggregate demand schedule upward by $100.

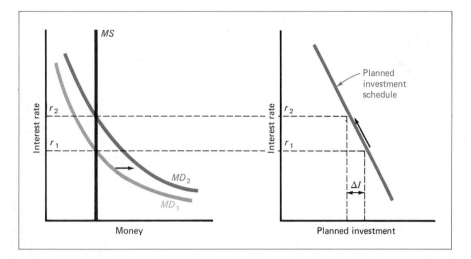

EXHIBIT 13.2
The crowding out effect

An increase in government purchases causes nominal national income to rise via the multiplier effect. The increase in income shifts the money demand curve from its initial position MD_1 to the new position MD_2. The equilibrium interest rate rises from r_1 to r_2. An amount of private investment equal to ΔI is "crowded out."

Planned expenditure now exceeds national product at the initial income level. This causes unplanned depletion of business inventories, to which firms respond by increasing output and/or raising prices. The level of nominal national income begins to rise.

Money Market Effect

As national income rises, the change in fiscal policy begins to affect the money market. The increase in nominal national income causes the money demand curve to shift rightward. In Exhibit 13.2, this is shown as a shift from the initial position MD_1 of the money demand curve toward a new position MD_2. The money demand curve shifts because when incomes rise, people tend to want more money in their portfolios. Because the money supply does not increase, these people's attempts to get more money by selling bonds simply drives down the price of bonds and drives up the rate of interest. Looking at all this together, we see that the effect on the money market of the increase in government purchases is to push up the rate of interest.

Crowding Out

Now let us shift our attention from the money market to the planned investment schedule, also shown in Exhibit 13.2. As the interest rate rises, firms find it more costly to undertake fixed investment projects and more costly to hold large inventories of raw materials or finished goods. They therefore reduce their planned investment expenditures, moving upward and to the left along the planned investment schedule. This decrease in planned investment expenditures, as an indirect effect of an increase in government purchases, is called the **crowding out effect.** The amount of investment crowded out is labeled ΔI in the exhibit.

Crowding Out Effect The tendency of expansionary fiscal policy to cause a drop in private planned investment expenditure as a result of a rise in the interest rate.

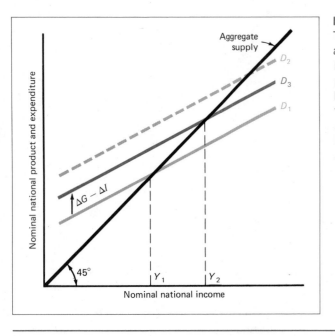

EXHIBIT 13.3
The crowding out effect in terms of aggregate supply and demand
Here the crowding out effect is shown from the perspective of aggregate supply and demand. Taken by itself, the increase in government purchases (ΔG) would have pushed the aggregate demand curve from D_1 to D_2. The crowding out effect chops ΔI off private investment, however, so the actual shift is only from D_1 to D_3, a distance equal to $\Delta G - \Delta I$.

Let us look at what has happened now in terms of aggregate supply and demand. The original position of the aggregate demand curve is shown as D_1 in Exhibit 13.3. Considered in isolation, the increase in government spending would have pushed the schedule all the way up to the position D_2. When we take crowding out into effect, though, it is apparent that the upward shift in aggregate demand is less than the amount of increase in government purchases. If we use ΔG to stand for the increase in government purchases and ΔI to stand for the amount of investment crowded out, the upward shift is reduced to $\Delta G - \Delta I$. This puts the final position of the aggregate demand curve at D_3.

Looking at Exhibits 13.2 and 13.3 together, now, we see that both income and the interest rate have changed. The new equilibrium interest rate r_2 and the new equilibrium nominal national income Y_2 are both higher than they were to begin with.

Crowding Out and the Multiplier

Because an increase in government purchases crowds out some private investment, national income does not rise by the full amount of the multiplier times the increase in government purchases. This fact does not, however, directly contradict the conclusion we reached in Chapter 10 and repeated at the beginning of this section. The trouble is that the earlier conclusion, which was based on partial equilibrium analysis, included the assumption that planned investment would not change when national income changed. The general equilibrium approach taken here shows that it is invalid to make that assumption. This means that we must modify the way we apply the multiplier theory to the analysis of fiscal policy. The multiplier must now be applied not just to the change in government purchases, but to the change in government purchases *minus* the induced change in private planned investment expenditure.

This new way of applying the multiplier theory to the analysis of fiscal policy can be put in the form of a simple equation. Using the symbol ΔY to represent the change in nominal national income resulting from a change ΔG in government purchases, we can write

$$\Delta Y = M(\Delta G - \Delta I)$$

M in this equation stands for the simple multiplier, as in Chapter 9.

Other Fiscal Policies

The crowding out effect applies to other types of fiscal policy as well as to changes in government purchases. When taxes are lowered, or when the level of government purchases is increased while the budget is kept in balance, nominal national income rises. This pushes the interest rate up, and crowds out some investment. That means that the overall effectiveness of these fiscal policies is somewhat less than would be predicted by the simple applications of the tax multiplier or balanced budget multiplier as outlined in Chapter 10.

It must also be remembered that when taxes are raised or government purchases lowered, as might be done to eliminate an expansionary gap from the economy, the crowding out effect works in reverse. The contractionary impact of fiscal policy is somewhat diminished, because as incomes fall, the demand for money and the interest rate fall too. These effects stimulate new private investment expenditure, somewhat offsetting the downward shift in the aggregate demand schedule that the contractionary policy produces.

Now let us look at the crowding out effect in a real-world situation.

CASE 13.1
The Wall Street Journal Looks at Crowding Out[1]

For American businessmen, the crowding out effect is not just an esoteric piece of economic theory, but a matter of serious practical concern. In 1975, the editors of *The Wall Street Journal* became concerned over the growth of the federal budget deficit, which was reaching record levels. They discussed the possibility that government borrowing to cover huge deficits "would force private borrowers out of the credit markets, reducing capital investment and offsetting or even reversing the supposedly stimulative effects of deficit spending."

By the spring of 1976, the editors concluded that their fears had at least in part been justified. In 1975, gross private domestic investment fell to 12.2 percent of GNP, the lowest rate in the postwar period. Fixed nonresidential investment (that is, investment in factories and machines) fell to 9.9 percent of GNP, well below the 12 percent rate the the Department of Commerce says is needed to meet legally established antipollution and energy independence goals, and still provide full employment in 1980. *The Journal* cited several items of evidence that the drop in investment was not just a coincidence, but was at least in substantial part a direct result of crowding out.

The editors summarized their fears for the future in these terms. "It is all very well for the Keynesians to tell us that the way to make up the shortfall in investment is to stimulate the economy and return to full employment rapidly. But how? Not by their standard prescription of a bigger deficit, if the above numbers have any meaning. Assuming for the moment that deficits can stimulate to begin with, the numbers suggest that they can stimulate only to the extent they fill in a naturally occurring fall in investment. Otherwise, they not only fail to stimulate, but detract from investment and future growth."

[1]Based on an editorial, "Crowding Out, Revisited," *The Wall Street Journal,* Tuesday, April 6, 1975, p. 22.

Monetary Policy and National Income

In Chapter 12 we looked at the effects of a change in the money supply from a partial equilibrium point of view, taking into account only what happens in the money market. Now we shall reconsider the effects of changes in the money supply in a general equilibrium context, taking into account the interaction of money and the multiplier theory of income determination.

To be specific, let us suppose that the Federal Reserve initiates an expansion of the money supply via an open market purchase of bonds. We need not give separate consideration to the expansion of the money supply by the use of other instruments of monetary policy because the effects are very little different than the effects of an open market operation.

Initial Effects

We have already analyzed initial effects of the open market purchase in Chapters 11 and 12. The open market purchase creates an increase in commercial bank reserves, and banks are induced to begin the process of deposit expansion. When the expansion is complete the money supply will have increased by an amount equal to the expansion in the reserves times the money multiplier. This is indicated in Exhibit 13.4 by the shift in the money supply curve from the position MS_1 to the position MS_2.

As the money supply expands, people find that they have more money than they want to hold in their portfolios at the original rate of interest.

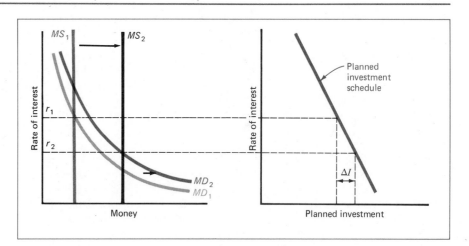

EXHIBIT 13.4

Money market and investment effects of an increase in the money supply
An increase in the money supply shifts the money supply curve from MS_1 to MS_2. The immediate effect of this is to cause a movement down along the money demand curve MD_1 toward its intersection with the new money supply curve. The interest rate then falls, and planned investment expenditure rises. That stimulates nominal national income via the multiplier effect. The rise in income in turn shifts the money demand schedule to a new position MD_2. That cuts short the fall in the interest rate, and a new equilibrium is established.

EXHIBIT 13.5
The effect of an increase in the money supply on aggregate demand and nominal national income
An increase in planned investment spending, caused by an increase in the money supply, shifts the aggregate demand curve upward. The amount of the shift is equal to the change in investment, ΔI. A new equilibrium is established with nominal national income increasing from Y_1 to Y_2.

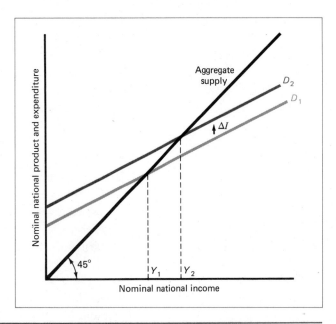

They attempt to reduce their money holdings by buying other assets, among them, bonds. This tends to push the price of bonds up and the interest rate down. In the diagram, this process is represented by a movement along the original money demand curve MD_1 toward its intersection with the new money supply curve.

Income and Expenditure Effects

As the interest rate begins to fall, business executives are encouraged to increase their level of planned investment, moving down and to the right along their planned investment schedule. The increase in investment expenditure shifts the aggregate demand schedule upward, as shown in Exhibit 13.5. Planned expenditure now temporarily exceeds national income, and by the familiar multiplier process, nominal national income begins to increase.

As national income increases, the money market is once again affected. Now the money demand curve begins to shift to the right, moving toward the position marked as MD_2 in Exhibit 13.4. This shift in the money demand curve cuts off the fall in the interest rate, and a new equilibrium interest rate is established where MD_2 and MS_2 intersect.

Once this equilibrium interest rate is established, planned investment stops expanding. The aggregate demand schedule comes to rest at a new equilibrium position D_2 in Exhibit 13.5. That means that the new equilibrium level of nominal national income will be higher than it was before the increase in the money supply.

In short, our general equilibrium analysis tells us that an increase in the money supply will result in new equilibrium values for both the interest rate and nominal national income. The interest rate will be lower than before the monetary expansion took place, and the level of nominal national income will be higher.

Transmission Mechanism   The whole set of ways in which monetary policy exerts an impact on the economy.

Transmission Mechanism

The ways in which monetary policy exerts an impact on the economy are together known as the **transmission mechanism.** Up to this point, our whole emphasis has been on one aspect of the transmission mechanism, namely, the tendency of expansionary monetary policy to lower interest rates, which in turn stimulates business investment. That is not quite the whole story. One or two other elements of the transmission mechanism also deserve to be mentioned.

For one thing, the effect of expansionary monetary policy on investment spending does not act solely through changes in the interest rate. When the money supply is tightly controlled, and banks have few if any excess reserves, individuals and businesses may find it difficult to borrow any money at all. Under such conditions, for example, banks may continue to post an interest rate of 9 percent for home mortgages, but potential home buyers may get the brush-off when they apply for money, or be told that there is a long waiting list. At another time, when easier monetary policy leaves banks with ample reserves, the waiting lists shorten and the standards by which the creditworthiness of borrowers is judged may be slackened a little. As a result, more loans may be made, and more construction and other types of investment may take place, even though the interest rates actually charged to borrowers do not change much.

Still another part of the transmission mechanism can help stimulate planned expenditure without directly affecting interest rates. When expansionary monetary policy puts excess money in people's portfolios, they will not necessarily try to exchange all of the excess for bonds, especially after the price of bonds rises and their yield becomes less attractive. They may also spend money to buy goods, including consumer durables, raw materials, and the like.

Economists are far from complete agreement over the nature of the transmission mechanism by which monetary policy affects the level of national income. For our limited purposes, we have concentrated on the interest rate-investment part of the mechanism. The reader should keep in mind, though, that this is only a convenient simplification.

Monetary versus Fiscal Policy

Because both fiscal and monetary policy affect the level of nominal national income, they are to some extent substitutes. If policy makers believe that there is an expansionary or contractionary gap to get rid of, which policy should they use? The question of monetary versus fiscal policy turns out to be one of the most debated issues in modern economics.

A Historical Note

Keynes' *General Theory of Employment, Interest and Money* was intended to be "general" in the sense that it would take both monetary and fiscal influences on the economy into account. However, in the first years after the publication of Keynes' book, it was not the general theory as a whole that dominated the thinking of the economics profession. Instead, some followers of Keynes tended to place a somewhat one-sided emphasis on planned expenditure, and to downplay the role of money in the economy. Early followers of Keynes interpreted the experience of the Great Depression as justifying the view that "money doesn't matter." They attributed the fact that monetary policy had failed to prevent both the 46 percent decline in nominal income and the increase in the unemployment rate to 25 percent of the labor force, which occurred between 1929 and 1933, not to poor conduct of monetary policy, but to its ineffectiveness. The fact that the Great Depression did not end until World War II brought on a massive increase in government spending appeared to support this view.

After the war, many of the early Keynesians forecast a new depression and economic stagnation. They thought that private investment opportunities would "dry up" with the disappearance of wartime government spending. Experience proved them wrong. Instead, the United States and the countries of Western Europe experienced rapid postwar recovery. Central banks in most of the major economies pursued "easy" monetary policies during these years, and inflation was a more widespread problem than depression. In fact, inflationary pressures were kept under control only by "orthodox" monetary policies. Economists began to wonder if perhaps "money mattered" after all and to look once again at the general theory as a whole.

The Monetarists

The reaction against the one-sided theories of the early Keynesians received major support from the empirical research of the **monetarists** led by Milton Friedman of the University of Chicago. Friedman's reinterpretation of the historical record led him to think that the primary causes of ups and downs in business activity are movements in the money supply. It seemed possible to explain even the Great Depression in this way.

Monetarists Economists who believe that movements in the money supply are the primary causes of ups and downs in business activity.

The New Economists

The economics profession did not become converted to monetarism, at least not in its extreme "only money matters" form. But out of the debate between the monetarists and the old Keynesians there developed a "new economics," an updated Keynesian economics that assigns important roles to both monetary and fiscal policy. This modern Keynesianism finally came into its own during the Kennedy and Johnson administrations. Then, for the first time, the actual conduct of economic policy began to be based on Keynesian economic theory as interpreted by a group of economists associated with the President's Council of Economic Advisors, including Walter Heller, James Tobin, and Gardner Ackley. Paul Samuelson of MIT, although not a member of the Council, was another outspoken proponent of the new economics brand of governmental activism in economic stabilization. The successful economic resurgence of the Kennedy and Johnson years added considerably to their prestige.

Today it is hard to find an economist who would take either an extreme "money doesn't matter" or an "only money matters" position. Instead, the question is how much money matters. There is a great deal of common ground between Keynesian economists and monetarists. Virtually all of what we have said in these chapters belongs to this common ground. Still, within the common theoretical framework, there is room for debate on the relative effectiveness of monetary versus fiscal policy.

Milton Friedman (1912–   )

In October 1976, Milton Friedman received the Nobel Memorial Prize in economics, becoming the sixth American to win or share in that prize. Few were surprised. The main surprise was that this most original and influential of economists had had to wait in line so long! The explanation is that Friedman has built his career outside the economics establishment—built it, in fact, by challenging virtually every major establishment doctrine.

Friedman was born in New York in 1912, the son of immigrant garment workers. His hard-working parents sent him across the river to Rutgers University in New Jersey, where Friedman came under the influence of Arthur Burns, then a young Assistant Professor. From Burns, Friedman learned the importance of empirical work in economics. Statistical testing of all theory and policy prescriptions became a key characteristic of Friedman's later work. From Rutgers, Friedman went to the University of Chicago for an M.A., and then East again to Columbia University, where he got his Ph.D. in 1946. With his degree in hand, he returned to Chicago to teach. There, he became the leading member of the "Chicago School," which provides the main intellectual counterweight to the Eastern Establishment in American economics today.

If we were to single out one single theme that underlies all of Friedman's work, it would be his conviction that the market economy works, and works best when left alone. This can be seen in his best-known work, *A Monetary History of the United States*. Written with Anna Schwartz, this work challenges two major tenets of orthodox Keynesian economics. These are, first, the idea that the market economy is inherently unstable without the guiding hand of government, and second, that monetary policy had been tried and found useless as a cure for the Great Depression. Friedman and Schwartz found both beliefs to be the opposite of the truth. "The Great Depression," Friedman later wrote, "far from being a sign of the inherent instability of the private enterprise system, is a testament to how much harm can be done by mistakes on the part of a few men when they wield vast power over the monetary system of the country."

Friedman strongly favors a "hands-off" policy by governments in almost every area, not just in monetary matters. The trouble, in his view, is not that government is evil by nature, but rather that so many policies end up having the opposite of their intended effects. "The social reformers who seek through politics to do nothing but serve the public interest invariably end up serving some private interest that was no part of their intention to serve. They are led by an invisible hand to serve a private interest." Transport regulation, the income tax, public education, agricultural subsidies, and housing programs are among the many policy areas where Friedman believes the government has done more harm than good, and where a free competitive market would do better.

Today, Friedman continues to take on new challenges. He promotes his ideas before Congressional committees, in professional journals, in his *Newsweek* column, and in face-to-face debate with his colleagues. Economics has never had a more respected heretic.

Part of the debate concerns the size of the crowding out effect. The size of the crowding out effect depends critically on the exact shapes of the money demand curve and the planned investment schedule. Exhibit 13.6 shows why. Suppose that the money demand curve has the shape shown by MD_1, indicating that the demand for money is not very sensitive to changes in the interest rate. If this is the case, the portfolio adjustments required when the money demand curve shifts relative to the money supply curve (as when nominal income changes) or when the money supply curve shifts relative to the money demand curve (as in the conduct of monetary policy) will bring about large changes in the rate of interest. Suppose that at the same time the planned investment schedule is relatively flat, like

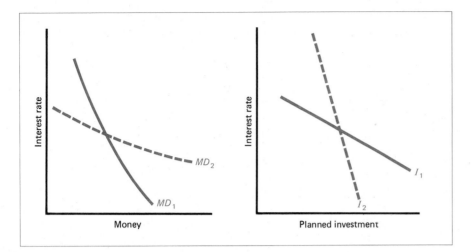

EXHIBIT 13.6

Alternative views of monetary and fiscal policy effectiveness.
If the money demand curve has a shape like MD_1 while the planned investment schedule is shaped like I_1, monetary policy will tend to be more effective than fiscal policy. A change in the money supply will have a big impact on planned expenditure, while fiscal policy will be severely hampered by the crowding out effect. On the other hand, a money demand schedule like MD_2 with a planned investment schedule like I_2 would give the advantage to fiscal policy. Changes in the money supply would have little impact on investment spending, and the crowding out effect would be small.

the curve I_1, so that a change in the rate of interest will induce a large change in planned investment expenditure. Taken together, the curves MD_1 and I_1 would tend to give the sort of results expected by monetarists. An expansion of government purchases would lead to a large increase in the rate of interest, a large drop in private investment spending, and hence a large crowding out effect. Also, an increase in the money supply would lead to a large decline in the rate of interest and a large increase in investment spending. Therefore, given curves of these shapes, fiscal policy would tend to be relatively ineffective and monetary policy would be relatively effective.

On the other hand, if the money demand curve had the shape MD_2 and the planned investment schedule the shape I_2, the situation would be just reversed. Fiscal policy would have relatively little impact on interest rates, and interest rates, in turn, would have relatively little impact on private investment. Changes in taxes or government purchases would then operate on aggregate nominal demand without much hindrance from the crowding out effect. At the same time, the economy would become much less sensitive to changes in the money supply. The world would behave more like a Keynesian would expect it to.

Transmission Mechanism

Another consideration bearing on the relative strength of fiscal and monetary policy is the nature of the transmission mechanism. If the transmission mechanism does not operate solely through interest rate changes, but instead allows monetary effects to bypass interest rate changes in some cases, then monetarist conclusions about the importance of monetary policy would tend to follow. If interest rate changes were the only mechanism by which monetary policy can affect expenditure, then money would matter less.

Interpretation

Why were these controversies not settled long ago by simply looking at the evidence? The reason is that there are problems in interpreting available data, some of which are quite technical, but others of which are not difficult to understand.

One difference in interpretation concerns the changes in the money supply that accompany economic downturns. For example, monetarists interpret the 25 percent decrease in the money supply that occurred from 1929 to 1933 as a major cause of the Great Depression. Some new economists disagree. They say instead that it was the Depression that caused the decline in the money supply. Their reasoning is that, in periods of depression, banks may be unwilling to make use of excess reserves in ways that will expand the money supply, because it will not appear attractive to them either to make new loans or to buy securities. The excess reserves of commercial banks did indeed grow substantially during the Great Depression. According to the new economists, this is evidence that trying to use expansionary monetary policy in a depression would be like "pushing on a string." New reserves pumped into the banking system would simply lie idle as excess reserves. Instead of the money supply changing, only the total reserves to money supply multiplier would change.

Counter Interpretation

Monetarists hotly deny this interpretation. They argue that the money multiplier has been quite stable, at least recently, and also that any fall in this multiplier can be offset by still greater expansion of reserves through open market purchases. They turn right around and argue that it is the new economists who have misinterpreted the historical record regarding the relative strength of monetary and fiscal policy. To be sure, they say, there has tended to be a correspondence between the size of the stimulus provided by the federal government budget surplus or deficit and the rate of growth of aggregate nominal demand. Yet they argue that much of this correspondence stems not from the effectiveness of fiscal policy, but from the tendency of the Federal Reserve to pursue what is called an **accommodating monetary policy.** When the government runs a large deficit, the Treasury needs to make heavy sales of bonds to the public. That puts upward pressure on interest rates. The Federal Reserve has often acted to offset such upward pressure on interest rates by making open market purchases of bonds. To the extent that this is done, the money supply grows faster as the deficit grows larger. According to monetarists, it is this monetary expansion, not the deficit itself, that provides the major part of the supposed stimulus of deficit spending.

Accommodating Monetary Policy
A policy under which the Federal Reserve expands the money supply in an attempt to keep interest rates from rising when the Treasury sells bonds to cover a budget deficit.

Evidence

How can this debate be settled? Two possible ways of bringing evidence to bear on the issue of monetary versus fiscal policy are discussed in the following case studies. One approach, discussed in Case 13.2, is to look at critical policy episodes when monetary and fiscal policy move in opposite directions. Unfortunately, this happens too infrequently to provide conclusive answers. The alternative approach, discussed in Case 13.3, is to use modern econometric techniques to sort out monetary from fiscal influences in periods when the two policies have worked in the same direction.

CASE 13.2
Critical Episodes in Recent Economic Policy

During the 1960s there were two important policy episodes in which monetary and fiscal policy moved in opposite directions. Both of these episodes have been interpreted as favoring the monetarist position. Both are easily identified in Exhibit 13.7.

The first episode occurred in the second half of 1966. In that year, the Federal Reserve became worried about possible overheating of the economy and suddenly cut the growth of the money supply from 6.4 percent per year to zero.

During the same period, the federal budget swung from surplus to deficit. President Johnson, who did not believe in the need for restraint, was angered by the Federal Reserve's policy. He called William McChesney Martin, then the Federal Reserve Board Chairman, down to the LBJ Ranch for consultation, but to no avail. Champions of the Federal Reserve's independence from political control have picturesquely dubbed this episode "the Fed's finest hour." The outcome of the Fed's finest hour was the "minirecession" of early 1967, apparently indicating that the restrictive monetary policy outweighed the effect of the rising federal deficit.

The second episode also occurred during the Johnson administration, but this time the lineup of forces was reversed. In mid-1968, Congress, at the request of the administration, passed a 10 percent income tax surcharge to cool off the economy. Exhibit 13.7 shows that this swung the federal budget very sharply from a strong deficit position to a strong surplus position. This time, the Federal Reserve feared "fiscal overkill" and continued through the end of 1968 to maintain a very rapid rate of monetary expansion. The outcome of this episode was that the tax surcharge failed to have its intended restraining effect on the economy. The growth of nominal GNP did not decline. This too is cited by monetarists as a demonstration of the relative strength of monetary and fiscal policy.

CASE 13.3
A Monetarist Analysis of the 1964 Tax Cut[2]

In Case 10.2, we recounted the history of the Kennedy tax cut of 1964. More than any other single episode of macroeconomic policy, the expansion that followed this tax cut bolstered the reputation of the new generation of Keynesian economists. Arthur Okun has written that the post-1964 expansion is an "insoluble mystery" unless one attributes it to the tax cut.[3] Another writer concluded that "the tax cut of 1964 should have convinced the last remaining skeptics that discretionary fiscal policy can be effective."[4]

Yet the skeptics have remained unconvinced. One of the unconvinced skeptics is Richard T. Froyen of the University of North Carolina. In 1974 he published an article challenging Okun's conclusion that the expansion of 1964 and 1965 could be explained only by the tax cut. Froyen points to the fact that monetary policy was also expansionary in the period surrounding the tax cut. In one statistical test, he shows that some 92 percent of the growth

[2]Richard T. Froyen "Monetarist Econometric Models and the 1964 Tax Cut," *Economic Inquiry,* Vol. XII, No. 2 (June 1974).

[3]A. M. Okun, "Measuring the Impact of the 1964 Tax Reduction," in W. W. Heller, (Ed.), *Perspectives on Economic Growth* (New York: 1968), as quoted in Froyen.

[4]M. K. Evans, *Macroeconomic Activity* (New York: 1969), as quoted in Froyen.

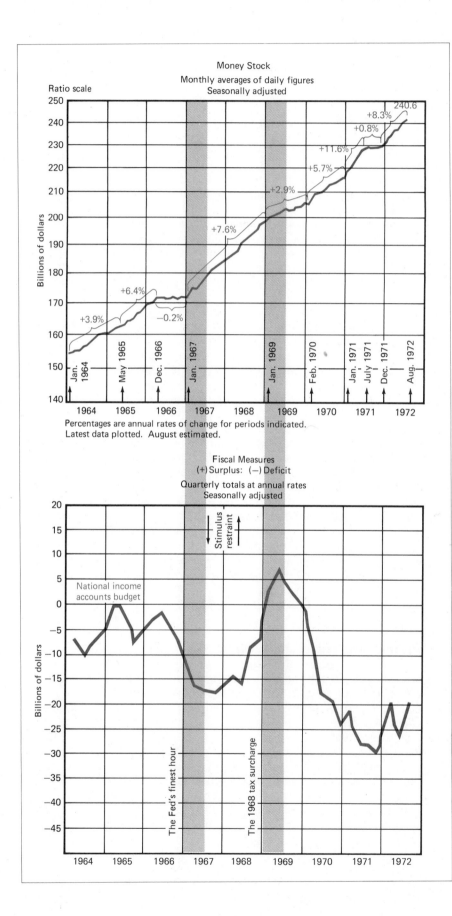

Money Stock
Monthly averages of daily figures
Seasonally adjusted

Percentages are annual rates of change for periods indicated.
Latest data plotted. August estimated.

Fiscal Measures
(+) Surplus: (−) Deficit
Quarterly totals at annual rates
Seasonally adjusted

EXHIBIT 13.7
Recent experience with monetary and fiscal policy
Twice during the 1960s fiscal and monetary policy moved in opposite directions. During
the "Fed's finest hour" of 1966, monetary restraint was applied while the budget
deficit grew. During the 1968 tax surcharge, in contrast, the money supply continued
to expand while the budget swung from deficit to surplus. On both occasions, monetary
policy appeared to dominate the outcome.
Source: U.S. Department of Commerce, Council of Economic Advisors and Federal Reserve Bank
of St. Louis. Latest data plotted: third quarter preliminary.

in GNP from January 1964 to mid-1965 could be explained by looking at
monetary policy and government purchases alone, without taking taxes into
account at all.

In another test, he compares his monetarist approach with two of the
most elaborate Keynesian studies, to see which would have best predicted
the effects of the tax cut if predictions had been made at the end of 1963
using all three methods. He finds that one of the Keynesian studies does a
slightly better job than his monetarist approach, and that the other one
does much worse.

Froyen concludes that accelerating rates of monetary growth provide a
plausible alternative explanation of the expansion that followed the tax cut.
It would be wrong, in his view, to interpret this dramatic episode as confirming the Keynesian view of how the economy works. Instead, it seems to
offer little conclusive evidence one way or the other. The debate goes on.

Conclusions

This brings us to the end of our long discussion of the determination of
nominal national income and product. Much ground remains to be covered,
though. In particular, we need to raise the issue of how a given change in
nominal GNP is split up between a change in prices and a change in real
output. Until we have a theory that can handle the split-up, we cannot
take up the highly important policy issues of inflation and unemployment.
It is quite likely that inflation and unemployment are the very issues that
got the reader interested in studying economics in the first place. Let us
turn to them, then, in the next four chapters.[5]

SUMMARY

1. In order to understand the interaction of money and the multiplier, we must
   move from partial equilibrium analysis to general equilibrium analysis. What
   happens in the money market affects aggregate demand because any change in
   the interest rate changes planned investment expenditure. What happens to
   aggregate demand affects the money market, because movements in nominal
   national income shift the money demand curve.
2. The money market and the circular flow can both be in equilibrium at once
   only if a certain pair of values for the interest rate and nominal income prevail.
   With the money supply, autonomous consumption, the marginal propensity to
   consume, net taxes, and the position of the planned investment schedule given,

[5]On a first reading, Chapters 14 and 17 can be read as a sequence without loss of con-
tinuity. Chapters 15 and 16 add much important detail on the theory of unemployment
and inflation.

the equilibrium values for nominal national income and the interest rate are unique.

3. An increase in government purchases has a somewhat weaker impact on the equilibrium level of nominal national income than a simple application of the multiplier theory predicts. The reason is that any growth in nominal income shifts the money demand curve and pushes up the interest rate. This in turn crowds out some private investment, partially offsetting the increase in government purchases.

4. An increase in the money supply has the initial effect of depressing the interest rate. This stimulates planned investment, and aggregate demand increases. As nominal national income rises, the money demand schedule shifts to the right, limiting but not completely cancelling out the fall in the interest rate. In the new equilibrium position, the interest rate will be lower and the level of nominal national income higher than before the monetary expansion.

5. Because monetary and fiscal policies both affect the equilibrium level of nominal national income, they are to some extent substitutes. Which type of policy is more effective is a matter of considerable debate, and has been for many years. The debate is not entirely resolved. Some evidence points one way and some the other.

DISCUSSION QUESTIONS

1. Suppose that you wanted to study the effect of variation in rainfall on the prices of three agricultural products: corn, soybeans, and hogs. Do you think a general equilibrium approach or a partial equilibrium approach would give you more insight into the problem?

2. Use the theory presented in this chapter to trace the effects of a tax increase through the economy. What happens to national income, the interest rate, investment, and consumption?

3. Use the theory presented in this chapter to trace the effects of an increase in required reserve ratios on demand deposits. What happens to national income, the interest rate, investment, and consumption?

4. Suppose that there is a contractionary gap in the economy. For the sake of discussion, let us assume that the government could with equal ease bring national income up to its target level by using expansionary monetary policy or by increasing government purchases. If the government also had a long-term goal of promoting rapid economic growth, can you think of any reason for them to use one policy rather than the other?

5. Would you say that Fed Chairman Arthur Burns is one of the four most powerful men in the United States? Would your opinion have been the same before you read this chapter? Before you started this course?

6. Suppose that the Fed decided on a policy of "pegging" the interest rate at some level r by smoothly expanding or contracting the money supply. (This policy could be represented graphically by drawing a horizontal rather than a vertical money supply curve.) How would this affect the effectiveness of fiscal policy? What would happen to the crowding out effect?

Appendix
The Elementary Algebra
of Money and
Income Determination

This appendix is a continuation of the appendix to Chapter 10, in which we developed a simple algebraic version of the multiplier theory. It adds no new theory to what has been presented in the body of Chapter 13. Nonetheless, those readers who feel comfortable with elementary algebra may find the approach presented here useful in consolidating their understanding of the general theory of income determination.

Aggregate Demand
The basic equation for aggregate demand is

$$AD = C + I + G \tag{1}$$

In the appendix to Chapter 10, we replaced the C in this equation with a consumption schedule, which we wrote as

$$C = \mathbf{a} + \mathbf{b}(Y - T) \tag{2}$$

where $\mathbf{a}$ and $\mathbf{b}$ were constants representing autonomous consumption and the marginal propensity to consume. Now we shall also replace I in Eq. (1) with a simple planned investment schedule:

$$I = \mathbf{c} + \mathbf{d}r \tag{3}$$

where I stands for planned investment, r for the interest rate, and $\mathbf{c}$ and $\mathbf{d}$ are constants. The constant $\mathbf{d}$ will have a negative value, because planned investment increases as the rate of interest falls.

Putting Eq. (1), (2), and (3) together, we get the following general expression for the aggregate demand schedule:

$$AD = \mathbf{a} + \mathbf{c} + \mathbf{b}(Y - T) + \mathbf{d}r + G \tag{4}$$

Money Demand
For a general equilibrium analysis of income determination, we also need a money demand schedule. The one used in Chapters 11 and 12 gave a money demand curve in the shape of a rectangular hyperbola. (Exhibit 12.2, for example, is based on the formula $MD = 0.6Y/r$.) To retain this kind of money demand schedule would involve us in quadratic equations and unnecessarily complicate our arithmetic, so we shall replace it with a linearized money demand schedule written as

$$MD = \mathbf{e}Y + \mathbf{f}r \tag{5}$$

where MD stands for the quantity of money demanded, r for the interest rate, Y for income, and $\mathbf{e}$ and $\mathbf{f}$ are constants. The constant $\mathbf{f}$ will be negative, because money demand decreases when the interest rate rises.

The reader is cautioned that this linear formulation of the money demand function has certain drawbacks. One is that, except for a certain central range of the variables, algebraic solution of the equilibrium equations (to be presented below) may produce negative values for income or the interest rate. Such negative values have no reasonable economic meaning. We shall be careful to stay within the safe range of values in the examples we give.

Numerical Values

Let us replace the constants in these equations with representative numerical values and see how our algebraic formulations of planned expenditures and money demand can be put to work. Using $\mathbf{a} = 150$, $\mathbf{b} = 0.5$, $\mathbf{c} = 200$, $\mathbf{d} = -2500$, $\mathbf{e} = 0.25$, and $\mathbf{f} = -1,250$, Eqs. (4) and (5) can be rewritten as

$$AD = 350 + 0.5(Y - T) - 2,500r + G \tag{6}$$

and

$$MD = 0.25Y - 1,250r \tag{7}$$

Equilibrium Conditions

As we saw in the text of Chapter 12, the economy as a whole can be in equilibrium only when both the money market and the circular flow are in equilibrium. Money market equilibrium requires that money demand equal money supply, and equilibrium in the circular flow requires that national product be equal to planned expenditure. These equilibrium conditions can be written as

$$MS = MD \tag{8}$$

for the money market, where MS stands for the money supply, and

$$Y = AD \tag{9}$$

for the circular flow.

Substituting Eqs. (6) and (7) into Eqs. (8) and (9), we get

$$MS = 0.25Y - 1,250r \tag{10}$$

and

$$Y = 350 + 0.5(Y - T) - 2,500r + G \tag{11}$$

which simplifies to

$$Y = 700 - T + 2G - 5,000r \tag{12}$$

Equilibrium in the economy is possible only for pairs of values of r and Y that simultaneously satisfy Eqs. (10) and (12).

Policy Variables

Besides r and Y, there are three variables in Eqs. (10) and (11) for which we have not yet specified numerical values. These are G (government purchases), T (net taxes), and MS (the money supply). These variables are collectively referred to as **policy variables,** because they stand for those elements of the economy that are under the direct control of the government. Let us turn to some problems now, to see how manipulation of these variables can be used by policy makers in their attempts to hit their economic targets.

Policy Variables Those elements of the economy that are under the direct control of the government.

Problem 1: Government policy makers set their policy variables at the values $G = 100$, $T = 100$, and $MS = 100$. Apply Eqs. (10) and (12) to determine the equilibrium values of r and Y.

Solution: Equation (10) becomes

$$100 = 0.25Y - 1,250r$$

and Eq. (12) becomes

$$Y = 700 - 100 + 200 = 5,000r$$

Simplifying and setting the equations equal to zero, we get

$$100 - 0.25Y + 1,250r = 0$$
$$800 - Y \quad\quad - 5,000r = 0$$

The usual methods for solution of simultaneous equations give the pair of values $r = 0.04$ and $Y = 600$ as the equilibrium levels for the interest rate and national income.

Problem 2: Using the solution to Problem 1 as a starting point, assume that the authorities want to raise the equilibrium level of national income to a target level of $700, using monetary policy alone. How much will the money supply have to be increased to accomplish this objective?

Solution: Substitute $Y = 700$, $G = 100$, and $T = 100$ into Eq. (12) in order to find the required equilibrium value for r.

The substitutions give

$$700 = 700 - 100 + 200 - 5,000r$$

which simplifies to

$$100 - 5,000r = 0$$

The solution to this last equation is $r = 0.02$.

Next substitute the equilibrium values $Y = 700$ and $r = 0.02$ into Eq. (10) in order to determine the money supply necessary to give a 0.02 rate of interest when national income is 700. This gives

$$MS = 0.25(700) - 2,500(0.02) = 150$$

The solution to the problem, then, is that the money supply must be increased by $50, from $100 to $150, in order to raise national income to $700.

Problem 3: Using the solution to Problem 1 as a starting point, show that an increase of $100 in government purchases will be more effective in raising the equilibrium level of national income if the Fed pursues an accommodating monetary policy than if the Fed leaves the money supply unchanged.

Solution: An accommodating monetary policy is one that expands the money supply enough to keep the interest rate unchanged—in this case, equal to 0.04. Substitute the values $T = 100$, $G = 200$, and $r = 0.04$ into equation (12) to get the new value that equilibrium national income will reach if accommodating monetary policy is pursued. Without going into details, the new equilibrium Y with accommodating monetary policy is 800. [Further substitution of $Y = 800$ and $r = 0.04$ into Eq. (10) shows that the money supply would have to be increased to $150 to achieve this result.]

Without accommodating monetary policy, the new values of Y and r are found by going through the same steps outlined in the solution to Problem 1, using $G = 200$. Again without going into details, the solution turns out to be $Y = 700$ and $r = 0.06$. Substitution of the new, higher value of the interest rate into the investment schedule ($I = 200 - 2,500r$) shows us that $50 of the original $100 in private planned investment is crowded out by the $100 increase in government purchases. This accounts for the lower equilibrium value of Y when accommodating monetary policy is not used.

CHAPTER 14
Unemployment and Inflation: The Problem and Some Traditional Answers

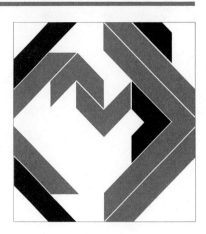

What You Will Learn in This Chapter
The two most important goals of American economic policy have long been full employment and price stability. The record for achieving those goals over the past twenty-five years, however, is not very good. In all but four years, there has been either excessive inflation or excessive unemployment. Even more disturbing, in most years since 1970 there have been both excessive inflation and excessive unemployment. In the past, several theories have been developed to explain this not-too-good record. Each is worth looking at, although none contains the whole truth.

For Review
Here are some important terms and concepts that will be put to use in this chapter. Be certain that you understand them, or review them before proceeding.

Theory of money demand (Chapter 12)
Monetarism (Chapter 13)
Expansionary and contractionary gaps (Chapter 10)

Inflation and Unemployment in the Postwar American Economy

Goals and Targets
In the past several chapters, we have often referred to some particular level of nominal income as a target adopted by economic policy makers. Now the time has come to look behind this income target to the more fundamental goals of economic policy that cause a particular target to be chosen.

The two overriding goals of economic policy in the postwar American economy have been full employment and price stability. Those goals are the things that policy makers, and the rest of us for that matter, really want, just as their opposites, unemployment and inflation, are what we really want to avoid. A national income target, by comparison, is something secondary and derivative. If fiscal and monetary authorities pursue policies aimed at a nominal national income target of $1.5 trillion in some particular year, it is not because that number of dollars would, in itself, produce economic bliss. Rather, the income target is chosen in the hope that aiming for it will have favorable effects on unemployment and inflation.

One of our aims in these next four chapters will be to move from an analysis of economic policy conducted in terms of a target level of nominal national income to an analysis conducted in terms of the goals of full employment and price stability. This will require us to understand how the goals themselves can be defined, and how inflation and unemployment are affected when fiscal and monetary policy are employed to manipulate the equilibrium level of nominal national income.

The Employment Goal

"Full employment" is well established in the American political vocabulary as a major goal of policy, but from an economist's point of view, the term is an unfortunate one. Taken at face value, the term "full employment" would seem to indicate a total absence of unemployment, yet it is quite impossible that the level of unemployment, as officially measured, should ever drop to zero. As we shall see in Chapter 15, the structure of the economy and the methods used to prepare unemployment statistics mean that some portion of the labor force will always be unemployed.

The Employment Act of 1946 uses more sensible language in setting as a goal the *maximum* level of employment consistent with the pursuit of other important objectives of government. There is room for legitimate difference of opinion as to what this means in terms of numbers. The most we can safely say is that the vast majority of economists would consider the employment goal to be adequately met if the official unemployment rate were as low as 3 percent of the labor force. On the other hand, a substantial number would begin to complain if the measured rate were to rise above 5 percent.

The Unemployment Record

Exhibit 14.1 shows the record of unemployment in the United States since 1950. Inspection of this exhibit shows that the unemployment rate has been above the 3 to 5 percent range in twelve of the last twenty-five years. Those who still maintain an unemployment goal of 4 percent or below can look with satisfaction only to the years of the Korean and Vietnam wars.

True, even the peaks of postwar unemployment look moderate compared to the Great Depression of the 1930s. In some years then, more than a quarter of the labor force was out of work, and the unemployment rate stayed over 10 percent for an entire decade. By any standards but comparison with the 1930s, however, the American unemployment record of the last quarter century is less than brilliant.

The Price Stability Goal

Unlike "full employment," price stability is technically achievable, even when taken literally. There is nothing inherently impossible in having periods when prices, as measured by official indexes, show no change one way or the other. Years of declining prices are also possible. It ought to be remembered, though, that the price indexes most commonly used in the American economy, especially the consumer price index, have moderate upward biases. As a practical matter, most economists would consider the goal of price stability to be fulfilled in years when the consumer price index rose 1 percent or less. In light of recent experience, a majority would probably be quite happy with anything under 2 percent.

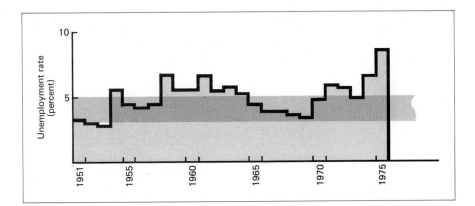

EXHIBIT 14.1

Unemployment in the United States since 1951

If the measured rate of unemployment could be kept in the range of 3 to 5 percent, most economists would accept that the full employment goal was being reasonably well served. As this exhibit shows, though, the unemployment rate has been above the 3 to 5 percent range in twelve of the last twenty-five years.

Source: Prepared by the Federal Reserve Bank of St. Louis.

The Inflation Record

Exhibit 14.2 shows the record of prices over the last twenty-five years in the American economy, as measured by the annual rate of change in the consumer price index. In comparison with the shaded 0 to 2 percent range, the record looks just slightly better than the unemployment record, but still, inflation exceeded 2 percent in more than half of these years.

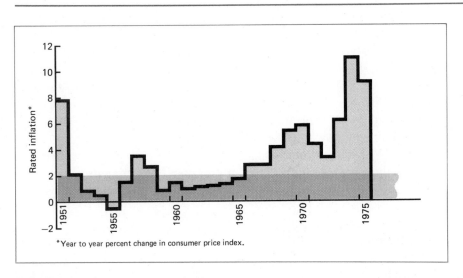

*Year to year percent change in consumer price index.

EXHIBIT 14.2

Inflation since 1951

Price stability, meaning a zero rate of change in official price indexes, is a technically possible goal. For practical purposes, however, most economists would say that the goal of price stability was being well served if inflation could be kept below 2 percent per year. In more than half of the last twenty-five years, inflation has been higher than the shaded 0 to 2 percent range.

Source: Economic Report of the President, 1976, Table B-46.

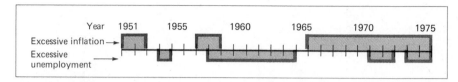

EXHIBIT 14.3
Combined inflation-unemployment record
As this exhibit shows, there have been only four years out of the last twenty-five when both the goal of price stability and the goal of full employment have been met within acceptable tolerances. What is more, in all but one year since 1971, neither goal has been achieved.

Combined Record

If we set the records on unemployment and inflation side by side, the picture is even less encouraging than when we look at either separately. Exhibit 14.3 gives a schematic representation of what has been achieved. This figure shows only four scattered years in which the goals of low unemployment and price stability were both achieved. The most ominous feature of Exhibit 14.3 is the almost unbroken string of years since 1971 in which neither goal was achieved. What is more, forecasts available at the time of this writing show this trend continuing at least into 1976 and 1977.

The economic problems of the 1970s have caused a considerable upheaval in macroeconomic theory. Before 1970, inflation and unemployment were conventionally thought of as problems that, although serious, at least came one at a time. Isolated bad years such as 1958 were thought only to represent ill-timed or badly handled transitions from one state to the other. Now much of earlier thinking is being reconsidered. Previously accepted explanations of unemployment and inflation are now seen to have been only partial truths.

Unfortunately, no completely worked out and generally accepted new theory of inflation and unemployment is yet available. That should not deter us, though, from following the rethinking process along as far as it has gone. With this in mind, we shall devote the remainder of this chapter to looking at some of the traditional theories of inflation and unemployment that provide the starting point for recent work. In Chapters 15 and 16 we shall look at some of the most fruitful new directions that macroeconomic thinking is now taking. Then, in Chapter 17 we shall discuss several important unresolved controversies of economic stabilization policy.

The Quantity Theory of Money

Velocity

The first theory of inflation we shall look at is also the oldest. The theory begins with the observation that in all modern economies, the quantity of money in existence at any time is less than a year's nominal national income for that economy. That does not mean that there is a shortage of money, however. The quantity of money is a stock and national income is a flow. As the circular flow of income and product churns around during the year, any given dollar, whether a dollar bill or an entry in a bank deposit, can be used again and again to conduct first one person's business and then another's.

It is easy to measure the average number of times each dollar is used for income-generating purposes during a year. All we need to do is divide gross national product, measured in nominal terms, by the quantity of money. The ratio of nominal GNP to the quantity of money is known as the **income velocity of money.** The income velocity of money is given by the formula

$$V = \frac{Y}{M}$$

where V stands for velocity, Y for nominal national income, and M for the quantity of money.

Exhibit 14.4 presents data on the income velocity of money in the United States over the last decade. The figure indicates that each dollar of currency and demand deposits now turns over about five times a year in the process of generating national income. The income velocity of money shows a gradual upward trend over this period, but no sharp year-to-year fluctuations.

Quantity Theory

So far we have no theory of anything—just a definition of the concept velocity. Two steps are needed to turn this definition, and the equation on which it is based, into a theory of inflation.

The first step is to rewrite nominal national income as the product of two separate elements, real national income and the price level. In Chapter 7 we defined a price index as the ratio of nominal GNP to real GNP. Using this definition, together with the definition of velocity, we can now write

$$V = \frac{Py}{M}$$

where P stands for the price index, and lowercase y for real national income.

Income Velocity of Money (Velocity) The ratio of nominal GNP to the quantity of money, hence, the average number of times per year each dollar of the money supply is used for income-generating purposes.

EXHIBIT 14.4
Income velocity of money, 1966–1975
The ratio of GNP to the money supply is known as the income velocity of money. As this exhibit shows, the income velocity of money has tended to rise over the last ten years, but is free of sudden year-to-year changes.

Year	Income Velocity*
1966	4.28
1967	4.26
1968	4.30
1969	4.47
1970	4.42
1971	4.48
1972	4.53
1973	4.76
1974	4.91
1975	5.11

*Ratio of GNP to M_1.
Source: Statistical Abstract of the United States.

The second step is to isolate the element of price on the left-hand side of the equation, and *then to assume that V is a constant.* This gives us the expression

$$P = \frac{MV}{y}$$

With *V* constant, this equation can now be interpreted as a theory that *explains* the price level in terms of the quantity of money. In a country with some predetermined level of real income, the price level is simply proportional to the quantity of money in circulation. The more money, the higher are prices; the less money, the lower are prices. This theory is called the **crude quantity theory of prices.**

Crude Quantity Theory of Prices (Quantity Theory) The theory that the price level in an economy is simply proportional to the quantity of money in circulation.

Does It Work?

The crude quantity theory of prices is an old idea. It was first suggested centuries ago, when prices rose in Europe following the great influx of Spanish silver and gold from the New World. Today, the crude quantity theory seems to fit the facts best in periods of very rapid inflation, called **hyperinflation,** as the following case study suggests.

Hyperinflation Very rapid inflation.

CASE 14.1
Money and Inflation in Latin America[1]

Hyperinflation has been a chronic problem in many Latin American countries. Some have experienced inflation rates of up to 200 percent per year in the worst years, and even averaged over long periods, rates of price increase have been high.

The wide variation in inflation rates makes Latin American experience a good illustration of the applicability of the crude quantity theory. Economist Beryl W. Sprinkel assembled the data shown in Exhibit 14.5. These figures support the crude quantity theory prediction that the rate of change in the price level (*P*) should be equal to the rate of growth in the ratio of money to real national income (*M/y*), with velocity (*V*) approximately constant.

[1]Based on Beryl W. Sprinkel, *Money and Markets. A Monetarist View* (Homewood, Ill.: Richard D. Irwin, 1971).

Despite its intuitive appeal and its applicability in extreme cases, the crude quantity theory of prices has a very limited usefulness as a tool for short-run economic forecasting and policy making in a developed economy. The main trouble is that movements in prices do not occur instantly in response to changes in the money supply. Evidence from recent American experience suggests that the rate of price change in any year depends in a complex fashion on the trend of changes in the money supply and other economic variables in several preceding years.

In recent years, economists of the monetarist school, whose theories we referred to at the end of the last chapter, have been hard at work developing a "sophisticated" quantity theory to replace the crude quantity theory described here. One major difference between the crude quantity theory and its modern cousin is that the modern theory does not treat velocity as a constant. Instead, velocity changes as the interest rate and a few other

EXHIBIT 14.5

Rates of change in money and inflation in seven Latin American countries, 1955–1968

The crude quantity theory of prices appears to do rather well as an explanation of inflation when very wide ranges of price variation are involved. These data for seven Latin American countries show that the rate of increase in the consumer price index very closely matched the rate of growth of the money stock, measured in relation to real GNP.

Country	Compound Annual Rate of Change in	
	Money Supply/Real Gross National Production (%)	Consumer Price Index (%)
Brazil	35.3	37.9
Chile	29.0	27.6
Argentina	22.6	26.6
Colombia	11.2	10.4
Peru	7.7	9.0
Ecuador	4.4	2.3
Mexico	3.8	3.6

Source: Beryl W. Sprinkel, *Money and Markets. A Monetarist View* (Homewood, Ill.: Richard D. Irwin, 1971), p. 189.

key economic variables change. What is important, according to monetarists, is not that velocity is fixed, but that it changes in a fairly predictable way. The predictability of velocity, they believe, greatly enhances the effectiveness of monetary policy.

We should note that in Chapter 12, we said a great deal about velocity without actually using the word. The income velocity of money, Y/M, is, after all, just the reciprocal of the ratio money to GNP. By looking at the money demand schedule given in Exhibit 12.2, the reader can easily calculate the income velocity of money for various levels of the interest rate in the simplified economy of our examples. Similarly, data on velocity for the postwar American economy can be calculated from Exhibit 12.3. The data given in Exhibit 12.3 suggest that the variations in income velocity shown here in Exhibit 14.4 can largely be explained in terms of changes in the interest rate.

This is not the place, though, for a long discourse on modern theories of income velocity. For the moment, it is enough to conclude that the crude quantity theory contains a part of the key to the inflation-unemployment puzzle, but only a part, and turn to another theory.

Unemployment, Inflation, and the Keynesian Cross

Keynesian Theory

During the first two postwar decades, when periods of high unemployment alternated with periods of inflation, most economics textbooks featured a theory of unemployment and inflation that was based on simple Keynesian multiplier analysis. Let us look at this theory, which for want of a better term we shall call the "crude Keynesian theory."

Exhibit 14.6 contains a Keynesian cross diagram of the familiar kind. Notice, though, that we have made one significant change. One point on the horizontal axis has been marked "full employment national income." That replaces the indication of a "target" level of national income that some of our earlier diagrams contained.

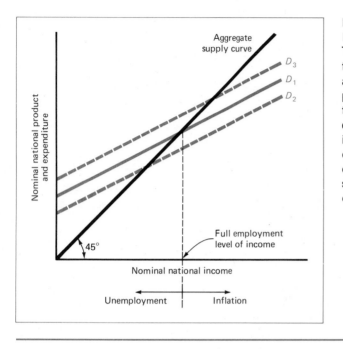

EXHIBIT 14.6
Inflation and the Keynesian cross
The crude Keynesian theory of inflation is based on this Keynesian cross diagram, plus some additional assumptions. When the aggregate demand curve is in position D_1, we assume that real GNP will be sufficient to keep everyone employed. If the aggregate demand curve shifts to D_2, it is assumed that the resulting fall in nominal GNP will all take the form of reduced real output and increased unemployment. If the aggregate demand curve shifts to D_3, it is assumed that all of the subsequent increase in nominal GNP will take the form of a price increase.

To get a theory of unemployment and inflation from this diagram, we reason like this: First, suppose that consumption, planned investment, and government spending are just sufficient to put the aggregate demand schedule at the level marked D_1. In this position, it intersects the aggregate supply schedule exactly at the "full employment" level of national income. By assumption, when equilibrium national income is at this level, just enough goods will be demanded to keep everyone busy who wants a job. (To put it less casually, just enough goods will be demanded to keep all but 4 or 5 percent of the labor force at work, as measured by official statistics.)

Next suppose that because of an error of policy, or some unexpected change in private consumption or planned investment, the aggregate demand schedule slips to the level marked D_2. This creates a contractionary gap. Applying the multiplier theory, we predict that this downward shift in planned expenditure will be followed by a downward movement of nominal national income. Now one more crucial assumption is added. That assumption is that in the short run, at least, all or most of the downward movement of nominal national income will take the form of a fall in real income and product, and not much if any will take the form of a decline in prices. Because the lower level of real output requires fewer workers to produce it, the economy will experience a period of relatively high unemployment and approximate price stability.

Finally, assume that for one reason or another, the aggregate demand schedule were to shift upward, reaching the position labeled D_3 in Exhibit 14.6. This high level of planned expenditure would produce an expansionary gap. In accordance with the multiplier theory, nominal national income would rise. Remember, though, that everyone, or almost everyone, who wants a job now has one. It is not physically possible to squeeze more than a little extra real output from the economy above the full employment level. The rise in nominal income that the multiplier theory requires can take place only in the form of an increase in the price level. As a result, the expansionary gap brings on a period of very low unemployment and inflation of the general price level.

Does It Work?

Like the crude quantity theory, the crude Keynesian theory has considerable intuitive appeal if applied in the proper time and place. In particular, the theory provides a fairly plausible reading of the American record of inflation and unemployment in the years 1951–1969. (See Exhibits 14.1–14.3.) Nonetheless, it cannot be judged to be entirely satisfactory, for several reasons.

First, proponents of this theory have always had difficulty explaining why downward movements in nominal income affected real output so much more strongly than prices, at least in the short run. A number of hypotheses were advanced by various authors, but no one of these was ever universally accepted. Also, it was sometimes difficult to rationalize the various hypotheses in terms of microeconomic theory.

Second, where expansionary gaps were involved, the crude Keynesian theory tells us at most how much prices will rise, but not how fast they will rise. Because inflation is by its nature a matter of the speed of change in the price level, the theory was incomplete here.

Finally, and clearly most serious of all, the crude Keynesian theory is altogether unable to explain how high (and even rising) unemployment can occur simultaneously with high (and even rising) rates of inflation. For this reason, the crude Keynesian theory has lost even its intuitive appeal as an explanation of unemployment and inflation in the 1970s.

As one would expect, Keynesian economists have not simply thrown up their hands in despair when faced with the lessons of recent experience. Instead, they are hard at work building sophisticated versions of Keynesian theory. These, it is hoped, will have superior explanatory powers.

The Phillips Curve

Early Empirical Work

Economists place a strong emphasis on empirical work—work based on real-world data—as well as on abstract theorizing. Sometimes a single empirical study can suggest a whole new direction for theory to take. A well-known research paper by the British economist A. W. H. Phillips, which we outline in the following case study, had such an impact.

CASE 14.2
A. W. H. Phillips and the Phillips Curve[2]

In 1958, A. W. H. Phillips published the results of some attempts he had made to test the simple hypothesis that wage rates tend to rise faster when unemployment is low than when it is high. The data he had available covered a very long period of the economic history of Britain, stretching from 1861 to

[2]A. W. H. Phillips, "The Relationship Between Unemployment and the Rate of Change of Money Wage Rates in the United Kingdom, 1861–1957," *Economica*, New Series Vol. 25 (Nov. 1958), pp. 283–299.

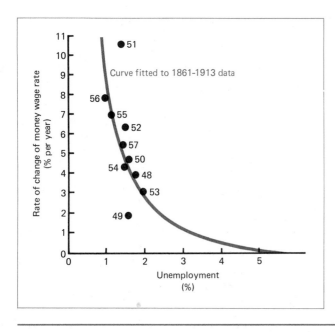

EXHIBIT 14.7
One of A. W. H. Phillips' original Phillips curves for the British economy

In 1958, A. W. H. Phillips published a very influential paper that looked at the relationship between unemployment and the rate of change in wages over a long period in Britain. He found that data from the period 1948 to 1957 fit rather closely a curve based on data from the period 1861 to 1913, as shown here. Curves like this have since come to be called *Phillips curves.*

Source: A. W. H. Phillips, "The Relationship between Unemployment and the Rate of Change of Money Wage Rates in the United Kingdom, 1861–1957," *Economica,* New Series Vol. 25 (Nov. 1958), pp. 283–299. Reprinted by permission.

1957. The statistical evidence he assembled seemed to support the idea that the rate of change in money wage rates can be explained by the level of unemployment.

Phillips presented his results in a series of charts, one of which is reproduced here as Exhibit 14.7. This diagram contains a curve that represents the average relationship between unemployment and the rate of change of wages during the period 1861 to 1913. The points scattered near the curve show wage and unemployment data for the years 1948 to 1957. The fit of the modern years in Phillips' study to the curve calculated on much earlier data is remarkably close.

Allan William H. Phillips
(1914–1975)

A. W. H. Phillips was an economist whose entire reputation was based on a single paper, published on the right topic at the right time. In the late 1950s, the relationship between inflation and unemployment ranked as the major unsolved problem of macroeconomic theory. The curves that Phillips drew in his famous article in *Economica* suggested a simple, stable relationship between inflation and unemployment. Phillips' paper offered little by way of a theoretical explanation of the relationship, but his curves became the peg on which all future discussion of the problem was hung. Almost immediately, every article on inflation and unemployment became a discussion of what was the shape of the "Phillips curve," what point on the Phillips curve was best as a policy target, how the Phillips curve could be shifted, and so forth. Today, the term is so well established that Phillips' name enjoys a sort of immortality even though his own interpretation of the famous curve has fallen into disrepute.

A. W. H. Phillips was born in New Zealand, but made London his base for most of his academic career. He taught at the London School of Economics during the 1950s and 1960s until moving to the Australian National University in 1967. Phillips was originally trained in electrical engineering, and this training seems to have influenced his approach to economic problems. This approach has been characterized as "scientist." In the mid-1950s he was suggesting the use of an "electric analog machine or simulator" as an aid to the study of economic dynamics. This idea perhaps foreshadowed the intensive use of electronic computers in contemporary economic research.

Since the publication of Phillips' article, curves like the one in Exhibit 14.7 have come to be called **Phillips curves.** In recent years, the use of the term "Phillips curve" has been broadened to include similar curves drawn on diagrams where the vertical axis measures the rate of change of prices (that is, the rate of inflation) instead of the rate of change of wages. Recent data for the United States will be presented in a Phillips curve framework in Chapter 16.

A Menu

Like the crude quantity theory and the crude Keynesian theory we have already examined, the intuitively appealing concept of the Phillips curve is open to serious misinterpretation when applied to economic policy. A tempting but misleading interpretation is to regard the Phillips curve as a menu of alternatives from which policy makers can choose a preferred compromise between the evils of inflation and unemployment.

Suppose, for example, that the President and his Council of Economic Advisors were presented with data that suggested the Phillips curve shown in Exhibit 14.8. We might easily imagine that if the administration were a Democratic one, strongly influenced by union labor or sympathetic to the plight of the unemployed, it might pursue expansionary policies and aim for a point high up and to the left, such as the point marked D in the figure. In contrast, a Republican adminstration, dominated by conservative businesspeople and dour bankers, might aim for a point such as R, near the intersection of the Phillips curve and the horizontal axis.

Drift

The trouble with interpreting the Phillips curve as a policy menu is that it may not stand still while the diners enjoy their meal. As the 1960s progressed, economists in the United States began to notice that inflation-

Phillips Curve   A curve showing the relationship between the rate of inflation and the level of unemployment. Inflation, usually placed on the vertical axis of such a figure, may be measured either in terms of the rate of change in wages or the rate of change in a price index.

EXHIBIT 14.8

The Phillips curve as a policy menu

The Phillips curve is sometimes misleadingly interpreted as a policy menu offering a fixed trade-off between inflation and unemployment. If the Phillips curve for the American economy had the shape shown here, we might imagine that Democrats would want to choose a point like D, where low unemployment would be "bought" at the price of high inflation, while Republicans might rather have a point like R. Unfortunately for this interpretation, the Phillips curve is not stable. Policies designed to produce movements along it can cause it to shift to a new position.

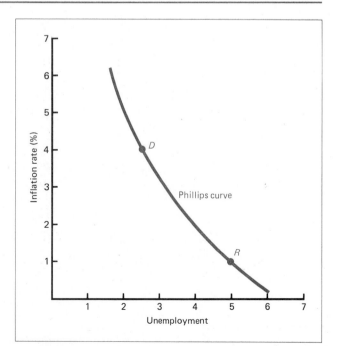

unemployment points for recent years did not fit the Phillips curves they had plotted using data from the 1950s. It became common to speak of an upward drift in the Phillips curve. The menu seemed to be getting less appetizing as time went by. If the upward drift had been entirely spontaneous, policy makers could simply have been told to make the best of disappointing circumstances, and still choose the point they liked best from the new, higher Phillips curve. If, however, it could be shown that shifts in the Phillips curve were caused by the particular policies chosen to move the economy *along* a supposedly fixed curve, the idea of the Phillips curve as a policy menu would have to be reevaluated altogether.

In fact, as we shall show in Chapter 16, it is now widely believed that the choice of particular inflation and unemployment goals does determine the position and rate of drift of the Phillips curve. The modern theory of inflation that economists are now developing does have a place in it for the Phillips curve, but the place is not quite the one that early interpreters envisaged.

Cost-Push Inflation

Demand-Pull

All three of the theories we have looked at so far share the common element that inflation is touched off by a rise in aggregate demand. In the quantity theory, the excessive aggregate demand results from an injection of new money into the economy. In the Keynesian theory it is represented by a shift in the aggregate demand schedule to a position high enough to produce an expansionary gap. And according to the Phillips curve analysis, inflation does not become serious until demand has risen enough to produce a shortage of labor. Because all these theories single out a rise in aggregate demand as the initial cause of a rise in the price level, they are collectively referred to as **demand-pull** theories of inflation.

Demand-Pull Inflation   Inflation that is initially touched off by an increase in aggregate demand.

Cost-Push

In the course of the 1950s and 1960s, economists began to realize that serious inflation could occur even when there was considerable slack in overall demand and a substantial level of unemployment. None of the demand-pull theories adequately explained this possibility, and it became increasingly popular to speak of a new kind of inflation, called **cost-push inflation.**

The most commonly heard version of the cost-push theory runs something like this. Suppose that, initially, the economy is enjoying a period of approximate price stability and moderate, but not unusually low unemployment. Then imagine that it comes time for some powerful labor union in an important basic industry (let us call it the steel industry, for the sake of illustration) to renegotiate its contract with employers. Through aggressive bargaining, and perhaps the threat or actual occurrence of a strike, the union wins a very generous raise for all its members.

Cost-Push Inflation   Inflation that is initially touched off by a spontaneous rise in wages, profit margins, commodity prices, or other elements of cost during a period of slack aggregate demand.

Suppose that the rise in wages is so big that it cannot be fully offset by increases in output per man hour. If so, the cost of making a ton of steel goes up. Citing the increase in cost as justification, the steel companies raise their prices. Steel is used to make cars, refrigerators, apartment buildings, and hundreds of other things, so costs rise in all those other industries. The makers of cars, refrigerators, and so forth all raise their prices, again citing the rise in costs as justification. The increase in the price of steel has now become a general increase in the price level.

As other union contracts expire, the bargaining becomes tougher and tougher. For one thing, the leaders of the auto workers, miners, teamsters, and so forth have their reputations on the line with their rank-and-file union members, who expect them to do as well as the steel workers did. On top of that, union negotiators are now able to point to the rise in the cost of living as additional justification for giving their workers a fat wage package. The cost-push mechanism is now in full swing, and the initial spark has touched off an inflationary wage-price spiral.

Adherents to the cost-push theory often point out that the process need not start with a rise in wages. Other powerful economic interests may fire the first shot. For example, it is often suggested that some large, highly concentrated industry like the automobile industry may initiate the cycle by unilaterally raising its prices simply to increase profits, even though there is no justification for such an increase in terms of rising costs or rising demand. The resulting inflation is then called **profit-push inflation** to distinguish it from the **wage-push inflation** of our first scenario.

Finally, the cost-push cycle may be touched off by a rise in the price of important basic commodities, such as oil or wheat. The initial source of commodity price rises may lie altogether outside the American economy, being found in such uncontrollable elements as Arab politics or the weather in Russia. Nonetheless, once under way, commodity price increases can spread throughout the economy by the cost-push mechanism, producing what can be called **commodity inflation.**

Does It Make Sense?

Does the cost-push theory of inflation make sense? The answer seems to be that, like the other theories we have examined, it contains an element of truth, but that element of truth is subject to strict qualifications. These qualifications are worth reviewing in detail.

The Cost-Push Illusion

The first qualification we must make is to distinguish between genuine cost-push inflation on the one hand, and the **cost-push illusion** on the other. Because of the cost-push illusion, ordinary demand-pull inflation may *look* like cost-push inflation to those who are actually caught up in it. Milton Friedman uses a vivid little example to illustrate the cost-push illusion. His story is based, in turn, on a much longer parable told by A. A. Alchian and W. R. Allen.

Profit-Push Inflation   A variety of cost-push inflation in which a spontaneous increase in profit margins is the initial source of price increases.

Wage-Push Inflation   A variety of cost-push inflation in which a spontaneous increase in nominal wage rates is the initial source of price increases.

Commodity Inflation   A variety of cost-push inflation in which a spontaneous increase in commodity prices is the initial source of general price increases.

Cost-Push Illusion   The phenomenon that demand-pull inflation often looks like cost-push inflation to those caught up in it, because inventories cushion the immediate impact of demand on prices at each link in the chain of distribution from producers to retailers.

CASE 14.3
The Cost-Push Illusion[3]
Let us suppose in a country in which everything else is fine all of a sudden there is a great craze for increasing the consumption of meat, and all the

[3]The story is quoted from Milton Friedman, "Unemployment versus Inflation?" Institute for Economic Affairs Occasional Paper No. 44 (London, 1975), pp. 34–35. Originally appeared in Armen A. Alchian and William R. Allen, *University Economics: Elements of Inquiry,* 2d ed., (Belmont, Calif.: Wadsworth, 1972).

housewives rush to the butchers to buy meat. The butchers are delighted to sell them the meat. They do not mark up the prices at all, they just sell out all the meat they have but they place additional orders with the wholesalers. The wholesalers are delighted to sell the meat. They clean out their inventories. They go back to the packing houses. The packing houses ship out their meat. The price is the same but the packing houses send orders to their buyers at the cattle market: ''Buy more beef!'' There is only a fixed amount of cattle available. And so the only thing that happens is that in the process of each packer trying to buy more beef, he bids up the price. Then a notice goes from the packer to the wholesaler. ''We are very sorry, but due to an increase in our costs we are required to increase the price.'' A notice goes from the wholesaler to the retailer. And the retailer finally says to the customer when she comes in to complain that beef has gone up, ''I'm terribly sorry, but my costs have gone up.'' He's right. But what started the increase in costs all the way up and down the line? It was the housewife rushing in to buy the meat.

The point of this example is that what is true for individual business-people is not necessarily true for the economy as a whole. All businesspeople may feel that they raise prices reluctantly, and only when placed under severe pressure by the rises of wages and costs. That may be true insofar as it goes. But where does the pressure come from? It comes from an increase in demand, say the critics of cost-push inflation.

What keeps the true cause of inflation from being obvious to everyone is the existence of inventories at every link in the chain from producer to consumer. The initial impact of an increase in demand is a decline in inventories, first at the retail level, then at the wholesale level, then at the factory level, and so forth. As businesspeople at each link in the chain increase their orders to replenish stocks, the process will eventually reach someone who cannot respond by pulling goods out of the inventories of the next person in line. This may be the packer who has to buy beef at auction, it may be the importer who has to bid for raw materials on world commodity markets, or it may be an employer who can find new workers only by bidding them away from other jobs. Sooner or later, the rise in demand encounters the inescapable fact of the scarcity of resources, and then a price rise starts to get passed back up the chain of distribution.

Monopoly Power

Monopoly Power A seller's power to raise the price of a product without losing all, or nearly all, of his or her customers.

A second qualification to the cost-push theory of inflation hinges on the concept of **monopoly power.** Economists say that a firm has monopoly power whenever it is able to raise the price of its product without losing all, or nearly all of its customers to competitors. Applied to the labor market, a union can be said to have monopoly power if it is able to obtain a substantial increase in the wages of its members without a serious loss of jobs to nonunion workers.

Most accounts of cost-push inflation depend on monopoly power to set the cost-price spiral in motion. Clearly, a union or a firm would not make the initial push in wages or prices if it did not think it could gain an advantage by doing so. Without monopoly power, making such a push would only result in a loss of jobs or sales to competitors. About the only exception to the rule that cost-push inflation has to begin in a relatively monopolistic part of the economy would be commodity inflation set in motion by bad weather, which in turn might lead to rising prices in the agricultural sector.

Now, a well-established proposition of microeconomic theory does tell us that, other things being equal, prices (or wages) will be higher in a market where sellers have substantial monopoly power than in a market where there is a high degree of competition. For any given degree of monopoly power, though, there will be a level beyond which prices cannot profitably be raised. In nontechnical language, this is a matter of "charging all that the market will bear." Once this profit-maximizing equilibrium price (or workers' welfare-maximizing wage) is reached, the prices (or wages) in a monopolistic market, although high, will stop rising.

Here, then, is the confusion that must be avoided. Monopoly power can cause *high* prices and wages, but there is no reason to expect it to cause *steadily rising* prices and wages. It follows that a firm or labor union with firmly established monopoly power is no more likely suddenly to push its prices or wages above the prevailing equilibrium level than one that operates in a fully competitive manner. Only a sudden *increase* in the degree of a firm's or union's monopoly power could cause the sudden *increase* in prices or wages needed to touch off the mechanism of cost-push inflation. No evidence has been found of any substantial increase in the monopoly power of either business or labor that could account for the steady acceleration of inflation over the last fifteen years.

Relative Prices

Even if we could identify a sudden increase in monopoly power as a source of cost-push inflation, one more qualification would still be needed. Let us grant, for the sake of discussion, that some major union (make it the steelworkers again) wins a sudden large rise in wages. Perhaps this is caused by the election of a new union leader, who is determined to bargain much more aggressively than the old one. The next question is why this should cause a general rise in prices and wages, and not just an increase in steel prices and steelworkers' wages relative to those in other sectors of the economy. Why will the increased prices and wages in the steel industry not be offset by lower prices and wages elsewhere?

Think of it this way. When the price of steel goes up, either the quantity of steel sold will be reduced, or the buyers of steel will have to spend more than before on the purchase of steel. Very probably both will happen. If the quantity of steel produced falls, some steel workers will be laid off. These will have to go hunt for work elsewhere, and the presence of these new job seekers will tend to depress wages outside the steel industry. If buyers of steel spend more to purchase steel, they will have less left over to purchase other things. The demand for other goods and the prices of other goods will thus tend to fall. Instead of a general wage-price spiral, then, all the economy would experience would be a shift in relative prices. The price of steel would go up and the prices of other things would go down. As measured by a price index, no significant inflation would occur.

This argument suggests that in order to have true cost-push inflation, something must prevent the smooth adjustment of relative prices and wages. Suppose that prices and wages in other sectors did not fall when steel prices and wages went up. Other sectors of the economy would not be able to absorb the newly laid off steelworkers, so they would have to stay home and draw unemployment. Real output would drop, and unemployment would rise. Price indexes would go up because steel prices are higher and no other prices are lower.

Cost-Push Summary

All these qualifications together greatly narrow the range of circumstances in which the cost-push theory of inflation can be made to work. First, we must eliminate all those cases of demand-pull inflation that masquerade as cost-push inflation as a result of the cost-push illusion. Second, there must be some factor or combination of factors that touches off the wage-price spiral. A rise in international commodity prices might be sufficient, but the simple presence of monopoly power is not by itself enough. Third, there must be some reason for inflexibility of wages and prices in all sectors of the economy, so that wage and price rises in one sector are not simply offset by declines in wages and prices elsewhere. These qualifications do not entirely undermine the validity of the cost-push theory, but they do indicate that we have quite a bit more work to do before we know how to apply it properly.

Conclusions

Each of the four traditional theories of inflation and unemployment that we have presented in this chapter has something to recommend it. Each seems to fit the facts in some particular time or place. None of them is a completely general theory of inflation and unemployment, however. They are like the separate pieces of a puzzle that we have not yet put together.

Putting together the unemployment-inflation puzzle is perhaps the most important single job for economists today. The job is by no means finished, but little by little the outlines of a picture are beginning to emerge. Perhaps the most fascinating feature of the emerging picture is that it appears to have room for all of the pieces. As we develop the modern theories of unemployment and inflation in the next two chapters, we shall find that, properly qualified and interpreted, none of the four theories of this chapter directly contradicts any other. Taken together, there is reason to hope that they provide a theory that can help policy makers to guide our economy back toward "full employment" and price stability.

SUMMARY

1. Price stability and full employment are the two most important goals of economic stabilization policy. For practical purposes, we can think of full employment as being somewhere in the 3 to 5 percent range of measured unemployment, and price stability as being somewhere in the 0 to 2 percent range of inflation. By these standards, the postwar record of economic stabilization for the American economy has been poor and is apparently getting worse.
2. The crude quantity theory of inflation has a very long tradition in economic thought. It is based on the assumption that the velocity of money is a constant, so that prices are proportional to the money supply when real output is given.

This theory appears to work fairly well during episodes of hyperinflation, but for practical short-run applications, a more sophisticated theory of velocity is needed.

3. The crude Keynesian theory of inflation and unemployment is based on the usual Keynesian nominal income determination theory, plus a few added assumptions. One assumption is that there is a particular level of nominal income that is associated with full employment. A second assumption is that below this level, movements in nominal income take the form only of movements in employment and real output, with prices unchanged. A third assumption is that above the full employment level, movements in nominal income take the form of pure price movements. The crude Keynesian theory does not allow for the possibility that high rates of inflation and unemployment might occur at the same time.

4. A Phillips curve shows the relationship between rates of inflation and unemployment for an economy. If the Phillips curve were stable, it would provide a "menu" from which policy makers could choose according to their tastes. However, the Phillips curve is not stable. It turns out that its position is partly determined by the very policies that government authorities pursue when they try to choose a particular point on the curve.

5. The idea of cost-push inflation was introduced to explain how prices could rise when there was substantial slack in employment and aggregate demand. According to the theory, inflation can be touched off by spontaneous increases in profits, prices, or wages. In applying the cost-push theory, it is very important to distinguish between genuine cost-push inflation and the cost-push illusion.

DISCUSSION QUESTIONS

1. In your own opinion, what levels of both inflation and unemployment would you consider to be excessive? Is either inflation or unemployment above your limit at the moment?

2. Milton Friedman writes, "long-continued inflation is always and everywhere a monetary phenomenon that arises from a more rapid expansion in the quantity of money than in the quantity of output." Why does he add the qualifying phrase "long-continued?" Can short-term inflation have other sources?

3. The crude Keynesian theory implies a sharply kinked, L-shaped Phillips curve. Can you explain why?

4. Some people maintain that unemployment is a painful human tragedy while inflation is just a matter of dollars chasing dollars. What sort of choice would such a person make if faced with a Phillips curve "menu" (assuming, for the sake of discussion, that the menu were a stable one)? Do you think that inflation, like unemployment, also affects *people?* If inflation is not "about people" but only "about dollars," why do we study it in an economics course?

5. Assume that in a country where everything else is fine, there is suddenly an outbreak of hoof and mouth disease that sharply decreases the supply of beef cattle. Would the resulting rise in the price of beef be true cost-push inflation? Trace this kind of inflation through the marketing chain for beef. At what points would it look different than demand-pull inflation? At what points would it be hard to tell the difference?

CHAPTER 15
A Closer Look at Unemployment

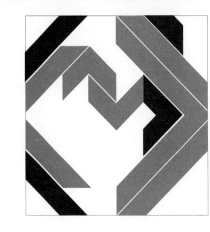

What You Will Learn in This Chapter

Most people think that "unemployed" means "not working" or "cannot find a job." It is not a simple matter, though, to translate those ideas into a single number, *the* unemployment rate, which can be used as a guide to policy. For some purposes, it is more interesting to look at the average duration of unemployment at a certain time. The duration of unemployment depends on how successful unemployed workers are in the process of job search. By looking at the impact of inflation on the process of job search, we get an important insight into the nature of the Phillips curve. Once unemployment is fully understood, we can begin to explore ways to reduce the unemployment rate to an acceptable level.

For Review

Here are some important terms and concepts that will be put to use in this chapter. Be certain that you understand them, or review them before proceeding.

The price system as a mechanism for utilizing knowledge (Chapter 2)

The Phillips curve (Chapter 14)

Measuring Unemployment

Unemployment statistics are perhaps the most closely watched numbers in the entire economy. The federal government is bound by law to keep unemployment at a low level. Newspapers and television make each monthly change of a fraction of a percentage point into headline news. Political careers can be made or broken by what happens to these magic numbers. The numbers are important enough, in fact, to make it worth knowing what they mean, and where they come from. We shall begin this chapter, then, by looking at how unemployment is measured.

What Is Unemployment?

Let us begin by looking not at what the Bureau of Labor Statistics officially means by "unemployment," but instead at two common sense meanings of the term. The first common sense meaning of "unemployed" is "not working," and the second is "cannot find a job."

Employed   According to the official Bureau of Labor Statistics definition, a person who (a) works at least one hour a week for pay, or at least fifteen hours per week as an unpaid worker in a family business, or (b) normally works the required number of hours, but is temporarily not working because of bad weather, illness, vacation, or a labor dispute.

If unemployed means not working, then an astonishing 62 percent of the U.S. population were unemployed in 1974. By working, official statisticians mean someone who works at least one hour a week for pay, or at least fifteen hours a week as an unpaid worker in a family business. By that definition, only 80.6 million people out of a total population of 211.4 million were working in an average week of 1974. Another 5.3 million people had jobs from which they were temporarily absent as a result of illness, bad weather, labor disputes, or vacations. These people are referred to as **employed** even though they are not working. The other 130.1 million Americans were not employed in an average week of 1974, but as we shall see in a moment, most of them were not officially *un*employed either.

Our other common sense idea of unemployment—"cannot find a job"— turns out to fit a surprisingly small number of people. In the average week of 1974, just 3.5 million people, or 1.6 percent of the population, could not find a job even though they were actively looking for one. About half of those had been looking less than a month. However, some people who were not unable to find a job were counted as unemployed too.

The Unemployment Rate

The official unemployment rate falls somewhere between these two common sense measures of unemployment. In 1974, it stood at 5.6 percent. Exhibit 15.1 will help us understand where this number comes from.

Starting at the top, we first divide the total population into three large groups. One group includes people under 16, plus those who are institutionalized or in the armed forces. They are not considered to be potential workers at all. The second group consists of adults who could potentially be workers, but who for one reason or another did not have a job and were not actively looking for one. Well over half of these were women who cited home responsibilities as their reason for not looking for work, and most of the rest were retired, disabled, ill, or in school. The remaining group—91 million people or 43 percent of the population in 1974—make up the **civilian labor force.**

Civilian Labor Force   All civilians aged 16 or over, who are either (a) employed, (b) actively looking for a job, (c) laid off from a job to which they expect to be recalled, or (d) waiting to start a new job that will begin within 30 days.

The **unemployment rate** as officially measured is the percentage of the civilian labor force that is not employed. The Bureau of Labor Statistics in cooperation with the Bureau of the Census obtains the data needed to make unemployment measurements from a monthly sample of about 50,000 randomly selected households. Field agents go to preselected houses and ask a series of specific questions about the job status of each member of the household. The questions include such things as: Did anyone work last week? Did anyone look for work? How long have they been looking for work? How did they go about looking? The result is that one headline-making percentage, plus a large array of supplementary tables that receive much less public attention.

Unemployment Rate   The percentage of the civilian labor force who are not employed.

Gray Areas

Clearly, there are a lot of gray areas in the measurement of unemployment. The official unemployment rate can equally well be criticized for understating or for overstating the "true" number of the unemployed.

Many gray areas come to light when we compare "unemployment" with "cannot find a job." People are counted as unemployed even though

EXHIBIT 15.1

Employment and unemployment, 1974

The Bureau of Labor Statistics bases its official unemployment rate on a complex breakdown of the population according to age and unemployment status. The Bureau defines the unemployment rate as the percentage of the civilian labor force who are not employed. This definition of the unemployment rate can be thought of as a compromise between the two common sense definitions of "not working" and "cannot find a job."

(a)

Millions of persons, 1974	
Total population	211.4
Civilian labor force	91.0
Employed	85.9
Working	80.6
Not working	5.3
Unemployed	5.1
Lost last job	2.2
Left last job	0.8
Reentered labor force	1.4
Never worked before	0.7
Not in labor force	57.6
Home responsibilities	32.7
In school	7.2
Ill health and disability	5.4
Retirement and old age	7.4
All other	4.6
Under 16, institutionalized, and armed forces	62.8

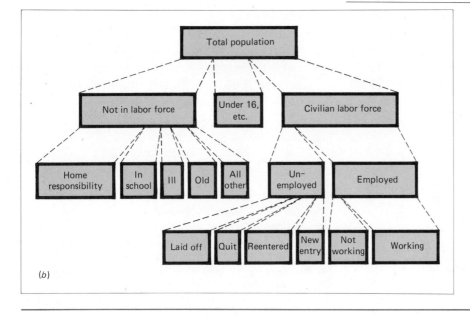

(b)

they are not looking for a job, if they are laid off from their job but expect to be recalled, or if they have found a job that they expect to start within thirty days. The label "cannot find a job" also does not seem very appropriate for a person who could have stayed on in his last job, but instead quit voluntarily, yet such people are counted as unemployed.

On the other hand, there are a certain number of people who really cannot find a job, and really would want one, but have become so discouraged with their prospects that they have gone a week or more without actively looking for one. Available data suggest that there is about one of these "discouraged workers" for every ten officially unemployed. Also, there are an unmeasured number of genuinely unemployed 14- and 15-year olds.

Some of these have been laid off from previous steady jobs and may even have dependents, but since 1967 they no longer count in the labor force so they cannot be unemployed. Finally, workers who want, need, and are actively looking for a *full-time* job are not counted as unemployed if they have worked even a single hour in the week before being surveyed. These workers are sometimes called "underemployed."

Unemployment Stocks and Flows

Wherever we draw the line between the employed and the unemployed, the unemployment rate measures a stock. The level of unemployment at any time, and changes in that level, depend on the size of the *flows* into and out of the stock of unemployed workers.

Exhibit 15.2 shows the relationships between the stock of unemployed workers and several key flows. Three ways to enter the stock of unemployed workers are shown. Employed workers can become unemployed either by quitting their jobs or by being laid off. Also, people not in the labor force can become officially unemployed if they begin seriously looking for work but do not find it immediately. Of course, some new entrants and reentrants find jobs right away, without going through a period of unemployment.

The exhibit also shows three ways for people to leave the stock of unemployed. They can be hired for a new job, or recalled to one from which they were laid off. Also, they can retire or withdraw from the labor force without ever having found a job.

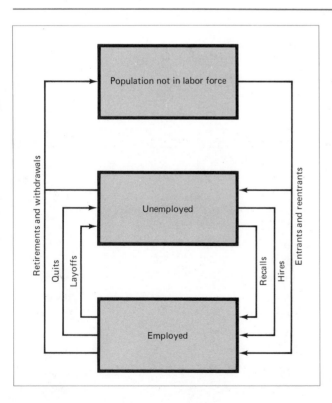

EXHIBIT 15.2
Labor market stocks and flows
The size of the stock of unemployed persons depends on the rates of flow of workers into and out of unemployed status. People can become unemployed by entering the labor force without finding a job immediately, or by quitting or being laid off from their last job and then looking for a new one. They can leave the stock of the unemployed by being hired for a new job or recalled to an old one, or by leaving the labor force in discouragement without ever having found a job.

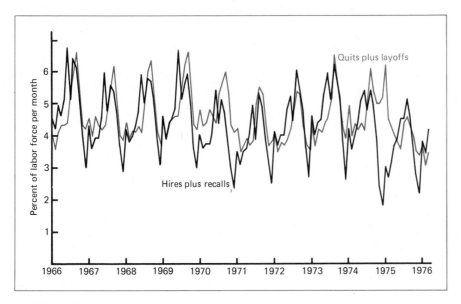

EXHIBIT 15.3
Quits, layoffs, hires, and recalls
The number of people unemployed at one time is fairly small compared to
the size of the flows into and out of unemployment. The monthly change in
the unemployment rate is equal to the difference between the rate of quits
plus layoffs, and the rate of hires plus recalls. Those flows are usually so
closely matched that the unemployment rate changes by less than half a
percentage point a month.

Balance

The number of workers actually unemployed at any time is rather
small compared to the size of the flows into and out of the stock of unemployed. This is clearly shown in Exhibit 15.3, which gives data on the major
flows identified in Exhibit 15.2. On the average, between 4 and 5 percent of
the labor force quit their jobs or are laid off each month, while a very nearly
equal number are hired or recalled to work.

Given these relatively large inflows and outflows, the unemployment
rate would fluctuate violently from month to month were it not for the fact
that the rate of quits plus layoffs and the rate of hires plus recalls is always
very nearly in balance. The rate of change in the unemployment rate is
equal to the difference between quits plus layoffs and hires plus recalls.
As Exhibit 15.3 shows, the difference is rarely as much as $\frac{1}{2}$ percent.

Frictional Unemployment

On the average, the total stock of unemployed workers "turns over"
every few weeks. That does not mean, of course, that every individual unemployed person in the stock is changed, but the picture of a quit or layoff,
followed by a brief stay among the unemployed, and then a hire or recall is
more the rule than the exception. Exhibit 15.4 gives figures on the average
duration of unemployment for selected years. In good years, well over half
the unemployed are out of work less than four weeks, and only one in

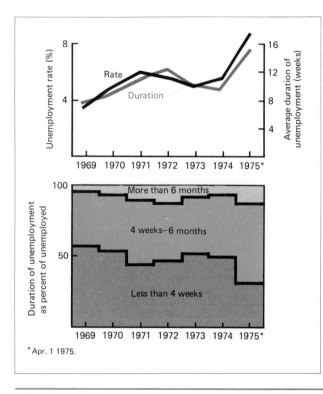

* Apr. 1 1975.

EXHIBIT 15.4
Duration and rate of unemployment
The unemployment picture is dominated by those spending a relatively short period between jobs. In a reasonably good year, well over half of the unemployed have been out of work less than four weeks. Even in a very bad year, only about one in eight of the unemployed has been out of work half a year or more. The average duration of unemployment closely follows the unemployment rate.

Source: U.S. Bureau of the Census, *Statistical Abstract of the United States, 1975* (Washington, D.C.: U.S. Government Printing Office, 1976).

twenty is out of work for more than six months. Even in years of high unemployment, the short-term unemployed dominate the picture.

Economists refer to that portion of unemployment accounted for by people spending relatively short periods between jobs as **frictional unemployment.** The presence of frictional unemployment is the major reason why the policy goal that we call "full employment" can never mean a zero measured rate of unemployment. Frictional unemployment is present in good times as well as bad, for the simple reason that as the economy picks up and layoffs are reduced, more people voluntarily quit their jobs to look for better ones. This tendency of people to switch jobs when times are good keeps the measured unemployment rate up, but it is nothing to worry about. Quite the contrary, a normal level of frictional unemployment is a sign of a healthy economy. It is the means by which each individual becomes matched with the best possible job.

Dual Labor Market

More serious policy problems are raised by that minority of workers who spend long periods in the ranks of the unemployed, or who become unemployed frequently. According to one often heard theory, these workers are victims of a **dual labor market.** The idea is that the primary sector of the labor market contains high-wage jobs with large, profitable firms. These jobs are likely to be unionized, to offer more opportunities for advancement, and to be less affected by ups and downs in business activity. The secondary sector of the labor market, in contrast, contains low-paying jobs with marginal firms, which are held by unorganized workers with unstable work

Frictional Unemployment That portion of unemployment accounted for by people spending relatively short periods between jobs.

Dual Labor Market The division of the labor market into a primary sector, containing good jobs with established firms, and a secondary sector, containing low-paid, unstable jobs with marginal firms.

patterns. These are largely "dead-end" jobs with few opportunities for advancement. They are heavily hit by cyclical swings in unemployment.

Because secondary-sector jobs are unattractive, workers who are not qualified for primary-sector jobs typically have short periods of employment often ending in quits rather than layoffs. These alternate with long periods of vainly trying to find something better. We shall return to the special policy problems raised by unemployment in the secondary labor market later in this chapter.

Unemployment and Job Search

We have seen that the unemployment rate depends on a delicate balance between flows of workers into and out of the stock of unemployed. We have also seen that these flows are large in relation to the number of workers unemployed at any time. It follows that anything that happens to change even slightly the average length of time a worker remains unemployed can have a very significant impact on the measured rate of unemployment.

For this reason, much recent work on the theory of unemployment has focused closely on the process of job search as a key to the average duration of unemployment, and hence to the measured unemployment rate. There are many variations of the job search theory of unemployment, and new ideas are still being put forth and tested. Certain basic assumptions, though, are shared by almost all economists working in this field.

Information

One basic assumption underlies all job search theories. That is the notion that workers looking for jobs and employers looking for workers operate without complete information of one another's needs or requirements, and without complete information about future economic trends. The job search process is essentially a matter of putting the labor market to work as a mechanism for obtaining knowledge.

Let us translate our discussion into more specific terms. Consider an individual unemployed worker who is looking for a new job. At the start of the job search, he or she knows that "somewhere out there" there are a number of employers looking for workers. The first necessity is to find out who and where these employers are, and what their jobs are like.

The jobs will not all be equally good. For one thing, some will pay better wages than others. In addition, some will offer pleasant surroundings and some not, some will be near and others far, and some will be stimulating, others dull. To keep things simple, we shall talk only about wage differences between different jobs, but the reader should remember that the job seeker will make mental adjustments in wage offers to allow for non-wage advantages and disadvantages of any job.

Our worker, then, sets out to sample the jobs available. Common sense tells us that people will not automatically take the first job offered. To play safe, even after getting one job offer, they would like to check a few more potential employers to see if something better turns up. On the average, the larger the number of jobs they include in their sample, the better will be the best wage offer they come across.

Reservation Wage   The wage (adjusted for nonmonetary advantages and disadvantages of a job) below which a person will not accept a job offer.

The Reservation Wage

There is a limit to the length of time a person will search for a job when jobs are available. That limit can be expressed in terms of the idea of a **reservation wage.** A person's reservation wage is the wage (adjusted for nonmonetary advantages of the job, as always) below which he or she will not accept an offer. A person who has a reservation wage of $150 per week, for example, will reject any offer of $149 a week or less, and take any job that comes along that offers $150 per week or more.

People's reservation wages tend to decline the longer their job search continues. There are at least two reasons for this. First, people may initially be very optimistic, overestimating their own worth in the eyes of potential employers, and then gradually they become more realistic as the hoped-for top-level offers do not materialize. Second, even if unemployment insurance is available, long periods without work tend to cut into people's savings, and financial pressure to get back to work increases. Case studies confirm the idea that reservation wages decline as the period of job search is lengthened.

CASE 15.1
Reservation Wages and the Duration of Unemployment

Several studies have been made of the effects of the duration of unemployment on the reservation wage. In one study,[1] Hirschel Kasper sampled 3,000 long-term unemployed workers in Minnesota during the 1961 recession. Their unemployment duration ranged from 0 to 20 months, with an average of 7.5 months. He found that workers initially asked for wages higher than their previous wages, but after about 6 months of unemployment they were willing to accept less. He also found that the faster the decline in the reservation wage, the sooner new employment was accepted.

Another study[2] was based on an incident in which the Boeing Company in Seattle laid off 7,700 workers when the Defense Department cancelled a big aerospace contract. Fourteen weeks after this huge layoff, some 69 percent of the former employees still had not found work. These were asked to respond to a questionnaire item saying "I need work that pays at least $_____ per month." The study revealed that, on the average, the reservation wage of these workers declined by 2.6 percent each month.

[1]Hirschel Kasper, "The Relation Between the Duration of Unemployment and the Asking Wage," unpublished Ph.D. dissertation, Department of Economics, University of Minnesota, 1963, and "The Asking Price of Labor and the Duration of Unemployment," *Review of Economics and Statistics* (May 1967). The data are used here as they are cited by Charles C. Holt in "Job Search, Phillips' Wage Relation, and Union Influence: Theory and Evidence," in Edmund S. Phelps (Ed.), *Microeconomic Foundations of Employment and Inflation Theory* (New York: W. W. Norton, 1970), p. 97.
[2]Data of the U.S. Arms Control and Disarmament Agency, as reported by Holt.

Duration of Unemployment

The idea of repeated sampling to find the best job offer plus the idea of a declining reservation wage gives us a simple theory of the duration of unemployment. Exhibit 15.5 gives a graphical presentation of the theory. An upward-sloping curve is drawn in the diagram to show that, on the average, a worker can find a better job offer by spending more time in job search. A downward-sloping curve is drawn to show how the worker's reservation wage falls as time goes by. The two curves come together the first time the worker gets a job offer that meets that worker's reservation wage. This

EXHIBIT 15.5

Determination of the average duration of unemployment
The longer people search for jobs, the better, on the
average, will be the best wage offers they uncover.
At the same time, the longer they search, the lower
their reservation wages tend to fall. In this exhibit, the
duration of unemployment is determined by the
intersection of the reservation wage curve and the
wage offer curve. That indicates the point at which
people first receive job offers that meet their reservation
wage.

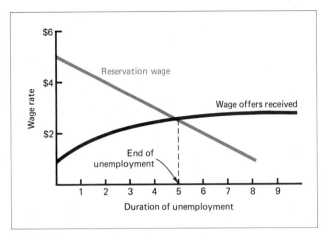

takes five weeks on the average as our figure is drawn. The worker takes the
job, and the period of unemployment is at an end.

We should stress two things about this figure. First, the curves express averages for workers of similar skills and experience. Individual
workers among them may, simply by good luck, find offers meeting their
reservation wage on the first or second try. Others, less lucky, may have to
look longer than average before they find something they will accept. Second, the positions of the curves, and hence the average length of job search,
may be very different for workers at different skill levels. In particular, for
workers in the secondary labor market, wage offers received are likely to be
very low. At the same time, hope for something better, even if unrealistic,
keeps the reservation wage from falling very rapidly. This can stretch out
the period of unemployment to many months.

Job Search and Inflation

The job search theory we have just given, simple though it is, can give
us some highly useful insights into what happens to unemployment when
economic conditions change. In particular, the job search theory supplies
a key piece to the unemployment-inflation puzzle that we introduced in
Chapter 14. Let us see what happens to the job search process when inflation comes on the scene.

Imagine an economy in which neither prices nor wages have been
changing in the recent past, and neither are expected to change in the
immediate future. Suppose that under these initial conditions, the average
duration of unemployment is five weeks, and the measured unemployment
rate is 5 percent. Suddenly, out of the blue, all prices and nominal wages
begin to rise. What will happen?

Let us look at things from the point of view of the unemployed job
searchers. By assumption, they do not expect prices to go up. It does not
occur to them that during the period they work at their new jobs, it will
cost them more to live than before. Also by assumption, they do not know
that wages *in general* have gone up, so they do not immediately reconsider their own estimates of their value to potential employers. Unexpected
inflation thus has no effect on their reservation wages. What does happen is

that before they have searched very long, they get nominal wage offers that look pretty good. Operating on their own, with incomplete information, job searchers are likely to consider such high wage offers to be isolated pieces of good luck. The jobs will quickly be accepted.

No individual job searcher realizes, of course, that many other job searchers are also experiencing "good luck" and taking less than five weeks, on the average, to find jobs. The decrease in the average duration of job search shows up as a drop in the measured unemployment rate. Our conclusion is that *unexpected* inflation causes unemployment to fall.

Expected Inflation

It will not take too long, of course, for workers to catch on to what is happening. Unexpected inflation then becomes expected inflation. The effect of expected inflation on unemployment is quite different.

Expected inflation does cause reservation wages to rise. If wages and prices begin rising by, say, 5 percent per year, and job searchers know it, it is easy to see what they will do. Expecting prices to be higher than before, they will reestimate the level of nominal wage they will need to keep up with the cost of living. Also, expecting wages to be higher than before, they will know that the first high nominal offer they get is not an isolated bit of good luck, but part of a general trend. They will not need to snap it up, because later offers may be even better.

In fact, if inflation is *fully* expected by all workers and employers, it will have no real impact on the labor market at all. Workers will know that by waiting, they will get better nominal wage offers, but that the cost of living will be going up just as fast. Employers will know that the higher nominal wages they have to pay each year will be entirely offset by the prices they will get for the products they sell. No one will be any better off or any worse off than if neither prices nor wages changed at all. Job searchers will behave no differently than they would if prices and wages were stable.

False Expectations

There is a third case to consider, that in which people *falsely* expect prices to rise when in fact they are stable. If wages and prices stopped rising, but workers still expected them to go up by 5 percent a year, their search for jobs would become more difficult. They would raise their reservation wages, thinking that they needed the extra money to cover a higher cost of living. They would expect nominal wage offers to rise also, but they would not. These workers, operating in isolation from one another, might well think that they were just having uncommonly bad luck. For a while, at least, they would keep looking and looking for jobs that met their expectations. Eventually, they would either really get lucky and find one, or become discouraged and lower their reservation wages to realistic levels. Meanwhile, though, the average duration of job search would have risen, and so would the measured unemployment rate.

The Natural Rate of Unemployment

Let us summarize what we have said now about inflation and unemployment. We have argued that unexpected inflation shortens the average duration of unemployment and lowers the unemployment rate. Falsely expected inflation, we said, lengthens the duration and raises the rate of unemployment. In the middle lie all cases where the expected rate of inflation and the actual rate are just equal. This middle ground includes the case where both the actual and expected rate of inflation are zero, that is, the case of price stability.

The case of price stability, when prices neither change nor are expected to, provides an important benchmark for economic policy. To emphasize its importance, we introduce a special term to refer to the rate of unemployment that prevails when prices are stable and expected inflation is zero. That rate is called the **natural rate of unemployment.** It is natural not, of course, in the sense that it is a God-given constant, beyond the influence of economic policy. Instead, it is natural in the sense that it is the rate of unemployment that prevails when everyone knows what is going on, and no one is fooled. Because it is the rate of unemployment that prevails when everyone has accurate knowledge of market conditions, we might alternatively call it the equilibrium rate of unemployment.

Natural Rate of Unemployment That rate of unemployment that would prevail if the expected rate of inflation were equal to the actual rate of inflation.

The Phillips Curve

In Chapter 14 we introduced the Phillips curve to represent the trade-off between inflation and unemployment. The Phillips curve contained an element of truth, we said, but the problem was that it seemed to drift over time. Now our job search theory of unemployment offers an explanation of why the Phillips curve can shift from one year to another.

Consider Exhibit 15.6. There we have sketched not one but three Phillips curves. Each of them represents the short-run trade-off between unemployment and inflation *for a given expected rate of inflation*. On each curve, unemployment is at the natural rate (here assumed to be 5 percent) when the actual rate of inflation and the expected rate are equal. If people expect the rate of inflation to be 2 percent, but in fact inflation accelerates

EXHIBIT 15.6

Expected inflation and the shifting Phillips curve
The position of the Phillips curve depends on the rate of expected inflation, and the rate of unemployment depends on the relationship between the expected rate of inflation and the actual rate. With expected inflation at 2 percent, for example, an acceleration of actual inflation to 3½ percent would lower the unemployment rate, moving the economy from point *A* to point *B*. Unemployment is at the natural rate whenever actual and expected inflation are equal.

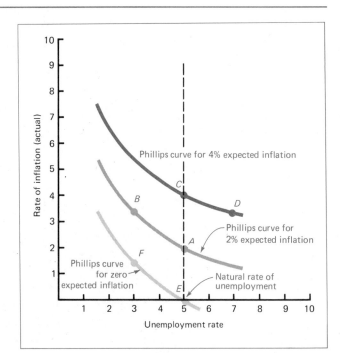

to $3\frac{1}{2}$ percent, the economy would move up and to the left along the middle Phillips curve, from point A to point B. If they expect the rate of inflation to be 4 percent but in fact it slows to $3\frac{1}{2}$ percent, they would move down and to the right along the top Phillips curve, from point C to point D.

Suppose that the economy had experienced a long period of price stability, so that actual and expected inflation were both zero. In that case, the bottom Phillips curve would provide a short-run "menu" from which policy makers might choose. If they wished, they might, for example, get unemployment down to 3 percent if they were willing to tolerate a bit of inflation, moving from point E to point F. They could do that only in the short run, however. After a while, people would notice that prices were going up. They would begin to expect them to continue to do so. As soon as that happened, the Phillips curve would begin to drift upward, and the policy menu would suddenly begin to look less appetizing.

By following this line of argument, we can construct a theory of inflation on the shoulders of our theory of unemployment. We shall do this in some detail in the next chapter. Before we leave our discussion of unemployment, though, there is one more important topic to cover. This is the question of what determines the natural rate of unemployment itself, and what, if anything, can be done to keep it down to an acceptable level.

Lowering the Natural Rate of Unemployment

To put the label "natural" on a rate of unemployment is not to say that such a level of unemployment is a good thing. During the 1960s, it was usual for economists to think of the natural rate as about 4 percent. That was the number used by Arthur Okun to represent full employment in his original formulation of Okun's law. For policy purposes, though, the Kennedy administration regarded even 4 percent as only an "interim" goal. It was to be bettered once it had been achieved.

Today 4 percent seems unrealistically low for the natural rate. Estimates based on the most recent data suggest that the natural rate may be as high as 5.36 percent. Certainly most guesses would now be closer to 5 than 4 percent. Yet 5 percent unemployment seems hard to accept as the best the American economy can do without runaway inflation. Must we live with such a high natural rate, and accept the social problems it may bring?

Unemployment as a Social Problem

To a considerable extent, the American fear of unemployment is a heritage of the Great Depression of the 1930s. In those days, when Keynes was writing his *General Theory,* unemployment meant millions upon millions of desperate people, thrown out of their jobs and into the breadlines where they waited hopelessly for work as months dragged into years.

The face of unemployment in the 1970s is no longer the same as in the Depression years. Now, even in a moderately poor year, some 90 percent of the unemployed are out or work less than six months. Well under half of the unemployed have been fired or laid off from their last job.

To understand unemployment as a social problem today, we have to look at it in terms of its impact on the specific types of people, or demo-

EXHIBIT 15.7

Unemployment by demographic categories
Unemployment is not distributed evenly among the
population. Some demographic categories are hit
harder than others. A high proportion of the members
of hard-hit groups are locked into the secondary labor
market. Statistical analysis suggests that unemployment
among these groups would remain high even in a very
tight labor market.

Demographic Category	Actual Unemployment Rate, 1971 (%)	Hypothetical Unemployment Rate with Tight Labor Market* (%)
Teenage† males	16.7	11.4
Teenage females	17.4	13.7
Teenage whites	15.2	10.8
Teenage nonwhites	31.8	24.5
Adult white males‡	4.0	1.7
Adult nonwhite males	7.3	3.3
Adult white females	5.3	3.2
Adult nonwhite females	8.7	6.1

*1.5 percent unemployed among white males 25 years and older.
†16 to 19 years.
‡Adult = 20 years and older.

Source: Martin S. Feldstein, "Lowering the Permanent Rate of Unemployment," (U.S. Congress, Joint Economic Committee, Sept. 18, 1973).

graphic categories, who are affected. Exhibit 15.7 shows the unemployment
rate for 1971 broken down by demographic categories.

The first column of that table shows actual unemployment rates for
1971. We see that not many adult white males were unemployed that year,
as their fathers may have been forty years before. Instead, unemployment
was concentrated among females, nonwhites, and teenagers, with any
group falling into two of those categories doubly hit. Teenage nonwhites
were a real disaster area. One thing that makes these high unemployment
rates a serious social problem is the fact that so many members of the
hardest-hit groups are trapped in the secondary labor market. Secondary-
sector unemployment tends not to fall as low as primary-sector unemployment even when the economy picks up. To show this, Harvard economist
Martin Feldstein estimated the unemployment rate that would prevail
for various groups in a "very tight" labor market. (Feldstein's idea of a
tight labor market was one in which overall unemployment would be
below the natural rate). His figures are given in the second column of
Exhibit 15.7. They are rather distressing. Adult white females and nonwhite males seem to gain substantially from the tight labor market conditions, but unemployment among teenagers and nonwhite females remains
at problem levels.

Policy and the Natural Rate

The high natural rate of unemployment in our economy poses a serious
problem for policy makers. Part of the problem is that certain existing
labor market policies act to increase the natural rate of unemployment.
When the government pursues other policies designed to lower it, different
government agencies end up working at cross purposes with one another.
Another part of the problem is that most of the measures that could be
taken to lower the natural rate of unemployment have unfortunate side
effects. To get an idea of some of the problems and trade-offs, let us look
first at some policies that tend to raise the natural rate, and then at some
that might lower it.

Minimum Wage Laws

For years, economists have argued that minimum wage laws, rather than easing the plight of the poor, increase unemployment and throw more people into poverty. The usual explanation of this perverse effect is that some people may have reservation wages lower than the minimum wage rate, but cannot legally be offered jobs at such low wages. This is not the whole story concerning the effects of minimum wage laws, however. They have another effect as well, which is to discourage on-the-job training. This may help explain the particularly high rate of teenage unemployment.

To see how this works, consider a hypothetical example. John Jones, a 17-year-old high school dropout, approaches the Atlas Company looking for a job. Jones is completely untrained, but he still claims to be worth $2.25 an hour, and is in fact worth that much. The Atlas Company offers him his choice of two jobs, that of stock boy, paying $2.25 per hour, and that of a machinist's assistant. Unfortunately, the Atlas personnel manager explains, a lot of his time in the second position would be spent learning about machines and not really producing very much. The company can only afford to pay him $1.50 per hour for that job. Jones realizes the advantage of on-the-job training, and takes the lower-paying job. Within a year, he has been promoted to machinist first class and is earning $6 per hour.

Now introduce a legal minimum wage of $2 per hour. The Atlas Company can still offer him the stock boy job, but not the machinist assistantship. The company would lose money paying him $2 per hour in that position, and is legally barred from paying $1.50. Jones takes the stock boy job, but soon finds it to be boring and a dead end and quits to look again for something better.

This example shows us how minimum wage laws can contribute to a vicious cycle of teenage unemployment. Employers expect unstable work behavior from teenagers and tailor available jobs accordingly. The teenage workers themselves are turned off by the dead-end jobs thus created and shift aimlessly from one employer to another. One direction to move in lowering the natural rate of unemployment would be to get rid of minimum wage laws and replace them, if need be, with other types of income-assistance programs having a less serious disincentive effect.

Unemployment Compensation

Unemployment compensation is a second government program that, like minimum wage laws, keeps the natural rate of unemployment high. To understand the employment effects of unemployed compensation, it will be helpful to look at a detailed example constructed by Feldstein.[3]

CASE 15.2
Employment Effects of Unemployment Compensation
Consider a worker in Massachusetts in 1971 with a wife and two children. He earns $500 per month, or $6,000 per year if he experiences no unemployment. She earns $350 per month, or $4,200 per year if she experiences no unemployment. If he is unemployed for one month, he loses $500 in

[3]Martin S. Feldstein, "Lowering the Permanent Rated Unemployment" (U.S. Congress, Joint Economic Committee, Sept. 18, 1973).

gross earnings but less than $100 in net income. How does this occur? A reduction of $500 in annual earnings reduces his federal income tax by $83, his social security payroll tax by $26, and his Massachusetts income tax by $25. The total reduction in taxes is $134. Unemployment compensation consists of 50 percent of his wage plus dependents' allowances of $6 per week for each child. Total unemployment compensation is therefore $302. His net income therefore falls from $366 for the month if he is employed to the $302 paid as unemployment compensation.

If he returns to work after one month, his annual net income is only $128 higher than if he returns after three months. Moreover, part of the higher increase in income would be offset by the cost of transportation to work and other expenses associated with employment.

This case is by no means extreme. If his wife were to lose her job while he remained employed, the loss of income would be even less in relation to the loss in earnings. In fact, it is not difficult to construct examples in which a short period of unemployment will actually *increase* a family's annual income—not to mention providing an opportunity to do some work around the house! Small wonder some unions are now bargaining for "reverse seniority" clauses in their contracts, whereby long-term employees are laid off first, rather than last, if a temporary lull in production occurs.

How does the labor market react to the distinctive effects of unemployment compensation laws? One reaction is obvious. These laws greatly reduce the cost of job search. If the man from Massachusetts did not expect to be rehired at his old job, he could take his time looking for a new one, because the opportunity cost of job search to him would not be the $125 per week implied by his gross wage but in fact only about $15 per week.

A second reaction to unemployment compensation is less obvious but also very important. It provides a subsidy to seasonal, cyclical, and casual employment. Consider the construction industry, for example. Construction costs are lower in the summer than in the winter because of the weather, so firms have a natural incentive to employ seasonal labor. However, in the absence of unemployment compensation, there would be an offsetting disincentive. Workers would be reluctant to go into the building trades, where they would work fewer weeks per year, unless their hourly wage rate when employed were higher than for steady work. Thus, it might pay construction firms to hire on a steady-work basis at a lower wage, and absorb the added expense of the special equipment and materials needed for winter construction.

With unemployment compensation, the picture is different. Workers need not be paid such a high premium to enter a seasonal occupation if they will get supplemental benefits from the state during the months they are laid off. Hence, employers will not adapt their construction methods to year-round work.

The seasonal component of unemployment averages around three-quarters of a percentage point. When we consider that similar effects hold true with respect to the incentives firms have for scheduling work over the course of the business cycle, or over periods of temporary high demand, the impact of unemployment compensation on the rate of unemployment is even greater than this.

Job Placement

Let us turn now from policies that raise the natural rate of unemployment to policies designed to lower it. One way to attack unemployment is through job placement programs. An area where job placement programs might have particularly beneficial impact is that of teenage unemployment. In his testimony to Congress, which we have cited before, Martin Feldstein recommended a nationwide Youth Employment Service. British experience with such a program suggests that by improving the quality of first jobs taken by young people leaving school, the cycle of teenage unemployment might be broken before it begins.

For low-skilled adult workers, the prospects for reducing unemployment through job placement alone is not encouraging. An experimental program tried in Boston is a case in point. The idea of this program was to refer long-term unemployed adults to jobs for which they were qualified, which usually meant secondary-sector jobs. Seventy percent of the workers referred to potential employers were offered jobs, but 45 percent of the job offers were rejected. Of those who did accept work, less than half remained on the job for as long as one month. A very high proportion of the separations in this period were voluntary.[4]

Manpower Training

Such experiences have led many economists to recommend another approach to handling unemployment among low-skilled adult workers. Instead of simply sticking them in jobs corresponding to their current skills, the idea is to enroll them in *manpower training programs* designed to upgrade their skills to match those required by better jobs. Unfortunately, despite some ten years of experience with these programs and some $10 billion of federal expenditures on them, no one has a very clear idea of how well they work. We simply do not know whether unemployment rates are lower for those who have enrolled in manpower programs than for those with the same demographic characteristics who have not. Isolated evaluations of particular local experiences suggest that such programs have positive, but small effects. The general picture is clouded by the existence of some notable success and some spectacular failures.

Public Employment

Still another alternative for reducing unemployment is the proposal to make the government itself an "employer of last resort." The idea is that any person who is unemployed and wants work will be given a government job of some kind. Public employment programs were used on a large scale by the Roosevelt administration during the Great Depression, and a number of smaller-scale programs are in operation now. Because it is likely that the public employment concept will continue to find favor with Congress, it is worth mentioning two serious problems that this type of policy tends to encounter.

The first problem of public employment programs is, what should the new public employees do? The easy answer is that they should be put to work at the most productive jobs that can be devised for them, given their skills and experience. Unfortunately, there are certain drawbacks to put-

[4]*Ibid.*

ting this easy answer into effect. In the first place, the more necessary and productive the jobs public employment programs offer, the more likely it is that participants in these programs will simply displace existing workers, with no net impact on unemployment. A particularly serious problem is the tendency of federal public employment programs to displace public employment at the state and local level. In the second place, to put public employees to work in highly productive jobs usually requires investing public money in the tools, buildings, and other capital equipment needed to do the jobs. That makes public employment programs very expensive.

Consideration of these difficulties has led some policy makers to propose an alternative "easy answer" to the question of what public employment workers ought to do: They should do jobs that would otherwise go altogether undone, and that require an absolute minimum of capital equipment. The trouble with that approach, though, is that the jobs that result are often pure make-work. They produce little real benefit and give the workers involved no useful training or experience.

Perhaps an even more serious problem with making the government the employer of last resort lies in a "ratchet effect" from which such programs suffer. Workers who enter the public payroll when times are hard often do not return to the private sector when good times return. With each up and down of the cycle, the total number of public employees moves up a notch. This would not be so bad if the new public employees were doing work that was as useful or productive as that which they could be doing in the private sector, but for the reasons outlined above, their public-sector work is likely to be less productive.

Conclusions

Our discussion has not led us to a set of solutions for the problem of a high natural rate of unemployment, but instead, has left us with a set of open questions:

Do minimum wage laws provide sufficient benefit to any lower-income group to justify their effects on unemployment? This question is a bit less open than the others. Enough evidence is in to suggest a negative answer.

Can unemployment compensation be reformed in ways that would limit its disincentive effects? This question has not received the attention it deserves.

How much can improved job placement contribute to solving the unemployment problem? Under what conditions can manpower training programs yield benefits that justify their costs? It is troubling that experience to date in these areas has not provided more encouraging answers.

Are expanded public employment programs, including the employer-of-last-resort concept, compatible with an efficient allocation of resources between the public and private sectors? A study of British experience, which offers encouragement in the area of job placement, would indicate great caution in the area of public employment.

Living with Unemployment?

In sum, it appears that there are three broad directions that unemployment policy can take. None of the directions is costless, but it is hard to see how a choice among them can be avoided.

First, the government can use conventional macroeconomic policy in an attempt to keep unemployment as far below the natural rate as possible. This is the policy that has most frequently been chosen by successive administrations and Congresses in the United States since at least the 1960s. The entire next chapter will be devoted to an analysis of the costs and the chances for success of this very important option.

Second, the government can pursue the whole range of policies designed to lower the natural rate of unemployment. In some cases, such policies conflict with the goal of providing high living standards for unemployed and low-paid workers. In other cases, they conflict with the goal of efficient resource allocation, which means that they conflict with the goal of providing high living standards for the rest of us. To know just how great the costs of this option are, we must have more accurate answers to the "open questions" listed above.

Finally, the government can adopt a policy of living with unemployment. The cost of this option is abandoning "full employment" as a major goal of macroeconomic policy. The social problems associated with unemployment (especially those associated with the very high unemployment rates of some subsections of the labor force) would become problems of *micro*economic policy, to be treated by measures similar to those chosen to treat the social problems of disability or old age. *Macro*economic policy would then be left free to pursue the goals of price stability, economic growth, and international economic balance.

None of these policy options is costless, or free of serious disadvantages. In dealing with unemployment, as everywhere else in economic life, we must remember the old economic principle: There ain't no such thing as a free lunch.

SUMMARY

1. Unemployment, as measured by the Bureau of Labor Statistics, does not quite conform to the common sense notions of "not working" or "can't find a job." Instead, the unemployment rate measures the percentage of the civilian labor force that is not employed. The official unemployment rate can be criticized for having either an upward or a downward bias. Some who want a job and cannot find one are not counted, among them, so-called discouraged workers. Others who are not really unable to find a job are counted as unemployed, including workers who have voluntarily quit their jobs, or who have found a job but not started it yet.

2. The unemployment rate measures a stock. Changes in the unemployment rate depend on a rather close balance of flows into and out of the stock of unemployed persons. Turnover among the stock of unemployed persons is fairly rapid. In normal years, half of the unemployed have been out of work less than four weeks, and only in the worst years does the average duration of unemployment go above three months.

3. The unemployment rate is closely correlated with the average duration of unemployment. Anything that affects the process of job search thus has an important impact on the unemployment rate. Workers look for a job until they find one that meets their reservation wage—a process that takes several weeks on the average. In periods when inflation proceeds at a rate faster than people expect it, this period of job search tends to be shortened. In periods when inflation is slower than expected, the period of job search tends to stretch out. The rate of unemployment that prevails when no one is fooled by the rate of inflation is called the natural rate of unemployment.

4. The theory of job search helps us explain why the short-run Phillips curve shifts from time to time. The position of the Phillips curve depends on the expected rate of inflation, since unemployment equals the natural rate whenever actual and expected inflation are equal. The actual rate of unemployment at any time depends on the relationship between the actual and expected rates of inflation.

5. To call one particular rate of unemployment "natural" is not to say that it is a good thing. The natural rate for the U.S. economy in the 1970s appears to be 5 percent or more, high enough to be considered a significant social problem. Sometimes government efforts to help the poor and the unemployed have the side effect of keeping the natural rate of unemployment high. Minimum wage laws and unemployment compensation do this. Job placement programs, manpower training, and public employment have been tried as methods of lowering the natural rate, but none of these has yet proved entirely satisfactory. In the end, we are faced with the fact that lowering the natural rate of unemployment involves some very hard trade-offs.

DISCUSSION QUESTIONS

1. Some people say that we should change the way we measure unemployment so that the official unemployment figure includes all those and only those who are suffering genuine hardship because of their inability to find a job. What specific changes in measurement techniques would be necessary in order to put this suggestion into effect?

2. Some countries do not use the household survey method to measure unemployment. Instead, they just count people who show up at unemployment offices to claim compensation or to look for jobs. What difference do you think this technique would make for the measured level of unemployment?

3. In addition to keeping an unemployment index, the government also makes periodic surveys of job openings. Suppose that you looked at these data and found that the number of job openings was equal to or greater than the number of unemployed persons. Would you be justified in thinking that there was no unemployment *problem* in a human sense? In a political sense? In an economic sense?

4. Communist countries regularly claim that they have no unemployment at all. Is that claim believable? Do you think that it is just empty boasting, or do you think that it may largely reflect different ways of measuring unemployment?

5. If you like working with graphs, try using the wage offer curve and reservation wage curve to explain how inflation affects the measured level of unemployment. How does expected inflation affect each curve? How does unexpected inflation affect each curve?

6. What do you think determines people's expected rate of inflation? Do you think it is reasonable, as a rough rule of thumb, to say that people expect inflation this year to be just what it was last year? Why or why not? What do you expect the rate of inflation to be next year? Next month? Make a note of your answer, and check yourself a month or a year later.

7. Suppose that unemployment compensation were simply abolished. What would that do to measured unemployment? What would it do to the reservation wage curve in Exhibit 15.5? What would it do to the natural rate of unemployment? What would it do to the position of the short-run Phillips curves in Exhibit 15.6?

8. Feldstein's analysis implies that raising unemployment benefits would increase the rate of unemployment. Consider this plan, though: The level of unemployment payments for unemployed persons would remain exactly the same as it is now, but unemployment payments would *continue* for six weeks *after* a person began a new job. What do you think that would do to the unemployment rate? Why?

CHAPTER 16
A Closer Look at Inflation

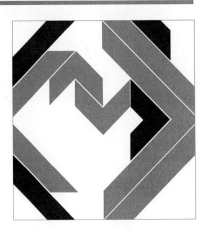

What You Will Learn in This Chapter
A theory of inflation must explain how any change in nominal national product will be split up between change in real output and change in the price level. A theory that can do this can tell us what effect monetary and fiscal policy measures will have on inflation and unemployment. We already have all of the ingredients for such a theory. Now we need only to assemble the pieces and put them to use.

For Review
Here are some important terms and concepts that will be put to use in this chapter. Be certain that you understand them, or review them before proceeding.
>Real and nominal values and the price index (Chapter 6)
>Okun's law (Chapter 7)
>Theory of nominal income determination (Chapters 8–13)
>The Phillips curve (Chapters 14 and 15)

Ingredients
We now have all the ingredients we need for a theory of inflation. Let us review briefly what we have.

First, from Chapter 6 we have a way of measuring the price level for the economy. The price index for any year is equal to the ratio of nominal national product to real national product in that year.

Second, from Chapter 7 we have Okun's law. That law relates real output to unemployment. More precisely, it says that each percentage point change in the measured unemployment rate will produce roughly a 3 percent change in real national product.

Third, from Chapters 8 to 13 we have a theory to tell us what determines nominal national product. In that theory, nominal national product can be controlled by the use of monetary and fiscal policy. What we did not do in those earlier chapters was show how a given change in nominal national product would be split up between changes in prices and changes in real output. That is what we shall do here.

Fourth, from Chapter 14 we have a theory of unemployment. That theory makes unemployment depend, among other things, on the actual and expected rates of inflation. In graphical terms, the theory implies a short-run Phillips curve that shifts as the expected rate of inflation changes. Chapter 14 also gave us the idea of the natural rate of unemployment, an important benchmark for our discussion of inflation.

A Theory of Inflation

Inflation and Real Growth

All we really have to do now is put the pieces together. Our first step will be to establish a simple relationship between inflation and the growth of real national product. The price level in any year is the ratio of nominal to real national product in that year. It follows that the rate of change in the price level, that is, the rate of inflation, depends on the rate of growth of nominal national product and the rate of growth of real national product. For a given rate of growth of nominal national product, the rate of inflation will be less, the higher the rate of growth of real national product.

Consider some examples. If real national product grows at the same rate as nominal national product, there will be no inflation at all. At the other extreme, if nominal national product grows while real national product does not change, the rate of inflation will be equal to the rate of growth of nominal product. These two cases and all those in between fit a general rule. That rule tells us that the rate of inflation must be equal to the rate of growth of nominal national product minus the rate of growth of real national product. A 10 percent rate of growth of nominal product will produce 5 percent inflation if real product grows at 5 percent, 3 percent inflation if real product grows at 7 percent, and so forth.

Okun's Law

Our next step is to translate this relationship between inflation and real growth into a relationship between inflation and unemployment. Okun's law tells us that the rate of growth of real output from one year to the next depends on how much the unemployment rate changes.[1] For each percentage point drop in unemployment, we get approximately 3 percent growth of real output. It follows, then, that for a given rate of growth of nominal national product, each percentage point drop in unemployment will reduce the rate of inflation by about 3 percent.

Let us put this in the form of a graph. Consider Exhibit 16.1, where we have placed inflation on the vertical axis and unemployment on the horizontal axis. Suppose that initially unemployment is at its natural rate, which we take to be 5 percent. Now let nominal national product begin to grow at a rate of 6 percent. The amount of inflation produced by this rate of nominal growth depends on what happens to unemployment. If unemployment does not change, there must be 6 percent inflation, as at point A in the exhibit. To keep prices stable, real output would have to grow by 6 percent each year. Okun's law tells us that this can happen only if the unemployment rate drops 2 percentage points in the year. That would put the economy at point B, with no inflation and 3 percent unemployment.

[1]Throughout this chapter, we ignore the effects of growth in labor productivity or in the labor force. This simplifies presentation of the basic theory. Once the theory is clearly understood it is not hard to adjust it to allow for growth of potential output.

EXHIBIT 16.1

The inflationary pressure curve

For a given rate of growth of nominal GNP, the rate of inflation depends on what happens to real GNP. For a given initial rate of unemployment, the growth of real GNP depends on what happens to unemployment (Okun's law). Here we assume a 6 percent growth of nominal GNP and an initial rate of unemployment of 5 percent. If unemployment does not change, there will be 6 percent inflation, as at point A. Each percentage point decrease in unemployment adds 3 percent to real growth, and hence trims 3 percent from the rate of inflation.

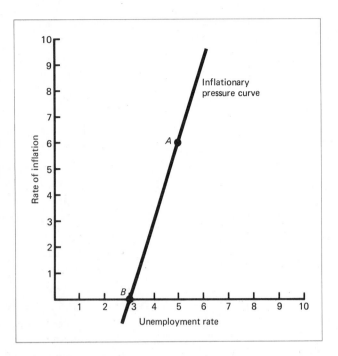

If unemployment decreased somewhat, but by less than 2 percentage points, there would be some amount of inflation between 0 and 6 percent.

The line drawn through points *A* and *B* in Exhibit 16.1 shows all the combinations of inflation and unemployment that are possible, given the assumed initial level of unemployment and the assumed rate of change in nominal national product. We shall call it an **inflationary pressure curve.** The inflationary pressure curve tells us that, other things being equal, each annual percentage point reduction in unemployment will trim about three percentage points from the annual rate of inflation.

An upward shift in the curve drawn in Exhibit 16.1 would indicate an increase in inflationary pressure. The position of the curve could change if either of two things happened. First, an increase in the rate of growth of nominal GNP would increase inflationary pressure. More real growth, and hence a bigger drop in unemployment, would be needed to hold inflation down to any given rate. Second, a lower initial rate of unemployment would also increase inflationary pressure. If the unemployment rate is high to begin with, there is a lot of room for improvement in real output. If it is already low, there is less room for further improvement. A drop in unemployment from 5 to 3 percent was enough to absorb a 6 percent growth of nominal GNP without inflation in Exhibit 16.1. If unemployment had been 3 percent to begin with, just keeping it at 3 percent would not have helped. Keeping inflation below 6 percent would have required cutting unemployment to an even lower level.

A simple rule makes it easy to sketch the correct inflationary pressure curve for any set of conditions. First find the point corresponding to the assumed initial level of unemployment and the assumed rate of growth of nominal national product (see point *A* in Exhibit 16.1). Then draw a line through that point with a slope of +3. That line will be the required inflationary pressure curve.

Inflationary Pressure Curve A graph, derived from Okun's law and the definition of the price level, that shows the amount of inflation associated with each rate of unemployment, given an initial unemployment rate and a rate of growth of nominal output.

Determining the Rate of Inflation

We have now almost finished putting the inflation-unemployment puzzle together. Our familiar multiplier theory tells us how monetary and fiscal policy affect nominal output. Given the growth of nominal output and the initial level of unemployment, the inflationary pressure curve sets out a possible range of rates of inflation. Each of these is tied to a certain level of unemployment. All we have left to do is show which of the points on the inflationary pressure curve will actually apply. The Phillips curve, as developed in Chapter 14, gives us this last missing piece.

Consider Exhibit 16.2. In drawing this exhibit, we have assumed that initially the economy is in a "standing start" position. By this we mean that in the immediate past, neither nominal nor real output has been growing, that there has been no inflation and no one expects any, and that unemployment is at the natural rate. Under these initial conditions, the inflationary pressure curve is in the position I_1, and the economy is at point A.

Next assume that the government applies a dose of fiscal or monetary policy big enough to start nominal output growing at 5 percent per year. Aggregate demand increases, and a familiar chain of events gets underway. Expenditures increase and firms unexpectedly find their inventories falling. Some respond by stepping up output, others by raising prices, and other by doing a little of both. Nominal national product rises, and pushes the inflationary pressure curve up to the position I_2 in Exhibit 16.2.

Now let us look at what happens in the labor market. Those firms that are stepping up their output go out to recruit new workers. Some will offer higher nominal wages, knowing that the rising level of demand will let them recoup these wages in higher prices and expanded sales volume. Job searchers will, on the average, be luckier in finding good offers. They

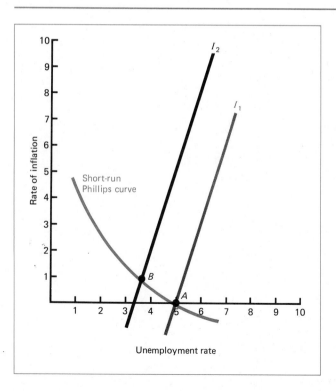

EXHIBIT 16.2
The determination of inflation and unemployment
Together, the Phillips curve and the inflationary pressure curve determine the rates of inflation and unemployment, given an initial level of unemployment and a rate of growth of nominal output. Here the economy begins from a "standing start" at A. There are no inflationary expectations, so the short-run Phillips curve is in the position shown. Raising the rate of nominal growth from 0 to 5 percent shifts the inflationary pressure curve from I_1 and I_2. Unemployment drops to just over 3½ percent, and inflation reaches a rate of just under 1 percent.

are not expecting any inflation, so they have not raised their reservation wages. The average duration of unemployment drops, and the economy begins to move away from point *A*, up and to the left along the short-run Phillips curve shown in Exhibit 16.2.

As the unemployment rate begins to drop, we have to watch what happens in terms of both the Phillips curve and the inflationary pressure curve at once. According to the Phillips curve, the more inflation there is, the less unemployment there will be. According to the inflationary pressure curve, the less unemployment there is, the less inflation there will be. *Together, the Phillips curve and the inflationary pressure curve determine both the level of unemployment and the rate of inflation.* The economy must end up at point *B*, where the inflationary pressure curve and Phillips curve intersect. As Exhibit 16.2 is drawn, this means just under 1 percent inflation and just over $3\frac{1}{2}$ percent unemployment.

No other combination of inflation and unemployment is possible under the conditions we have assumed. Suppose, for example, that inflation were only one-half of 1 percent. The Phillips curve shows us that that would barely get unemployment down by one percentage point. A 1 percent drop in unemployment means only a 3 percent rise in real output. But 5 percent nominal growth with only 3 percent real growth would mean 2 percent inflation, not $\frac{1}{2}$ percent. Assuming a $\frac{1}{2}$ percent rate of inflation thus leads to a contradiction.

By much the same reasoning, we can show that unemployment cannot be lower than what is shown by the intersection of our two curves. Suppose that we wanted unemployment to be 3 percent. The Phillips curve shows us that this would require inflation of about $1\frac{1}{2}$ percent. Three percent unemployment, though, would mean a 6 percent growth of real output. To have 6 percent growth of real output and 3 percent inflation, nominal output would have to grow not by 5 percent, but by 9 percent. Once again we have a contradiction.

To repeat, only one combination of inflation and unemployment is possible once the growth of nominal output and the initial unemployment rate are given. Our theory of inflation is complete.

Economic Policy and the Dynamics of Inflation

We now have a simple but powerful set of tools for determining the effects of economic policy. Chapters 8 through 13 gave us the theory we need to know how fiscal and monetary policy affect nominal national income and product. Now the Phillips curve and inflationary pressure curve tell us how any given change in nominal output will be split up between change in real output and change in the price level. In the remainder of this chapter, we shall use these new tools to explain how certain patterns of economic policy, extending over a period of years, can produce the dynamic swings of inflation and unemployment that take place in the economy around us.

Acceleration

The first pattern we shall examine is the repeated application of expansionary monetary or fiscal policy over a series of years. Let us go back to Exhibit 16.2. There we saw that, beginning from a standing start, a 5 percent expansion of nominal GNP produced a drop in unemployment of almost 1½ percent at the cost of less than 1 percent inflation. Policy makers would have every reason to be very pleased with those results. They would be so pleased, in fact, that they would surely want to try another dose of the same medicine. In the second year, unfortunately, a further 5 percent expansion of nominal GNP would not be split up so favorably between inflationary and real output effects. There are two reasons for this.

First of all, to get continued growth of real output, it is not enough just to keep unemployment at a low level. We need a further drop in unemployment. Yet the farther to the left we go along the Phillips curve, the steeper the curve gets. This means that a bigger dose of unexpected inflation is needed to give each percentage point reduction in unemployment.

Also, in the second year of expansionary policy, the government no longer has the advantage of a standing start. People have experienced some inflation, even though mild, and some of them may be alert enough to realize that continued expansionary policy will bring more. Once people come to *expect* inflation, the short-run Phillips curve begins to shift upward. That too makes the inflation–unemployment trade-off less attractive than in the first year.

We see, then, that although a second year of expansionary policy is likely to produce some further gain in unemployment and real output, the cost in terms of inflation will be higher than before. In subsequent years, the trade-off will get less favorable still. Soon it will not be enough just to repeat the original policy of 5 percent growth of nominal output. Nominal output will have to expand faster and faster. The economy will then have reached the situation shown in Exhibit 16.3, where the inflationary pressure curve has to shift up each year just to keep even with the upward drift of the short-run Phillips curve.

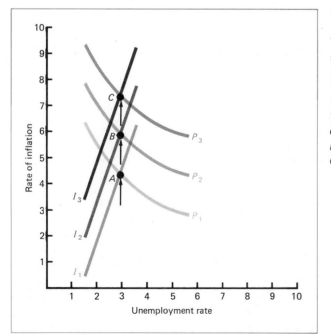

EXHIBIT 16.3

The effects of prolonged acceleration.
To keep unemployment below the natural rate for a sustained period requires a continuous acceleration of inflation. The actual rate of inflation must always be higher than the expected rate. Here, as rising inflationary expectations push the Phillips curves up from P_1 to P_2 to P_3, accelerating growth of nominal output shifts the inflationary pressure curve from I_1 to I_2 to I_3. A, B, and C are successive positions of the economy as acceleration continues.

EXHIBIT 16.4

The Kennedy-Johnson acceleration

During the Kennedy and Johnson administrations, the economy expanded almost without interruption. (Exceptions were the hesitation over Kennedy's tax cut in 1963, and the "Fed's finest hour" in 1966.) Accelerating inflation pulled unemployment well below the natural rate and kept it there for several years in a row.

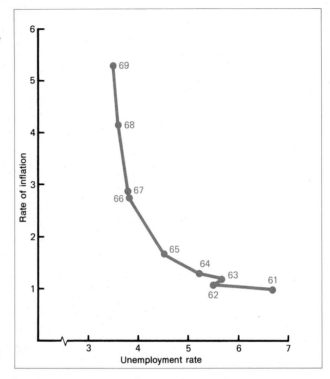

Source: Data from *Economic Report of the President* (Washington, D.C.: U.S. Government Printing Office, 1976).

We can put what we have learned in the form of an important generalization: *To keep unemployment below the natural rate for a sustained period requires a continuous acceleration of inflation.* A case study will show this principle in action.

CASE 16.1
Acceleration in the Kennedy-Johnson Era

As we have mentioned before, John Kennedy came to office in 1960 with the declared intention to "get the country moving again" after two recessions late in the Eisenhower administration. President Lyndon Johnson, who succeeded him, was equally determined to pursue an expansionary policy. Economists are still debating the relative importance of the Kennedy tax cut, heavy defense spending, and rapid monetary growth, but there is no doubt that in combination these policies were as expansionary as anyone could have wished. The result was what Johnson proudly called "the longest peacetime (*sic*) expansion in American history."

Exhibit 16.4 shows the unemployment-inflation record for the economy during the Kennedy-Johnson era. The pattern is much what our theory would lead us to expect. Expansionary policy at first produced substantial gains in employment with little inflation penalty. From the year of the Kennedy tax cut on, though, each successive reduction in unemployment was accompanied by a bigger jump in prices. By the end of Johnson's term in office, inflation was rising higher and higher each year just to keep unemployment where it was, substantially below what anyone would consider its natural rate.

Deceleration

In theory, there is no limit to the number of years that unemployment can be held below its natural rate by continued acceleration. In practice, though, political pressures eventually build up to "do something" about inflation. The most obvious thing to do is to put on the monetary and fiscal brakes, and decelerate the growth of aggregate demand. It is not necessary actually to cut aggregate demand in nominal terms—just to reduce its rate of growth.

As might be expected, the effects of deceleration are much like the initial effects of expansion, taken in reverse. As deceleration begins, aggregate demand will not grow as fast as firms have foreseen when making their production, pricing, and inventory plans. The result will be unplanned inventory accumulation. As stocks of unsold goods pile up, some firms will react by cutting prices (or at least raising them less than they had planned), while others will cut back production.

The production cutbacks will mean fewer job openings. They will also mean that those firms still taking on workers will be able to get the personnel they want without offering such high wages as they would otherwise have had to. Remember, though, that the deceleration is at first unexpected. Workers who have become used to low unemployment and steady inflation will set out to look for jobs with high reservation wages. At first, they will not realize that conditions in the labor market as a whole have changed. Each will attribute his difficulty in finding a job to individual bad luck. The average duration of job search will lengthen, and the unemployment rate will rise.

A word should be said about the unionized sector of the labor market. Inflationary expectations play an important role in labor-management negotiations. If, as deceleration begins, both parties expect prices to continue rising as before, they are likely to agree on nominal wage increases that fully reflect those expectations. To the extent that nominal wages in unionized industries continue to rise rapidly, however, job openings in these industries will become even scarcer than they otherwise would be, as demand falls off. High wage settlements in unionized industries will thus make the job search prospects of the unemployed that much more difficult.

Inflationary Recession

Inflationary Recession A period of rising unemployment during which the rate of inflation remains high, or even continues to rise.

What happens next can be called an **inflationary recession.**[2] Unemployment goes up, real output goes down, and prices continue to rise, perhaps temporarily even faster than before.

Exhibit 16.5 gives a graphical interpretation. This diagram starts where Exhibit 16.3 left off, at the end of a sustained acceleration. Expected inflation of 6 percent has pushed the short-run Phillips curve up to the position P_1. Policy makers have raised the rate of growth of nominal output to $7\frac{1}{2}$ percent, which puts the inflationary pressure curve at I_1. The economy is at point A. Actual inflation is still running ahead of expected inflation, and unemployment is a full two percentage points below its natural rate.

Then the brakes are applied. The next year, growth of aggregate demand is cut back to 3 percent, shifting the inflationary pressure curve to I_2. Inflationary expectations are still moving up. Last year people expected

---

[2]The phenomenon of inflationary recession is new enough that there is no single established name for it. News writers often employ such unpleasant-sounding hybrid words as "stagflation" or "slumpflation."

EXHIBIT 16.5
Inflationary recession

This exhibit begins where Exhibit 16.3 left off, at the end of a period of prolonged acceleration. Expected inflation is initially 6 percent with actual inflation even higher, 7½ percent, putting the economy at *A*. Then the rate of growth of nominal output is cut from 7½ percent to 3 percent, shifting the inflationary pressure curve to *I*₂. Inflationary expectations, based on last year's actual rate, push the Phillips curve up to *P*₂, so the economy moves from *A* to *B*, an inflationary recession.

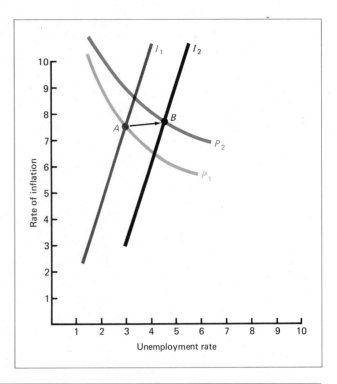

inflation to be only 6 percent when in fact it was 7½ percent. This year they expect inflation to be at least that high, which moves the Phillips curve up to the position P_2. The inflationary expectations are vindicated. The economy moves from point *A* to point *B*. Deceleration has brought on an inflationary recession.

Cost-Push Inflation

During an inflationary recession, cost-push inflation becomes important. In Chapter 14 we saw that two conditions must be met for true cost-push inflation (as distinct from the cost-push illusion) to occur. The first condition is that some force must be present that will touch off a rise in wages or prices when demand is not rising. The second is that something must prevent prices and wages in competitive markets from falling when wages or prices in more monopolistic markets rise.

During inflationary recession, just the conditions we need are present. In highly concentrated and highly unionized industries, inflationary expectations cause wages and prices to keep rising, even when demand begins to slow down. These wage and price increases mean fewer jobs in the sectors affected. We cannot count on falling wages in nonunionized sectors to take up the slack in employment. Any decline in wage offers that occurred while inflationary expectations continued to push up reservation wages would only lengthen the average period of job search and raise unemployment still further.

The cost-push theory of inflation comes into its own during an inflationary recession. In such a period, demand-pull and cost-push inflation are not conflicting interpretations of the same thing. Instead, the latter occurs as an aftereffect of the former.

Continued Deceleration

An inflationary recession is the worst of all possible worlds. It occurs when expected inflation rises while actual inflationary pressure is decreasing. Once people begin to realize that the brakes have been applied, things stop getting worse and start getting better. Once inflation peaks, the Phillips curve stops shifting upward, and begins to fall. Continued moderate growth of aggregate demand can then begin to slow inflation without making unemployment worse. In principle, by holding unemployment above the natural rate for an extended period, the economy could be brought to a "soft landing." Inflationary expectations could be reduced to zero, and then unemployment could be eased back to the natural rate with prices stable. Such a prolonged deceleration would be the downside equivalent of the continued acceleration we showed in Exhibit 16.3.

Reflation

Reflation An expansion of aggregate demand after a period of high unemployment and decelerating inflation. Reflation brings substantial short-term gains in employment with little or no inflationary penalty.

In the real world, though, a "soft landing" is difficult to achieve. Just as prolonged acceleration generates political pressure to "do something" about inflation, prolonged deceleration brings pressure to "do something" about unemployment. It is always politically tempting to respond to these pressures and **reflate.** In the first stages of a reflation, before inflationary expectations are rekindled, it is possible to get a big increase in real output with little penalty in terms of prices. In fact, if renewed expansion of aggregate demand starts while the Phillips curve is still drifting downward, it is perfectly possible to enjoy a few months when both inflation and unemployment are falling. Reflation is thus the mirror image of inflationary recession.

Stop-Go

Although reflation brings the best of all possible economic worlds, its effects are only temporary. As soon as expectations adjust to what has happened, higher inflationary penalties will once again have to be paid, just to hold on to the gains in unemployment. We are back in familiar territory, having completed a cycle.

Stop-Go Policy A cycle of acceleration, inflationary recession, deceleration, and reflation brought about by alternating political pressures to "do something" first about inflation and then about unemployment.

The cycle of acceleration, inflationary recession, deceleration, and reflation is popularly known as **stop-go policy.** Unlike the traditional business cycle, which economists have known about for more than a century, the origins of the stop-go cycle are more political than economic. Perhaps we can even say that the stop-go cycle is a peculiarity of democratic politics (little "d," not big "D"—Republicans are not immune). In an election year, it is particularly difficult to resist the short-run gains of reflation, or to take the initial steps to end run-away acceleration.

Inflationary Bias

To add the final touch to our discussion of stop-go, we must mention a possibility we have not yet considered. It may be that, on the average, the political system is more sensitive to the type of political pressures that arise from unemployment than to those arising from inflation. If this is the case, the symmetry of the stop-go pattern is destroyed. We shall not work through all the details of what happens when an inflationary bias is added to a policy of stop-go stabilization, but Exhibit 16.6 gives a sketch of the process. The economy goes into an upward spiral because the upward push

EXHIBIT 16.6
Stop-go with an inflationary bias
The so-called "stop-go" cycle means the alternation of acceleration, inflationary recession, deceleration, and reflation, as political pressure builds up first to "do something" about inflation and then to "do something" about unemployment. If the pressures to reduce unemployment are, on the average, stronger than the pressures to control inflation, the stop-go cycle may be given an upward bias. Each time around, the cycle spirals higher, as this sketch indicates.

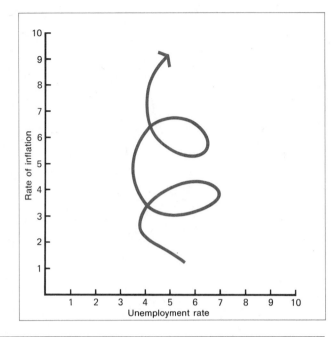

that the economy is given during the acceleration phase of the stop-go cycle is longer and more vigorous than the downward push it receives during the recessionary phase.

Conclusions

Sometimes economists construct theories purely for their own sake. The most interesting economic theories, though, are the ones that help us to interpret actual economic events. The theory of inflation presented in this chapter appears to be one of these. As simple as it is (lots of qualifications and elaborations would be added in an advanced course), it gives us some very useful insights, as one last case study will show.

CASE 16.2
Recent American Experience with
Unemployment and Inflation
Exhibit 16.7 presents actual data on inflation and unemployment in the American economy from 1954 to 1975. We have already examined one part of this record, the Kennedy-Johnson acceleration. Now let us look at some other features.

The overall impression one gets from the figure is that of a series of roughly triangular clockwise loops. Although the lengths and strengths of successive accelerations and decelerations are rather irregular, it does not take much imagination to see an upward spiral of sorts. There is at least a rough resemblance of this figure to the one we drew in Exhibit 16.6.

Although the rate of inflation has drifted up over the years, it has not moved up over every single cycle. Consider the period following the recession of 1957. The recovery from this recession was very weak. The vertical line drawn between the points for 1959 and 1960, which forms the upward side of the next triangular loop, is shorter and farther to the right than most. This weak recovery seems to have happened because Eisenhower had been

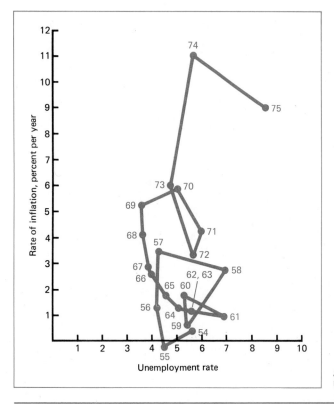

EXHIBIT 16.7
Recent U.S. experience with inflation and unemployment
Since 1954, inflation and unemployment have spiraled upward in a series of roughly triangular loops. One cycle, that which followed the 1957 recession, was cut off before the previous peak of inflation had been reached. In 1973–1974, inflation reached an especially high peak because internationally generated commodity inflation was added to domestic inflationary pressures. Inflation is given as year-to-year percentage increase in the consumer price index.

Source: Data from *Economic Report of the President* (Washington, D.C.: U.S. Government Printing Office, 1976).

frightened by the inflation of 1956 and 1957, and did not want to repeat the experience. Tight monetary policy cut the recovery off before the previous peak of inflation was reached.

The last loop in the series, in contrast, is extraordinarily stretched out. In part, the new highs in the inflation can be blamed on the fact that the 1972 recession did not last long enough to purge inflationary expectations entirely. Reflation began from a higher level than it ever had before. That is not the whole story, however. In the years 1973 and 1974, some special cost-push elements must be taken into account.

First, 1973 and 1974 saw a "price bulge" as an aftereffect of Nixon's 1971–1972 price and wage controls. (These controls will be discussed more fully in the next chapter.) On top of this came two strong sources of commodity inflation. One of these was the fourfold rise in oil prices after 1974. The other was the near-doubling of food prices, also largely touched off by events outside U.S. borders. Finally, a decline in the exchange rate at which the dollar traded against foreign currencies added still more cost-push pressure. Exhibit 16.8 attempts to give some rough estimates of the importance of each of these cost-push elements. According to the numbers shown there, inflation would have been a little higher in 1971 and 1972 without controls. In 1973 and 1974, by comparison, inflation would have been considerably less if outside influences had not combined so forcefully.

SUMMARY

1. For a given rate of growth of nominal GNP, the rate of inflation depends on what happens to real GNP. For a given initial level of unemployment, the growth of real GNP depends on how unemployment moves (Okun's law).

EXHIBIT 16.8

Actual and estimated changes in percent rates of inflation*

Inflation in 1973 and 1974 was worse than it would otherwise have been because of several special cost-push factors. One was the "price bulge" following the end of Nixon's wage and price controls. Another was the oil crisis. A third was devaluation of the dollar in international exchange markets, and a fourth the rise in other commodity prices, especially food. These figures should not be taken as exact, but they do indicate the relative importance of the various special influences.

	1971	1972	1973	1974	Total
	Actual Change				
	4.3	3.3	6.2	11.0	24.8%
	Change due to				*Total Changes*
Oil crisis	0	0	0	+2.0	+2.0%
Wage and price controls	−0.5	−2.0	+0.5	+2.0	0
Depreciation of exchange rates		+0.5	+2.0	+0.5	+3.0%
Internationally generated non-oil commodity price increases		+0.5	+1.0	+1.5	+3.0%
Total changes	−0.5	−1.0	+3.5	+6.0	+8.0%

*Calculated from annual averages of the consumer price index.

Putting these two propositions together gives us the inflationary pressure curve, which relates inflation to unemployment, given the rate of nominal growth and the initial unemployment rate. The inflationary pressure curve has a slope of about + 3, indicating that each percentage point reduction in unemployment cuts three points off the inflation rate. An increase in the rate of growth of nominal output, or a reduction in the initial rate of unemployment, shifts the inflationary pressure curve to the left. Opposite changes shift it to the right.

2. Together, the inflationary pressure curve and the Phillips curve determine the rates of inflation and unemployment *given* (a) the rate of growth of nominal national product, as determined by monetary and fiscal policy; (b) the initial rate of unemployment; and (c) the level of inflationary expectations, which determines the height of the Phillips curve. To assume levels of inflation or unemployment other than those shown by the intersection of the two curves must lead to a contradiction.

3. To keep unemployment below the natural rate requires that the actual rate of inflation must be higher than the expected rate of inflation. Because people tend to expect what has happened in the immediate past to continue to happen in the future, inflationary expectations tend to catch up with the actual rate of inflation. Only by continually accelerating the rate of inflation, so that expectations never catch up with actuality, can the unemployment rate be kept below the natural rate for a prolonged period.

4. An inflationary recession is the worst of both worlds. Fiscal or monetary brakes cut the rate of growth of nominal output, but past inflationary experience continues temporarily to push up inflationary expectations and the Phillips curve. The result is a combination of rising unemployment and high or even increasing inflation. Once people become aware that the brakes have been applied and inflation has been checked, inflationary expectations will fall and eventually the economy can be decelerated to a "soft landing."

5. During a prolonged period of acceleration, political pressures build up to "do something" about inflation. Similarly, during a prolonged deceleration, pressures build up to take action on unemployment. The result can be a stop-go cycle of alternating acceleration, inflationary recession, deceleration, and reflation. If the political system is, on the average, more sensitive to unemployment than to inflation, the stop-go cycle can be given an upward bias, sending the rate of inflation spiraling upward over time.

DISCUSSION QUESTIONS

1. If after a long period of relatively steady prices there is an increase in aggregate demand, why would the initial increase in prices be strictly demand-pull inflation? Why would cost-push elements not appear right away?

2. In some periods and some countries, the government has used the acceleration technique to keep unemployment low for long periods. All the time they were doing it, however, they continually issued statements to the effect that they were keeping a watchful eye on prices, that they viewed price stability as an important goal, and so on. Do you think such statements might serve any actual economic purpose? Do you think it would make any difference if the government just announced, "OK, it is our policy to keep unemployment low, so we are going to let the rate of inflation climb each year by 2 percent above what it was the year before"?

3. Suppose that some private economic research organization discovered a 100 percent accurate and reliable method of forecasting next year's rate of inflation. Why might the government want to prevent this forecast from being published? What do you think would be the effect on the shape of the Phillips curve if the forecast were widely published, and were widely known to be accurate.

4. What effect do you think shortening the period between national elections would have on economic policy? What effect would lengthening the period have? What effect would there be if the government could call an election any time it wanted, as in some parliamentary systems? Under the last option, under what economic conditions do you think the government would most frequently decide to call an election?

5. Go to the newspaper, or to some government source such as the *Survey of Current Business* or the *Economic Report of the President,* and find inflation and unemployment statistics for 1976 and beyond. Include forecasts for the current year if you can find them. Plot these new data on Exhibit 16.7. Do they fall where you expect? Write a paragraph interpreting the newest data.

Appendix
Inflation and
the Money Market

This appendix is an extension of Chapters 11 through 13, where we discussed the role of money in the economy. It explains how our theory of money and aggregate demand can be modified to take inflation into account. Here, as throughout Chapters 15 and 16, inflationary expectations play an important part in the story.

Real and Nominal Rates of Interest

Let us begin by looking at a person who is about to lend $100 for one year. Suppose that he wants a 5 percent rate of return. If he receives $105 in principal plus interest at the end of the year, and there has been no inflation, he will be satisfied. But what if there has been 5 percent inflation? The $105 our lender is repaid would then be worth no more than the $100 he loaned. Although he would still have earned $5 measured in nominal terms, his *real* return would have been zero.

This example suggests that when there is inflation, we need to distinguish between real and nominal rates of interest. By the nominal rate of interest, we mean the rate of interest measured in current dollars, and by the real rate, we mean the nominal rate adjusted for inflation. There is a well-known theory to explain how the real and nominal rates are related. This theory was first set forth by Yale economist Irving Fisher at the turn of the century. In Fisher's theory, the nominal rate of interest will be approximately equal to the real rate of interest plus the expected rate of inflation.

This theory clearly makes sense. If a lender were willing to part with his money only if guaranteed a 5 percent rate of return when he expected no inflation, it stands to reason that he would ask for a 10 percent nominal return if he expected prices to rise by 5 percent. Experience seems to bear out the theory, at least roughly. Interest rates have been higher than ever before in recent years of record inflation. It is true that interest rates have not risen enough to protect real rates of return fully against increases in prices, and that in some years, actual real interest rates have been negative. Such facts, however, do not directly contradict Fisher's theory. It could simply be that in the worst years, inflation was higher than it was expected to be.

Interest and Investment

The theory of aggregate demand set forth in Chapter 13 did not use the distinction between real and nominal rates of interest. For periods of zero or low inflationary expectations, this does not make much difference, but the theory should be slightly modified to apply to inflationary periods.

First, the theory of money demand. The process of adjusting portfolios between bonds and money, which underlies the theory of the demand for money, works in terms of nominal rates of interest. It is the nominal rate that indicates the relative advantage of holding bonds rather than money.

Suppose that the nominal rate is 10 percent and inflation is zero. The real cost of holding money in such a case is the loss of an opportunity to earn a 10 percent real rate of return on bonds. Alternatively, suppose that the nominal rate is 10 percent, but expected inflation is 5 percent. In this case, the real cost of holding money is the loss of an opportunity to earn a 5 percent real rate of return on bonds, plus a second cost in the form of a 5 percent per year deterioration of the purchasing power of the money itself. Together the two costs total 10 percent. In either case, the relative attractiveness of bonds and money is the same. It follows that when we draw a money demand curve, we should label the vertical axis the nominal rate of interest.

In contrast, for planned investment, it is the real rate that counts. Suppose that a firm is willing to borrow $1,000 at 5 percent to buy a doughnut machine when the price of doughnuts (and of everything else) is expected to remain unchanged. Will the firm not then be willing to borrow $1,000 at a nominal 10 percent if it expects the price of the doughnuts it sells (and of everything else) to rise at 5 percent per year? Investment plans are made in terms of the real rate of interest, so it is the real rate that should go on the verticle axis when we draw a planned investment schedule.

In order to modify our theory of the determination of aggregate nominal demand to fit inflationary periods, then, we must use the nominal rate of interest in the money market and the real rate for the planned investment schedule. The reader can easily see how the diagrams of Chapter 13 could be changed to do this. All we would have to do would be to subtract the expected rate of inflation when numbering the vertical axis of the planned investment schedule.

Paradox

The distinction between the real and nominal rate of interest can be used to explain an apparent paradox of monetary policy. Our theory of Chapters 12 and 13 suggested that increasing the money supply would lower the rate of interest. Yet consider a period such as the late 1960s for the U.S. economy. From 1965 to 1970 the Federal Reserve allowed the money supply to grow at a rate of over 5 percent per year (contrasted to an average rate of growth from 1952 to 1964 of less than 2 percent). Nonetheless, the market yield on corporate bonds rose from under 5 percent to over 8 percent.

This "paradox," of course, has a simple resolution. The expansion of the money supply led to a rise in the rate of inflation from 1.9 percent per year in 1965 to 5.5 percent per year in 1970. The accelerating inflation widened the gap between the real and nominal rates of interest. With the real rate roughly steady during the period, the nominal rate went up. We see then that, in the long run, as inflationary expectations adjust to observed rates of inflation, expansionary monetary policy can actually cause the nominal rate of interest to rise rather than fall.

Error

Failure to keep in mind the distinction between real and nominal rates of interest can lead to serious errors in interpreting monetary policy. Traditionally people have tended to watch market rates of interest—that is, nominal rates—for an indication of the direction of monetary policy. A drop in rates was taken to indicate expansionary policy, and a rise to indicate restrictive policy.

This is all quite reasonable for a noninflationary world. In an inflationary period, though, market rates of interest do not give an accurate picture of monetary policy at all. In the late 1960s, for example, many people, apparently even including some at the Fed itself, were misled. They thought that because market interest rates were rising, monetary policy was taking a restrictive course and hence helping to combat inflation. In fact, exactly the opposite was true. The rapid growth in the money supply was helping to contribute to inflation. Because interest rates can be misleading in inflationary periods, it is now becoming more and more accepted to concentrate on rates of change of the money supply itself as an indicator of the direction of monetary policy, rather than to concentrate on market interest rates.

CHAPTER 17
The Future of Stabilization Policy

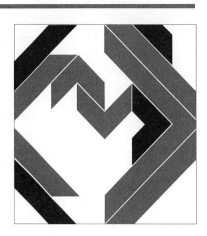

What You Will Learn in This Chapter
The postwar economic record has not been good. This has given rise to the charge that economic stabilization through the management of aggregate demand has failed. Our theory of inflation and unemployment helps us understand what truth there is to these charges. So does an understanding of lags in policy making. Now many economists are looking beyond demand management to new tools of economic stabilization. Two such tools are incomes policy and indexing.

For Review
Here are some important terms and concepts that will be put to use in this chapter. Be certain that you understand them, or review them before proceeding.
> Fiscal and monetary policy (Chapters 8–13)
> The Phillips curve (Chapter 14)
> Cost-push inflation (Chapter 14)

The Great Depression of the 1930s had many lasting effects on economic policy and economic thought. One of those effects was to give the government increased responsibility for economic stabilization. The Employment Act of 1946 made this the law of the land. Influenced by the work of Keynes, economists chose **demand management** as the key tool of stabilization policy. If the economy slumped and too many people were out of work, a boost to aggregate demand would plug the contractionary gap and fix things up. If a boom got too hot and prices rose too fast, putting the damper on demand would cool things off. Given the political will, there seemed reason to hope that the economy could be "fine-tuned" for prosperity without inflation.

Sad to say, the postwar economic record has not been good. Perhaps we could forgive some early policy mistakes if there were a clear trend toward increasing stability, but there has been no such trend. By the 1970s, the economy was in worse shape than at any time for forty years. This experience has cast doubt on the whole idea of stability through demand management.

Demand Management A general term for the fiscal and monetary policies used to control aggregate demand for purposes of economic stabilization.

In this chapter we shall look at the source of those doubts, and at the new directions that economic thinking is taking in response to them. First we shall recap the theory we have developed in the last three chapters. Using that as a basis, we shall look at two competing philosophies of demand management: fine tuning and policy rules. Finally, we shall discuss some ideas that look beyond demand management for an answer to our problems.

Inflation, Unemployment, and Aggregate Demand—A Recap

To understand recent economic events, we must know how demand management policies affect inflation and unemployment. Let us begin, then, by restating what we have learned. The four traditional theories that we introduced in Chapter 14 will give us a framework for this brief recap.

Nominal Income Determination

The first two traditional theories we looked at were the crude quantity theory of inflation and the crude Keynesian theory. Neither of these theories gives a complete explanation of inflation and unemployment. Put together and brought up to date, though, they do give us a pretty good idea of how demand management policies determine nominal national income and product. That is an important first step.

Expectations and the Phillips Curve

The next traditional theory we looked at was the Phillips curve. The Phillips curve tells us that, in the short run at least, there is a trade-off between inflation and unemployment. Demand management can give us more jobs if we can stand a rise in prices, or it can cut the rate of inflation if we do not mind seeing a few more people out of work. In the long run, though, the Phillips curve does not give us a simple, stable trade-off. That is because it is not so much the rate of inflation that matters for unemployment as *changes* in the rate of inflation.

One idea more than any other helps us to understand how the Phillips curve really works. That is the idea that people make their plans for working and producing on the basis of what they *expect* to happen, not on the basis of what is actually happening. They must do this for the simple reason that they do not find out about what is actually happening until after it has happened.

Think of what goes on, then, when the rate of inflation changes. When inflation speeds up, employers offer workers fatter wage deals than they expected to get, and workers snap up the jobs. Unemployment goes down for a while, until people find out what prices are really doing. Higher prices mean that the workers' big new paychecks do not buy any more than before. Once workers come to expect inflation, they start shopping around for even better jobs, and unemployment rises again.

On the down side, something similar happens. When inflation first starts to drop, people will be caught unaware. Firms will still be willing to meet high wage demands because they expect to get the money back in higher prices. Instead, it turns out that they cannot sell as much as they had hoped at the higher prices, so they cut back output and lay workers off. Only when they come to expect the lower inflation will they get their plans straightened out and get production back to normal.

Cost-Push

This brings us to cost-push, our fourth traditional theory of inflation. The idea of expectations helps us see how cost-push fits into the picture. When inflation stops going up and starts coming down, workers and union negotiators will be taken by surprise at least for a while. They will keep demanding big pay increases to keep up with the inflation they think is going to get worse. Firms will grant those increases because they also think that inflation is still going up. Remember that true cost-push inflation requires that there be some force to push prices and wages up even when demand is not rising. Now we see that when expectations are slow in adjusting to an actual slowdown of inflation, just the right conditions for cost-push are created.[1]

Markets and the Use of Knowledge

This, then, is a rough outline of the theory of inflation and unemployment we have built in the last three chapters. Now that all the pieces are in place, we can see that this theory builds on the fundamental insight that markets are mechanisms for putting knowledge to use. In the best of times, we know that the plans of businesspeople, workers, and consumers do not always mesh. Some people make mistakes, while other lucky ones make windfall gains. Lots of little errors tend to cancel one another out.

Sudden changes in the rate of inflation, though, add something new to the picture. Such changes can mean that, for a while, *everyone will tend to make mistakes in the same direction at once*. When inflation speeds up, not just a few workers, but a great many will accept pay deals that turn out not to be so good after all. When inflation slows down, not just a few firms but many will find themselves stuck with wage bills and price lists that are higher than they ought to be. These widespread errors give rise to the changes in unemployment that are the familiar by-product of changes in the rate of inflation.

Are we saying, then, that people are fools? Not at all. People are smart. They learn from experience. All we are saying is that learning does not take place at the speed of light. A little time passes after actual events change their course before people adjust their plans and expectations to new conditions. In the meantime, people may be led to do things they would not do if they had complete knowledge of economic conditions.

Policy Implications

Our understanding of inflation and unemployment contains some important implications for economic policy. We discussed these in detail in Chapter 16, but it is worth listing three of them here again.

1. Unexpected increases in the rate of inflation pull the rate of unem-

---

[1]Another kind of cost-push inflation has also been important recently. That is commodity inflation brought about by increases in the international prices of oil, food, and some other goods. See Case 16.2 for a discussion of recent commodity inflation.

ployment below what it otherwise would be. It follows that if policy makers allow inflation to run faster and faster year after year, they can keep unemployment low for quite a while.

2. When inflation slows after a long period of acceleration, we end up in the worst of all possible worlds. Inflationary expectations generate cost-push inflation while the slowdown of demand pushes up unemployment. The worse the inflation, the more distasteful is the cure.

3. Recession cures inflation, but only slowly. After the cure is underway and prices are falling, a quick step-up of aggregate demand (reflation) temporarily brings the best of both worlds. Until expectations adjust to the reversal of policy, we get the best of all possible worlds: falling unemployment without rising inflation.

With these conclusions in mind, let us turn now to the debate over the future of demand management.

Fine Tuning versus Policy Rules

When economists express a fear that demand management has failed, they do not mean that it has failed to have any effect on the economy. Everyone grants that the level of aggregate demand, measured in nominal terms, has a powerful influence on economic life. Disputes about the relative importance of monetary or fiscal tools of demand management should not obscure this agreement. Instead, doubts about demand management are doubts about whether the particular policies that have been pursued have had a *stabilizing* effect. The fear is that the powerful tools of demand management, if misused, can have results opposite to those intended.

Much of the debate over demand management revolves around two different philosophies of how such policies should be used. One group of economists takes an activist line. They think that the federal government should make frequent and vigorous use of both fiscal and monetary policy tools in order to *fine-tune* the economy. That way we can hope to get just the desired mix of high employment, high real growth, and price stability. Others argue that attempts to fine-tune usually do more harm than good. They should be replaced by a policy of "steady-as-you-go," governed by *rules* that remain unchanged over long periods.

The Case for Fine Tuning

The case for fine tuning is based on three beliefs about the economic and political system of a modern democracy like the United States. The first is the belief that, left to itself, the private economy is unstable. The second is the belief that the tools of demand management work fairly rapidly and predictably. The third belief is that, with careful scientific argument and patient persuasion, government authorities can be educated to use the tools of demand management in the best long-run interest of the public at large.

The belief that the private economy is unstable has a long history. For nearly two hundred years there have been alternating periods of boom and depression in market economies. By World War II, a whole branch of economic theory had grown up to support this view, under the name of business-cycle theory. The Great Depression reinforced the idea of instability in the minds of all those who lived through it.

The idea that fiscal and monetary policy are quick and predictable in their effects on the economy is part and parcel of the Keynesian tradition. It is supported by much of the theory presented in Chapters 8 through 13 of this book.

Then there is the idea that in a democratic nation political power will end up in the hands of politicians who will use the tools of policy wisely. This is an outgrowth of the American liberal tradition as it has developed from Franklin Roosevelt's New Deal to John Kennedy's New Frontier.

Experience

The fine-tuners came into their own in the Kennedy-Johnson era. Initially, their policies met with success. The years 1961 to 1969 saw the longest period of "peacetime" expansion in the history of the United States. Since that time something has gone wrong. Economic instability has increased. A stop-go policy cycle has pushed the economy into widening swings of unemployment and inflation. It looks, then, as if at least part of the fine-tuner's argument must be incorrect. Either the tools of activist monetary and fiscal policy do not work as quickly and predictably as they should, or else the tools have been badly mishandled. Let us see what the opponents of fine tuning have to say.

The Case against Fine Tuning

Opponents of fine tuning challenge every aspect of the case we have just set forth. They claim that their historical studies show the private economy to be less unstable than is often thought. They are sceptical that politicians have the courage to keep long-run economic goals in mind when faced, in the short run, with the need for reelection. But the most telling point in the case against fine tuning is a challenge to the idea that the effects of demand management are either quick or predictable.

Lags

In recent years, economists have begun to worry more and more about lags and delays in the operation of fiscal and monetary policy. There are two major kinds of lags. First, there is the so-called **inside lag,** which is the delay between the time policy action is needed and the time action is taken. Second, there is the **outside lag,** which is the delay between the time policy action is taken and the time its effects on the economy are felt.

The inside lag has several sources. An important one is the time it takes to gather accurate economic statistics. During the famous episode of "the Fed's finest hour," President Johnson would probably have resisted tight monetary policy less if he had known how fast demand was already expanding. In late 1972 and early 1973, both monetary and fiscal policy might have been tighter if people in Washington had known in time of shortages that were developing in key industries. And in 1974, restrictive policy might have been relaxed earlier if it had been known how rapidly business inven-

Inside Lag The delay between the time a policy action is needed and the time policy action is taken.

Outside Lag The delay between the time policy action is taken and the time its effects on the economy are felt.

tories were piling up.[2] A second source of inside lag is the legislative process of Congress. This is particularly serious for fiscal policy. (Recall that the Kennedy tax cut took over two years to reach the statute books.) Because the Federal Reserve Board is independent of Congress, the inside lag for monetary policy is probably a little shorter than for fiscal policy.

The causes of the outside lag for fiscal and monetary policy are not really very well understood, but it is well established that the lag is a serious one. For monetary policy, it is likely to be at least six months before the first important effects of a policy change are felt, and perhaps two years before all the effects have worked through the system. It is sometimes thought that fiscal policy suffers from a shorter outside lag, although just how much shorter is not clear.

Destabilization

Lags make fine tuning very hard. You can understand this if you have ever stood under a shower when the water pressure changed. First you are scalded. When you try to adjust the taps, you find that there is a lag of a few seconds between the time you turn them and the time the water coming out changes in temperature. You overreact to the scalding and are next frozen. By the time you get the system fine-tuned again, the water pressure is probably back where it was in the first place anyway. You might just as well have stepped aside and waited.

The point is that when there are lags, policy actions can have a destabilizing rather than a stabilizing effect. A policy that is intended to speed recovery from a recession may take effect only in time to make inflation worse when recovery is already under way. An action intended to cool off a boom may take hold in the bottom of the next recession when it is least wanted.

Rules

What do the opponents of fine tuning offer in its place? Specific suggestions vary. A common theme, though, is that demand management should be made subject to explicit, long-term rules rather than being left to the discretion of policy makers.

Milton Friedman has for years tried to popularize the idea of a monetary policy rule. He suggests that the Fed should be required by law to keep money growth to the same steady pace year after year. Friedman thinks the constancy of the pace matters more than the specific rate, but suggests that a good target would be equal to the long-run growth of potential GNP. That would be somewhere in the neighborhood of 4 percent per year.

Full Employment Balanced Budget A rule under which tax and spending policy would be adjusted so that the federal budget would be in balance if the economy were at full employment.

The most often mentioned idea for a fiscal policy rule is the **full employment balanced budget.** Under such a rule, Congress and the President would decide the level of government purchases solely on the basis of the actual needs they see for defense, housing, health care, and so forth. No attention would be paid at this stage to the macroeconomic effects of

[2]These examples are given by Herbert Stein, who served as Chairman of the Council of Economic Advisors under President Nixon, in *Economic Planning and the Improvement of Economic Policy* (Washington: The American Enterprise Institute, 1975), p. 28.

these policies. Then, having made the spending decisions, they would adjust taxes so that the budget would be in balance if the economy were at full employment. Because actual net taxes change with the size of nominal income, there would still be actual budget deficits in times of recession and surpluses in times of exceptionally high employment. Fiscal policy of a sort of "automatic" variety would exist. This, it is hoped, would have a stabilizing effect on real output.

Discretionary Authority

Needless to say, fine-tuners think that the ideas of monetary rules and full employment balanced budgets are nonsense. Some think instead that more discretion and flexibility are needed, not less. For example, some recommend that the independence of the Federal Reserve be done away with, so that monetary and fiscal policy might be coordinated by the executive branch of government more closely than is now possible. Also, it has often been suggested that the President be given some degree of discretionary fiscal authority. The inside lag would be shortened by letting him order immediate tax cuts or surcharges, or increase or decrease government spending, without prior approval of Congress. But demands for more discretionary policy are heard less often now than they once were. Instead, one gets strong statements of what economic policy cannot do from the highest levels of the economics profession. A significant case study in changing attitudes is provided by this passage from the 1976 *Economic Report of the President:*

CASE 17.1
Humility Comes to the
Council of Economic Advisors

There is a lesson to be drawn from past policy mistakes. The history of monetary and fiscal policies demonstrates that we have a great deal to learn about implementing discretionary policy changes. Our ability to forecast is at best imperfect, especially in an increasingly complex and interdependent world, and the difficulties in forecasting grow larger as we extend the period for which the forecast is made. This is a significant problem because of the time lags involved in altering the pace of economic activity through discretionary monetary and fiscal actions. There is a perception lag in diagnosing the problem, a reaction lag in selecting the appropriate response, and an implementation lag in having the policy prescription accepted and put into effect through our political and administrative processes.

We also lack reliable estimates of how long it takes before the economy responds to policies once they are undertaken and how large the response will be. This is especially true now because the high rates of inflation in recent years have made price expectations much more important . . . than they formerly were, but there has not been sufficient experience to pin down how inflationary processes affect key relationships within the economy. With respect to fiscal policy there is the additional complication that countercyclical increases in Government expenditures are difficult to check during later upswings. Because countercyclical policy changes may be slow to take hold and then hard to reverse, their effects may extend well past the time when they are most needed. Consequently a significant danger exists that, instead of smoothing economic fluctuations, discretionary changes in policy aimed at demand management may themselves become a source of economic instability. . . .

The proper conclusion is not that we should forswear the use of discretionary policy. . . . Discretionary policies do have an important function in our economic system. But we must be mindful of the great difficulties in successfully executing countercyclical policies.

What is called for in our judgment is a steadier course in macroeconomic policies than has been followed in the past. We should set policies broadly consistent with sustainable long-term noninflationary growth and try to limit the size and duration of any policy deviations that promise short-term benefits but risk interfering with our long-run goals.

Beyond Demand Management

In this section we turn our attention to two tools of stabilization policy that we have not yet discussed. These are incomes policies and indexing. The two have a common starting point in the assumption that demand management, at least as practiced in the past, has failed.

Incomes Policies

Incomes Policy   A policy of directly controlling wages, salaries, earnings, and prices in order to fight inflation.

By an **incomes policy,** we mean any policy that directly controls wages, salaries, and earnings for the purpose of fighting inflation. Ordinarily, such policies also include direct controls on wholesale and retail prices. The United States has experimented with incomes policies. Such policies have become a permanent feature of economic life in many Western European countries, Great Britain and Sweden being especially notable examples. It will be worth our while to look at how these policies work, and why they are highly controversial.

Theory of Controls

Let us begin by looking at policies that control prices and wages from a theoretical point of view. The case for controls is strongest as a temporary measure to fight inflationary recession. We have said that when policy makers put on the brakes after a long period of accelerating inflation, we are thrown for a time into the worst of all possible worlds. Workers and employers base their plans on the expectation of more inflation, yet aggregate demand is actually tailing off. Until expectations adjust to reality, wages, prices, and unemployment all rise at once.

Now enter the timely use of an incomes policy. Suppose that just at the moment the fiscal and monetary brakes are put on, the government announces a program of strict price and wage controls. This is done with great fanfare and a show of grim determination to lick inflation once and for all. What is hoped is that workers and businessmen will *believe* that controls are going to stop inflation. If they do, they will revise their inflationary expectations downward much more rapidly than if they had to wait to learn from experience. This revision of expectations will get rid of the cost-push element of the inflationary recession. Workers will know that they do not have to push for high wages to beat inflation, so they will accept the controls. Firms will know that they will not have to pay higher wages, so they will keep their prices in line and concentrate on increasing their sales. The readjustment to price stability and full employment will be more rapid and less painful than it would be without an incomes policy.

Problems with Controls

So much for theory. We may grant that controls are helpful in squeezing the cost-push element out of an inflationary recession. Does that mean that they are a cure-all for the economic problems of our time? Not really. The problem is that controls can be of help in correcting past mistakes in demand management policy, but they cannot work as a substitute for sound demand management. Unfortunate things can happen if we try to use an incomes policy to fight inflation without also slowing the growth of aggregate demand, or if we leave controls in force after a recession is over and a new boom gets underway.

If aggregate demand rises in nominal terms, one of three things must logically happen. First, national product (aggregate supply) could rise in real terms to meet the increased nominal demand without a rise in prices. Second, prices could rise to meet the increase in nominal demand without an increase in output. Finally, neither prices nor output might rise, in which case the aggregate quantity of goods demanded would exceed the aggregate quantity of goods supplied, and there would be an overall shortage of goods. A combination of these three alternatives may sometimes occur, but no fourth alternative is logically possible.

Naturally, the first alternative is the most attractive. That would mean real economic growth without inflation. Real economic growth can come from only two sources, however. One is an increase in potential GNP, which we can hope for at about 4 percent per year in the long run. The other is a fall in unemployment. This source of growth is temporary, because unemployment would soon reach a level below which it could fall no further. In the long run, then, *real growth without inflation or shortages is possible only if demand management limits the growth of nominal GNP to the long-term rate of growth of potential GNP.*

An incomes policy cannot buy us real growth without inflation or shortages if that rule of demand management is not followed. All it can do is determine which of the second two alternatives we get. If aggregate demand is allowed to run away without controls, we get runaway inflation. If controls are applied and demand still runs away, we get shortages, rationing, and black markets.

American Experience with Controls

There have been two major experiments with wage and price controls in the American economy. One was during World War II. Then huge wartime government spending made it impractical to control aggregate demand. The effects of controls in those conditions were as predicted. Rationing was introduced, and there were widespread shortages and black markets. All this was tolerated because people felt rationing to be the fairest way to distribute essentials during the emergency. As soon as the war had been won, controls were abandoned with a sigh of relief.

The other major experiment with an incomes policy took place during the Nixon administration. This case is much more relevant to future policy, and deserves a closer look.

CASE 17.2
Nixon's Wage and Price Controls
On August 15, 1971, President Richard Nixon announced a dramatic "new economic policy." The new policy was prompted as much by international as by domestic events, but the part of the program that got the most attention was domestic. That was a strict 90-day freeze on all prices and wages, announced to combat inflation.

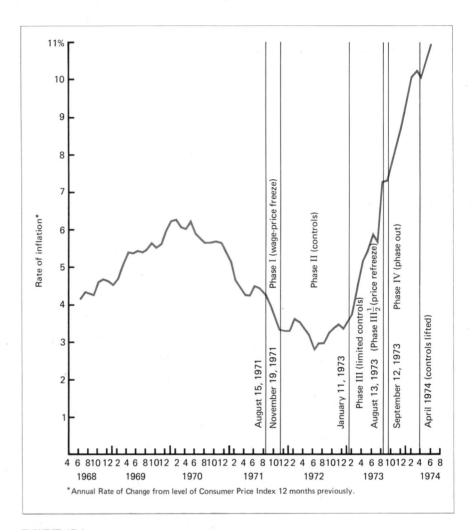

EXHIBIT 17.1
Inflation and price controls
Source: Federal Reserve Bank of St. Louis. Appeared in *Economic Report of the President* (Washington, D.C.: U.S. Government Printing Office, 1976).

The freeze later became known as Phase I of what proved to be a protracted experiment with controls. It was followed by Phase II, a full-fledged incomes policy lasting until January 11, 1973. Under Phase II, firms could raise prices to cover increases in costs, but could not increase their profit margins. Wage increases were limited to 5.5 percent except in special circumstances.

Phase I and II came at the sort of time when price controls can be expected to work best. As Exhibit 17.1 shows, inflation had been on the decline for almost two years. Phase I clearly speeded the fall of inflation while it lasted, although some of the gains were lost in a post-freeze "bulge." By mid-1972, the bulge had been overcome, and the rate of inflation had fallen further.

It is hard to say how much Phase I and Phase II actually speeded the decline of inflation. An eyeball interpretation of Exhibit 17.1 shows that what happened during the first year of controls was a steady continuation of what was already happening. There is no real way to tell whether inflation would have come down as fast without controls or not. At any rate, little harm had been done. There were a few isolated cases of shortages, mainly in lumber, but nothing alarming or widespread.

Believing that Phases I and II had done their job, Nixon wisely followed the orthodox prescription and began to put incomes policy back on the shelf. In January 1973, Phase II was replaced by Phase III. This imposed slightly looser standards and emphasized self-enforcement. Unfortunately, by the time Phase III came into effect, a strong recovery of aggregate demand was under way. Prices began to rise more rapidly, as Exhibit 17.1 clearly shows. Looking back on this period, it is now clear that the looser controls of Phase III did not *cause* this rise in prices, but at the time they were thought to have. Political pressure built up to "get tough." Nixon responded in August 1973 with a refreeze of prices and wages, which came to be called Phase III½.

Taken together, Phases III and III½ fit the principle that controls will not work when aggregate demand is not controlled. During Phase III, when controls were weak, inflation went up at a very rapid pace. During the refreeze of Phase III½ inflation was temporarily halted, but serious shortages and distortions began to show up. Contractors could not build because they could not get reinforcing bars for their concrete. Miners could not mine because they could not get the bolts they needed to strengthen their mineshafts. Publishers had to shift to expensive high-quality paper because cheap low-quality paper became hard to get. Firms began to hoard inventories of raw materials in fear of more shortages to come.

It was judged that the distortions of Phase III½ were too great a price to pay for artificially keeping inflation down. In September 1973, Nixon switched to Phase IV, which was a phase-out. By April 1974, controls were so unpopular that Congress let the authority for them expire, with little opposition from either party.

The Future of Controls

The Nixon experiment with controls was a mixed success at best. As long as inflation was falling anyway, the controls may have helped a little, and at least provided useful political window dressing. When inflation began to rise again, they proved useless and then worse than useless. Given the record shown in Exhibit 17.1, it seems likely that in the future, people will not even *expect* controls to do any good, so that even their psychological effect would be lost.

Not everyone is willing to give up yet on the idea of controls, though. A very bold British experiment with incomes policy, underway as of this writing, is being watched closely. The British incomes policy of 1976 has one novel feature. In return for accepting lower wage increases, the government has promised to cut taxes for wage earners. The idea is that this will protect workers' real incomes without making labor power so expensive that firms cannot afford to hire new workers. In combination, the wage controls and tax incentives are hoped to cut both inflation and unemployment at the same time. Arthur Okun has backed a similar scheme for the U.S. economy, which he calls "real wage insurance." Incomes policy is likely to be talked about and experimented with as long as inflation remains at its recent unacceptable levels.

Indexing

Let us turn now from controls to a very different kind of policy that also goes beyond demand management. That is the policy called **indexing.** Indexing means inflation-proofing wages, taxes, debts, savings, and a host of other things by using "escalator clauses" to adjust nominal values when prices change. Indexing is viewed partly as a way of combatting inflation, and partly as a way of easing some of its worst effects when it does occur

Indexing A policy under which wages, interest payments, taxes, and other things expressed in nominal terms are revalued upward to keep pace with inflation.

The best-known advocate of indexing has been Milton Friedman.[3] His program for indexation features five specific measures. The first three, which apply to government, would be compulsory. They are as follows:

1. Indexing income taxes. That means that if, say, the consumer price index went up 10 percent in a year, the personal exemption would automatically go up from $700 to $770, the $5,000–$6,000 income bracket would become the $5,500–$6,600 bracket, and so forth. Corporate income taxes would be indexed the same way.

2. Indexing capital gains for tax purposes. If you bought a house for $30,000 in 1976 and sold it for $40,000 in 1978, you now have to declare a capital gain of $10,000. If prices had gone up by 15 percent in the meantime, though, $4,500 of that would be only "paper" gain, not real capital gain. Under Friedman's plan, you would pay taxes only on the remaining $5,500.

3. Indexing government bonds. U.S. savings bonds would be written so that they would pay some fixed rate of interest (say 3 percent) *plus* the annual rate of inflation. If the consumer price index went up by 8 percent in a year, your bond would earn $3 + 8 = 11$ percent that year, and so forth.

In addition to these actions by government, Friedman would hope for additional voluntary actions in the private sector. These would include:

4. Indexing of private corporate bonds, mortgage loans, and perhaps even some savings deposits. This would work just like the indexing of government bonds.

5. Indexing of wages and salaries. Many union contracts already have "escalator clauses" that do this. If the consumer price index went up by 5 percent, wages would also rise by 5 percent under such a contract. Friedman hopes that these contracts become more widespread.

Effects of Indexation

How would indexation help? Proponents argue that there would be three beneficial effects.

First, indexation would, like wage and price controls, help squeeze the cost-push element out of inflationary recession. As things are now, when inflation slows down, workers want to keep pushing wages up because they fear that they will need the higher wages to offset expected inflation. With indexation, workers would no longer have to fear inflation. If prices went up, they would be protected by escalator clauses, and if they did not go up, the protection would not be needed. There would be no need to push wages up artificially.

Second, indexation would reduce the government's temptation to let aggregate demand run out of control. As things are now, the government gains enormously by inflation. People and corporations are pushed into higher tax brackets. People are taxed for capital gains that are really only "paper" gains. And the real cost of paying off the national debt goes down, which means that people who bought government bonds in the past are

---

[3]The following account of Friedman's indexing scheme is based on his pamphlet, "Monetary Correction," London: Institute for Economic Affairs Occasional Paper 41, 1974.

forced to pay an inflation "tax" too. Friedman estimates the government's revenue from such inflation "taxes" to be $25 billion in 1973 alone. With indexation, government could not get these huge windfall gains. Policy makers would thus have less incentive to pump up aggregate demand.

Finally, indexation would relieve some of the burdens of inflation even if it did not halt inflation altogether. Now, inflation robs people of the real value of their savings, and confers windfall gains on those lucky enough to be deep in debt. Wealthy people with clever accountants and financial advisors can already find ways to shelter their savings from inflation. People in lower and middle-income brackets now have no refuge. This is a special hardship on the old who have saved for retirement. Indexed government bonds would give them the protection they need.

Prospects for Indexation

Indexation is not a new or untried idea. In the United States, social security payments, federal retirement benefits, and wages of some government workers are already indexed. Many unions, including the huge auto workers union, have escalator clauses in their contracts. In Canada and Australia, the personal income tax is now indexed. In Brazil, almost everything in the economy is indexed. If inflation continues in the United States it is likely that indexation will become still more widespread here.

Indexation, like incomes policy, is no cure-all. Even its strongest supporters do not say it is. It is just one of a number of ideas that some economists think may make it easier to recover from the consequences of past errors of demand management, and escape a repetition of these errors.

Conclusions

The End of Macroeconomics?

Macroeconomics as we know it was born in the crisis of the Great Depression. Before that time, the distinction between what we now call macro- and microeconomics was not as sharp as it later became. Part of what made Keynes' ideas catch on was their *macro* quality. To the followers of Keynes, it seemed that the really important features of national economic life could be captured in a few key relationships between broad aggregate quantities. Macroeconomics meant building with big blocks, labeled "consumption," "investment," "aggregate supply," "money," and so forth. The demand management policies of the 1960s grew out of this macroeconomic approach.

Now, in the mid-1970s, there is not yet any one thing to replace macroeconomics. It is far from agreed, even, that the term should be given up. Yet one thing more than any other unites the critics of the theory and policy of the past. That is a belief in the great importance of understanding the detailed microstructure of economic life. This is as true of economists who are liberals as of those who are conservatives. It is as true of neo-Keynesians as it is of monetarists. And it is true of those who simply look for the truth with no labels attached. The exciting topics of macroeconomics today are such micro questions as these: How can we understand unemployment in terms of the job search decisions of individual workers?

How is cost-push inflation generated in concentrated as compared with competitive industries? Which particular sectors of the economy are affected first and which only after a long lag when new money is injected into the economy? How do individual workers, consumers, and businesspeople form their expectations and plans for the future?

We are back, it seems, to the theme with which we began this book. Economics is about people. It is not about aggregate demand, or expansionary gaps, or Phillips curves except when these things are understood as expressions of the way individual people think and act and plan. Macroeconomics is not yet dead and it need not die, but the more *people* are brought into it, the more the distinction between macro and micro will continue to blur.

SUMMARY

1. Modern theories of inflation and unemployment place major emphasis on the role of expectations in determining how demand management policies affect the economy. When there are unexpected changes in the rate of inflation, many workers and employers make mistakes, and do things they would not otherwise have done. These mistakes show up as changes in the unemployment rate.
2. If inflation gets faster and faster each year, unemployment can be kept low for a long period. When inflation does slow down, though, an inflationary recession is likely to be the result. Recession cures inflation, but only slowly. When aggregate demand first begins to grow again after a recession, unemployment may fall sharply with little increase in inflation.
3. There are important lags in the use of fiscal and monetary policy. There is an inside lag between the time a policy is needed and the time it is enacted, and an outside lag between that time and the time it takes effect. If lags are long enough, attempts to fine-tune the economy can have destabilizing rather than stabilizing effects. For this reason, some economists frown on fine tuning and advocate steady-as-you-go policy rules instead.
4. Incomes policies (wage and price controls) are one kind of stabilization policy that goes beyond demand management. There is good reason to believe that temporary controls may be helpful in easing the effects of inflationary recession. But an incomes policy cannot work as a substitute for good demand management.
5. Indexing seeks to fight inflation by tying the nominal values of taxes, bonds, mortgages, wages, and other things to the purchasing power of the dollar. Indexing is hoped to have three beneficial effects. It may, like wage-price controls, help squeeze the cost-push element out of inflationary recession. It may also lessen the incentive that government now has to inflate. And indexing may make it easier for retired and middle-class people to protect their savings against rising prices.

DISCUSSION QUESTIONS

1. In what sense does an abnormally high or low rate of unemployment indicate that the market is not performing its function of distributing knowledge very well?
2. What specific reforms in government can you think of that would slow the inside lag of economic policy? The outside lag?
3. Herbert Stein is a relatively conservative economist, who does not usually support spending large amounts of money to expand the federal bureaucracy. Yet he advocates spending large amounts of money to improve the quality

of economic statistics available to government, and the speed with which they are collected. Why does he think the data-gathering branch of government is so important?

4. If you feel ambitious, go to your library and see if you can find the *Economic Report of the President* for any of the years during President Kennedy's term of office. Do you think those reports generally reflect a confidence in the ability of policy makers to fine-tune the economy? Find some specific passage to contrast with the passage from the 1976 report quoted here as Case 17.1.

5. In 1975, Senators Hubert Humphrey and Jacob Javits introduced a bill called the "Balanced Growth and Planning Act." One of their reasons for introducing it was the belief that comprehensive economic planning would help avoid future errors of stabilization policy. Do you think they are right? What do you think "comprehensive economic planning" means?

PART THREE
The Economics of Life on a Small Planet

In recent years, economists have devoted increasing attention to the interrelated questions of pollution, population, and resource depletion. These questions take on an increased urgency as our planet Earth seems to shrink year by year. Each year there seem to be fewer clean and unpolluted areas remaining. Each year the ratio of the Earth's surface area to its population declines. And each year we burrow deeper into our planet's mines and wells to extract scarce resources that can never be replaced. What does the future hold in store?

Economics, as the "science of scarcity," has much to say about pollution, population, and resource depletion. The more scarcity presses upon us, the more important it is to use what we have wisely. Economics can help in three ways. First, it can help us formulate realistic standards of wise use against which to measure the actual allocation of resources. Second, economics can help identify the sources of past and present errors in resource use. And third, economics can help us to formulate improved policies that will allow us to meet the challenge of the future successfully.

We shall begin in Chapter 18 with the problem of pollution. Here we shall be able to put our familiar tools of supply and demand to work in a novel way to analyze the supply and demand for pollution opportunities. This will give us a framework for comparing several different strategies of pollution control.

Next, in Chapter 19, we shall turn to the problems of population and resource depletion. The problem of population, in particular, has a long history in economic thought. The classical economists of the eighteenth and early nineteenth centuries were, in a sense, pessimists on the question of population. They foretold imminent economic stagnation as population outran food supplies. For a century or more thereafter, such fears seemed groundless. Now, when our world supports more billions of people than the classical economists would ever have dreamed possible, population pessimism is returning.

In both Chapters 18 and 19, we discuss the problems of our shrinking planet largely from the perspective of the United States and other industrialized countries. It is in the countries of the third world, though, that these problems are the most pressing. In Chapter 20, we examine the problems and prospects of less developed economies.

CHAPTER 18
The Economics of Pollution

What You Will Learn in This Chapter
The problem of pollution can be considered from many points of view, but to the economist, it is simply a problem in resource allocation. Disposal of waste products always involves opportunity costs. Either we must suffer a deterioration of the environment, or we must reduce our consumption of material goods, or we must use scarce factors of production in costly efforts at pollution abatement. Our familiar tools of economic analysis, including supply and demand, can help us understand why there is a pollution problem in the first place, and help us to compare alternative policies for controlling pollution.

For Review
Here are some important terms and concepts that will be put to use in this chapter. Be certain that you understand them, or review them before proceeding.
    Opportunity cost (Chapter 1)
    The margin, marginal (Chapter 1)
    Market justice and distributive justice (Chapter 1)

Pollution as an Economic Problem

Pollution and Scarcity

Everyone has something to say about pollution. There are as many different ways of looking at the problem as there are people. Ecologists look at pollution in terms of the disruption of complex systems of plant and animal life. Politicians look at pollution in terms of votes. Moralists look at it in terms of good and evil. Economists also have their own point of view.

From the economic point of view, pollution is a problem of scarcity. The critical scarce resource is the waste disposal capacity of the environment. That capacity is not unlimited. Air, water, and land areas can absorb human wastes to a certain extent without adverse effects. Some production by-products can be incorporated into natural cycles. Small amounts of pollutants can be diluted to imperceptible concentration. However, these capacities for natural recycling and dilution are smaller than the waste output of our economic system in many areas now. Once we have identified pollution as an economic problem, we can apply familiar tools of economic analysis to it. In the discussion that follows, we shall show how such economic ideas as opportunity cost, marginalism, and supply and demand can help us understand the problem of pollution, and find ways to deal with it.

Opportunity Costs

Economists think of environmental issues in terms of *trade-offs* and *opportunity costs*. Some trade-offs involve converting wastes from one form into another. Most methods of pollution abatement do not really *get rid* of wastes, but merely change their physical form. Production and consumption are, after all, subject to the law of the conservation of matter. Scrubbing systems on factory smokestacks convert airborne wastes into waterborne wastes, but they do not reduce the total tonnage of wastes. Sewage treatment systems convert waterborne wastes into solid wastes, but some place must still be found to dump the sludge. Incineration gets rid of solid wastes, but creates airborne wastes.

Recycling

Recycling is often pictured as a way out of these trade-offs. Recycling converts wastes into useful substances rather than other wastes. Yet even recycling involves opportunity costs. To gather bottles and cans and remelt them, or to remove sulfur from the smoke of burning coal and oil requires a lot of energy. Using energy produces waste heat. Ultimately, recycling means trading off *material* pollution for *energy* pollution.

Of course, this does not mean that waste treatment and recycling are futile. It is just *because* wastes cannot be made to vanish that it is very important to release them into the environment in the least destructive way. Changing wastes from one form into another allows us to make the maximum use of scarce environmental waste disposal capacities under a variety of local conditions.

Product Trade-Offs

There is also a second important set of trade-offs bearing on the pollution problem. Pollution can sometimes be reduced by substituting one *product* for another. We can, for example, substitute unleaded for leaded gasoline. We can produce fewer material goods and more services. We can reduce pollution still further by giving up marketable goods and services in favor of such nonmarket goods as increased leisure and the direct enjoyment of nature through outdoor recreation.

The Marginal Principle

All these trade-offs mean a lot of decisions. We cannot make these pollution control decisions without some general standards. To economists, it seems natural to express many of the important standards in *marginal* terms. As an example, let us consider the decision of *how much* pollution should be tolerated. This decision, we can show, requires us to find a balance between two margins.

EXHIBIT 18.1
The marginal social cost of pollution
The marginal social cost of pollution is the total cost to all members of
society that results from a one-unit increase in pollution. At low levels of
pollution, within the natural absorptive capacity of the environment, the
marginal social cost of pollution may be zero. As the quantity of pollution
increases, the marginal social cost of pollution probably tends to increase for
most pollutants.

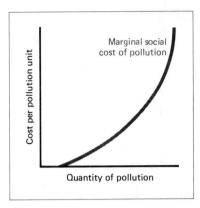

Social Cost

The first margin is the **marginal social cost of pollution.** For a given
type of pollution, this means the total cost to all members of society of an
additional unit of pollution. Suppose, for example, that in a community of
1,000 people, each additional pound of sulfur dioxide emitted cost *each*
person 0.003 cent in the form of damage to painted surfaces, and 0.004
cent in terms of personal discomfort. The marginal social cost of sulfur
dioxide pollution in this community could thus be $1,000 \times (0.003 + 0.004)$
= 7 cents per pound.

For most kinds of pollution, it is likely that the marginal social cost of
pollution increases as its quantity increases. A graph of the marginal cost
of pollution would thus have the form shown in Exhibit 18.1. Marginal
social cost begins at zero for pollution within the natural absorptive capacity of the environment. As pollution concentrations become first unpleas-
ant and then dangerous, marginal social cost rises to a high level.

Marginal Social Cost of Pollution
The total cost to all members of
society of an additional unit of
pollution.

Abatement Cost

The second margin is the **marginal cost of pollution abatement.**
This means the economic cost of reducing pollution of a given kind by one
unit. Other things being equal, the marginal cost of pollution abatement
tends to rise as the level of pollution decreases. For example, in controlling
automobile exhaust emissions, relatively cheap devices can cut pollution
by half. Somewhat more complicated and expensive devices are required
to cut it in half again, to the level of 75 percent abatement. Very elaborate
and costly methods must be installed to cut it in half a third time, to 87.5
percent abatement, and so forth. With such examples in mind, we draw
marginal abatement cost curves with downward slopes, as in Exhibit 18.2.

**Marginal Cost of Pollution Abate-
ment** The cost of reducing a
given kind of pollution by one unit.

Optimum

In Exhibit 18.3, now, we draw both schedules in one diagram. This
allows us to identify the point where the marginal cost of abatement is
equal to the marginal social cost of pollution. That happens at the point
where the two curves intersect. As far as economics is concerned, this is the
optimal quantity of pollution. Pollution in excess of this amount represents
a misallocation of resources. The damage done by additional pollution then
exceeds the cost of eliminating it. Excessive abatement, which means oper-

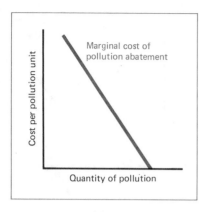

EXHIBIT 18.2

The marginal cost of pollution abatement

The marginal cost of pollution abatement is the cost of reducing pollution by one unit. The cost of eliminating pollution tends to increase as the percentage of all pollution eliminated increases. That gives the marginal cost of pollution abatement a downward slope.

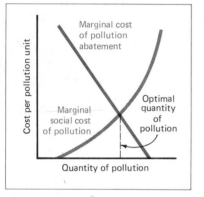

EXHIBIT 18.3

The optimal quantity of pollution

The optimal quantity of pollution is determined by the intersection of the marginal cost of pollution abatement curve and the marginal social cost of pollution curve. To the left of that point, the benefits of further reductions in pollution do not justify the high cost of abatement. To the right of the intersection, the cost of abatement is less than the cost imposed on society by additional pollution.

ating to the left of the intersection point, is also wasteful. It also represents an unnecessary reduction in human welfare. If the marginal cost of pollution abatement exceeds the marginal social cost of pollution, we can gain by trading a small reduction in environmental quality for a relatively large increase in material production.

Measurement Problems

This marginal analysis gives a simple theoretical standard for pollution control. The standard is not so easy to apply in practice, however. There are severe problems of measurement, especially on the side of social cost. Attempts to measure the social cost of pollution usually concentrate on such things as damage to property, health cost measured in terms of medical expenses and time lost from work, and the value of wildlife and crops killed. Actual estimates suffer from several defects.

First, data on the costs of pollution are at best fragmentary. There are many gaps, which must be filled by pure guesswork. Second, it is difficult to account for purely subjective costs. These include offenses to aesthetic sensibilities and discomforts not actually resulting in damage to the health. Yet these subjective costs have a very real economic value. The fact that many people spend hard-earned money to avoid the effects of pollution by leaving polluted areas shows such costs to be real. Finally, estimates of the social cost of pollution rarely give more than the average cost figures. Yet it is marginal cost data, much more difficult to obtain, that are really relevant to pollution policy decisions.

There are problems too in estimating the costs of pollution abatement. One major problem is that calculations must take into account not only the direct costs of getting rid of one form of pollution, but also the social costs of any different forms of pollution produced as a result. Measuring these is subject to all the problems of measuring the social cost of any kind of pollution. We shall have to keep these practical difficulties in mind when we consider policy alternatives.

Economic Strategies for Pollution Control

Supply and Demand

Controlling pollution is a problem of economic policy. As in many other cases, we can use our old friends supply and demand to explain where the problem comes from, and to compare alternative solutions. Let us see how supply and demand analysis can be applied to pollution.

Look at Exhibit 18.4. We have drawn the marginal cost of pollution abatement curve again there, but now we have given it a new name: the *demand curve for pollution opportunities*. It is very easy to understand why the same schedule serves both purposes. Simply ask how much a firm would be willing to pay, if necessary, for the opportunity to dump an additional unit of untreated waste directly into the environment. The answer is that it would pay any sum smaller, but never any sum larger, than the cost of pollution-free waste disposal.

So much for the demand curve. In Exhibit 18.4 we have drawn the supply curve for pollution opportunities as a straight line lying right along the horizontal axis. That indicates that unlimited pollution opportunities are available without paying any price at all. The equilibrium quantity of pollution is found where the two curves intersect. Unless the social cost of pollution is also zero, which is not the case, this equilbrium is not where we want to be. What can be done?

EXHIBIT 18.4

Supply and demand for pollution opportunities

The marginal cost of pollution abatement curve can also be called the demand curve for pollution opportunities. The position of the supply curve for pollution opportunities depends on how much firms must pay in order to discharge wastes into the environment. If they do not have to pay at all, the supply curve will coincide with the horizontal axis as shown here, and the equilibrium quantity of pollution will be greater than the optimum quantity.

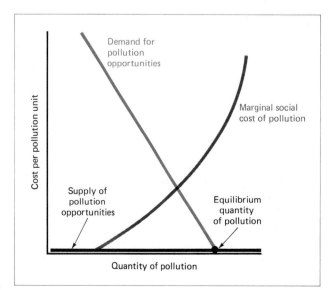

The Regulatory Approach

Most current government policies for controlling pollution take a regulatory approach. Congress sets up some agency with authority to control pollution of particular types or in particular areas. Sometimes the regulators simply set a maximum amount of pollution permitted from each source, and leave the choice of abatement method up to the polluter. In other cases, regulators specify that certain abatement procedures must be followed. Regulation such as this has the effect of rationing pollution opportunities. It can prevent the economic system from ending up on an equilibrium like that shown in Exhibit 18.4, where there is too much pollution.

Although the regulatory approach has in many cases been effective, economists often find fault with it. For one thing, regulations can be written too rigidly, so that they do not give polluters enough incentive to search for the least-cost method of cleaning up their wastes. For another, regulation does not always ensure that the burden of cleaning up will be efficiently allocated among various pollution sources. Critics of the regulatory approach have suggested some alternative strategies for pollution control that more directly make use of supply and demand. Let us examine some of these alternatives.

Residual Charges

Residual Charges Charges of a fixed amount per unit of waste imposed on all sources that discharge a given kind of waste into the environment.

One nonregulatory strategy for controlling pollution works by shifting the pollution opportunity supply curve with **residual charges.** Residual charges, are, in effect, waste disposal taxes. There are charges of a fixed amount per unit of waste, imposed on all sources of a given kind of waste. As an example, consider a residual charge on sulfur dioxide emissions. Suppose that all sources of this type of pollution had to pay a fee of $.05 per pound for all sulfur emitted into the atmosphere.

Exhibit 18.4 shows the effect of such a residual charge. The charge

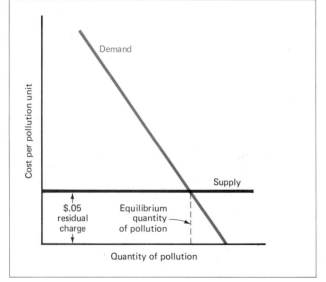

EXHIBIT 18.5
The effect of a residual charge
A residual charge makes it necessary for polluters to pay for the opportunity to discharge wastes into the environment. Here, the charge is set at $.05 per unit. The residual charge moves the pollution opportunity supply curve upward to the position shown, and forces polluters up and to the left along their demand curve, thus reducing the equilibrium quantity of pollution.

EXHIBIT 18.6

An optimal residual charge

Ideally, a residual charge could be set just high enough to reduce pollution by the optimal amount. Here, the supply curve for pollution opportunities cuts the demand and marginal social cost curves just at their point of intersection. In practice, such fine tuning of residual charges is quite difficult.

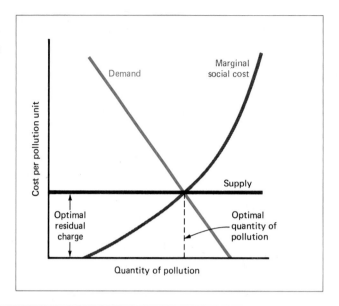

shifts the pollution opportunity supply curve up from its position along the horizontal axis to a position $.05 higher. Polluters would react to the tax by moving back along their demand curve to a new equilibrium where there is less pollution. They will do this because it will pay them to use all pollution abatement methods that can remove a pound of sulfur from stack gases for $.05 or less.

By raising or lowering the amount of charge, any desired degree of pollution control can be achieved. Ideally, the charge would be set so that the pollution opportunity supply curve passes exactly through the intersection of the marginal abatement cost curve (demand curve) and the marginal social cost curve. This ideal situation is shown in Exhibit 18.6. Unfortunately, there is no easy way to determine just where this intersection is, and hence just what the charge should be. The agency responsible for setting the rate of the residual charge is faced with the measurement difficulties we mentioned above.

Objections to Residual Charges

Pollution taxes and residual charges are likely to figure prominently in future policy debates. Let us take a moment to look at some objections one often hears to residual charges. The objections come from three principal sources: industry, consumers, and environmentalists. Industrialists sometimes say that residual charges would impose an "unfair double burden" on industry. They would have to pay the charge at the same time that they are undergoing the expense of installing pollution abatement equipment. Consumers object that industry would be able to pass the burden of the charge along in the form of higher product prices. Environmentalists protest that residual charges mean granting a "license to pollute." They fear that industry would just put up the money and keep right on despoiling the environment as before. Let us take up each of these objections in turn.

Double Burden

The "double burden" objection is the weakest of the three. No industry is ever forced by a residual charge to pay a double burden. Any polluter always has the option of paying the charge and making no effort to reduce pollution at all. In this case, it bears just one burden, that of the charge itself. Any money it spends on pollution abatement equipment will be spent for one reason only. That will be if it is *cheaper* to install the equipment than to pay to pollute. Far from being a second burden added on top of the tax, abatement expenditures represent a way to escape from the tax and hence reduce the total burden.

Passing the Burden

The argument that residual charges can be shifted to consumers has more of an element of truth in it. Exhibit 18.7 shows why. Let D represent the demand curve for a commodity and S the market supply curve, before there is any pollution control policy. These conditions give an equilibrium at E, with a price p and a quantity of output q. A residual charge will raise the marginal cost of production. The increase will be either the amount of tax paid per unit of production or the cost of the abatement equipment needed to avoid payment, whichever is smaller. This will shift the whole supply curve up to the new position S'. The vertical distance between the old and new supply curves is equal to the per unit burden of the charge. With the new supply curve S', equilibrium is at E' with price and quantity p' and q', respectively. The difference between the new price and the old one shows the share of the burden passed along to the consumer. As the figure is drawn, this is about half the burden of the tax. The exact share passed on will vary from product to product, depending on the shapes of the supply and demand curves.

We see, then, that at least part of the burden of a residual charge can be passed along to consumers. But does this really constitute a valid criticism of the policy? A strong argument can be made that it does not. We must remember that *someone* always pays the price of pollution. Different

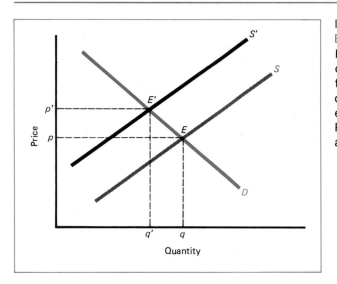

EXHIBIT 18.7

Effect of a residual charge on product price

Here we see the effects of a residual charge in terms of the supply and demand for a product produced by a firm that must pay the charge. The product supply curve is shifted up from S to S'. This causes the equilibrium price of the product to rise from p to p'. Part, but not all, of the cost increase is thus passed along to the consumer.

policies only change *who* pays for it. Under current conditions, producers and consumers of pollution-intensive goods both get a free ride. They shift the burden to innocent third parties. If we want to lift the burden from these third parties, why should consumers expect to be able to continue their free ride?

Higher prices for high-pollution products would actually be beneficial. They would stimulate consumers to make the trade-offs that must be made if the environment is to be protected. If the prices of relatively "dirty" products rise compared to relatively "clean" products and services, consumers would shift their spending patterns accordingly. If firms could not pass along to consumers a part of the pollution taxes imposed upon them, it is not easy to see how the necessary change in consumption habits would come about.

License

The third objection, that residual charges are just a "license to pollute," is open to more than one interpretation. Depending on how it is interpreted, it may be wholly invalid or partially valid.

Sometimes the argument is made to imply that residual charges would have no effect on pollution. It is said that businesses would just pay the charge and carry on as before. But this is flatly incorrect, unless one is going to deny that supply and demand applies to waste disposal as it does to other business activities. At other times, the "license to pollute" argument is meant as an objection to the fact that the taxes would eliminate only a part, and not all of pollution output. In this application, too, the argument violates good economic reasoning. To eliminate *all* pollution regardless of cost, as some environmentalists advocate, would involve greater sacrifices of material welfare than we could justify in terms of consumer satisfaction. Instead we have argued that pollution control should proceed only up to the point where the marginal cost of pollution abatement begins to exceed the marginal social cost of pollution.

A third interpretation of the "license to pollute" argument makes more economic sense. The problem is that no direct compensation is offered to those downwind or downstream of any pollution sources that do continue polluting even after imposition of the charges. To these remaining victims, it seems unjust that a firm can legally continue to make life miserable just by paying a fee to the government. Polluters, it is argued, should pay compensation to their victims, not taxes to the government.

Pollution Control and Property Rights

The question of who should be compensated for pollution damage raises the whole issue of pollution and property rights. The basic idea is this: From the point of view of property rights, pollution is *theft*. If you use the airspace in and around my home as a dumping ground for your unwanted combustion products, you are stealing waste disposal services from me. If you use my living room as a reverberation chamber for noise from your truck or motorcycle, you are robbing me of my right to peace and quiet. As owner, I ought to have the right to prevent you from using my property in these ways, unless you negotiate with me in advance to buy my permission. If you do not, I should be able to bring civil or criminal action against you in a court of law.

Unfortunately, the law, as it now stands, is stacked against property owners and in favor of polluters. Certain changes could be made, however, to redress the balance. It could, for example, be made easier for private citizens to initiate lawsuits when their property is attacked by pollution. At present, property owners often must wait for local governments to take legal action on their behalf. If the polluters have more "pull" in the state-house or city hall than their victims do, the victims may wait in vain. Also, it could be made easier for large groups of citizens to act jointly, through class action suits or other means, to gain legal redress for damages done to them.

What would be the economic effect of laws permitting property owners to protect themselves from pollution? One possible effect would be the creation of a private market for pollution rights. In this market, people would sell pollution opportunities to firms in return for a price high enough to compensate for the damage done. If all individuals sold pollution rights at prices equal to the marginal cost to them of pollution damage, the pollution market would look as it does in Exhibit 18.8. The pollution opportunity supply curve would follow exactly along the marginal social cost curve. The equilibrium quantity of pollution would be exactly the economically optimal amount.

Objections

Of course, the legal protection of private property rights as a method of pollution control is open to certain practical objections, just like all other methods. One objection is that not all environmental resources that are open to pollution damage are privately owned. Would this mean that polluters would retain unlimited opportunities to dump their wastes in public waterways, world oceans, publicly owned wilderness areas, and the like? One way to overcome the problem would be to auction off all rivers, oceans, national parks, and the like to private owners. The private owners

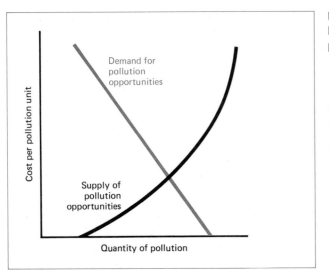

EXHIBIT 18.8
Pollution opportunities with perfect protection of private property
If all property were privately owned and if polluters always had to compensate victims for damage to persons or property, a private market in pollution opportunities would be created. Ideally, the supply curve in this market would exactly coincide with the marginal social cost of pollution curve. The equilibrium quantity of pollution would then equal the optimal quantity.

could then protect them from damage. Short of this radical proposal, taxes and user charges could be used to protect such public resources, while private law protected privately owned resources.

There is a second objection to giving private owners blanket rights to protect their property against pollution. Such a policy might result in excessive reduction in pollution levels. A potential polluter located in a densely populated area might have to negotiate pollution opportunity contracts with tens of thousands of individual small property owners before emitting even a single puff of smoke. The expense of doing this would be prohibitive, even if the actual charges paid to each owner were in themselves reasonable. To avoid these expenses a firm might spend far more than the economically optimal amount on pollution abatement. Perhaps, of course, we have suffered from too much pollution for so long that it would be a pleasant novelty to suffer from too little. Speaking more practically, though, we might concede that the property-rights approach probably works best when the impact of pollution is relatively concentrated. Some type of residual charge scheme may be a better answer when damages are very widely dispersed.

Conclusions

The main objective of pollution control, as we have discussed it in this chapter, has been to improve the efficiency of resource allocation. A complete analysis of environmental policy should look at the normative implications of these policies as well. In concluding our discussion, let us look at pollution control policies in terms of market justice and distributive justice.

By the standard of market justice, the effects of pollution control policies of almost any kind appear to be beneficial. Pollution is theft. It is a form of coercion through which producers enjoy unjustifiably high profits, and consumers of high-pollution products enjoy unjustifiably low prices. Third parties, as victims of pollution, are unwillingly forced to bear the costs without sharing in the benefits. Policies that put a price tag on pollution help to correct these injustices by making everyone pay the full cost of the things produced and consumed.

Strictly speaking, according to the standard of market justice, a policy should not only impose penalties on polluters, but should also provide compensation to its victims. Policies based on enforcement of private property rights, including the right of pollution victims to sue for damages, do this, while residual charges do not.

From the point of view of distributive justice, the effects of pollution control policies are more problematical. If one's notion of distributive justice is simply increased equality of real incomes, antipollution measures may well make things worse. We would have to study carefully the exact distribution of the costs and benefits of various alternative policies in order to be certain on this point. Without such study, we can only make some conjectures. These conjectures suggest, however, that low-income groups might not fare well. They might bear a disproportionately large share of the costs of pollution control policies, and receive a disproportionately small share of the benefits.

One result of effective pollution control policies, as we have seen, must be to raise the prices of goods to consumers. Low-income groups spend a larger portion of their budget on material goods and devote a smaller portion to consumption of services and to savings. The burden of pollution taxes might thus be expected to rest more heavily on them in proportion to their incomes.

At the same time, it seems likely that the benefits of pollution control policies are less valuable to the poor than to the rich. Suppose that the benefits of pollution control were equally distributed in *physical* terms. For example, suppose that the level of air pollution were lowered just as much in low-income as in high-income neighborhoods. This does not mean that the benefit would be equally distributed in *economic* terms. Clean air and other environmental amenities are to a considerable extent "luxury goods." They have a high value to those who already have a generous supply of material goods, and a relatively low value to those who do not. How many pounds of beef, or pairs of shoes, or dollars, would poor people be willing to give up in order to reduce by half the sulfur dioxide content of the air they breathe? How much would wealthy people be willing to sacrifice for the same purpose? It is easy to see that, at least beyond a certain point, pollution control policies may reflect the tastes only of the relatively well-to-do.

SUMMARY

1. Pollution can be viewed as a problem in the allocation of scarce resources. In this case, the scarce resource is the waste-absorption capacity of the environment. Once this capacity is exceeded, further waste disposal must incur opportunity costs of one kind or another. If wastes are discharged untreated into the environment, the opportunity costs take the form of a less healthy and pleasant world in which to live. If costly pollution abatement techniques are used, scarce factors of production must be diverted from other uses. No policy can help us avoid these trade-offs altogether. The economic problem of pollution is how to balance the social cost of pollution against the economic cost of pollution abatement.

2. Supply and demand analysis can be applied to the problem of pollution control. The marginal cost of pollution abatement curve can be thought of as a demand curve for pollution. If there are no pollution controls of any kind, the supply curve for pollution opportunities is a horizontal line at zero height. The equilibrium quantity of pollution will be too high when the supply curve has that shape. All pollution control policies aim in one way or another to limit the supply of pollution opportunities.

3. The regulatory approach to pollution abatement is, in effect, a form of administrative rationing for pollution opportunities. It has been effective in some cases, but economists often criticize it as inefficient. Residual charges are an alternative pollution control method. Under a residual charge scheme, the supply curve for pollution opportunities becomes a horizontal line at a height equal to the charge per unit of waste. Still another approach to pollution control is through the enforcement of private property rights. Ideally, if all property were privately owned, and polluters had to compensate owners for all damage to persons and property, the supply of pollution opportunities curve would coincide with the marginal social cost of pollution curve. Each approach has its advantages and its practical difficulties. For the moment, it seems worthwhile to experiment with all methods.

4. Pollution raises normative as well as positive issues. One such issue is that of compensating victims of pollution. The regulatory and residual charge approaches to pollution control do not compensate victims. Pollution control via defense of private property rights appears to be superior in this respect. Another normative question concerns the distributive impact of pollution control. In the absence of firm evidence to the contrary, it seems plausible to think that the costs of pollution control may be borne more than proportionately by the poor, and the benefits of pollution control may accrue more proportionately to the well-to-do.

DISCUSSION QUESTIONS

1. Why has pollution become a major national policy issue only recently? Is pollution worse that it used to be? Do the cars of New York City today discharge more waste each day than the horses of New York City did in 1901? Has our high standard of living actually caused more pollution, or has it made us less willing to tolerate it than we used to, or has it done both?

2. Can you think of circumstances in which the marginal social cost of waste disposal for a firm is also a part of its explicit private costs of production? Of its implicit private costs? Of neither its implicit nor its explicit costs?

3. When does "waste disposal" become "pollution"? How do you distinguish between the two? Is the distinction a matter of positive economics or of normative economics?

4. Many environmentalists are uncomfortable with the concept of an economically optimal amount of pollution. They tend to think that less pollution is always better. Do you agree? Do you think that the difference between these environmentalists' viewpoint and the viewpoint set forth in this chapter is one of values or of analysis?

5. Suppose that you are a member of Congress when a bill comes up to abolish all specific pollution control regulations for automobile exhausts. In place of the present regulations, there would be a residual charge of $.01 per mile placed on all driving. The rate of charge would be reduced appropriately for those drivers who could prove that their cars were equipped with effective emission control devices. Would you favor this measure? Why or why not? If your only objection is that you think $.01 per mile is too low a charge, how high do you think the rate should be?

6. Many of the Great Lakes have become seriously polluted. Among the people damaged by this are the owners of lakefront property. Do you think that these owners ought to be permitted to bring suit against any company polluting the lake where their property is located? If such suits were permitted, do you think many would be brought? Should property owners who win their cases against polluters be able to obtain a cease-and-desist order stopping all further pollution, or should they simply be awarded monetary damages?

CHAPTER 19
Population, Resources, and the Economic Future

What You Will Learn in This Chapter
In recent years the economic future has become a subject of increasing public concern. Certain problems must be overcome in order to ensure continued long-term economic growth. The problem of pollution is one of them. Other problems are population growth and the depletion of nonrenewable resources. These problems are at least partly economic in nature. A study of population movements in the past, and their relation to economic development, can help us assess our prospects for the future. We also need to understand how markets allocate nonrenewable resources over time, and how they respond to the increasing scarcity of such resources.

For Review
Here is an important concept that will be put to use in this chapter. Be certain that you understand or review it before proceeding.
    Resource allocation (Chapter 2)

We have spent many chapters in this book discussing the questions of *what, how, who,* and *for whom.* In recent years, increasing attention has been drawn to a fifth great economic question: *how long?* How long will scarce resources last? How long can economic growth continue? How long will we be able to continue feeding ourselves? The question of *how long* brings kinds of scarcities to our attention that we have not paid much attention to up to now. These are scarcities that arise from the limited size of the planet Earth itself. There is room on our planet for only a finite number of human beings. The mineral resources of the planet can last only a finite length of time at present rates of consumption. The economic future cannot simply be an endless extrapolation of past economic trends.

In part, our economic future depends on whether we learn to deal successfully with the problem of pollution, discussed in the last chapter. If pollution does not do us in, there remain two other major problem areas, population growth and resource depletion. We shall discuss these two in what follows.

The Economics of Population

Population Arithmetic

We can begin by reviewing some of the simple arithmetic of population growth. For a population to increase, it is obvious that more people must be born than die each year. (In saying this and in what follows, we ignore immigration and emigration.) The number of people born into a population per 1,000 per year is the **crude birth rate** for that population. The number who die per 1,000 per year is the **crude death rate.** The difference between the two is called the **rate of natural increase.**

Exhibit 19.1 shows crude birth rates, crude death rates, and rates of natural increase for a selection of countries, according to the latest available data. In interpreting data such as these, it sometimes helps to translate rates of natural increase into population doubling times. We have done this in the last column of the table. The faster the rate of natural increase, the shorter the period of time required for the population to double in size.

Growth Curves

A population that grew indefinitely at a constant rate of natural increase would double each time a fixed number of years elapsed. It would reach 2, 4, 8, 16, 32, 64 (and so forth) times its original size, following the

Crude Birth Rate The number of people born into a population per 1,000 per year.

Crude Death Rate The number of people in a population who die per 1,000 per year.

Rate of Natural Increase The current rate of growth of a population calculated as the crude birth rate minus the crude death rate.

EXHIBIT 19.1
Birth rates, death rates, and natural increase of population for selected countries, 1969–1970
The current rate of population growth for a country can be found by subtracting the crude death rate from the crude birth rate. The faster the rate of population growth, the shorter the time period required for the population to double.

Country	Crude Birth Rate	Crude Death Rate	Rate of Natural Increase	Approximate Doubling Time of Population (years)
Ecuador	44.9	11.4	33.5	21
Mexico	43.2	9.7	33.5	21
Pakistan	50.9	18.4	32.5	21
Algeria	49.1	16.9	32.2	22
Kenya	47.8	17.5	30.3	23
Zambia	49.8	20.7	21.9	24
India	42.8	16.7	26.1	27
Afghanistan	50.5	26.5	24.0	29
Egypt	36.8	14.4	22.4	31
Cuba	29.6	7.5	19.1	37
Argentina	22.5	8.6	13.9	50
Japan	18.8	6.9	11.9	59
Australia	20.4	8.7	11.7	60
USSR	17.0	8.1	8.9	79
United States	17.9	9.5	8.4	83
Italy	17.5	10.1	7.4	95
France	16.7	11.4	5.3	132
United Kingdom	16.7	11.9	4.8	148
Czechoslovakia	15.5	11.2	4.3	163

Source: UN Statistical Yearbook, 1973.

EXHIBIT 19.2
Typical S-shaped curve of population growth
A living population cannot grow indefinitely in a finite environment. Under laboratory conditions, populations of bacteria or fruitflies or other organisms tend to follow S-shaped growth curves such as the one shown here. In the long run, it seems inevitable that the growth curve of human population will also begin to decrease.

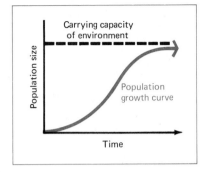

same sort of growth path as that followed by the value of a sum of money invested at compound interest. Normally, however, living populations are not able to grow exponentially without limit. Suppose that bacteria are allowed to multiply in a jar of nutrient, or a population of fruitflies is allowed to grow in a glass cage or a room of fixed size, or a breeding pair of dogs is introduced on an island previously inhabited only by rabbits. Under such conditions, the growth of the population of bacteria, fruitflies, or dogs typically follows the kind of S-shaped growth curve shown in Exhibit 19.2. At first, the population will expand at an exponential rate. The biological characteristics of the species in question determine the population doubling time under optimal conditions. Sooner or later, though, the population will begin to fill up its jar or cage or island or whatever. Then, under more crowded conditions, the time needed to double the population will increase. Eventually, overcrowding will bring population growth to a halt.

Must the growth of human population also be subject to this S-curve pattern? In the long run, it surely must. Estimates of the maximum human population of earth vary widely, but no one doubts that there is some finite ceiling. (One admittedly fanciful estimate places the limit as high as 20 million times the present world population. This would require people to live 120 to the square meter in a 2,000-story building covering the entire earth. Even that limit would take only 890 years to reach at the present rate of growth of world population!)

In the short run, though, the growth of human population has not followed the simple S-curve pattern. In fact, over as long a period as any kind of population estimates can be made, the world rate of natural increase has been accelerating, not slowing down. World population has doubled in about the last 45 years, and will double again in the next 35, if the current rate of growth continues. The last preceding doubling of population took about 80 years, from 1850 to 1930. The doubling before that took some 200 years. It is hard to imagine that this trend will continue. We must be living at present very close to the bend in the world population curve, after which the rate of population will begin to decline.

Population Equilibrium

There is really no doubt whatever that the level of human population is headed for an equilibrium state in which births will just balance deaths. The really interesting question is what will that equilibrium look like? Let us explore some possibilities.

First, imagine a market economy in which people earn money to buy the necessities of life only by selling factor services. The population begins to approach some fixed limit to population growth, defined, for example, by the food supply. Income is distributed unequally in this society. As population nears the ceiling, the price of food will rise relative to the wage rate. The lowest-income groups will find their standard of living reduced, and this will eventually affect their birth and death rates. At some point there will begin to be an excess of deaths over births among the poorest classes. This will be accompanied by a balance between births and deaths for those living just at the margin of subsistence. An excess of births will be possible only among the well-to-do. When enough people have finally been pushed down to or below the margin of subsistence, population growth as a whole will cease. We can call the result a *marginal subsistence equilibrium* for population.

A marginal subsistence equilibrium assumes great inequality. It implies affluence for a few against the backdrop of destitute masses, whose members are continuously replenished by the excess children of the rich driven down into poverty. If we remove the assumption of inequality, the result is a second type of population equilibrium, which we can call the *absolute subsistence equilibrium.* Under this solution, as crowding begins to lower the living standards of a population, taxes and transfers are used to share the burden equally among all. This equality permits population growth to go on longer; no one is starved or crowded to the point that they cannot reproduce until everyone is starved or crowded to that point. The total number of people living in poverty in the absolute subsistence equilibrium is greater than in the marginal subsistence equilibrium.

Dismal Economics

Population projections like these were what once caused economics to be called the "dismal science." As long ago as 1798, Thomas Malthus forecast a marginal subsistence population equilibrium for humanity. This would come about through operation of the **law of diminishing returns,** as a growing population caught up with a fixed supply of agricultural land. According to Malthus' theory, only the landlords who owned the means of producing precious food would escape eventual poverty. Even the capitalists would eventually be ground down and their profits reduced to zero.

Malthus' prophecy has not come true for Great Britain, the United States, or other advanced industrial countries. These countries have instead achieved, or nearly achieved, a nonsubsistence population equilibrium with low birth rates, low death rates, and high living standards. The process by which this has been achieved is a good illustration of how economic and demographic processes interact.

The Demographic Transition

In a preindustrial society, birth rates and death rates are both very high, and the rate of natural increase of population is low. With industrialization and economic development, per capita incomes begin to rise. The first demographic effect of rising income is a reduction in the death rate. This is brought about by better nutrition, better hygiene, and better medical care. With the birth rate remaining high, the drop in the death

Diminishing Returns (Law of) If the output of some good is increased by increasing the quantity of one variable input while the quantity of other inputs used remains fixed, then a point will eventually be reached beyond which the quantity of output produced by each additional unit of the variable input will diminish.

Thomas Robert Malthus was born in England in 1766, and received what was, for his time, a radical upbringing. His father was an admirer of Rousseau and Condorcet. One of his tutors was imprisoned for expressing the wish that the French revolutionaries would invade and liberate England. He studied at Cambridge, took holy orders, and became a curate.

In 1793 a book appeared that had a great impact on the circles in which young Malthus moved. The book was *Enquiry Concerning Political Justice and Its Influence on Morals and Happiness* by the anarchist and socialist William Godwin. As a result of many lively debates over this book and subsequent essays by Godwin, Malthus decided to write down his own view that population growth constituted an insurmountable barrier to a society of absolute equality and abundance. This writing appeared as *An Essay on the Principle of Population* in 1798.

The heart of Malthus' argument was the doctrine that population tended to grow in geometric progression (2, 4, 8, 16, and so forth) while the means of subsistence grew only in arithmetic progression (2, 4, 6, 8, and so forth). As population increased, increasingly less-fertile land would have to be brought into cultivation. Population would outstrip food production, and wages would be driven down to the subsistence level.

Famine, vice, misery, and war could be avoided only if people engaged in "moral restraint," that is, later marriages with fewer children per family. Schemes such as the Poor Laws or subsidized housing for the poor were worse than useless. They simply encouraged population growth, and hence led to an actual deterioration of conditions.

Malthus' views influenced Darwin in developing his "survival of the fittest" doctrine in the nineteenth century. More than anyone else, it was Malthus who was responsible for earning political economy the name of the "dismal science." Not everyone has interpreted Malthus in such a negative light, however. John Maynard Keynes placed Malthus firmly in "the English tradition of humane science . . . a tradition marked by a love of truth and a most noble lucidity, . . . and by an immense disinterestedness and public spirit."

Thomas Robert Malthus
(1766–1834)

---

rate increases the rate of natural increase. Population enters a phase of very rapid growth.

If there are sufficient natural resources, and if there is enough investment in new capital, economic growth can outstrip population growth. Per capita income then rises. This has happened in all the major industrialized countries of the world. In these countries, rising per capita incomes have eventually caused the birth rate to fall. Population growth has then slowed, and population equilibrium has been approached.

The whole cycle, from falling death rates to rapid population growth to falling birth rates and equilibrium, is called the **demographic transition.** Exhibit 19.3 provides a graphical representation of the demographic transition. Part *a* of this exhibit represents the course of the crude birth rate and death rate over time. Part *b* shows what happens to the rate of natural increase as it first rises and then falls. Part *c* shows the familiar S-curve pattern of population growth that results from the demographic transition. The human population growth curve shown there differs in an important respect from that of flies in a cage or dogs on an island. The difference is that it levels off at an equilibrium population below the biologically maximum level set by subsistence requirements.

The crucial part of the demographic transition is the fall in birth rates produced by rapid economic development. Demographers do not completely

Demographic Transition A population cycle that accompanies economic development, beginning with a fall in the death rate, continuing with a phase of rapid population growth, and concluding with a decline in the birth rate.

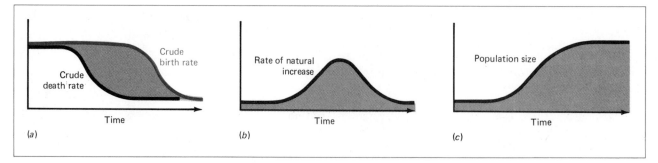

EXHIBIT 19.3
The demographic transition
In a preindustrial society, both birth rates and death rates are high, so that population growth is slow. The first effect of economic development is a drop in the death rate. This brings on a period of rapid population growth. As economic development continues, the birth rate begins to fall. Population growth decelerates and eventually may fall to zero.

understand the mechanisms that bring about this decline in birth rates. In large part, the decline is probably caused by increasing urbanization. Traditionally, a large number of children is an economic asset to a farm family, because children can contribute to production from an early age. In the city, children tend to be an economic burden. There is no guarantee of remunerative jobs for them, and their food, clothing, and housing cannot be produced at home. More subtle changes in life styles and attitudes toward family life, which occur as income rises, also seem to be involved in the demographic transition.

Net Reproduction

To complete the demographic transition and approach an equilibrium population takes many decades. To understand why the transition takes so long, we need to know more about population growth than crude birth rates and crude death rates alone can tell us.

Crude birth rates and death rates can be misleading because they depend on both the underlying reproductive behavior of a population and its age structure. A more direct measure of reproductive behavior is the **net reproduction rate** for a population. The net reproduction rate is the average number of daughters born to each female child in the population over her lifetime. If the net reproduction rate is equal to one, then the population is, in the long run, just replacing itself. If it is greater than one, then the population has a long-run tendency to grow. If it is less than one, it has a long-run tendency to shrink.

In the short run, the rate of natural increase in a population may be positive even when the net reproduction rate is one or less. In particular, this will happen when population growth has been slowing in the recent past. The present population of the United States provides a case in point. The net reproduction rate in the United States is now very close to one, but it has fallen to that level only recently. The elderly people now in high mortality brackets are members of the relatively small generation born around the turn of the century. Those in the high fertility range are mem-

Net Reproduction Rate The inherent long-term rate of growth of a population, measured as the average number of daughters born to each female child over her lifetime.

bers of the much larger generation who were born immediately after World War II. The disproportion in the size of the generations causes the crude death rate to be lower than it will eventually be in the long-run equilibrium, and the crude birth rate to be higher. If there is no further change in reproductive behavior, and the net reproductive rate remains approximately equal to one, it will take some 40 to 60 years for the rate of natural increase to fall to zero. Only at that date will the demographic transition in this country be altogether complete.

Population Policy

In a country where the net reproduction rate is as low as it is in the United States, there is really no pressing problem of population policy. True, some people who think the country is already overcrowded would prefer immediate zero population growth. As an immediate objective, however, zero population growth would require fairly drastic policies, such as licensing of motherhood or compulsory contraception. Most people would probably prefer gradually coasting to a halt as we now appear to be doing.

Population growth *is* a serious problem for economic policy, though, in all those countries that have not completed the demographic transition. That includes most of the world outside the advanced industrial economies of the Northern Hemisphere. We shall return to a discussion of the particular problems of population and economic development in the next chapter.

The Economics of Running Out

Let us turn now to another aspect of the question *how long?* This is the scarcity of resources that are limited primarily in terms of their stocks rather than their flows. Using up these resources means eventually running out of them.

Sources and Sinks

The things we are running out of can be classified as **sources** and **sinks.**[1] Sources are naturally occurring stocks of useful productive inputs. Sinks are naturally occurring means of disposing of useless or harmful by-products and consumption. Both are scarce.

The sources whose scarcity is of greatest concern are those of metals and fossil fuels. The currently usable sources of some of these things appear to be in startlingly short supply relative to current rates of use. Charts like the one shown in Exhibit 19.4 have received wide publicity. This chart shows that currently exploitable sources of at least eleven vital raw materials will not last out the lifetime of students now in college. A number of important sources, it appears, will not even last out the lifetime of those students' dogs and cats!

Comparable figures for the most important natural sinks are more difficult to come by. Some natural sinks—the capacity of lakes and rivers

Sources Naturally occurring stocks of useful productive inputs.

Sinks Naturally occurring means of disposing of useless or harmful by-products of production and consumption.

---

[1]The theory we are about to look at applies only to sources and sinks that are privately owned. Many sources, including mines, oil wells, and the like are in fact privately owned. Many sinks, in contrast, are not. The problem of intelligent use of such natural sinks as the air and large bodies of water, when these are not private property, were discussed in the chapter on pollution.

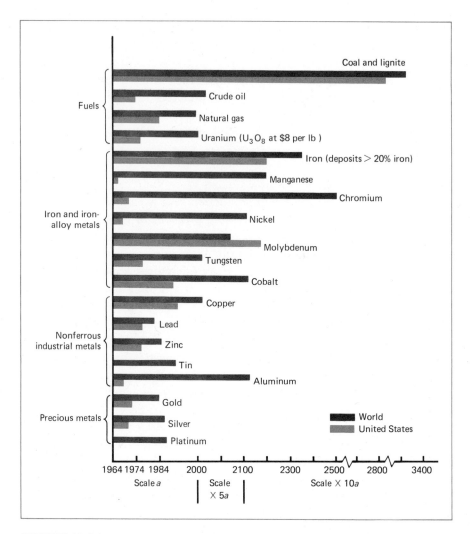

EXHIBIT 19.4

Estimated lifetimes of recoverable mineral resources

This exhibit shows lifetimes of estimated recoverable reserves of mineral resources. Reserves are those that are of high enough grade to be mined with today's techniques. Increasing population and consumption rates, unknown deposits, and future use of presently submarginal ores, are not considered.

Source: From p. 71 of *Population, Resources, Environment: Issues in Human Ecology,* 2nd ed., by Paul R. Ehrlich and Anne H. Ehrlich. W. H. Freeman and Company. Copyright © 1972. First appeared in Preston E. Cloud, Jr., "Realities of Mineral Distribution," *Texas Quarterly,* Vol. 11 (1968), pp. 103–126. Reprinted by permission.

to bear human and industrial wastes, for example—have already been exhausted in places. They must be replaced by costly artificial means of disposal. Of more concern for the long run are three sinks for which no known artificial substitutes are available.

The first of these is the earth's capacity to absorb waste heat from energy-using economic activities. At present rates of growth of energy use, the production of waste heat is estimated to reach the danger level in about 100 years. If drastic climatic effects are to be avoided, we shall have to begin before that point to rely on so-called invariant energy sources. These are sources like solar, wind, wave and geothermal power, which only redirect energy naturally present in the environment, unlike fossil fuels, nuclear fission, and nuclear fusion, which make net additions to the earth's energy balance.

The second sink that is a long-run concern is the ability of the atmosphere to absorb carbon dioxide. Since 1880, the carbon dioxide content of the atmosphere appears to have increased by about 12 percent. A significant part of this increase is believed to have been caused by combustion of fossil fuels. Beyond some point, excessive carbon dioxide in the air would have serious climatic effects, because atmospheric carbon dioxide limits the rate at which the earth can radiate excess energy into space.

There is a third troublesome kind of sink that no one quite knows what to do about. This is the kind of sink needed to dispose of the radioactive by-products of nuclear power production. Many nuclear by-products are so toxic that they will have to be kept sealed away from contact with the environment for 1,000 years or more. That is why nuclear engineers sometimes call the disposal of radioactive wastes the "thousand-year problem." Engineers are hoping that they will be able to solve the thousand-year problem sooner or later, but for now, many radioactive wastes are being stored in temporary facilities.

Market Allocation over Time

The main economic problem that arises in connection with depletable sources and sinks is how to allocate them over time. Should they be used up as fast as possible, in the hope that something will be there to replace them when they run out? Should they be severely rationed so that they will last as long as possible? Should their rate of use be gradually tapered off year by year? As a starting point for answering these questions, let us look at how the market allocates resources over time.

Suppose that there is some resource that exists in a known, limited quantity and costs very little to extract from the sources where it is found. Let us use natural gas, just for the sake of example. The owners of natural gas wells can either sell their gas now, or conserve it to sell in the future. Each alternative has its advantages. If they sell their gas now, they can use the revenue they take in to invest in stocks or bonds, to provide them an interest income after their gas supplies are exhausted. On the other hand, if some resource owners conserve their gas while others sell now, the owners who hold back may be able to sell at a higher price later. Gas will then be even scarcer than it is at present. Which should owners do: sell now, or wait?

It is not hard to figure out what will happen if this decision is left to the market. Enough gas will be sold now to ensure that the price will be pushed up in the future, as less and less is left. Enough gas will be conserved, however, so that the *expected rate of increase in price will not exceed the market rate of interest.* To confirm this, suppose for a moment that it were not true. Let us say that the price next year is expected to be 15 percent higher than this year, but that the market rate of interest is only 10 percent. Any one resource owner can hold back $1,000 worth of gas, and sell it next year for $1,150. His alternative would be to sell now, and invest the $1,000 in securities that will be worth $1,100 next year, including accumulated interest.

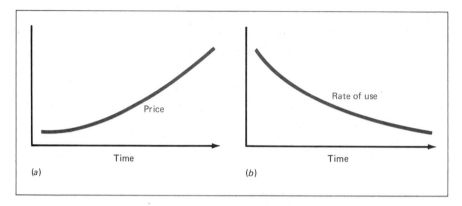

EXHIBIT 19.5
Market allocation over time of a nonrenewable resource
The market price of a nonrenewable resource tends to rise over time. Supply
and demand conditions limit the rate of depletion, so the price will not rise
at a rate faster than the rate of interest. As the price rises, the rate of use
falls, other things being equal.

The alternative of holding back is clearly the more profitable. As some producers begin to turn off their production valves, though, the quantity of gas currently supplied will decrease. That will cause the current price to be bid up by supply and demand. At the same time, the larger quantity of gas left in reserve will tend to depress the expected price next year. Only when the spread between this year's and next year's price has diminished to 10 percent will owners stop switching from current production to conservation.

In short, when there is a resource that exists in a known, fixed quantity, and whose cost of extraction is low, the market will allocate that resource over time as shown in Exhibit 19.5. The price will rise over time at a rate equal to the rate of interest. Other things being equal, the rate of use will fall as the price rises.[2]

Qualifications

The preceding argument puts a maximum on the rate at which the price of a scarce resource will increase and the rate at which it will be used up. There are circumstances under which the rate of use and of price increase would be less rapid than the rate of interest. In particular, this would be the case if the resource were costly to extract, or if high prices stimulated a search for new reserves or for substitutes. Let us consider some examples.

First, suppose that the current price of a resource is equal to the current marginal cost of extracting it. In that case, the quantity supplied will be limited by the quantity demanded at the current price rather than by the expected effect of current use on future prices. The quantity demanded may very well not be high enough to deplete the resource fast enough to push its future price up at a rate equal to the interest rate.

---

[2]If economic growth or population growth cause the demand curve for the resource to shift steadily to the right as time goes by, this pattern may be somewhat modified. The rate of price rise will still not exceed the rate of interest, but the rate of use could, for a time, increase before it begins to taper off.

Second, consider the possibility that there are reserves of a resource that cannot be profitably exploited now, but that can be used if the price rises a little. The presence of those reserves may limit the rate of price increase, because they will increase expected future supply. In practice, the usable reserves of many important resources do appear to increase quite elastically as demand and prices rise. Partly this is because higher prices make it worthwhile to spend more money on exploration, and partly because they make it worthwhile to exploit known low-grade reserves. The tendency of reserves to expand and prices to increase makes data like those given in Exhibit 19.4 of little use for serious planning of resource policy. Oil reserves are a case in point. Between 1950 and 1968, oil production expanded by 280 percent, but proved reserves increased by 420 percent. It would have been an error to have based policy in the early 1950s on the assumption that the world's reserves of oil would be exhausted by the early 1960s.

Finally, we must consider the possibility that high prices for natural resources will stimulate the production of substitutes. The following case study describes how this can happen.

CASE 19.1
Commercial Development of Alternative Energy Sources

As oil prices increased during the 1970s, a great interest in alternative energy sources developed. Congress voted funds for long-range studies of wind power, solar power, geothermal power, and even wave power. The price increase did more than just stimulate activity in Congressional committee rooms, however. It brought a response from the market as well. Entrepreneurs, some operating on a large scale and others working in their own basements, moved to exploit the new price conditions. The American Solar Heat Corporation (AMSOLHEAT) of Danbury, Connecticut, is a typical example of this kind of entrepreneurship.

Note the emphasis on relative price changes in the AMSOLHEAT advertisement reproduced in Exhibit 19.6. The firm offers nothing really new in the way of technology. It uses techniques that were already in use during the 1940s and 1950s, before cheap energy made them uneconomical. Now, at current prices for oil and gas, solar hot water heat is again economical. It can be sold not as a plaything, but as a practical way for homeowners to save money on their energy bills.

None of what we have said guarantees, of course, that we shall always have unlimited supplies of all resources we want. The point is rather that, in a market economy, we do not have to worry about just "running out" some day, like falling off a cliff. As natural resources reserves are depleted, prices will rise. The price rise will slow the rate of growth of consumption. This interaction between reserves and current prices is the market's way of looking ahead, and can be counted on to produce a smooth transition to changing circumstances.

Conclusions

Can we conclude that we live in the "best of all possible worlds," in which we do not need to worry about a population explosion or the depletion of scarce natural resources? Unfortunately, we cannot. Two worries remain.

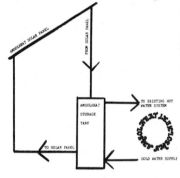

EXHIBIT 19.6

A market response to the energy crisis

When the oil embargo pushed the cost of energy up, entrepreneur Joseph Heyman of Ridgefield, Connecticut, responded by founding the American Solar Heat Corporation (AMSOLHEAT). His product uses technology that has long been known, but was uneconomical while conventional fuels were cheap.

Source: American Solar Heat Corp., Danbury, Conn.

One worry is that resource owners will be stupid and short sighted, and will allow their resources to be depleted at a rate faster than the rate that will give them the highest possible income in the long run. Anecdotal evidence suggests that in years past, especially in the frontier era when people thought that natural resources were altogether unlimited and would never run out, this kind of private short sightedness may sometimes have occurred. Today we presumably have less to fear from the failure of resource owners to pursue their own self-interest.

A second, more serious worry arises from the fact that not all natural resources are under the control of private owners. In the last chapter, we saw how scarce natural sinks could sometimes be polluted up to and beyond their absorption capacity when those sinks were publicly owned and left free for every user. Much the same thing can happen when depletable sources of minerals or fossil fuels are controlled by political rather than market forces.

The American government's policy on oil and natural gas is a clear case in which political forces have operated more short sightedly than market forces. For years, the Federal Power Commission, which regulates natural gas prices, acted in the short-run interest of powerful consumer groups by forcing gas producers to sell at a regulated price below the market equilibrium price. As a result, natural gas has been used extremely wastefully. It has even been used for electric power generation, where more efficient substitutes are available. Natural gas reserves are now far below what they would be if control of pricing and production had been left to the market. More recently, the same mistake has been repeated with oil prices. Fearing political repercussions, Congress has legislated artificially low prices for petroleum products. Again, the result is predictable. Depletion of scarce known reserves will be accelerated, existing supplies will be used wastefully, and research on alternative energy sources will be retarded.

We must conclude with a final warning about a possible misinterpretation of the economic theory of resource markets. Economic theory tells us that the market can reasonably be relied on to guarantee efficient use of depletable natural resources. That does not mean, however, that the scarcity of natural resources imposes no limit to economic growth. Even if resources were used with perfect efficiency, the world could eventually face a decline in output and living standards as things run out.

There is no doubt that the depletion of natural resources puts a drag on economic growth. Up to now, that drag has been more than compensated for by advances in technology and the accumulation of capital, both of which permit higher levels of output per unit of natural resource input. However, no purely theoretical consideration can guarantee that technology and capital accumulation will always advance fast enough to save us. A sufficient rate of capital accumulation is a particularly important requirement for continued growth. It takes more investment per unit of output to build solar power stations than oil-fired power stations. It takes more investment per unit of output to build nonpolluting factories than to use natural sinks for waste disposal. It takes more capital per unit of resources to extract metals from low-grade than from high-grade ores. Economists can only hope that capital accumulation and technological progress will win the race against depletion. No promises can be made.

SUMMARY

1. A population grows whenever its crude birth rate exceeds its crude death rate. In a finite environment, living populations cannot grow indefinitely. If the birth rate does not fall to the death rate, overcrowding will force the death rate up to the birth rate.

2. Population growth in developed countries has undergone a process known as the demographic transition. In preindustrial society, both birth and death rates were high. As industrialization began, death rates fell, and a period of rapid population growth began. Economic growth was even more rapid than population growth, however, so per capita incomes rose. This brought death rates down and reduced the rate of population growth.

3. In a market economy, the forces of supply and demand limit the rate at which nonrenewable natural resources are depleted. Too rapid depletion would drive current prices down and push expected future prices up so that the expected rate of price increase would exceed the rate of interest. Resource owners would then find it to their advantage to reduce current supply in order to sell later when the price was higher. The rate of price increase for a nonrenewable resource in a market economy thus tends to be equal to or less than the rate of interest. This encourages a proper balance between capital accumulation and resource conservation as alternative ways of preparing for the economic future.

DISCUSSION QUESTIONS

1. Do you agree that we must be near the bend in an S-shaped world population curve, even though every bit of evidence from the past points to continuous acceleration of world population growth? If so, why? If not, explain how you think continued acceleration of population growth can continue.

2. In early phases of industrialization, urbanization seems to be a major factor in bringing birth rates down. Today, birth rates are still falling in the United States, even though the degree of urbanization is no longer changing rapidly. What other factors do you think are at work causing the continued decline in birth rates?

3. One method to limit population growth in the United States works like this. Each person, when born, would be given one birth permit allowing him or her to have a child. Each couple could then have two children if they wanted. If they wanted fewer than two children, they could sell their excess certificate or certificates to couples who wanted more than two. Would you favor such a proposal under current conditions? Would you favor such a proposal in comparison to other population control policies if changing circumstances seemed to make overpopulation a much greater danger for this country than it is now? Assume now that the proposal were implemented, and that the net reproduction rate in this country remained below one. What would you expect to happen to the market price of birth permits?

4. Suppose that you are due to inherit $1 million when you graduate from college. You take a course in environmental studies, and your professor convinces you that short-sighted capitalists are using up mineral and energy resources at far too fast a rate, so that we shall soon run out of many important ores and minerals altogether. Would this give you any ideas about profitable ways to invest your million? Do you think your professor believes firmly enough in his predictions to invest his own savings the same way?

5. Review the AMSOLHEAT advertisement reproduced in Exhibit 19.6. How much is your hot water bill each year? (If you do not pay your own hot water bill, ask your parents or your professor what a typical family in your town pays for hot water.) If you could cut this bill by 70 percent, would it pay you to spend $1,260 on a solar hot water heater? (Assume that you can finance the project with a 12 percent home improvement loan from your local bank.) If your answer is no, how low would the interest rate have to be to make the solar heater pay, given the size of your hot water bill? How big would your water bill have to be, given a 12 percent rate of interest?

CHAPTER 20
Economic Development in a World of Scarcity

What You Will Learn in This Chapter

Less developed countries face even more serious problems of population, resources, and environment than do developed countries. They are also less well equipped to surmount them. For one thing, these countries have not yet gone through the demographic transition. Many of them are in danger of being caught in a "population trap" that could bring economic growth to a halt. The capital resources of less developed countries are also very limited. They cannot do everything at once, and face a difficult choice between a development strategy emphasizing industry and one emphasizing rural development.

For Review

Here are some important terms and concepts that will be put to use in this chapter. Be certain that you understand them, or review them before proceeding.

Sources of economic growth (Chapter 7)
Demographic transition (Chapter 19)

For two chapters now, we have looked at the problems of pollution, population, and resources that cloud the economic future for the world's advanced industrial countries. These problems pose some serious challenges for economic policy. Mistakes have been made in the past that must not be repeated in the future. Nonetheless, the picture is not entirely one of gloom. The developed countries face the future with some big advantages. Most of them have completed the demographic transition and left acute population problems behind. They also have the potential for capital formation that they will need to replace natural resources with synthetic substitutes.

In the less developed countries of the world, things are going to be more difficult. These countries must deal with the same problems of pollution, population, and resources, plus some others of their own, and are less well equipped to do so. Let us turn now to an examination of the problems and prospects for the economic future of the "third world." We begin with an attempt to understand just what economic development is.

Three Faces of Development

Economic Development as Growth

The less developed countries that constitute what we call the third world have many differences, but also many things in common. The most conspicuous thing they have in common is low per capita income. No magic number divides the developed from the less developed countries, but development economics tends to focus on those with per capita gross national products of less than $500 per year. In Asia, China, India, and Bangladesh, with their vast populations, all fall in this poorest group. On the African continent, only Libya and South Africa escape unqualified less developed status. In South America, many countries, including Brazil, Bolivia, Haiti, Guatemala, and several others remain below the $500 mark. (Others, including Argentina, Chile, Venezuela, and Mexico are enough above the line to be counted as members of an intermediate group.) All in all, the less developed countries contain some two-thirds of the world's population.

To draw these distinctions in terms of per capita incomes is to say that economic development equals economic growth. That is the traditional view of the matter, and it is a view that still has much truth to it. Economic growth can occur without bringing a better life to everyone, but it is hard to see how a better life for all can come without at least some growth. This is especially true for those least developed countries that have less than $100 of gross national product per capita.

Much of development economics, then, focuses on ways to enable a country to grow. Growth-oriented development studies usually emphasize capital accumulation as the great key. Capital accumulation has accounted for only about 15 percent of economic growth in the United States in recent years, but it is more important for less developed countries. In such countries there is a great shortage of capital. Typically, saving and investment are only 5–7 percent of gross national product. This compares with over 15 percent in the United States, and 35 percent in Japan and the Soviet-type economies. Without capital accumulation, it is difficult to put unemployed and underemployed people to work. Without capital it is equally difficult to improve the level of education, or to take advantage of imported technology. Yet although capital accumulation and growth are important, they are not the whole story of economic development. Development has other faces too.

Development as Industrialization

The developed countries are not only richer than the less developed countries, they are also more highly industrialized. Developed countries typically have between a fifth and a quarter of their populations engaged in manufacturing industry. In the less developed countries, the proportion is likely to be 10 percent or less. A second interpretation of economic development, then, is that it means industrializing just as the advanced countries have done in the past.

The view that development means industrialization, like the view that development means economic growth, has much truth to it. The less developed countries have large and growing urban populations. Only industrialization offers these much hope of employment. As incomes rise in a developing country, the demand for manufactured goods increases rapidly. It makes sense to meet many of these needs with domestic sources of supply. Many less developed countries have valuable raw materials that they now export for processing. These could be processed domestically instead. Still, despite all this, the importance of industrialization to development should not be exaggerated.

For one thing, an overemphasis on industrialization may cause resources to be wasted on ill-conceived "showcase" projects. Not every less developed country needs a steel mill and an automobile works. Even small-scale industrial projects may be inappropriate if they mean building an exact replica of some plant originally designed for Manchester or Milwaukee, where relative factor scarcities and other market conditions are completely different.

What is more, an overemphasis on industrialization can lead to the neglect of other development objectives. To see why, let us take a look at a third face of economic development.

Development as Depauperization

It is a widely shared opinion that a major goal of economic development should be a better life for the poorest of the poor. These are the people at the low end of the income distribution in the poorest countries. They are the true paupers. They lack adequate food, often lack all access to medical care, and not infrequently lack even the most primitive shelter.

Development economists once were confident that the benefits of growth and industrialization would automatically "trickle down" to the poorest of the poor. Unfortunately, this optimism may not be justified, as

Irma Adelman was born in Cernowitz, Roumania. After coming to the United States, she studied at the University of California at Berkeley, receiving a Ph.D. in economics in 1955. She taught at Stanford, Johns Hopkins, and Northwestern University, before moving to the University of Maryland in 1972.

Professor Adelman has earned a reputation as one of the foremost writers on the subject of development economics. In all of her writings, she stresses the extreme complexity and interrelatedness of the phenomena of economic development. There is no simple explanation for underdevelopment, such as a deficiency of capital, or a lack of entrepreneurial talent, or an adverse ratio of population to natural resources, or a hostile international environment.

Because of the complex nature of underdevelopment, there can be no single key to development. Gradualist approaches to development policy are likely to fail. Instead, what is needed is some large shock that will significantly change the way the people of a less developed society behave. Adelman believes that the government must play a large role in administering these critical shocks.

Irma Adelman has employed quantitative methods widely in her studies of development. These quantitative studies led her to the disturbing discovery that very often in the early stages of development, the poorest 60 percent of the population become even poorer, both in relative and absolute terms, as the economy grows. Rather than the "trickle down" effect that earlier writers hoped for, there can instead be a "trickle up." She concludes that governments are choosing the wrong goals in economic development. There is a trade-off between sheer growth of GNP, on the one hand, and depauperization, on the other. For moral as much as for economic reasons, Adelman believes that governments ought to adopt depauperization as their primary development goal.

Irma Adelman (1930–   )

recent research of Irma Adelman and C. T. Morris has shown.[1] Their recent work focuses on the range of development from sub-Saharan Africa to the poorest countries of South America, that is, from about $100 to $500 per capita income. In these countries, development tends to bring both relative and absolute impoverishment to the poorest 60 percent of the population. At very low levels of development, there appears to be no "trickling down" at all. The poor begin to benefit only after an intermediate level of development has been reached.

Adelman and Morris have concluded that the policies needed to benefit the poor are different than those needed to maximize growth rates. The ideas of development as growth or industrialization, they say, should be replaced with the idea of **depauperization.** Depauperization means not only providing the necessary material basis for life, but also access to education, status, security, self-expression, and power. Depauperization stresses the removal of social, political, and spiritual deprivation as much as physical deprivation. It has as much to do with equity as with growth.

Depauperization Economic development of a kind that benefits the poorest of the poor, providing them not only with the material necessities of life, but also with access to education, status, security, self-expression, and power.

Two Strategies

The choice of development goals strongly influences the strategy that can best promote the development process. The Soviet Union represents one extreme. For Soviet planners, development meant industrialization above all else. Through high rates of saving, they sacrificed consumption to achieve rapid growth. Through collectivization, they sacrificed the growth of agriculture to achieve the growth of industry. Eventually, the benefits of successful industrialization began to trickle down to the population at large. Initially, though, living standards declined, and the overall distribution of income shifted in favor of industrial workers and against peasants.

Even where industrialization as an end in itself is not made a higher priority than overall growth, the benefits of development may be spread very unevenly. Many less developed countries suffer from what is called a **dual economy.** In such an economy, a modern, Westernized industrial sector provides high wages for better educated workers and a tax base to pay a middle class of civil servants. Meanwhile a secondary, traditional sector remains largely untouched. Sometimes, the overall growth rate of GNP can be maximized by concentrating available development resources on the modern sector, at least in the short run. Often also foreign aid and the investments of multinational corporations are concentrated on the modern sector of dual economies.

Dual Economy A less developed economy that is sharply divided into a modern, Westernized industrial sector capable of rapid growth, and a traditional rural sector that remains stagnant.

There is a second kind of development strategy that contrasts with the industry-first approach. Instead, it emphasizes redistribution and mass education first, and growth later. Redistribution in the context of less developed countries means most importantly the redistribution of land ownership. Education means mass education in literacy and general knowledge, rather than just specialized training for participation in the modern sector. If this strategy works, redistribution can provide the basis for rural development and education can provide the basis for the growth of

[1]Irma Adelman and C. T. Morris, *Society, Politics, and Economic Development,* (Baltimore: Johns Hopkins, 1967).

broadly based, labor-intensive industry. Adelman and Morris cite Israel, Japan, South Korea, Singapore, and Taiwan as countries that have successfully followed this strategy. China should probably be added to the list. In the last century, American economic development followed this strategy much more nearly than did economic development in Europe.

Population and Development

Death Control and Birth Control

Whatever development strategy they choose, all less developed countries face certain common problems that they must somehow overcome. None are more serious than the closely related problems of death control, birth control, and population growth. In Chapter 19 we introduced some basic concepts of population economics. Now let us see how these apply specifically to less developed countries.

Traditional societies of the past had high birth rates, high death rates, and relatively stable populations. In developed economies, both deaths and births are controlled by the techniques of modern medical science, and population growth rates are also low. Today's less developed countries lie between these two demographic patterns. They have successfully imported modern methods of death control, especially the control of epidemic disease, but birth control has not fully taken hold. As a result, population growth rates are very high.

Turn back for a moment to Exhibit 19.4, which gives population growth data for a selected group of developed and less developed countries. The countries are ranked in order of their rates of population growth. Near the middle of the table we find Afghanistan which, with both the highest crude birth rate and crude death rate of all listed countries, most closely fits the traditional pattern. Even there, though, modern medicine has had an effect on the death rate. The rate of natural increase of population is very substantial, at 22.4 per 1,000 per year. At the bottom of the table are the United Kingdom and Czechoslovakia, where birth rates and death rates are very nearly in equilibrium. At the top are Ecuador and Mexico—by no means the poorest of less developed countries—where death rates are as low as those in the United States or Great Britain, but birth rates are nearly as high as in the poorest parts of Africa. These are the countries where, to use the popular phrase, the "population bomb" is ticking away.

The Population Trap

Birth rates, death rates, economic growth, and income levels are in very delicate balance during economic development. We explained in Chapter 19 that countries that develop successfully undergo a process called the demographic transition. During the demographic transition, rising income levels first depress death rates, causing population growth rates to accelerate, and then depress birth rates, causing population growth to slow.

Exhibit 20.1 shows what happens to per capita income and population growth, assuming steady economic growth during the demographic transition. In part *a,* the vertical axis measures the level of per capita income. We suppose that when income is below the level *A,* people are so poor that

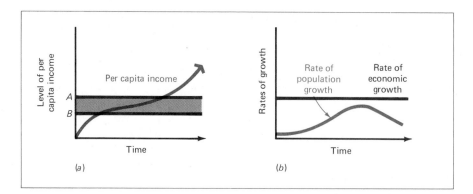

EXHIBIT 20.1

The demographic transition

Here we show the effects of the demographic transition in terms of economic growth and population growth. We assume that death rates begin to fall once per capita reaches the level *A,* and that birth rates begin to fall once per capita reaches the level *B.* During the transition, the growth of population speeds up and that of per capita income slows. Economic growth always stays above population growth, however.

Population Trap A situation in which the rate of population growth rises above the rate of economic growth, halting the growth of per capita income and aborting the demographic transition.

death rates are high, and when it is above *B,* people are prosperous enough that birth rates are low. (Of course, things are really more complicated than this. There are not really any sharp cutoff levels of income, but our simple assumption will serve to make the point.) In part *b,* the vertical axis measures growth rates of total GNP and of population. Note that population growth never exceeds the growth of GNP. The curve of per capita income in part *a* always moves upward, although it rises less rapidly in the zone between *A* and *B* while the demographic transition is under way.

Can today's less developed countries complete this process as the developed countries have done? It is to be hoped that they can, but it is by no means certain. There is a real danger that they will get caught in a **population trap,** and their attempt to make it through the demographic transition will abort.

Exhibit 20.2 shows schematically how a country could fall foul of the population trap. Suppose that such a country begins development normally, as did the country represented in Exhibit 20.1. This time, though, either population growth is more rapid or economic growth slower. At time *T,* the growth of population begins to exceed the growth of income, and per capita income starts to fall. Instead of completing the demographic transition, the country falls back into a subsistence equilibrium with birth and death rates both high and per capita income stagnant.

Escape

In the nineteenth century, when Western Europe and North America were industrializing, death rates fell only slowly, and only after living standards had already begun to improve. Population growth rates did not rise above 1 percent per year in most cases. Today, modern death control techniques have reached almost every corner of the globe, no matter how poor. That makes it more difficult for today's less developed countries to

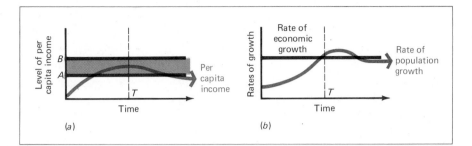

EXHIBIT 20.2
The population trap
If at some point during the demographic transition the rate of population growth exceeds the rate of economic growth, a country may be caught in a "population trap." As this exhibit is drawn, the country enters the trap at time *T*. At that point, per capita income begins to fall, and the demographic transition is absorbed.

escape the population trap. During the nineteenth century, the American economy experienced growth rates of GNP in the range of 3.5 to 4.5 percent per year. Rates of growth in that range are no longer good enough for less developed countries, where population itself can grow as fast as 3.5 percent per year. Any growth rate for GNP slower than 6 to 7 percent per year gives little hope for escaping the population trap just by outrunning it. Countries like South Korea or Taiwan may make it, but those like Haiti, Chad, or Dahomey, where per capita incomes are already falling, will not.

The only other way to escape the population trap is to bring down the birth rate while incomes are still low. There is some evidence that in countries where the benefits of growth have been widely shared among the population, birth rates have begun to fall at per capita income levels as low as $200. In other countries, highly publicized birth control campaigns have had little if any effect. India is one country where voluntary programs of birth control have consistently fallen short of targets. As India now retreats from democracy, the government there seems to be moving toward a get-tough policy. In some cases subsidized housing and other social benefits are withdrawn from families that have a third child. In other cases, the government is threatening compulsory sterilization. It remains to be seen whether such programs will have an effect, and whether they will be copied in other less developed countries.

Food and Development[2]

Hunger

We now turn to the aspect of economic development that causes the greatest concern of all. That is the problem of hunger.

Hunger comes in varying degrees. People are said to be undernourished if they suffer from a quantitative lack of calories. They are said to suffer

[2]This section draws at many points on the useful survey *World of Hunger,* by Jonathan Power and Anne-Marie Holenstein (London: Temple Smith, 1976).

from malnutrition if the food they do get contains insufficient protein and other nutrients, even if energy requirements are met. Undernourishment leads to actual starvation. In recent years it has been a major problem in the countries just south of the Sahara in Africa, India, Bangladesh, and Sri Lanka in Asia, and in Bolivia, Haiti, and El Salvador in the Americas, to list only a few. Malnutrition is much more widespread, and has long-run effects that are hardly less devastating. A protein insufficiency in the diets of young children and breast-feeding women is especially dangerous, because it retards brain development. People who survive a malnourished childhood are likely to suffer from lethargy and lack of productive ability in later life. These are hardly the traits required for the labor forces of poor countries struggling to achieve development.

Accurate statistics on world hunger are hard to come by. Definitions vary, and the governments of some of the worst-hit countries are reluctant to supply information. Some who have studied the problem believe that as many as two-thirds of the world's population may suffer from undernourishment or malnutrition in some form. The data in Exhibit 20.3 are based on much more conservative methods of estimation, but they still show an appallingly serious problem.

Hunger and Population

The relationship between hunger and population is complex. It is natural to think of overpopulation causing hunger, with a Malthusian growth of numbers of people outstripping food production. Hunger can be a spur to population growth, too, however. Malnutrition leads to high infant mortality. High infant mortality, in turn, leads to the desire to have a large family, so that at least some children will survive. Perhaps the relationship between malnutrition and desired family size is part of the reason why birth rates have fallen earliest in those countries that have distributed the benefits of development widely among their populations.

When the world food problem is presented as a race between production and the growth of demand, the results are sobering. Information presented at the World Food Conference in 1974[3] placed 71 less developed countries in three groups according to food and population trends during the period 1953–1971. In 24 of these countries, the rate of increase in food production fell short of population growth. In an additional 17, the rate of increase of food production exceeded the rate of growth of population, but fell short of the rate of growth of domestic demand. Because rising incomes permitted people to eat more, these countries had to increase food imports (or in some cases, decrease food exports), thus making things harder yet for the countries in the first group. In the 30 remaining countries, the rate of growth of food output exceeded the rate of growth of demand, but even some of these countries experienced regional problems because of maldistribution within their borders.

What can be done about the world food problem? In the remainder of this section, we shall examine some possible approaches.

---

[3]Preliminary Assessment of the World Food Situation, World Food Conference, 1974, UNIE/Conf. 65/Prep./6. Data also presented as Table 7 in Power and Holenstein, *World of Hunger*.

EXHIBIT 20.3
Estimated numbers of people with insufficient protein/energy supply, by regions, 1970
According to the relatively conservative estimates reported in this table, some 388 million people had less than minimum standards of nutrition in 1970. Some observers think that nearly two-thirds of the world's population may suffer from malnutrition to some extent.

Region	Population (billions)	Percentage Below Lower Limit (percent)	Number Below Lower Limit (millions)
Developed regions	1.07	3	28
Developing regions excluding Asian centrally planned economies	1.75	20	360
Latin America	0.28	13	37
Far East	1.02	22	221
Near East	0.17	20	34
Africa	0.28	25	68
World (excluding Asian centrally planned economies)	2.83	14	388

Source: Jonathan Power and Anne-Marie Holenstein, *World of Hunger* (London: Temple Smith, 1976). Reprinted by permission.

Food Aid

In 1954, the American Congress passed the Agricultural Trade Development and Assistance Act, commonly known as PL480. This act has been the heart of world food aid efforts. During the 1960s, the United States gave up to 84 percent of all world food aid. The less developed countries were able to rely on food aid for 30 to 45 percent of their food imports.

Under Title 1 of PL480, food was sold on favorable terms to governments. Under Title 2, food went free to governments and to the United Nations World Food Program. Title 2 food aid was aimed at the especially underprivileged, and at disaster relief. At the same time the populations of less developed countries were benefitting from PL480, American farmers were benefitting. The program was thus a combination of idealism and self-interest, but the combination for a long time seemed to work well.

Problems of Food Aid

Despite the very substantial benefits to countries receiving food aid, PL480 and the food aid programs of other governments have had their critics. It is important to realize why food aid alone is not likely to provide a long-run answer to the world food problem.

First of all, because American food aid is based on a mixture of charity and self-interest, it is liable to disruption from the self-interest side. When American farmers were producing huge grain surpluses, voters and consumers were happy to see the surpluses given away. Now that the chronic surpluses have disappeared, giving food hurts more than it used to. For one thing, there are now plenty of paying customers for American grain exports.

Also, grain prices have risen so high that further increases in exports put serious pressure on domestic food prices. Such exports thus now meet opposition from consumer groups. Since 1972, the total volume of American food aid has declined. In 1974, the amount of food delivered under aid programs fell to a third of the 1972 level. PL480 has thus proved least reliable just when it has been needed most.

There is a second serious problem in the tendency of some receiver governments to rely on food aid as a substitute for domestic agricultural development. In some cases, the motivation has been political. Necessary agricultural reforms would have threatened the privileges of entrenched ruling classes, so that getting American aid seemed like an easier way out. In other cases, food aid has disrupted domestic markets. Food aid kept prices low in the less developed countries. This was fine for the landless poor, but it greatly reduced incentives to farmers. Sometimes, the effect of food aid on relative prices made nonfood cash crops more attractive to grow than food crops.

Finally, many critics of food aid are unhappy about the standards by which recipients have been selected. The countries receiving greatest aid in recent years have been those such as South Vietnam, Chile, South Korea, Jordan, Syria, and Israel that have been crucial to American foreign policy. India, Bangladesh, and Sri Lanka, where need has been greatest, have gotten only something like a fifth of the total. The power that food exports give to the American government is certain to grow in coming years. Soon perhaps this food power will exceed even the power wielded by oil exporters. It is small wonder that the less developed nations are looking for ways to reduce their dependence.

Need for Rural Development

Throughout the world, less developed countries are urbanizing rapidly—far more rapidly than today's developed countries did at comparable stages of their own growth. The reasons for this urbanization are complex. Partly the modernity and the promise of a better life in the city attracts new population. Partly the problem is education systems that do not emphasize agricultural topics. Whatever the causes, cities are not able to meet the aspirations of all those who arrive in them. Urban unemployment rates are very high. Many of those who are employed work in tertiary services, from shining shoes to hustling, that contribute little to economic development or to the development of those individuals. Huge shanty towns surrounding third world cities are the rule rather than the exception.

Current rates of urbanization far exceed the potential for industrial development in most poor countries. A recent OECD study[4] calculated that, just to keep urban unemployment from rising in a typical less developed country, industrial output would have to grow at 18 percent per year. Even in Brazil, which has had outstanding success with industrialization and urban development, industrial growth has run at only 15 percent per year. To get rid of the 20 to 25 percent unemployment common in cities of less developed countries, industry would have to grow at something like 30 to 35 percent per year for a decade.

[4]David Turnham, *The Employment Problem in Less Developed Countries,* (Paris: Organization for Economic Cooperation and Development, 1971), as cited by Power and Holenstein, *World of Hunger,* pp. 74–75.

When urban unemployment and the food problem are considered together, it is not surprising that many development economists believe that the real hope for the less developed countries lies in the countryside. The hope is to hold people on the land, and make them productive there within a meaningful community structure. If the third world nations can do that, they may be able to feed themselves, distribute what little they have more equitably, meet the nonmaterial aspirations of their populations, and retain their independence. That, at least, is what the advocates of rural development say. They all recognize that there are problems, though.

Technological Problems

Rural development does not mean just the introduction of new agricultural methods. It also means the growth of small-scale industry in villages and towns. These are necessary to meet local needs and provide employment for those whom even the most ambitious land reform program would leave landless. Is the technological basis for such development available?

In some respects, technological progress has been remarkable. The most talked-about development is the appearance of new, high-yield varieties of wheat and rice. Under laboratory conditions, these new varieties can triple food output per acre. They provide the best hope for less developed countries to escape from the sheer shortage of land.

Unfortunately, high-yield wheat, rice, and other grains cannot just be stuck in the ground and expected to do their magic. The secret of their success lies in their ability to absorb huge quantities of fertilizers. If ordinary varieties of grain are overfertilized, they produce only luxuriant growth of stems and leaves, or seedheads so heavy that they break the stalk of the plant. With high-yield varieties, extra fertilization produces growth where it is needed. Without such fertilization, the new varieties actually produce less than traditional crops. (In many cases, heavy use of pesticides and irrigation are needed as well.)

As the use of high-yield varieties has spread, less developed countries have become more dependent on imported fertilizers. They now produce barely half their own fertilizer needs. What is worse, fertilizer production depends critically on oil. This is particularly true of nitrogen fertilizers, which make up half the total used. These are made almost entirely from natural gas and petroleum products. The "green revolution" has been extremely hard hit by high oil prices, because outside the Middle East, few less developed countries have their own oil supplies.

Rural industrial development faces technological problems that are, if anything, greater than those faced by agricultural development. Western industrial research has developed technology designed to use cheap capital and save expensive labor. The opposite conditions prevail in rural areas of the third world. Very little research has gone into the development of simple but sophisticated labor-intensive ways of doing things.

Institutional Problems

A number of institutional problems also threaten rural development. Chief among these are the problem of land reform and the problem of supplying credit to rural areas.

Advocates of rural development support land reform. Land reform means buying (or sometimes confiscating) the large holdings of absentee landlords, and distributing the land in the smallest feasible parcels among those who actually till the soil. The effects of land reform, if it works, are threefold. First, a small landowner has a greater incentive than a tenant farmer to improve the land and introduce better production techniques. Second, wide distribution of ownership means wider distribution of the product, with all the benefits this is believed to bring. Third, land reform can lead to more stable rural community structures. This helps stop the rush to the city. It also helps provide the dignity and sense of personal worth that are part of the process of depauperization.

Many countries have carried out thorough land reforms, but many others have not. Two problems hold back further land reform. One major problem is political. The land-owning classes often dominate the political structures of less developed countries, and are reluctant to relinquish this hold. The second is economic. Under some circumstances, technological considerations may make it more productive to consolidate land holdings into bigger farms to realize economies of scale. To some extent, land reform can involve a trade-off between growth and depauperization.

The other major institutional weakness that holds back small-scale rural development is a weakness of credit markets. In many less developed countries, small farmers have no access to banks and other modern credit facilities. They must rely on local money lenders or merchants, who charge extremely high rates of interest.

High-yield crops have made the credit problem more serious than ever. The green revolution can actually work against the small farmer. Higher yields drive land rents up, and put downward pressure on output prices. The new varieties cannot be used without expensive fertilizers and pesticides, but buying these only puts the small farmer more at the mercy of the money lender. Thus if land reform is carried out without credit reform, land reform can in fact retard the introduction of new techniques.

Conclusions

The tone of much of this chapter has been pessimistic. There is no doubt that the problems of the less developed countries will be very difficult to surmount, and that some countries will fail. There is every doubt of the ability and the will of the industrialized countries to carry the burden of development. Nonetheless, there are places where things are going right rather than wrong. It is fitting to end this chapter with one of these success stories.

CASE 20.1
The Fondo Negro Project[5]

In the Dominican Republic, a fascinating experiment is attempting to get around the barriers to credit distribution in the rural areas of less developed countries. Convinced that small farmers could make use of credit if given proper backup with agricultural expertise, the Dominican Development Foundation (a private, nongovernment organization) has tried to find a way that is nonbureaucratic, simple, and above all, appealing to small farmers. They have done this by working through groups of farmers rather than individuals.

---

[5]Based on Jonathan Power and Anne-Marie Holenstein, *World of Hunger* (London: Temple Smith, 1976). Reprinted by permission.

Farmers who want to receive credit must set up an association. They receive money in the name of the group and agree to be responsible as a group for the repayments of individual members. Banks have found that 10 percent or more of small farmers default on their loans. The Foundation has got the default rate down to 4.2 percent. The social pressure of not letting the group down works astonishingly effectively.

The groups vary enormously. Some of them are quite loosely knit. Individual members operate independently and get together only to receive the loan. In others the collective system works at nearly every level of production. For example, a tomato farm is worked by a group of thirty families. They share the land and the cost of a large pump to bring water up from the river. They organize the planting, weeding, and reaping operations so that everyone takes an equal part of the load. This project—the community of Fondo Negro—has established itself in one of the driest and most impoverished parts of the Dominican Republic. The annual rainfall is only 650 mm, and average monthly temperatures vary from 25 to 30°C. Yet these peasant farmers have cultivated 115 hectares of land and have made in the first year a net profit of $263 per hectare. That is some $1,052 per family! Before they were set up in business by the Foundation and given the credit to prime their operations, the yearly income had been about $100 per family.

Here is a detailed breakdown of the economics of the project: The project consisted of putting 115 hectares of land into the cultivation of tomatoes. A yield of 546 cwt (hundredweight) per hectare was obtained. The total crop was 62,790 cwt. Sold at $1.50 per cwt, this brought in the sum of $94,185 in the first agricultural year.

Costs per hectare were $557.20. Direct costs of cultivation totalled $66,389. Out of this, $4,320 was paid to the 30 agricultural workers participating as a labor force, at the rate of $2 per day during 24 days per month over a period of 3 months and $62,050 was spent on other operational costs and agricultural expenses.

The capital investment reached $18,292.77, of which $3,060.00 related to enclosures and piping and $15,232.77 to irrigation and plant. There was a depreciation for this period of $1,829.28, taking 10 years as the time of use for the capital investment. Hence the direct profits from the cultivation were $25,997.72, or $225.89 per hectare. The economic surplus for the group was $30,297.72, if we add profit and the amount they obtained as payment for their labor. This gives an average profit of $263.46 per hectare.

The Foundation's more advanced groups are now having their loan applications transferred to commercial banks. Convinced that these small farmers will not default after all, the big banks have been persuaded to take them on as normal customers. So far 105 groups are receiving loans in this way, and the default rate is down to 1 percent.

SUMMARY

1. Economic development is a complex phenomenon. A major part of development is sheer economic growth—increasing the size of GNP as a whole. Development also means industrialization. In countries that have developed in the past, industry has grown more rapidly than agriculture. In extreme cases, such as that of the Soviet Union, the agricultural sector has actually been stripped of resources to aid the more rapid growth of industry. A third aspect of economic development is depauperization. This means not only growing, but distributing the benefits of growth to the poorest classes. An industry-first growth strategy may hamper depauperization.
2. Virtually all less developed countries face serious population pressures. Modern death control techniques have been introduced to all corners of the globe, no matter how poor. Where birth rates are still high, population growth rates are more rapid than they ever were during the demographic transition in developed

countries. If the growth rate of GNP does not keep up with the growth of population, a country may be caught in a population trap. In order to complete the demographic transition successfully, many countries will have to find a way of lowering birth rates while per capita incomes are still at a very low level.

3. Some observers believe that as many as two-thirds of the world's population suffer from undernourishment or malnutrition in some form. In many developing countries, population growth is outstripping food production, making the problem worse. In the past, food aid has provided an important stopgap, but food aid alone is not a long-run solution. Rural development is needed if less developed countries are to be able to feed themselves. Technological advances, including high-yield grains, provide a potential basis for rural development. Economic and institutional problems remain, however. Some way must be found to provide the fertilizers, pesticides, and capital needed to make the best use of high-yield grains. Land reform and credit reform are also necessary parts of successful rural development.

DISCUSSION QUESTIONS

1. In what ways are the problems faced by the less developed countries similar to the problems faced by the United States 100 or 200 years ago? In what ways are they different? Will today's less developed countries follow a similar path to economic development, or is a different route more promising?

2. Less developed countries are short on capital. Foreign firms are often willing to invest in such countries. Is foreign investment a good way for them to solve their capital shortage? What would you think might be the advantages and disadvantages of such foreign investment?

3. Less developed countries tend to have less equally distributed incomes than do developed countries. Why do you think this is so? Why do you think development sometimes increases rather than reduces inequality?

4. Do you see any similarity between the "dual economy" of some less developed countries, and the "dual labor market" that some economists believe exists in this country?

5. Americans eat huge quantities of meat. Each pound of meat requires up to 10 pounds of grain to produce. It is sometimes said that Americans could help the world food problem simply by eating less meat. Suppose that this advice were taken to heart, and Americans cut their meat consumption in half, eating more bread instead. Would the grain that was thus saved ever actually reach the hungry poor in the developing countries? If so, explain how shifts in market prices and changes in supply and demand conditions would operate to get it there. If not, explain why the market would fail to move the grain in the desired direction.

6. It is sometimes said that it is pointless just to give money to developing countries to buy food, because this money will just end up lining the pockets of Kansas farmers without doing the less developed countries themselves any real good. Is this concern wholly justified, partly justified, or wholly unjustified? Why?

PART FOUR
International Economics

Up to this point, we have studied micro- and macroeconomics solely within the context of a single national economy. We have not yet mentioned a whole area of economic theory, the theory of international trade.

The first question that we need to ask about this area of economics is why a separate theory of international trade is necessary. Does it really make that much difference that buyers and sellers in certain markets live on opposite sides of national boundaries? The differences between international and national markets are small enough so that most of our familiar tools of analysis apply to both, but there are enough differences to require that these tools be applied in new ways and to new problems. A separate body of theory is thus justified.

From a microeconomic point of view, the most significant feature of international markets is that finished products tend to move more easily in them than do factors of production. Land, with its natural resource deposits and associated climate factors, is the most immobile of factors. Labor also tends to be fairly immobile because of cultural, political, and linguistic barriers. Capital tends to be the most internationally mobile factor of production, but even it does not move as unrestrictedly between countries as within.

Factor immobility is significant because it causes persistent differences in relative and absolute costs of production between nations. With factors immobile, goods that make intense use of labor tend to be cheaper in countries where labor is relatively abundant, agricultural commodities tend to be cheaper in countries with good climates, and so forth. Were factors more mobile, countries with high labor costs would hire more foreign workers until their costs for labor-intensive products had fallen. Countries with bad growing conditions would import soil and sunlight to equalize the costs of agricultural production. In general, internation differences in production costs would be minimized. The microeconomic part of international trade theory will be discussed in Chapter 21.

From a macroeconomic point of view, the main point distinguishing international from national economics is the fact that different countries have different currencies. These fluctuate in value relative to one another. Different currencies make it possible for countries to pursue independent macroeconomic policies. This can mean inflation in one place and deflation across the border, differences in economic growth rates, and a variety of other things. When it comes to studying problems of international currency markets and the balance of payments, these differences become crucial. These macroeconomic issues are discussed in Chapter 22.

CHAPTER 21
International Trade and Comparative Advantages

What You Will Learn in This Chapter
The principle of comparative advantage lies at the heart of the theory of international trade. A country is said to have a comparative advantage in producing a good whenever it can produce that good at a lower opportunity cost than its trading partners. A country can hold a comparative advantage in production of a good even though its absolute production costs, measured in terms of factor inputs, may be higher than costs elsewhere. International specialization according to comparative advantage brings mutual gains to trading countries. Despite the promised benefits of free trade, however, many arguments are heard in favor of protecting domestic industry against foreign competition.

For Review
Here is an important concept that will be put to use in this chapter. Be certain that you understand it, or review it before proceeding.
   Distributive justice (Chapter 1)

The Theory of Comparative Advantage
If we are to study international trade from a microeconomic point of view, we must begin with the theory of comparative advantage. In a sense, international trade theory starts here historically as well as logically. The theory was first clearly set forth by David Ricardo early in the nineteenth century. Ricardo wanted to show why it would be to England's advantage to maintain active trade with other countries. To do so, he used an example very much like the following.

An Example
Let us imagine two countries, which we shall call "Norway" and "Spain." Both countries have farms and offshore fishing beds, but the moderate climate of Spain makes both the farms and the fishing beds more productive. The number of labor hours required to produce a ton of each product in the two countries is shown in Exhibit 21.1. For simplicity, we

	Spain	Norway
Fish	4	5
Grain	2	5

EXHIBIT 21.1
Labor hours per ton of output in Spain and Norway
The figures in this table show the number of labor hours required to produce each ton of fish and grain in Spain and Norway. Spain has an absolute advantage in the production of both goods. Norway has a comparative advantage in fish and Spain has a comparative advantage in grain.

Absolute Advantage   In international trade theory, the ability of a country to produce a good at absolutely lower cost, measured in terms of factor inputs, than its trading partners.

Comparative Advantage   In international trade theory, the ability of a country to produce a good at a lower opportunity cost, in terms of other goods, than its trading partners.

shall consider only labor costs in this example. We shall think of other costs as proportional to labor costs. Also, we shall assume per-unit labor costs to be constant for all levels of output.

This table reveals two kinds of differences in the cost structure of the two countries. First, we notice that *both* fish and grain require fewer labor hours to produce in Spain. Spain is said to have an **absolute advantage** in the production of both goods. Second, we notice that there are differences in the opportunity costs between the two countries. Let us look at the cost of each good in each country, not in terms of labor hours, but in terms of the other good. In Norway, producing a ton of fish means foregoing the opportunity to use 5 labor hours in the fields. A ton of fish thus has an opportunity cost of 1 ton of grain there. In Spain, producing a ton of fish means giving up the opportunity to produce 2 tons of grain. In terms of opportunity costs, then, fish is cheaper in Norway than in Spain, and grain is cheaper in Spain than in Norway. The country in which the opportunity cost of a good is lower is said to have **comparative advantage** in producing that good.

Pretrade Equilibrium

If no trade takes place between Norway and Spain, equilibrium in fish and grain markets in the two countries will be established independently. We have simplified things by ignoring all costs but labor costs, and assuming these to be constant. In pretrade equilibrium, the ratio of the price of fish to the price of grain in each country will thus be equal to the ratio of labor inputs needed to produce the goods. In Norway, where a ton of grain and a ton of fish both take the same labor to produce, the price of fish will be equal to the price of grain. In Spain, where a ton of fish takes twice as much labor to produce as a ton of grain, the equilibrium price of fish will be twice the price of grain.

Suppose that each country has 1,000 labor hours available for production of fish and grain. The way this will be divided between the two products in each country will depend on demand and consumer tastes. Let us suppose that demand conditions are such that in Norway, 100 tons of grain and 100 tons of fish are produced, while in Spain, 350 tons of grain are grown and 75 tons of fish are caught. The quantities produced and consumed in pretrade equilibrium are noted in Exhibit 21.2.

The Possibility of Trade

The stage is now set to consider the possibilities for trade between Norway and Spain. A superficial look at labor costs in the two countries might make us think there were no possibilities for trade. Norwegians might

David Ricardo, the greatest of the classical economists, was born in 1772. His father was a Jewish immigrant and a member of the London stock exchange. Ricardo's education was rather haphazard, and he entered his father's business at the age of 14. In 1793 he married, abandoned strict Jewish orthodoxy, and went into business on his own. These were years of war and financial disturbance. The young Ricardo developed a reputation for remarkable astuteness, and quickly made a large fortune.

In 1799, Ricardo read the *Wealth of Nations,* and first developed an interest in questions of political economy. In 1809, his first writings on economics appeared. These were a series of newspaper articles on ''The High Price of Bullion,'' which appeared the next year as an influential pamphlet. Several other short works added to his reputation in this area. In 1814, he retired from business to devote full time to political economy.

Ricardo's major work was *Principles of Political Economy and Taxation,* first published in 1817. This work contains, among other things, a pioneering statement of the principle of comparative advantage, as applied to international trade. With a lucid numerical example, Ricardo shows why it is to the mutual advantage of both countries for England to export wool to Portugal and import wine in return, even though both products can be produced at absolutely lower costs in Portugal.

But international trade is only a sidelight of Ricardo's *Principles.* The book covers the whole of economics as then known, beginning with value theory, and progressing to a theory of economic growth and evolution. Ricardo, like his friend Malthus and later follower John Stuart Mill, held that the economy was growing toward a future ''steady state.'' In this steady state, economic growth would come to a halt, and the wage rate would be depressed to the subsistence level.

Ricardo's book was extraordinarily influential. For more than half a century thereafter, much of economics as written in England was an elaboration of or commentary on Ricardo's work. The most famous of all economists to fall under the influence of Ricardo's theory and method was Karl Marx. Although Marx eventually reached revolutionary conclusions that differed radically from any views Ricardo held, his starting point was Ricardo's labor theory of value, and Ricardo's method of analyzing economic growth.

David Ricardo (1772–1823)

like to get their hands on some of those cheap Spanish goods, but why should the Spanish be interested? After all, can they not produce everything at home more cheaply than it can be produced abroad? If so, how could they gain from trade? A closer analysis shows us that this superficial view is incorrect. Absolute advantage turns out to be unimportant in determining patterns of trade. Only comparative advantage matters.

EXHIBIT 21.2
Pretrade equilibrium outputs of fish and grain in Spain and Norway

If Spain and Norway do not engage in trade, each country will have to meet all its needs from its own resources. The quantities of goods produced in each country depends on the strength of domestic demand. The relative prices of the two goods in each country will be determined by their labor costs, as shown in Exhibit 21.1.

	Spain	Norway	World Total
Fish	75	100	175
Grain	350	100	450

It is not hard to show that possibilities for trade exist. Imagine that an enterprising Norwegian fishing party decides to sail into a Spanish port with a ton of their catch. Spanish merchants in the port where they arrive will have been used to giving 2 tons of grain, or its equivalent, for a ton of fish. The Norwegians will have been accustomed to getting only an equal weight of grain for each ton of fish. Any exchange ratio between 1 and 2 tons of grain per ton of fish will seem more than normally attractive to both parties. For instance, a trade of $1\frac{1}{2}$ tons of grain for a ton of fish will make both the Spanish merchants and the Norwegian fishing party better off than they would have been had they traded only with others from their own country.

Gains from Specialization

The opening of trade between Spain and Norway will soon begin to have an effect on patterns of production in the two countries. In Norway, farmers will discover that instead of working 5 hours to raise a ton of grain from their own rocky soil, they can fish for 5 hours instead, and trade their catch to the Spaniards for $7\frac{1}{2}$ tons of grain. In Spain, people will find that it is no longer worth their while to spend 4 hours to catch a ton of fish. Instead, they can work just 3 hours in the fields. The $1\frac{1}{2}$ tons of grain that they grow will get them a ton of fish from the Norwegians. In short, the Norwegians will find it worth their while to specialize in fish and the Spanish will find it worth their while to specialize in grain.

Suppose now that trade continues at the ratio of $1\frac{1}{2}$ tons of grain per ton of fish until both countries have become completely specialized. Spain no longer produces any fish, and Norway no longer produces any grain. Norwegians catch 200 tons of fish, half of which is exported to Spain. The Spanish grow 500 tons of grain, 150 of which are exported to Norway. Exhibit 21.3 summarizes this posttrade situation.

A comparison of this table with Exhibit 21.2 reveals three noteworthy things. First, it shows that Norwegians are better off than before. They have just as much fish to eat, and 50 tons more grain than in the pretrade equilibrium. Second, it shows that Spaniards are better off. They have just as much grain to consume as ever, and more fish. Finally, comparing the last columns of the tables shows that total world output of both grain and fish has risen as a result of trade. Everyone is better off, and no one is worse off.

		Spain	Norway	World Total
Fish	Production	0	200	200
	Consumption	100	100	200
Grain	Production	500	0	500
	Consumption	350	150	500

EXHIBIT 21.3
Posttrade production and consumption of fish and grain in Spain and Norway
In this table, we assume that Spain and Norway have traded fish for grain at a ratio of 1½ tons of grain per ton of fish. Both countries have become entirely specialized. Comparing this table with that in Exhibit 21.2, we see that consumers in both countries have more of both products than they did in the absence of trade. We note also that total world production of fish has risen from 175 to 200 tons, and total world production of grain from 450 to 500 tons.

Generalized Mutual Advantage

The principle of mutual advantage from international trade is perfectly general. It applies to any situation where one country has a comparative advantage over another in producing some good. Wherever there is a comparative advantage, international specialization can increase consumption in each trading country, and world output as a whole.

A complete analysis of international trade would add many details. We would have to allow for cases in which only one country became fully specialized, and for cases in which our constant cost assumption did not hold. No part of the more detailed theory, however, would undermine our basic conclusion: International trade and specialization promote world economic efficiency and generate mutual advantages to all trading nations.

Protectionism and Trade Policy

Free Trade Challenged

There is a strong theoretical case that free international trade promotes world efficiency and consumer welfare. Nonetheless, many nations pursue policies that actively thwart such trade. We refer to policies that interfere with international trade by the general term **protectionism.** The most common protectionist policies are the imposition of **tariffs,** which are taxes levied on imported goods, and **import quotas,** which are limitations on quantities imported. The American government imposes tariffs and quotas on a number of goods.

In what follows, we shall look at some of the more commonly heard arguments in favor of protectionism. Some of them, as we shall see, are altogether false. Others are partly valid in terms of positive economics. Still others focus primarily on normative considerations.

Protectionism A policy of shielding domestic industry from foreign competition.

Tariff A tax levied on imported goods.

Import Quota A limitation on the quantity of a good that can be imported in a given time period.

Cheap Foreign Labor

One common argument against free trade sees a threat in imports from countries where wages are lower than in the United States. At the same time, though, workers in those countries fear competition from American workers backed by heavy capital investment. If one argument were true, both ought to be. If both were true, then trade must be making everyone worse off.

Fortunately, both arguments are false. It is exactly such differences in factor supplies and comparative costs that create opportunities for mutual advantage. The fallacious "cheap foreign labor" argument implies that trade is *best* conducted with countries differing as little as possible from our own. The theory of comparative advantage suggests, in contrast, that trade with such countries is likely to offer the *least* benefit. There is sometimes (but not always) an element of truth in the "cheap foreign labor" argument if it is applied to specific groups of workers, as we shall see below. But applied to average standards of living, as it often is, it is false.

Infant Industries

The famous "infant industry" argument is a second weapon in the protectionist arsenal. It runs like this: Suppose that a certain country has a comparative disadvantage in the production of tacos, but wishes to establish a domestic taco industry. To do so, it prohibits imports. This permits the domestic taco industry to expand and mature. Production costs fall and efficiency increases. Eventually, the country achieves a true comparative advantage in tacos. At that time, consumers will recoup the losses they must suffer in the meantime while the industry "grows up."

This sequence of events is not, in fact, wholly impossible. Nonetheless, it does not justify protection. If the present value of future gains to consumers more than offsets near-term losses, the taco industry ought to be able to grow without protection. It can borrow money to cover short-term operating losses while it competes with cheap foreign tacos. Eventually, when the industry matures and gains its comparative advantage, it can pay off the loans and have some left over. No special protection is needed to ensure the emergence of a domestic taco industry.

Suppose, though, that such borrowing would not be profitable for the taco industry. That, then, would be a sign that the future gains are so small, or so distant, that they do not offset current losses. In that case, to protect the industry would be to promote misallocation of resources over time. Sometimes it is suggested that imperfections in the credit market might make it difficult for an "infant industry" to borrow the funds it needs to finance expansion. But if true, this would at most create a case for government-sponsored loans to the infant industry. It would still not constitute a case for tariffs.

Terms of Trade

A third well-known protectionist theory is the "terms-of-trade" argument. This has some respectable basis in positive economics. The argument applies to a country that exercises **monopoly** or **monopsony** power in the international market. For example, suppose that America is the world's largest exporter of wheat and the largest importer of textiles. Restricting wheat exports and textile imports would then drive the world market price of wheat up and the world market price of textiles down. If the price movement were great enough, the improved terms of trade would more than compensate for the decrease in the volume of trade.

The terms-of-trade argument is valid (at least as a possibility) as it stands. Two things should be noted about it, however. First of all, it does not quite challenge the doctrine of comparative advantage head-on. What it really says is that by clever market manipulation, a country may be able to get a larger share of the gains from trade than it would if international markets operated unrestrictedly. Second, it cannot be applied to both sides of a market at once. If all countries try to play the terms-of-trade game, all of them lose. For one to play it openly invites mutually self-defeating retaliation.

Macroeconomics

Another partially valid protectionist argument suggests that trade may not be beneficial in times of macroeconomic disequilibrium. The basic idea is this. When a country is experiencing widespread unemployment, cutting off imports in a key sector may increase domestic employment. This may "prime the pump," and put the economy on the road to macroeconomic recovery at the expense of only small microeconomic losses. The

Pure Monopoly A market structure in which one firm accounts for 100 percent of industry sales.

Monopsony A market in which there is only one buyer. (From Greek *mono*, single, plus *opsonia*, buying.)

best rejoinder to this argument is that there are more sophisticated tools of macroeconomic policy that can do the same job with less microeconomic damage.

Multiple Factors

Our discussion up to this point has been limited to an economy in which there is only one factor of production, labor. Removing this assumption has some interesting implications. To see what these are, let us modify our earlier Spain-Norway example. We shall assume from now on that fishing requires a relatively large capital investment per worker, and farming a relatively small one. In the accepted terminology, fishing is said to be *capital intensive* and farming *labor intensive*.

We shall still assume that in the absence of trade, the opportunity cost of fish would be higher in Spain than in Norway. The theory of comparative advantage still applies, regardless of the number of factors of production with which we deal. International trade will still make it possible for total world production of both fish and grain to increase. It will still enable the quantities of both goods available for consumption in both countries to increase. Now, a new question arises concerning the gains from trade. How will they be distributed internally within each country?

Internal Distribution

To answer this question, we need to look at what happens in factor markets as trade brings about increasing specialization in each country. In Norway, production shifts from farming to fishing. As grain production is phased out, large quantities of labor and relatively small quantities of capital will be released. The shift in production will thus create a surplus of labor and a shortage of capital. Factor markets can return to equilibrium only when wages fall relative to the rate of return on capital. Only then will fisheries adopt relatively more labor-using methods of production. Meanwhile, in Spain, an opposite process occurs. The shift from fishing to farming depresses the rate of return on capital, and increases the wage rate. This causes Spanish farmers to use more capital per worker than before.

These changes in relative factor prices determine how the gains from trade are distributed among the people of each country. Spanish workers and Norwegian ship owners will gain doubly from trade. They will gain first because trade increases the size of the pie (that is, the total available quantity of goods), and second because the factor price shifts give them a relatively larger slice of the larger pie. For Norwegian workers and Spanish farm owners, in contrast, one of these effects works against the other. They still benefit from the growth of the pie, but they get a relatively smaller piece of it than before. They may or may not end up better off on balance as a result of trade. Suppose that the comparative advantage in the pretrade situation were large, and that the difference in factor intensity between the two countries were small. Norwegian workers and Spanish farm owners would then still gain from trade in an *absolute* sense, even though they would lose ground *relative* to others in their own country. If conditions were not so favorable, however, they could end up absolutely worse off than before trade began.

Mobility

In the preceding section, we considered only two broadly defined factors of production, labor and capital. What we said there applies even more forcefully when we turn our attention to narrowly defined factors of production. Suppose that we think not in terms of labor in general, but in terms of farmers and fishermen, and not in terms of capital in general, but in terms of boat owners and tractor owners. Then it becomes even more likely that trade will have a strongly uneven impact on incomes. The more specialized and less mobile factors of production are, the more relative factor prices will shift as a result of trade. The more likely it then will be that some specific groups will be harmed by trade.

Let us take an example nearer to home than that of Norwegian farmers and Spanish fishermen. Consider instead the effects on the American economy of increased imports of Japanese textiles. We can divide the impact of increased textile imports into three parts. First, all consumers in the country will benefit because textiles will be cheaper than before. Second, the Japanese will increase their purchases of American goods. This will benefit Americans who work in export-oriented industries. Finally, American textile workers and manufacturers will suffer a decreased demand for their products. Those with relatively mobile skills or assets can escape most of the impact by moving to other industries. For example, a truck driver working for a textile firm could switch to hauling peaches, or a plant making shirt boxes could switch to making shoe boxes. Some workers, however, would be less mobile because of their personal circumstances or the specialization of their skills. They would be likely to suffer a loss of income that would more than offset the benefits they would receive as consumers from cheaper textiles. Imagine a middle-aged, highly specialized spinning machine operator, with all his savings tied up in a house in a small textile town. He would derive slim consolation from being able to buy a cheap Japanese raincoat to wear on his weekly visits to the unemployment office.

In aggregate terms, the loss to the group adversely affected is more than offset by the gains to others in the economy. But this fact is not likely to make much practical impression on unemployed textile workers. They will see free trade as a threat, and will campaign for protection. The government will then have a hard political decision to make. Which group of interests should it look after? How much weight should it place on the widespread gains from trade, and how much on the complaints of particular people who do not share in those gains? Is there any way to reconcile these conflicting interests?

Distributive Justice

These are questions of normative economics. If the people who lose from free trade are more deserving than those who gain, then the principle of distributive justice might call for protection. Protection will not necessarily advance distributive justice, however. The immediate impact points in that direction, but a number of things must be taken into account before we can make a balanced judgment.

First, to protect textiles would benefit textile workers. Suppose that these workers were relatively low paid and had lower than average mobility. If one's idea of distributive justice emphasized support for the incomes of low-paid workers, the impact of a protectionist policy would be beneficial.

Second, the tariff or quota would also benefit the owners of other factors used in the textile industry. These would include stockholders, other investors, executives, and owners of real estate in textile communities. On the average, ownership of nonlabor resources tends to be concentrated in the hands of people with relatively high incomes. It is hard to say that with these other factors owners would gain more or less from protection than workers would. That could be discovered only by empirical study. It is very likely that this part of the impact, considered separately, would tend to increase inequality.

Third, protecting textiles would hurt consumers at large by raising textile prices. Again, it is hard to be sure about the distributional impact of this without detailed study. We would have to know whether high-or low-income groups tend to spend the greater share of their incomes on textile products. A seat-of-the-pants guess is that the pinch of higher textile prices would be felt more keenly by low-income groups.

Finally, even if we determined that the benefits of protection were concentrated on groups meriting special consideration, and adverse effects on less meritorious groups, one difficulty remains. We know that the losses to those harmed by protection will be greater in aggregate than the benefits to those helped. Does the gain in equality, if any, more than offset this loss in efficiency? In short, protecting a certain industry *might* improve things from the point of view of distributive justice, but this result is far from certain.

Alternative Policies

Let us suppose, for the sake of argument, that we were happy with the distributional impact of protecting textiles. Suppose even that we judge this favorable result to outweigh the necessary loss in efficiency. Would this make us support protectionism? Not yet. Before we come to any definite conclusion, we should compare the policy of protection with any alternative policies that might have the same beneficial distributive effects. One such alternative might be to subsidize the retraining and relocation of textile workers who lose their jobs. Another would simply be to pay these workers cash compensation.

How would these alternatives rate? In the terms of efficiency, they are not perfect, but probably they are better than tariffs or quotas. In terms of distributive justice, they seem to offer two advantages. One is that benefits are more precisely concentrated on the people we want to get them. The other is that the tax burden required to fund the alternative programs is likely to be distributed more equitably than the burden of high textile prices would be.

Conclusions

The debate over the merits of free trade versus protectionism has gone on for centuries. Adam Smith himself was one of the early spokesmen for free trade, with his doctrine that a highly developed division of labor depended on the widest possible market. Since his time, protectionism has never been widely popular in the economics profession. Among politicians, however, the pendulum has swung back and forth several times. There have been great eras of free trade, alternating with severe tariff wars. Today, it is hard to think of a major industrial country that does not have politically strong protectionist sentiment. Still, protectionists have not really had their way. Grudgingly, and against strong opposition, the world has moved toward freer trade in many ways in recent years. Trade policy will continue to be a source of political controversy in years to come. That is the only safe prediction.

SUMMARY

1. A country is said to have a comparative advantage in the production of any good that it can produce at a lower opportunity cost than its trading partners. Trading nations can realize mutual benefits if each specializes in products for which it has a comparative advantage. Such specialization can give consumers in each country more of all goods than they would have without international trade.

2. Some arguments against free trade are based on considerations of positive economics. Of these, the "cheap foreign labor" and "infant industry" arguments have little merit. The "terms of trade" argument establishes that a country with monopoly or monopsony power in international markets can gain by imposing tariffs on imported goods—but only if its trading partners do not retaliate. Trade restrictions are sometimes used to combat domestic unemployment in periods of macroeconomic disturbance, but conventional tools of macro policy are likely to be superior for such a purpose.

3. Other protectionist arguments emphasize normative considerations. In a world of multiple factors of production, many of which may be highly specialized, certain groups of workers or capitalists can gain by the exclusion of foreign competition. Their gains are more than offset, however, by losses to others of their fellow citizens.

DISCUSSION QUESTIONS

1. Suppose you learned that Vladimir Horowitz, the great pianist, was also an amazingly proficient typist. Knowing this, would it surprise you to learn also that he hired a secretary to type his correspondence, even though he could do the job better and faster himself? What does this have to do with comparative advantage?

2. Turn to Exhibit 21.1. Suppose that new, high-yield grains were introduced in Norway, so that the number of labor hours needed to grow a ton of grain there were cut from 5 hours to $2\frac{1}{2}$ hours. What would happen to trade between Norway and Spain? Would it still pay for Norwegians to import their grain from Spain? If the labor hours per ton of grain in Norway fell all the way to 2, what would happen to the pattern of trade?

3. A few years ago, President Nixon announced something called "Project Independence" that was intended to free this country from dependence on imported oil through development of domestic energy resources. What would be the benefits of that policy? Would everyone in the country potentially benefit from such a policy, or only some groups? What disadvantages would Project Independence have, compared with continued dependence on foreign oil?

4. Suppose that you became President of the United States, and that you were a convinced advocate of free trade. Would your policy be to cut out all U.S. tariffs and quotas at once, or would you bargain with your trading partners, saying that you would cut U.S. tariffs only if they cut their own tariffs? Why would a mutual reduction be better than a one-sided reduction?

5. Simple trade theory suggests that countries will export goods in which they have a comparative advantage and import goods in which they have a comparative disadvantage. In fact, countries often import the same kinds of goods they export. For example, most countries that are big exporters of automobiles are also big importers of automobiles. Why do you think that happens?

CHAPTER 22
The Balance of Payments and the International Monetary System

What You Will Learn in This Chapter
The macroeconomic branch of international trade theory focuses on problems of the balance of international payments. A country runs a balance of payments deficit if it pays out more to foreigners than it takes in from them. If the situation is reversed, the country runs a balance of payments surplus. Because there are many different kinds of international transactions, there are several different ways of measuring a country's balance of payments. The effects of a payments imbalance on exchange rates and on the domestic economy depend on the rules of international monetary institutions. In recent years there have been dramatic changes in the structures of these institutions. The future of the international monetary system is still uncertain.

For Review
Here are some important terms and concepts that will be put to use in this chapter. Be certain that you understand them, or review them before proceeding.
    Money and national income determination (Chapter 13)
    Tariffs and quotas (Chapter 21)

Of all the economic news that makes the headlines, that involving the balance of payments is probably the least well understood. Even well-informed people, who read news reports of inflation and unemployment with at least a basic understanding of what is going on, may have only the haziest idea of how the international monetary system works. This makes our job in this chapter in some ways a hard one. In a few short pages, we must try to deal with an area of economics that is properly the subject of a specialized course itself. At the same time, we cannot fairly assume that the reader has much of a head start. We shall try to meet these difficulties by limiting our objectives, concentrating on the basics, and omitting all but a bare minimum of technicalities.

The Balance of Payments

Domestic Trade and Payments

We shall begin by presenting some basic terms and concepts relating to the balance of payments. To get a better understanding of the balance of payments among nations, we shall first look at the balance of payments among states.

Suppose that two states, say Illinois and Wisconsin, trade only with each other. Wisconsin sells food to Illinois and acts as a vacationland for Illinois residents. Illinois sells manufactured goods to Wisconsin. If the dollar value of Illinois imports (Wisconsin exports) equals the value of Illinois exports (Wisconsin imports), the quantity of money in each state will remain unchanged. The amount spent on food and travel by Illinois residents will be offset by the amount earned by other Illinois residents who sell manufactured goods. The same will be true in Wisconsin. Bank deposits in both states will remain unchanged. Payments will be in balance.

Deficit and Surplus

Balance of Trade Deficit (Surplus) A country runs a balance of trade deficit (surplus) if the value of goods and services that it imports exceeds (falls short of) the value of goods and services that it exports.

Next, suppose that people living in Illinois buy more from Wisconsin than they sell. This creates a **balance of trade deficit** for Illinois and a **balance of trade surplus** for Wisconsin. Initially, Illinois residents can make up the deficit by running down their dollar holdings. Banks in Illinois will notice that deposits are declining, and banks in Wisconsin will notice that deposits are increasing. If the deficit persists, people and banks in Illinois will find themselves low on dollars. They may borrow from Wisconsin banks or merchants in order to continue their purchases. Illinois banks that are short on dollars may borrow from Wisconsin banks that have excess dollars. These funds in turn may be lent by Illinois banks to customers planning to buy goods from Wisconsin or planning to vacation there. In sum, a deficit state can finance a balance of trade deficit either by running down its stocks of currency or by short-term borrowing. If such borrowing is used, it is referred to as a **short-term capital flow.**

Short-Term Capital Flows Loans to or from foreigners, payable within one year or less.

Suppose now that the balance of trade in goods and services is corrected. Let us consider some different kinds of transactions. Suppose that Wisconsin residents buy stock in Illinois firms, and wealthy Illinois doctors buy farms in Wisconsin. These transactions are called **long-term capital flows.** If Illinois doctors spend less on farms than Wisconsin residents spend on stocks, we say that Illinois has a **capital account surplus** and Wisconsin a **capital account deficit.** A capital account deficit can be financed in much the same way as a trade deficit is financed. Wisconsin residents can draw down their holdings of dollars. They can also borrow from individuals or banks in Illinois, or they can borrow from their own banks which, in turn, borrow from banks in Illinois.

Long-Term Capital Flows Long-term loans to or from foreigners, or transactions with foreigners involving capital assets.

Capital Account Deficit (Surplus) A country runs a capital account deficit (surplus) if the value of long-term capital flow to foreigners exceeds (falls short of) the value of long-term capital flows from foreigners.

International Trade and Payments

Now let us turn to trade and payments between countries. We shall replace the state of Illinois in our example by the United States, and the state of Wisconsin by Mexico. All the movements of goods and services and capital assets that were possible between states are also possible between nations. There is just one major difference. *Each country has its own cur-*

rency. Mexico has the peso and the United States has the dollar. At the outset, let us assume that $1 is worth 12 pesos, without asking for the moment just why.

When Mexican goods are sold to foreigners, Mexican merchants will want to be paid in pesos. That is how they must meet their payrolls and pay their other expenses. Likewise, Americans doing business with Mexico will want to be paid in dollars. Each international transaction will thus require an intermediate step not necessary in trade between states: a visit to the **foreign exchange market.** By the foreign exchange market, we mean the whole family of institutions (including Mexican and American banks, specialized foreign exchange dealers, and official agencies of both governments) through which dollars may be exchanged for pesos and pesos for dollars.

Suppose that trade between the two countries is in balance, and there are no movements of long-term capital. The value of dollars brought to the foreign exchange market by Americans wanting to do business in Mexico will then be the same as the value of pesos brought by Mexicans wanting to do business in the United States. Trade is not always in balance, however. If the United States runs a trade deficit with Mexico, the value of dollars brought to the market will exceed the value of pesos taken there. In that case, any of a variety of things may happen. For a time, Americans may be able to finance the deficit by running down any stocks of pesos they have accumulated in the past. If that is not possible, Americans may ask Mexican exporters to accept deferred payments. That is the same as asking them for a loan. It is a type of short-term capital flow. Alternatively, American importers or their banks may get loans of pesos from Mexican banks. That is another type of short-term capital flow.

Foreign Exchange Market The whole group of institutions, including banks, specialized foreign exchange dealers, and official government agencies, through which the currency of one country may be exchanged for the currency of another.

Goods Balance

The first line of Exhibit 22.1 gives the **goods** or **merchandise trade balance.** It is the difference between exports and imports of tangible goods. We can see from the table that the United States exported more than it imported in the years 1961 and 1966. By 1971, the situation was reversed. For the first time in the postwar period, we imported more than we ex-

Merchandise Trade Balance (Goods Balance) The difference between exports and imports of tangible goods.

EXHIBIT 22.1

U.S. balance of payments (billions of dollars)
Because there are so many different kinds of international transactions, there are many different ways of measuring a country's balance of payments surplus or deficit. Here are six common measures for the United States for selected recent years.

	1961	1966	1971	1974
Goods (merchandise trade balance)	5.6	3.8	−2.7	−5.3
Goods and services	5.6	5.2	0.7	3.8
Current account	3.1	2.3	−2.8	−3.3
Current account and long term capital (basic balance)	0	−1.7	−9.4	−10.7
Net liquidity balance	−2.3	−2.2	−22.0	−18.9
Official settlements balance	−1.3	0.2	−29.8	−8.4

Balance of Goods and Services
The merchandise trade balance plus the balance of services.

Current Account Balance The balance of goods and services plus net private and government transfers.

Basic Balance The current account balance plus long-term capital flows.

Net Liquidity Balance The basic balance plus short-term capital flows.

Official Settlements Balance The net liquidity balance plus private liquid capital flows.

ported. (This caused great alarm in U.S. government circles.) The second item in Exhibit 22.1 includes services as well as goods. It is called the **balance of goods and services.** Services, or "invisibles" as they are sometimes called, include tourist expenditures, shipping, insurance, and income from foreign investments. All of these are "net"; that is, they are the difference between foreign purchases of American services and American purchases of foreign services. Investment income is the difference between the income received by Americans from their overseas investments and the income received by foreigners from their investments in the United States. By comparing lines 1 and 2 of the exhibit, we see that the service balance was zero in 1961 and positive in 1966, 1971, and 1974. The change was due primarily to a growth in income from direct American investments abroad.

Current Account Balance

The third item in Exhibit 22.1 is the **current account balance.** It includes goods and services, plus net private and government transfers. When an American sends a check to a relative or charitable organization abroad, that is a private transfer. When the American government extends foreign aid, a government transfer occurs. As one would expect, the United States transfers more abroad than foreigners transfer to Americans.

Other Balances

The fourth line of Exhibit 22.1 adds long-term capital flows to the current account balance. This item is called the **basic balance.** The table indicates that American investment abroad has exceeded investment by foreigners in the United States. This difference has been getting larger over time. Private short-term capital flows and government actions must offset any positive or negative basic balance.

The fifth item is the **net liquidity balance.** This balance is frequently used as an overall indicator of our balance of payments position. The net liquidity balance adds short-term capital flows to the basic balance. (An "errors and omissions" item is also included.) Short-term capital, for accounting purposes, is anything maturing in less than a year. As we saw earlier, short-term capital flows can balance a payments deficit or surplus. Short-term capital transactions can also arise because of interest rate differentials between countries. In each of the years examined in Exhibit 22.1, the short-term capital account (net) contributed to a further imbalance in the balance of payments. The "errors and omissions" item is normally small, usually $1 billion or less. However, in 1971 it jumped to nearly $11 billion and is the factor most responsible for the large disparity between the basic balance and the net liquidity balance.

The final entry in Exhibit 22.1 is the **official settlements balance.** It differs from the liquidity balance mainly by including private liquid capital flows. Normally, if foreigners are financing a U.S. deficit by acquiring dollars, this item is positive. However, in 1971, this item was negative. The reason was that foreigners expected a fall in the value of the dollar. In order to profit by the change, they reduced their holding of dollars. More will be said about this later.

The official settlements balance, as its name implies, must be offset by government actions. The government of a deficit country can finance the remaining imbalance by encouraging governments of surplus countries to accumulate its currency. It can also run down its holdings of currency of the surplus country. In the past, the dollar was sought by many governments as a reserve asset, so the United States had little trouble persuading surplus countries to hold dollars. In recent years, things have changed. By 1971 it took a great deal of arm twisting, and ultimately some corrective action by the United States, to get foreign governments to hold dollars.

Foreign Exchange Markets and Exchange Rates

Foreign Exchange Markets

We are now ready to take up a question we previously had set aside. What is it that determines the rate at which one currency exchanges for another? Why is a dollar worth 12 pesos, rather than 10 or 14 or some other number of pesos? To arrive at an answer, we must first take a closer look at the foreign exchange market, to which we have previously referred only casually. Following this, we shall discuss alternative international monetary systems. Each of these is characterized by a different set of rules that governments pursue in intervening in the foreign exchange markets.

Foreign exchange markets, like so many other markets, can be analyzed in terms of supply and demand. To illustrate, let us return to the foreign exchange market in which pesos are bought and sold. The supply and demand curves for this market are shown in Exhibit 22.2.

Demand

We have drawn the demand curve for pesos with a negative slope. In practice, the slope depends on what happens to the demand by foreigners for Mexican goods when the exchange rate changes. Consider, for example, a piece of leather luggage made in Mexico that carries a domestic price of 500 pesos. If the rate of exchange were $1 per peso, an American would have

---

EXHIBIT 22.2

The foreign exchange market for pesos and dollars

The foreign exchange market for pesos and dollars is the whole complex of institutions, including banks, foreign exchange dealers, and official government agencies, through which pesos may be exchanged for dollars and dollars for pesos. The equilibrium rate is determined by the intersection of the supply and demand curves for a currency in the foreign exchange market.

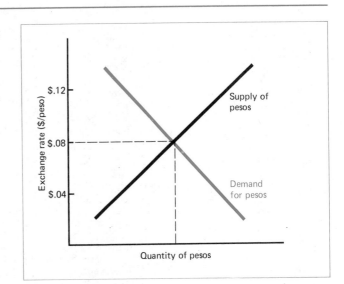

to put up $500 to obtain the luggage. Not much luggage would be sold, which means that not very many people would need to buy pesos. On the other hand, if a peso costs only $.10, the luggage would carry a price tag of only $50 to a U.S. buyer. Many such buyers would rush to exchange their dollars for pesos to take advantage of the bargain.

Supply

We have drawn the supply curve for pesos with an upward slope for similar reasons. Imagine that Mexicans are interested in buying American cars. If a peso is worth only $.10, a Mexican buyer would have to put up 30,000 of them to buy a car costing $3,000 in the United States and might think twice about the matter. But if a peso were worth $1, a car would cost only 3,000 pesos, and many more Mexican citizens could afford one.[1]

Shifts

Now let us consider some factors that can shift the demand and supply schedules. First, demand. Two important factors affecting demand are the price level in Mexico and Mexican interest rates. Should the price level in Mexico rise, say, by 10 percent, the Mexican luggage, which previously sold for 500 pesos, would now sell for 550 pesos. At each exchange rate, foreigners would need 10 percent more dollars to buy Mexican goods. They thus would demand fewer pesos at each rate of exchange, and the demand curve would shift to the left.[2] Alternatively, an increase in Mexican interest rates would increase the yield on investments made in Mexico and make Mexican assets more attractive to foreigners. This would increase the demand for pesos at any given exchange rate, and shift the demand schedule to the right. The demand curve for pesos can thus be shifted either by factors affecting Mexico's trade account or by factors affecting its capital account. In addition, the demand curve for pesos can be influenced by economic events outside Mexico's borders. If there is a sharp upturn in the American economy, for example, American consumers' demand for all goods and services will rise. This includes their demand for Mexican luggage, Acapulco vacations, and other Mexican exports. To get these things, they must trade in more dollars for pesos, and the peso demand curve will once again shift to the right.

From what we have said about demand, it is not hard to guess what factors might shift the supply curve of pesos. Only the names of the two countries need to be exchanged. A fall in the price level or a rise in the interest rate in the United States could induce Mexicans to bring more pesos to the market to offer for dollars. So will an upturn in nominal incomes in Mexico. These things would shift the supply curve rightward. On the other hand, inflation in the United States, a fall in American interest rates, or a recession in Mexico would all cause the supply curve of pesos to shift to the left.

---

[1]To be precise in this matter, an upward-sloping supply curve for pesos requires that Mexicans have an *elastic* demand for American goods. In a more detailed treatment of foreign exchange markets, we would have to consider also the possibility of an inelastic Mexican demand for American goods, and thus a backward-bending supply curve for pesos.

[2]Here we assume the American demand for Mexican goods also to be elastic. See footnote 1 above.

What happens when supply and demand curves shift around in the foreign exchange market? That depends on the rules of the game, as determined by international monetary institutions. Before describing the actual rules that have governed the international monetary system in recent years, let us examine two theoretically possible "pure" systems. These will teach us some important elements of theory, and provide a framework of reference from which to discuss the real systems.

The Gold Standard

The first international monetary system we shall look at is one in which the exchange rates of one currency for another are rigidly fixed. This would be the case if both Mexico and the United States were on a strict **gold standard.** For the two countries to be on a gold standard means that "peso" and "dollar" are really just terms for differing quantities of gold, that is, local names for gold coins of different sizes with pictures honoring different sets of dictators and colonial slaveowners. Suppose that 12½ of the coins called "peso" weigh the same as one of those called "dollar." The value of a peso would then be $.08.

With these circumstances in mind, let us look at the foreign exchange market. Turn to Exhibit 22.3. Suppose that initially the market is in equilibrium with the supply curve in the position S, and the demand curve in the position D_1. Then suppose that for some reason, say, an increase in American incomes, the demand curve for pesos shifts to the right to the position D_2. This creates a surplus of pesos, as shown by the horizontal gap between the supply and demand curves at the exchange rate of $.08 per peso. American citizens are bringing more dollars to the exchange markets than Mexican citizens are willing to sell.

Imbalance

Since both countries are on the gold standard, it is easy for the Mexican government to deal with the imbalance. It buys the excess dollars, melts them down, remints them as pesos, and sells them to Americans wanting to

Gold Standard An international monetary system in which the currencies of different countries are simply names for differing quantities of gold.

EXHIBIT 22.3

Foreign exchange market adjustments under a gold standard

An increase in American demand for Mexican goods shifts the demand curve for pesos from D_1 to D_2. This creates a balance of payments surplus in Mexico. Under a gold standard, this surplus leads to an increase in the Mexican money supply. That pushes up Mexican prices and cuts Mexican interest rates, shifting the demand curve back to D_3. It also stimulates Mexican demand for American goods and assets, shifting the peso supply to S_2. These demand and supply curve shifts restore equilibrium at the original exchange rate.

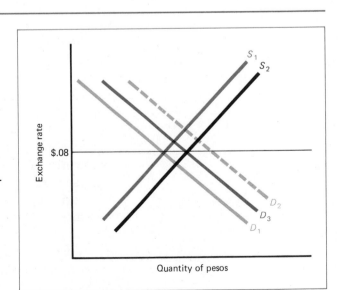

do business in Mexico. This action by the Mexican authorities has immediate repercussions. The newly minted pesos increase the Mexican money supply. An increase in the money supply tends to (1) raise prices, (2) lower interest rates, and (3) stimulate economic activity. Higher prices and lower interest rates in Mexico shift the demand curve for pesos to the left, because Mexican goods and securities become less attractive to American buyers. At the same time, rising nominal incomes in Mexico shift the supply curve of pesos to the right, as Mexicans buy more imports from the United States.

Meanwhile, the U.S. money supply falls as dollars flow into the Mexican mint. The resulting macroeconomic events north of the border reinforce the movements of the supply and demand curves. Sooner or later the curves will shift to positions like S_2 and D_3, where supply and demand are once again equal at the fixed exchange rate. When this happens, money supplies in both countries are once again stabilized, and equilibrium is reestablished.

Restoration of Equilibrium

We see, then, that a gold standard system contains a built-in mechanism that restores equilibrium automatically in the event of changes in supply and demand. This mechanism works in three steps. First, imbalance in the foreign exchange market causes changes in the money supplies of the trading countries. Next, changes in domestic money supplies cause changes in prices, interest rates, and nominal incomes in the domestic economics. Finally, these changes in turn cause corrective shifts in supply and demand curves in the foreign exchange market.

Flexible Rates

The second possible international monetary system we shall consider is one based on completely flexible exchange rates. "Peso" and "dollar" are now no longer names for differing quantities of gold. They are the names of two completely independent paper currencies issued by the Mexican and U.S. governments. Let us see how this system operates in the face of changing conditions in international markets.

Suppose once again that the foreign exchange market is initially in equilibrium and that payments in both countries are in balance. The demand curve is at D_1, the supply curve is at S_1, and the equilibrium price of pesos at \$.08 as shown in Exhibit 22.4. Once more an increase in nominal incomes in the United States causes the demand curve to shift to D_2. What happens? This time the excess demand for pesos meets with no action on the part of either government. American importers bid against one another for the limited supply of pesos that Mexican citizens are willing to sell and drive the price of the peso upward to an equilibrium level around \$.12. As the exchange rate rises, Mexicans are encouraged to buy more American goods, moving up along the peso supply curve in the process. At the same time, Americans are partially discouraged from buying more Mexican goods. They move up and to the left along their new demand curve. These movements restore payments to balance on both sides, with no action taken by government and no changes in the domestic money supply in either country.

EXHIBIT 22.4

Foreign exchange market adjustments under flexible rates

An increase in American demand for Mexican goods shifts the demand curve for pesos from D_1 to D_2. That creates a balance of payments surplus for Mexico. Under a system of flexible exchange rates, the surplus is corrected by a movement along the supply curve to a new equilibrium exchange rate where S_1 and D_2 intersect. No changes in the Mexican money supply need occur.

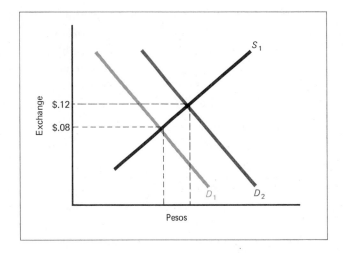

The Postwar International Monetary System

Bretton Woods

After World War II, the major trading nations of the world favored neither a rigid gold standard nor a perfectly flexible system of exchange rates. Instead, meeting under United Nations auspices at Bretton Woods, New Hampshire, in 1944, they established a mixed system. The International Monetary Fund (IMF), with headquarters in Washington, D.C., was established to administer the new system. At the present time, 124 nations are members of the IMF.

Adjustable Peg

The system established at Bretton Woods was based on the idea of an "adjustable peg." Let us look in brief at the rules of the international monetary game as it was played under the watchful eye of the IMF from 1944 until early 1973. So-called **par values** were established for each currency in terms of the U.S. dollar. Exchange rates were "pegged" at the par values. This means that they were allowed to fluctuate under the influence of supply and demand within a narrow band ranging from 2.25 percent above par to 2.25 percent below par. (The limits were only 1 percent until December 1971.) When the value of a currency rose to the upper limit or fell to the lower one, the government of the country in question was obligated under IMF rules to intervene and prevent further movement. A government faced with an excess demand for its currency at the limit rate had to sell enough of its own currency in exchange for dollars to soak up the excess demand. A government faced with an excess supply of its currency had to buy it in exchange for dollars if necessary to keep its price from slipping below the limit.

If the government of a deficit or surplus country got tired of intervening in the exchange market, it had another option under the rules of the game. It could "adjust the peg," that is, change the par value of its currency. This might be done in either of two slightly different ways. One was

Par Values Under the monetary system run by the International Monetary Fund from 1944 to 1973, the par value for a currency was the official exchange rate around which the actual exchange rate was permitted to fluctuate only within a narrow band.

immediately to declare a new par value above or below the initial value. The other was temporarily to *float* the currency. That means letting it find a new equilibrium value under the influence of supply and demand without government intervention. A new par value would later be fixed at the market-determined rate when things seemed to have settled down. (A few countries, notably Canada, let their currencies float for years at a time in the postwar period. This, however, was considered to be a violation of at least the spirit, if not the letter, of IMF rules.)

Adjustable Peg in Action

Let us look at the IMF system in action using our example of the United States and Mexico once again. Exhibit 22.5 shows the initial position, with supply at S_1 and demand at D_1. Equilibrium is achieved at an exchange rate of $.10 per peso. We shall assume this to be the par value. The upper and lower limits of permissible fluctuation are indicated by the shaded band from $.1025 to $.0975. (The width of the band has been exaggerated in the exhibit to make it easier to read.)

Now suppose that persistent inflation in Mexico begins to shift the demand curve for pesos to the left. Until the demand curve reaches the position D_2, the exchange rate floats downward as in a system of fully flexible rates. If inflation persists, however, and the demand curve shifts as far as position D_3, the Mexican government must do something. Its first recourse is to draw on its reserve of dollars in order to soak up the excess supply of pesos. This action tends to decrease the domestic money supply. The excess pesos put into the exchange market now go to the Mexican government treasury rather than going to American importers or tourists, who would buy Mexican goods from Mexican merchants, who would redeposit the pesos in Mexican banks. As in the case of the gold standard, this fall in the Mexican money supply would have a deflationary effect on the Mexican economy. The demand and supply curves would shift back to a point where they would intersect within the permissible exchange rate band.

What if the Mexican government does not have any reserves of dollars with which to buy pesos and support their price? Or what if after a period of supporting the peso, it runs out of dollars? As a stopgap measure, it had the right, under the rules set up at Bretton Woods, to borrow dollars from the IMF and continue its support efforts. If it did not want to do this, or if it borrowed up to the limit without eliminating the excess supply of pesos, it could devalue. That would mean letting the par value of the peso fall to the intersections of S_1 and D_3 in Exhibit 22.5. New limits of fluctuation would then be set up around that value.

Avoiding Adjustment

Under the postwar adjustable peg system, adjustments were not entirely automatic, even when exchange rates reached their permissible limits of fluctuations. The two possible mechanisms for restoring equilibrium in the foreign exchange markets—changes in the domestic money supply, or changes in par values—could both be short-circuited. Let us see how this could be done.

EXHIBIT 22.5

The foreign exchange market with an adjustable peg
Under the adjustable peg system, small shifts in supply
or demand simply cause exchange rates to fluctuate
within a narrow band around the par value of a currency. A shift in the demand curve for pesos from D_1
to D_2 would thus cause the value of the peso to fall
from its par value to its lower limit, $2\frac{1}{2}$ percent below
the par value. If there were a larger shift in demand,
such as from D_1 to D_3, the Mexican government would
have to intervene in the foreign exchange market, buying enough pesos to keep their value from falling
below $.0975.

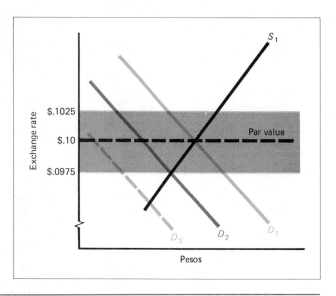

Refer once again to Exhibit 22.5. Suppose that when the demand curve
shifts to the position D_3, the Mexican authorities do not want to float or
devalue the peso. For domestic political or economic reasons, however,
they do not want the deflationary consequences of a decrease in the domestic money supply either. For the time being, they could avoid both
devaluation and deflation by an operation known as **sterilization.** For
each peso taken out of circulation by their support actions, they could
put a brand new peso back into circulation by any of the usual tools of
domestic monetary policy. This action "sterilizes" or short-circuits any
effect of the exchange markets on the domestic economy. (Sterilization,
of course, could also be used by surplus countries wanting to avoid increases
in the domestic money supply.)

Sterilization   A policy of using domestic monetary policy to offset
the effect of a balance of payments deficit or surplus on the domestic money supply.

Sterilization, unfortunately, has one serious drawback. Because it
thwarts the automatic mechanism that would restore payments balance to
an economy, there is no assurance that a country will not have to keep
supporting and sterilizing forever once it starts! This unappealing prospect
often drives governments to desperate measures.

Trade Restrictions

Suppose that a government is faced with a persistent balance of payments deficit, and does not want either to deflate or devalue. When it begins
to run out of foreign reserves and IMF borrowing rights, it can reduce the
excess supply of its currency by imposing direct restrictions on foreign
trade. Such restrictions come in several kinds and varieties. Among the
most commonly employed are the following:

1. Tariffs, which we discussed in the last chapter, are special taxes
   levied on imports at their point of entry. They accomplish their
   objective by raising the price of foreign goods to domestic buyers.
   If Mexico imposes tariffs on American goods, the supply curve
   for pesos will shift to the left.

2. Quotas, which we also encountered in Chapter 21, are legal limits on the quantity of particular types of goods that can be brought into a country in a given period of time. If Mexico imposes quotas on American goods, the supply curve of pesos will shift to the left.

3. Exchange controls are another type of trade restriction. One common form of exchange control is for the government to assume a legal monopoly on buying and selling foreign exchange. Importers and tourists must then apply to the government for foreign exchange rather than buying in the international market. The government can ration the available quantity of foreign currency as it sees fit. (In diagrammatic terms, a government that adopts exchange controls in effect replaces the supply curve of its currency with a vertical line that can be moved about at will.)

4. A final type of trade restriction is the use of export subsidies. Subsidies to exports make it possible for domestic firms to sell their goods at prices more attractive to foreigners. In our example, if Mexico were to adopt export subsidies, the demand curve for pesos would shift to the right.

The trouble with all these policies is that they invite retaliation by foreign countries. Such retaliation can cancel out any beneficial effects on the balance of payments. The end effect of a general imposition of trade restrictions is a decline in the total volume of international trade, and a decline in the efficiency and prosperity of the world economy as a whole.

Weaknesses of the System

Although the adjustable peg system established at Bretton Woods lasted nearly thirty years, it suffered from some elemental weaknesses that led eventually to its downfall. The main weakness of the system was that it was crisis-prone. Because adjustments were never fully automatic, governments often resisted making small adjustments when they would have been only slightly painful. Instead, they waited for pressures to build up that eventually tore the system apart.

In outline, here is the scenario for the kind of international monetary crisis that repeatedly occurred under the Bretton Woods rules. Some country, let us say the United Kingdom, runs a persistent balance of payments deficit. A chronic excess supply of British pounds sterling appears on the world's exchange markets. The British government is forced to support the pound. It does not want to deflate, so it sterilizes. (Or else it does deflate, but not enough to do any lasting good.) Gradually dollar reserves are run dangerously low, and the British government is forced to borrow from the IMF or the U.S. Treasury. It may try imposing exchange controls or other trade restrictions, but these meet with threats of retaliation and domestic political resistence. It becomes harder and harder to keep the pound from breaking through the floor.

Speculation

At this point *speculation* enters the picture. Let us interrupt our scenario for a brief digression on speculation. Speculators are active all the time in international currency markets. Their game works like this: Suppose the pound is floating around happily between its upper limit of

$2.45 and its lower limit of $2.35, changing a bit from day to day. If I buy £100,000 today at $2.40, and tomorrow the vagaries of supply and demand carry the rate up to $2.41, I can change them back into dollars and pocket a clear profit of $1,000. The problem is that in normal times no one can quite be sure whether the pound is on its way up or its way down. I might just as easily lose $1,000. Heads you win, tails you lose. Speculators are professional risk takers who perform a number of useful economic functions. In normal times, though, they do not play a very big role in the international payments picture.

Now back to our scenario where the British government is hanging desperately on the brink of a forced devaluation. At this point, speculators are faced with the kind of situation they are always looking for, but are rarely lucky enough to find. That is a situation in which it is *heads you win, tails you break even*. The question of the day is, will the pound hold at $2.35, or will it be devalued? Suppose that I sell all the pounds I can get my hands on, borrowing them if necessary. If the pound is devalued to $2.10 tomorrow, I can buy pounds back to pay off the loans and make a huge profit. If the British government somehow muddles through, and the pound holds, I lose practically nothing. At the very worst, the pound will rise a cent or two off its floor and I will have to pay a few days' or weeks' interest on the loans.

The final scene in the sterling crisis is set when speculators start to pour hundreds of millions of pounds into the foreign exchange market. The excess supply of sterling becomes overwhelming, and the last straw forcing an *actual* devaluation is the speculative pressure occurring in *anticipation* of the devaluation.

Crisis and Reform

In early 1973, an especially severe crisis occurred, involving the U.S. dollar, the German mark, and the Japanese yen. In response to this crisis, the major trading nations took the bold step of abandoning the adjustable peg, and allowing their currencies to float vis-à-vis one another. The relative value of the yen, the dollar, and the mark were allowed to find their own levels under the influence of supply and demand.

The international monetary system that emerged from the crisis of 1973 is still a mixed system. It contains a number of features that do not conform exactly to a pure flexible rate system. It usually is referred to as a flexible rate system because it is so much more flexible than the adjustable peg, but two important restrictions must be kept in mind.

First, not every currency floats against every other currency. Rather, the system is one in which major blocks of currencies float against one another. A major group of countries of Western Europe tried pegging their currencies against one another in an arrangement colorfully known as "the snake." Countries with strong trading ties with the United States have pegged their currencies to the dollar. Those with strong ties to Britain have pegged theirs to the pound. Movements between blocks have been substantial, though. Because increased flexibility has been introduced, several currencies have swung by as much as 20–30 percent. Occasionally there have been swings of 2 or 3 percent in a single day.

Second, movements of exchange rates have been characterized by the active but largely uncoordinated intervention of central banks. Movements in exchange rates are often resisted, either because of their possible effects on domestic inflation or because of their possible impact on particular politically sensitive sectors of the domestic economy. A float of a currency with sporadic central bank intervention is sometimes called a "dirty float." This term aptly distinguishes the current system from the perfectly flexible system of economic theory.

Conclusions[3]

The new world of the "dirty float" has not been with us long enough to allow any really conclusive evaluation. Enough has been learned, though, to be able to say that flexibility has worked much better than its opponents feared, although not as well as its strongest advocates had hoped. Here are some tentative conclusions that can be drawn from the first two years of experience with the new system.

First, it does appear that flexible rates have permitted countries to correct payments balances. In the days of the adjustable peg, critics of flexible rates often argued that demand elasticities for goods traded internationally might be so low that changes in exchange rates would have hardly any effect on nations' balance of payments. Not all the evidence is in, but what there is seems not to confirm the worst fears of these "elasticity pessimists."

Second, flexible rate advocates are dissappointed that the new system has not led to a reduction in the use of trade restrictions. Critics of the adjustable peg used to argue that trade restrictions were desperation measures forced on governments by the inflexibility of the old system. Unfortunately, no tendency toward a withering away of trade restrictions can yet be seen.

Third, the new system has not been as effective as some thought it would be in freeing domestic macroeconomic policy from the influence of world monetary effects. This can be seen as either a good or a bad thing, depending on one's point of view. Under the old system, governments often damaged their domestic economies by deflationary policies aimed at maintaining unrealistic parity values for their currencies. Now they are a little less likely to do so, although they remain under some pressure in that direction. On the other hand, under the old system international pressures sometimes restrained governments from pursuing recklessly inflationary policies. That was seen as a plus. It is probably fortunate that the new system has not led to complete autonomy of domestic policy from international effects, so that exchange rates still provide some degree of anti-inflationary discipline.

Finally, some observers of the new system have been surprised at the size of the impact that exchange rate movements have had on domestic inflation. When devaluation of a country's currency leads to domestic inflation, the effectiveness of that devaluation is reduced. The problem of

---

[3]This section draws on a useful paper by Marina V. N. Whitman, "The Payments Adjustment Process and the Exchange Rate Regime: What Have We Learned?" *American Economic Review*, May 1975.

transmitting inflationary problems from one country to another is at the same time made worse. In theory, it should be possible for exchange rate movements to take place with no significant effect on domestic price levels. Things have not worked out this way in practice.

There is no point in even pretending to forecast what the future will bring. A return to an adjustable peg system, or some slightly more flexible variant of it, is by no means out of the question. The European "snake" is an example of a movement in that direction.

There is also a small but vocal group of economists who favor a return to a strict gold standard. They see the inflationary effects of either floating rates or an adjustable peg as a great danger. They view the prospect of taking the weapon of discretionary monetary policy away from national governments as beneficial to the world economy. But gold standard advocates are a definite minority.

A recent survey of experience with flexible rates concluded modestly that "flexible rates are a second best in a world where the efficiency advantages of integration and a single international money must yield place to nations' insistence on individual sovereignty in the determination of domestic targets and policy instruments."[4] The writer added that it is hard to imagine any workable alternative to flexible rates in a world where nations experience high and widely varying rates of inflation. At the moment, the betting must be that flexible rates will be with us for some time to come, but nothing is certain. Readers of this chapter are advised to pay attention to the newspapers.

SUMMARY

1. If a country imports a greater value of goods and services than it exports, it runs a balance of trade deficit. Such a deficit can be financed by drawing down domestic holdings of foreign currency, or by short-term borrowing from foreigners. A capital account deficit occurs if purchases of capital assets from foreigners exceed sales of capital assets to foreigners. Such a deficit can be financed in the same way as a balance of trade deficit.
2. The exchange rates between different currencies are determined in foreign exchange markets. Changes in incomes or prices or interest rates in a country will affect the demand for that country's currency. Changes in foreign incomes or price levels or interest rates will affect the supply of a country's currency.
3. Under a gold standard, an automatic mechanism restores equilibrium whenever a country runs a payments deficit or surplus. Such an imbalance causes the money supply of a deficit country to fall. That leads to lower prices, higher interest rates, and lower nominal incomes in the deficit country. Those effects stimulate the demand for and reduce the supply of the country's currency on foreign exchange markets, thus restoring equilibrium. Opposite effects are felt in a surplus country.
4. Under a system of flexible exchange rates, a balance of payments deficit or surplus is corrected entirely by movements in exchange rates. No government action need be taken, and no changes in domestic money supplies need occur.
5. The postwar international monetary system established at Bretton Woods in 1944 was neither a gold standard nor a purely flexible system. It featured an "adjustable peg," that is, an official par value for each currency around which fluctuations were permitted within a narrow range. Temporary payment surpluses or deficits could be corrected by government intervention in foreign

[4]*Ibid.*

exchange markets. Persistent payments imbalances could be corrected by changes in par values. The system worked tolerably well for many years, but it was always crisis-prone. The adjustable peg was abandoned in 1973 after a particularly severe series of crises.

6. Under the current international monetary system, major currencies or blocs of currencies float against one another in a system of essentially flexible exchange markets. The system does not work perfectly, but it seems to work better than the critics of flexible rates feared prior to 1973.

DISCUSSION QUESTIONS

1. Have you seen any news items lately that concern the balance of payments surplus or deficit between your state and neighboring states? Why is the balance of payments between states of less interest than the balance of payments between nations?

2. A country that runs a trade deficit is often said to have an "unfavorable" balance of payments. What is unfavorable about such a situation? Are not the citizens of a country better off if they are able to consume many foreign goods without having to give up an equivalent value of goods in export?

3. Trace the effects of each of these kinds of transactions in terms of the balance of payments accounts given in Exhibit 22.1:
   a. A London businessman buys $1 million in stock in General Motors through the New York Stock Exchange.
   b. A woman in Cleveland sends $100 as a Christmas gift to her aunt in Poland.
   c. You fly to Japan on an American carrier, and spend $1,000 on photographic equipment while you are there. You bring the goods back with you when you return.
   d. While you are on vacation in Mexico, the owner of a local movie house hires you to distribute advertising leaflets to your fellow American tourists. He pays you 100 pesos. You save the money, and change it into U.S. dollars when you return home.

4. Suppose that the British demand for foreign goods is unit elastic and the foreign demand for British goods is perfectly inelastic. (Check these terms in the glossary.) Could the British government then correct a balance of trade deficit by devaluing the pound? If not, is there any other way for it to correct a balance of trade deficit?

5. If a government wishes to "peg" its exchange rate, what does it have to do? Does it just announce the par value it wants to maintain, or does it have to back up its announcement with actions? What kind of actions?

Glossary

Absolute Advantage   In international trade theory, the ability of a country to produce a good at absolutely lower cost, measured in terms of factor inputs, than its trading partners.

Accelerator Effect   The tendency of increases in national income to induce new investments, which in turn fuel further increases in national income.

Accommodating Monetary Policy   A policy under which the Federal Reserve expands the money supply in an attempt to keep interest rates from rising when the Treasury sells bonds to cover a budget deficit.

Aggregate   In economics, an adjective used to describe any quantity that is a grand total for the whole economy.

Aggregate Demand   The total value of all planned expenditures of all buyers in the economy.

Aggregate Demand Schedule   A schedule showing what the nominal level of total planned expenditure (aggregate demand) will be at each possible level of nominal national income.

Aggregate Supply   The total value of all goods and services supplied in the economy; identical to national product.

Aggregate Supply Schedule   A table or graph showing the level of nominal national product (aggregate supply) associated with each level of nominal national income.

Allocation   The distribution or assignment of things to specific uses. In economics, the term *resource allocation* means determining what will be produced, how it will be produced, who will produce it, and for whom it will be produced.

Anarcho-Capitalism (Radical Libertarianism)   A capitalist system in which no state exists at all, with all goods and services, including defense, police, and court services, supplied by private firms.

Antitrust Laws   A series of laws, beginning with the Sherman Act of 1890, which define government policy toward monopoly.

Ascetics   People who try to achieve happiness by purposely limiting their desires.

Autonomous Consumption   The level of consumption shown by a consumption schedule for a zero disposable income level.

Balance of Goods and Services   The merchandise trade balance plus the balance of services.

Balance of Trade Deficit (Surplus)   A country runs a balance of trade deficit (surplus) if the value of goods and services that it imports exceeds (falls short of) the value of goods and services that it exports.

Balanced Budget Multiplier   A multiplier showing how much equilibrium nominal national income will change in response to a change in government purchases matched dollar for dollar by an offsetting change in net taxes. The value of the balanced budget multiplier is always exactly 1.

Base Year   For measurement of real GNP, the year from which prices are used in evaluating both base year and current year outputs.

Basic Balance   The current account balance plus long-term capital flows.

Bilateral Monopoly   A market in which both buyer and seller exercise monopoly power, and neither passively accepts the demands of the other.

Bonds   Certificates issued by a borrower that entitle the lender (called the bondholder) to receive fixed periodic payments of interest, plus a larger final payment when the bond "matures" after a set number of years.

Breakeven Analysis   A business decision-making technique that relates fixed and variable costs to revenue per unit in order to identify the minimum level of output needed to break even on a project.

Capital   As a factor of production, all manufactured productive resources such as tools, industrial equipment, structures, and artificial improvements to land.

Capital Account Deficit (Surplus)   A country runs a capital account deficit (surplus) if the value of long-term capital flows to foreigners exceeds (falls short of) the value of long-term capital flows from foreigners.

Capital Budgeting The area of business decision making that focuses on long-run investment decisions.

Capital Market In the narrowest sense, the market in which manufactured means of production (capital) are bought, sold and rented. By extension, also those markets in which funds for the purchase of capital goods are borrowed and loaned, that is, credit markets.

Capitalism An economic system based on private ownership of all factors of production, receiving its name from the fact that, by and large, it is owners of capital who act as entrepreneurs in such an economy.

Capitalization (of a rent) The capitalized value of a rent is equal to the value of that sum of money that would earn a periodic interest return equal to the rent if invested at the current market rate of interest.

Cartel A group of firms that acts cooperatively to exercise monopoly power in a market.

Centralized Socialism A socialist system in which all capital and natural resources are owned by the government, which plans all production as if the economy were one big firm.

Circular Flow of Income and Product The flow of goods from firms to households and factor services from households to firms, counterbalanced by the flow of expenditures from households to firms and factor payments from firms to households.

Civilian Labor Force All civilians aged 16 or over, who are either (a) employed, (b) actively looking for a job, (c) laid off from a job to which they expect to be recalled, or (d) waiting to start a new job that will begin within 30 days.

Classical Liberal Capitalism A capitalist system in which the economic role of the state is limited to protecting private property rights and providing a court system to resolve private disputes.

Cobweb Effect A tendency for agricultural prices to rise above and then fall below the equilibrium level in alternate years, producing a pattern like a cobweb on a supply and demand diagram.

Commodity (1) In a general sense, any good or service produced to be sold in any market; (2) in a more particular sense, any of a number of basic industrial raw materials and agricultural products, such as gold, silver, wheat, corn, cattle, or hogs, that are traded in organized future markets.

Commodity Inflation A variety of cost-push inflation in which a spontaneous increase in commodity prices is the initial source of general price increases.

Comparative Advantage In international trade theory, the ability of a country to produce a good at a lower opportunity cost, in terms of other goods, than its trading partners.

Complements A pair of goods for which an increase in the price of one good causes a decrease in the quantity demanded of the other, other things being equal.

Concentration Ratios The percentage of all industry sales contributed by the four or eight largest firms in an industry. Used as a measure of the competitiveness of a market.

Conglomerate Mergers Mergers between firms in unrelated lines of business, for example, between an aircraft maker and a sporting goods manufacturer.

Consent Decree In antitrust cases, an agreement between the government and the offending company in which the latter is not brought to trial and does not admit guilt, but does have to modify its objectionable practices.

Constant Returns to Scale Said to be experienced when there are neither economies nor diseconomies of scale.

Consumer Equilibrium A state of affairs in which consumers cannot increase the total utility they obtain from a given budget by shifting expenditure from one kind of good to another. In consumer equilibrium, the marginal utility of dollar's worth of one good must be equal to the marginal utility of a dollar's worth of any other.

Consumer Price Index A price index based on a "representative market basket" of about 400 goods and services purchased by urban wage earners and clerical workers. This index is calculated using base year quantities.

Consumption Opportunity Line (Budget Line) A line showing the various combinations of goods that can be purchased at given prices with a given budget.

Consumption Schedule A graphical or numerical representation of the way in which nominal consumption expenditure varies as nominal income varies, other things being equal.

Contractionary Gap The gap between planned expenditures and the national product at the target level of national income when aggregate supply exceeds aggregate demand at that level.

Corporation A firm in which the ownership is divided into equal parts called shares, with each shareholder's liability limited to the amount of his or her investment in the firm.

Cost-Push Inflation Inflation that is initially touched off by a spontaneous rise in wages, profit margins, commodity prices, or other elements of cost during a period of slack aggregate demand.

Cost-Push Illusion The phenomenon that demand-pull inflation often looks like cost-push inflation to those caught up in it, because inventories cushion the immediate impact of demand on prices at each link in the chain of distribution from producers to retailers.

Craft Union A union of skilled workers all practicing the same trade.

Credit Markets A general term of the complex of financial institutions, including commercial banks, savings and loan associations, the stock and bond markets, insurance companies, and others that act as intermediaries between households which save and firms which invest.

Crowding Out Effect The tendency of expansionary fiscal policy to cause a drop in private planned investment expenditure as a result of a rise in the interest rate.

Crude Birth Rate The number of people born into a population per 1,000 per year.

Crude Death Rate   The number of people in a population who die per 1,000 per year.

Crude Quantity Theory of Prices (Quantity Theory)   The theory that the price level in an economy is simply proportional to the quantity of money in circulation.

Current Account Balance   The balance of goods and services plus net private and government transfers.

Currency   Coins and paper money.

Deficit (of the government budget)   An excess of government purchases over net taxes.

Deficit Spending   A policy of purposely allowing government purchases to exceed net taxes, with the difference being made up by borrowing from the public or creating new money.

Demand Curve   A graphical representation of the relationship between the price of a good and the quantity of that good demanded.

Demand Deposits   Deposits at commercial banks that permit the depositor to make payments to others by writing a check against the deposit. Demand deposits are what we commonly call checking accounts.

Demand Management   A general term for the fiscal and monetary policies used to control aggregate demand for purposes of economic stabilization.

Demand Schedule   A table showing the quantity of a good demanded at various prices.

Demand-Pull Inflation   Inflation that is initially touched off by an increase in aggregate demand.

Demographic Transition   A population cycle that accompanies economic development, beginning with a fall in the death rate, continuing with a phase of rapid population growth, and concluding with a decline in the birth rate.

Depauperization   Economic development of a kind that benefits the poorest of the poor, providing them not only with the material necessities of life, but also with access to education, status, security, self-expression, and power.

Diminishing Marginal Utility (Principle of)   The greater our rate of consumption of some good, the smaller the increase in utility we get from a unit increase in our rate of consumption.

Diminishing Returns (Law of)   If the output of some good is increased by increasing the quantity of one variable input while the quantity of other inputs used remains fixed, then a point will eventually be reached beyond which the quantity of output produced by each additional unit of the variable input will diminish.

Discount Rate (in the Banking System)   The interest rate paid by commercial banks to borrow reserve funds from the Fed.

Discounting   A method of comparing the value of recipts or outlays made at different points in time. See **Present Value.**

Diseconomies of Scale   Said to be experienced whenever long-run average cost increases as output increases.

Disposable Personal Income (disposable income)   Personal income minus personal income taxes.

Dissaving   Negative saving; the difference between disposable income and consumption expenditure when consumption exceeds disposable income.

Dissolution   In antitrust cases, a remedy requiring the offending company to be broken up into several smaller companies, or to sell off some of its subsidiaries.

Distributive Justice   The principle of distribution according to innate merit or, roughly, the principle of "from each according to his abilities, to each according to his needs."

Dual Economy   A less developed economy that is sharply divided into a modern, Westernized industrial sector capable of rapid growth, and a traditional rural sector that remains stagnant.

Dual Labor Market   The division of the labor market into a primary sector, containing good jobs with established firms, and a secondary sector, containing low-paid, unstable jobs with marginal firms.

Econometrician   An expert in the statistical analysis of economic data.

Economic Ideology   A set of judgments and beliefs concerning efficiency, market justice, and distributive justice as goals of economic policy, together with a set of prejudices or beliefs concerning matters of positive economics.

Economies of Scale   Said to be experienced whenever long-run average cost decreases as output increases.

Efficiency   The property of producing or acting with a minimum of expense, waste, and effort.

Effective Demand   The quantity of a good that purchasers are willing and able to buy at a particular price.

Egalitarianism   The principle that economic goods should be distributed equally among all members of society.

Elastic (Demand or Supply)   An elasticity numerically greater than 1.

Employed   According to the official Bureau of Labor Statistics definition, a person who (a) works at least one hour a week for pay or at least fifteen hours per week as an unpaid worker in a family business, or (b) normally works the required number of hours, but is temporarily not working because of bad weather, illness, vacation, or a labor dispute.

Entrepreneur   In general, anyone who is alert to opportunities for buying low and selling high in order to make a profit. More particularly, someone who undertakes to buy factors of production and organizes them for the production of useful goods or services in the hope that those goods or services can be sold at a profit.

Excess Quantity Demanded   The amount by which the quantity demanded of a good exceeds the quantity supplied, when the price of the good is below the equilibrium level.

Excess Quantity Supplied   The amount by which the

quantity supplied of a good exceeds the quantity demanded when the price of the good is above the equilibrium level.

Excess Reserves Commercial bank reserves in excess of the minimum legally required levels.

Expansionary Gap The gap between planned expenditures and national product at the target level of national income when aggregate demand exceeds aggregate supply at that level.

Expected Rate of Return The annual net improvement in a firm's cost or revenue that it expects to obtain by making an investment expressed as a percentage of the sum invested.

Expenditure Approach A method of estimating aggregate economic activity by adding together the nominal expenditure of all economic units on newly produced final goods and services.

Explicit Private Costs All costs that a firm must cover by explicit payments to outsiders.

Extensive Growth Growth based predominantly on the mobilization of increasing quantities of factor inputs.

Factors of Production The basic inputs of natural resources, labor, and capital used in the production of all goods.

Featherbedding The practice of insisting on purposely inefficient work rules, so that more workers will be needed to do a job.

Federal Reserve System (Fed) The central banking system of the United States, which provides banking services to government and commercial banks, and regulates the activities of commercial banks.

Fiscal Policy The policies that determine the levels of government purchases and taxes.

Fixed Inputs Those inputs whose quantities cannot be varied in response to short-run changes in output.

Fixed Investment Purchases by firms of newly produced capital goods, such as production machinery, newly built structures, office equipment, and so forth.

Flows Processes occurring continuously through time, measured in units per time period.

Foreign Exchange Market The whole group of institutions, including banks, specialized foreign exchange dealers, and official government agencies through which the currency of one country may be exchanged for the currency of another.

Frictional Unemployment That portion of unemployment accounted for by people spending relatively short periods between jobs.

Full Employment Balanced Budget A rule under which tax and spending policy would be adjusted so that the federal budget would be in balance if the economy were at full employment.

Future Markets A market in which buyers and sellers agree to deliver or take delivery of some commodity at a specified future date and at a price currently agreed on.

General Equilibrium Analysis An approach to the study of markets in which we say "if such-and-such an event occurs, the effect on the market for good X will be so-and-so, provided that other markets also adjust fully to the event in question."

Gold Standard An international monetary system in which the currencies of different countries are simply names for differing quantities of gold.

Government Purchases of Goods and Services (government purchases) Expenditures made by federal, state, and local governments to purchase goods from private firms and to hire the services of government employees.

Gross National Product (GNP) The dollar value at current market prices of all final goods and services produced annually by the nation's economy.

Homogeneous Having the property that every unit is just like every other unit.

Horizontal Mergers Mergers between firms engaged in the same line of business, for example, a merger between two steel mills.

Human Capital A name for the productive potential of an individual person. The term calls attention to the fact that this productive potential can be increased by "investing" in education or job training.

Hyperinflation Very rapid inflation, on the order of 1 percent per week or more increase in prices.

Implicit Private Costs The opportunity to a firm of using resources that the firm itself owns.

Import Quota A limitation on the quantity of a good that can be imported in a given time period.

Income Approach A method of estimating aggregate economic activity by adding together the incomes earned by all households.

Income Deficit The difference between a family's total money income from all sources and the official low-income level for that family.

Income Effect That part of the change in quantity demanded of a good whose price has fallen that can be traced directly to the change in real incomes resulting from the price change.

Income Velocity of Money (Velocity) The ratio of nominal GNP to the quantity of money, hence, the average number of times per year each dollar of the money supply is used for income-generating purposes.

Incomes Policy A policy of directly controlling wages, salaries, earnings, and prices in order to fight inflation.

Indexing A policy under which wages, interest payments, taxes, and other things expressed in nominal terms are revalued upward to keep pace with inflation.

Indifference Curve A graphical representation of an indifference set.

Indifference Set A set of consumption alternatives each yielding the same utility, so that no member of the set is preferred to any other.

Industrial Union A union of all workers in an industry, including both skilled and unskilled workers and workers practicing various trades.

Inelastic (Demand or Supply) An elasticity numerically less than 1.

Inferior Good A good for which an increase in the income of buyers causes a leftward shift in the demand curve.

Inflationary Pressure Curve A graph, derived from Okun's law and the definition of the price level, that shows the amount of inflation associated with each rate of unemployment, given an initial unemployment rate and a rate of growth of nominal output.

Inflationary Recession A period of rising unemployment during which the rate of inflation remains high, or even continues to rise.

Injunction In antitrust cases, a remedy leaving the offending company intact, but forbidding it from carrying out specific anticompetitive acts or practices.

Inside Lag The delay between the time a policy action is needed and the time policy action is taken.

Intensive Growth Growth based predominantly on improvements in the quality of factor inputs and in the efficiency with which they are utilized.

Interlocking Directorates Cases where the same person is on the board of directors of two or more firms.

Inventory Investment Changes in the stocks of finished products and raw materials firms keep on hand. If stocks are increasing, inventory investment is positive; if they are decreasing, it is negative.

Investment The sum of fixed investment and inventory investment.

Joint Marginal Benefit Curve A curve showing the dollar value of the total benefits that would be received by all members of a community as the result of a $1 increase in spending on a government-supplied good or service.

Keynesian Cross A graph that shows how the equilibrium level of nominal national income is determined. The "cross" is formed by the intersection of the aggregate demand and aggregate supply schedules.

Kolkhoz The Soviet collective farm, formally organized as a producer cooperative.

Labor As a factor of production, the contributions to production made by people working with their minds and their muscles.

Law of Demand The quantity of a good demanded by buyers tends to increase as the price of the good decreases, and tends to increase as the price decreases, other things being equal.

Linear Programming A mathematical decision-making technique widely applicable in business decision making.

Liquidity A property that an asset is said to have if it can be acquired and disposed of quickly and easily without the danger of a loss in nominal value.

Long-Run Average Cost The cost per unit of producing a given output when the quantities of all inputs have been adjusted to reduce that cost to a minimum.

Long-Run Perspective Any time perspective long enough that the quantities of all of a firm's inputs can be varied.

Long-Term Capital Flows Long-term loans to or from foreigners, or transactions with foreigners involving capital assets.

Low-Income Level The officially calculated dividing line between the poor and nonpoor, varying according to size of family, age of family members, and place of residence.

Lump Sum Taxes Taxes that do not vary as income varies.

M_1 The money supply defined as currency plus demand deposits.

M_2 The money supply defined as M_1 plus time deposits at commercial banks.

Managerial Calculation The kind of decision making needed by a firm operating in markets that are in equilibrium, with given production methods, prices, and demand conditions.

Margin, Marginal Terms referring to the effects of making a small increase in any economic activity. See specific glossary entries under *marginal cost, marginal product,* etc.

Marginal Average Rule The rule that marginal cost must be equal to average cost when average cost is at its minimum.

Marginal Cost The rate at which total cost increases as output increases. Alternately, the cost of producing one additional unit of output.

Marginal Cost of Pollution Abatement The cost of reducing a given kind of pollution by one unit.

Marginal Factor Cost The amount by which a firm's total factor cost must increase in order for it to obtain an additional unit of that factor.

Marginal Physical Product (of a factor) The increase in output resulting from a one-unit increase in the input of some factor of production, when the quantity of all other factors used remains unchanged.

Marginal Productivity Theory of Distribution A theory of the functional distribution of income, according to which each factor receives a payment equal to its marginal revenue product.

Marginal Propensity to Consume The fraction of each added dollar of disposable income that goes to added consumption.

Marginal Propensity to Save The fraction of each added dollar of disposable income that is not consumed.

Marginal Rate of Substitution The rate at which one good can be substituted for another without gain or loss in satisfaction. Equal to the slope of an indifference curve at any point.

Marginal Revenue   The change in a firm's total revenue that results from a one-unit change in total output.

Marginal Revenue Product (of a factor)   The change in revenue resulting from the sale of the product produced by one additional unit of factor input.

Marginal Tax Rate   The net increase in taxes paid or decrease in transfers received by a family for each $1 increase in the family's earned income.

Marginal Social Cost of Pollution   The total cost to all members of society of an additional unit of pollution.

Markets   A general term referring to all of the various arrangements that people have for trading with one another.

Market Equilibrium   A condition in which the separately formulated plans of buyers and sellers of some good exactly mesh when tested in the marketplace, so that the quantity supplied is exactly equal to the quantity demanded at the prevailing price.

Market Justice   The principle of distribution according to acquired merit. The observance of property rights and the honoring of contracts. Roughly, the principle of "value for value."

Market Structure   The important structural characteristics of a market, including such things as the number of firms that operate there, the extent to which the products of different firms are diverse or homogeneous, and the ease of entry into and exit from the industry.

Merchandise Trade Balance (Goods Balance)   The difference between exports and imports of tangible goods.

Merit Goods   Goods that are produced by government and supplied free of charge on the grounds that each citizen merits his or her fair share.

Monetarists   Economists who believe that movements in the money supply are the primary causes of "ups" and "downs" in business activity.

Money Demand Schedule   A schedule showing the quantity of money that people desire to hold in their portfolios given various values for the interest rate and the level of nominal income.

Money Multiplier   The ratio of the money supply (M_1) to total reserves.

Monopolistic Competition   A market structure in which there are many firms producing a strongly differentiated product.

Monopoly Power   A seller's power to raise the price of a product without losing all, or nearly all of his or her customers.

Monopsony   A market in which there is only one buyer. (From Greek *mono*, single, plus *opsonia*, buying.)

Multiplier Effect   The ability of a $1 shift in the aggregate demand schedule to induce more than a $1 change in the equilibrium level of nominal national income.

Multiplier (Simple)   The ratio of an induced change in the equilibrium level of national income to an initial change in planned expenditure. Also known as the simple multiplier, to distinguish it from other specialized terms. The value of the multiplier is given by the formula $M = 1/(1 - \text{MPC})$.

National Income   The total of all incomes, including wages, rents, interest payments, and profits, received by households.

National Product   The total value of all goods and services supplied in the economy.

Natural Monopoly   An industry in which total costs are minimized by having just one producer serve the entire market.

Natural Rate of Unemployment   That rate of unemployment that would prevail if the expected rate of inflation were equal to the actual rate of inflation.

Natural Resources   As a factor of production, land with its original fertility and mineral deposits.

Negative Income Tax   A general term for any of a number of transfer programs that would pay benefits or collect taxes from families according to a schedule based on earnings, while keeping marginal tax rates low enough to avoid serious disincentive effects.

Net Exports   The value of all domestically produced goods and services sold to foreigners less the value of all goods and services bought from foreigners; exports minus imports.

Net Liquidity Balance   The basic balance plus short-term capital flows.

Net National Product (NNP)   A measure of national product adjusted to exclude the value of investment expenditures that merely replace worn out or obsolete capital goods. Officially, NNP equals GNP minus the capital consumption allowance.

Net Present Value Approach   A capital budgeting technique based on a comparison of the present values of the net cash flows generated by alternative projects.

Net Reproduction Rate   The inherent long-term rate of growth of a population, measured as the average number of daughters born to each female child over her lifetime.

Net Tax Multiplier   A multiplier showing how much equilibrium nominal national income will change in response to a change in net taxes. The formula for the net tax multiplier is $M_T = \text{MPC}/\text{MPS}$.

Net Taxes   Total tax revenues collected by government at all levels minus total transfer payments disbursed.

Nominal Values   Measurements of economic values made in terms of actual market prices at which goods are sold.

Normal Good   A good for which an increase in the income of buyers causes a rightward shift in the demand curve.

Normative Economics   That part of economics that is devoted to making value judgments about what economic policies or conditions are good or bad.

NOW Accounts   Accounts that permit checks to be written on interest-bearing time deposits. NOW stands for "negotiable orders of withdrawal."

Official Settlements Balance The net liquidity balance plus private liquid capital flows.

Okun's Law A rule of thumb that says that for each percentage point by which the unemployment rate rises above the "full employment" benchmark (traditionally taken to be 4 percent measured unemployment), actual output will fall below potential output by about 3 percent.

Oligopoly A market structure in which there are two or more firms each of which has a large share of total sales.

Open Market Operations Purchases or sales of government securities between the Fed and the public, used as an instrument of monetary policy.

Opportunity Cost The cost of doing something as measured by the loss of the opportunity to do the next best thing instead with the same amount of time or resources.

Output Gap The difference between actual real GNP and potential real GNP in any year.

Outside Lag The delay between the time policy action is taken and the time its effects on the economy are felt.

Par Values Under the monetary system run by the International Monetary Fund from 1944 to 1973, the par value for a currency was the official exchange rate around which the actual exchange rate was permitted to fluctuate only within a narrow band.

Parity Price Ratio The ratio of an index of prices that farmers receive to an index of prices that farmers pay, using the years 1910–1914 as a base period.

Partial Equilibrium Analysis An approach to the study of markets in which we say "if such-and-such an event occurs, the effect on the market for good X will be so-and-so, provided that other markets are not disturbed from equilibrium."

Participatory Socialism A socialist system in which the means of production are owned collectively by the workers of individual firms, who participate democratically in the process of management, and share the profits of their firms.

Partnership A firm formed by two or more persons to carry on a business as co-owners. Each partner bears full legal liability for the debts of the firm.

Payback Period Analysis A capital budgeting technique based on calculation of a project's payback period, that is, the length of time required for a project's net cash flows to repay the project's initial investment cost.

Perfect Competition A market structure characterized by a large number of relatively small firms, a homogeneous product, good distribution of information among all market participants, and freedom of entry and exit.

Perfectly Elastic (Demand or Supply) The situation where the quantity demanded or supplied can vary without a change in price. Corresponds to a hori-

zontal demand or supply curve. Elasticity undefined numerically.

Perfectly Inelastic (Demand or Supply) An elasticity numerically equal to 0. No quantity change in response to a price change.

Permanent Income Hypothesis A hypothesis that reconciles a high, long-run marginal propensity to consume with a low, short-run marginal propensity to consume, by saying that people are likely to consume less out of transitory increases in income than out of those increases that they consider to be permanent.

Personal Income The total of all income, including transfer payments, actually received by households before payment of personal income taxes.

Phillips Curve A curve showing the relationship between the rate of inflation and the level of unemployment. Inflation, usually placed on the vertical axis of such a figure, may be measured either in terms of the rate of change in wages or the rate of change in a price index.

Planned Investment Schedule A graphical representation of the way in which the rate of planned investment for the economy as a whole varies as the rate of interest varies, other things being equal.

Policy Variable Those elements of the economy that are under the direct control of the government.

Political Equilibrium The quantity supplied of a public good or merit good at which political pressures for increased expenditure just balance pressures for decreased expenditure.

Political Supply Curve A curve showing the distribution of voter opinion on a public spending issue. The height of the curve at any point indicates the percentage of voters who support spending at least that much on the good or service in question.

Population Trap A situation in which the rate of population growth rises above the rate of economic growth, halting the growth of per capita income and and aborting the demographic transition.

Portfolio Balance The idea that people try to maintain a balance among the various kinds of assets they own, including money, consumer durables, stocks, and bonds, shifting from one kind of asset to another as economic conditions change.

Positive Economics That part of economics that is limited to making scientific predictions and purely descriptive statements.

Potential Output (potential real GNP) The level of output that the economy could in principle achieve if it were operating on the production possibilities frontier. Potential output can be estimated from actual real output using Okun's law.

Present Value The present value V_p of a future sum of money V_t discounted for t years at r percent interest is the sum that, if invested today at r percent, would grow to the value V_t in t years. The formula for calculating present value is $V_p = V_t/(1 + r)^t$.

Price Discrimination A practice of offering different

prices to different purchasers of the same good, when such price differences are not based on differences in grade, quality, and quantity of the same product, or on tangible differences in selling costs.

Price Elasticity of Demand (Elasticity of Demand) The percentage change in the quantity of a good demanded, divided by the percentage in the price of the good.

Price Elasticity of Supply (Elasticity of Supply) The percentage change in the quantity of a good supplied, divided by the percentage change in the price of the good.

Price Leadership A situation in which one firm in an oligopolistic industry, the price leader, can count on the others to match its price changes whether they are up or down.

Price Index In the most general sense, the ratio of current-year nominal GNP to current-year real GNP. See also *consumer* and *wholesale price indexes*.

Price Taker A firm that takes the prices at which it buys its inputs and sells its outputs as fixed, determined entirely by forces outside its own control.

Production Possibility Frontier A curve showing the possible combinations of goods that can be produced by an economy, given the quantity and quality of factors of production available.

Profit Income earned by buying low and selling high. Includes the case in which an entrepreneur buys factors of production and uses them to make something that can then be sold for more than the cost of obtaining the factor inputs.

Profit-Push Inflation A variety of cost-push inflation in which a spontaneous increase in profit margins is the initial source of price increases.

Progressive Tax One that takes a larger percentage of income from people whose incomes are high.

Protectionism A policy of shielding domestic industry from foreign competition.

Public Goods Goods or services having the two properties that (1) they cannot be provided to one citizen without being supplied also to his neighbors, and (2) once provided for one citizen, the cost of providing them to others is zero.

Pure Economic rent The income earned by any factor of production that is in perfectly inelastic supply.

Pure Monopoly A market structure in which one firm accounts for 100 percent of industry sales.

Rate of Natural Increase The current rate of growth of a population calculated as the crude birth rate minus the crude death rate.

Real GNP A measure of aggregate economic activity obtained by evaluating current-year quantities in terms of the prices of some base year.

Real Values Measurements of economic values that include adjustments for changes in prices between one year and another.

Reflation An expansion of aggregate demand after a period of high unemployment and decelerating inflation. Reflation brings substantial short-term gains in employment with little or no inflationary penalty.

Regressive Tax One which takes a larger percentage of income from people whose income is low.

Regulatory Lag The length of time, sometimes several years, that it takes a regulatory commission to review a firm's performance and react to changes in market conditions.

Required Reserve Ratios Legally required minimum quantities of reserves, expressed as ratios of reserves to various types of deposits.

Reservation Wage The wage (adjusted for nonmonetary advantages and disadvantages of a job) below which a person will not accept a job offer.

Reserves (of Commercial Banks) Money held by commercial banks as cash or non-interest-bearing deposits with the Federal Reserve.

Residual Charges Charges of a fixed amount per unit of waste imposed on all sources that discharge a given kind of waste into the environment.

Saving Schedule A graphical or numerical representation of the way in which nominal saving varies as nominal income varies, other things being equal.

Scarcity As used in economics, not having enough to fill all subjective wants.

Scientific Prediction A conditional prediction having the form "if *A*, then *B*, other things being equal."

Shortage In technical economic terminology, an excess quantity demanded.

Short-Run Perspective Any time perspective short enough that the quantities of at least some of a firm's inputs cannot be varied.

Short-Term Capital Flows Loans to or from foreigners, payable within one year or less.

Sinks Naturally occurring means of disposing of useless or harmful by-products of production and consumption.

Socialism Any of a number of doctrines that include the tenets that: (1) some major share of nonlabor factors of production ought to be owned in common or by the state; and (2) that justice requires incomes to be distributed at least somewhat more equally than under classical liberal capitalism.

Sole Proprietorship A firm owned and usually managed by a single person, who receives all profits of the firm and who personally bears all of the firm's liabilities.

Sources Naturally occurring stocks of useful productive inputs.

Speculative Demand (for Money) The part of money demand arising from the advantages of money as an asset with a fixed nominal value, which offers protection against the danger of capital loss in periods when it is feared that the prices of other assets may fall.

Speculator A person who buys something now at a low price, hoping to be able to sell it later at a high price.

State Capitalism A capitalist system in which government intervenes widely in the market, and provides an alternative to the market as a means by which individuals and firms can win control over resources.

Sterilization A policy of using domestic monetary policy to offset the effect of a balance of payments deficit or surplus on the domestic money supply.

Stocks Accumulated quantities existing at a particular time, measured in terms of simple units.

Stop-Go-Policy A cycle of acceleration, inflationary recession, deceleration, and reflation brought about by alternating political pressures to "do something" first about inflation and then about unemployment.

Substitutes A pair of goods for which an increase in the price of one good causes an increase in the quantity demanded of the other, other things being equal.

Substitution Effect That part of the increase in quantity demanded of a good whose price has fallen that can be traced directly to the principle of diminishing marginal utility, not taking into account the change in real income resulting from the change in price.

Supply Curve A graphical representation of the relationship between the price of a good and the quantity of that good supplied.

Supply Schedule A table showing the quantity of a good supplied at various prices.

Surplus In technical economic terminology, an excess quantity supplied.

Surplus (of the government budget) An excess of net taxes over government purchases.

Survivorship Principle The principle that business decisions are more often made by people with good judgment, because those with good judgment make profits and survive, whereas the incompetents soon loose their decision-making positions.

Target Level of National Income The level of nominal national income that policy makers think will permit their main economic goals (full employment, price stability, economic growth, or whatever) to be best realized.

Tariff A tax levied on imported goods.

Tax Incidence The matter of who bears the economic burden of taxation.

Time Deposits Interest-paying accounts at commercial banks against which it is not ordinarily possible to write checks. Both passbook savings accounts and certificates of deposits are included, except for certain very large certificates of deposit used by corporate depositors.

Total Private Costs Explicit plus implicit private costs.

Transactions Demand (for Money) The part of money demand arising from the usefulness of money as a generally acceptable medium of exchange.

Transitivity The principle that tells us that if A is preferred to B, and B is preferred to C, then A must be preferred to C.

Transfer Payments All payments made by government to individuals that are not made in return for goods or factor services currently supplied. Social security benefits, welfare payments, and unemployment compensation are major forms of transfers.

Transmission Mechanism The whole set of ways in which monetary policy exerts an impact on the economy.

Tying Contracts Contracts for the sale of a firm's products that include an agreement that the purchaser will not use or deal in the products of a competitor.

Unemployment Rate The percentage of the civilian labor force who are not employed.

Unit Elastic (Demand or Supply) An elasticity numerically equal to 1.

Utility The economist's term for the pleasure, satisfaction, and need fulfillment that we get from the consumption of material goods and services.

Variable Inputs Those inputs whose quantities can be varied in response to short-run changes in output.

Vertical Mergers Mergers between two firms, one of which is a supplier or customer of the other, for example, a merger between a newspaper and a paper manufacturer.

Wage-Push Inflation A variety of cost-push inflation in which a spontaneous increase in nominal wage rates is the initial source of price increases.

Wholesale Price Index A price index based on a sample of about 2,500 goods purchased in large quantities in transactions between firms. This index is calculated using base-year quantities.

Workable Competition Any market structure in which, taking into account structural characteristics and the dynamic factors that shaped them, no clearly indicated change can be effected through public policy measures that would result in greater social gains than social losses.

Suggestions for Further Reading

Preface

Boulding, Kenneth E., *Economics as a Science* (New York: McGraw-Hill, 1970).

Bowen, William G., "Econometrics," in *Perspectives in Economics,* Alan A. Brown, Egon Neuberger, and Malcolm Palmatier, eds. (New York: McGraw-Hill, 1971).

Brown, Alan A., and John E. Elliot, "Scope and Method of Economic Analysis," in *Perspectives in Economics,* Alan A. Brown, Egon Neuberger, and Malcolm Palmatier, eds. (New York: McGraw-Hill, 1971).

Ebenstein, William, *Today's Isms: Communism, Fascism, Capitalism, Socialism,* 6th ed. (Englewood Cliffs, N.J.: Prentice-Hall, 1970).

Kirzner, Israel M., *The Economic Point of View: An Essay in the History of Economic Thought* (Princeton, N.J.: Van Nostrand, 1960).

Olson, Mancur, Jr.; "Economics, Sociology, and the Best of All Possible Worlds," *The Public Interest,* Vol. 12, (1968).

Robbins, Lionel C., *An Essay on the Nature and Significance of Economic Science,* 2d rev. ed. (London: MacMillan, 1935).

Part One

Economic Report of the President, transmitted to the Congress of the United States, 1966. Section on twenty years of policy experience with the Full Employment Act, pp. 170–186.

Phelps, Edmund S., ed., *Private Wants and Public Needs: Issues Surrounding the Size and Scope of Government Expenditure,* rev. ed. (New York: Norton, 1965).

Posner, Richard A., *Economic Analysis of Law* (Boston: Little, Brown, 1972).

Smithies, Arthur, "Economic Analysis of the Public Sector," in *Perspectives in Economics,* Alan A. Brown, Egon Neuberger, and Malcolm Palmatier, eds. (New York: McGraw-Hill, 1971).

Part Two Chapters 5–7

Abraham, William I., *National Income and Economic Accounting* (Englewood Cliffs, N.J.: Prentice-Hall, 1969).

Beckerman, Wilfred, *Two Cheers for the Affluent Society* (New York: St. Martin's 1974).

Cole, H. S. D., et al., eds., *Models of Doom: A Critique of the Limits to Growth* (New York: Universe Books, 1973).

Kuznets, Simon S., "Problems of Interpretation of National Income Accounts," in *National Income: A Summary of Findings* (New York: National Bureau of Economic Research, 1946).

Meadows, Dennis L., et al., *The Limits to Growth* (Washington, D.C.: Potomac Associates, 1972).

Part Two, Chapters 8–10

Heilbroner, Robert L., and Peter Bernstein, *A Primer on Government Spending* (New York: Random House, 1963).

Heller, Walter W., *New Dimensions of Political Economy* (Cambridge: Harvard University Press, 1966).

Part Two, Chapters 11–13

Board of Governors of the Federal Reserve System, *The Federal Reserve System: Purposes and Functions,* 6th ed. (Washington, D.C.: Board of Governors of the Federal Reserve System, 1974).

Campbell, Colin, and Rosemary Campbell, *An Introduction to Money and Banking,* 2d ed. (Hinsdale, Ill.: Dryden Press, 1975).

Friedman, Milton, and Walter W. Heller, *Monetary versus Fiscal Policy* (New York: Norton, 1969).

Friedman, Milton, and Anna Schwartz, *A Monetary History of the United States, 1867–1960* (Princeton, N.J.: Princeton University Press, 1963).

Samuelson, Paul A., "Monetarism Objectively Evaluated," in *Readings in Introductory Economics,* John R. McKean and Ronald A. Wykstra, eds. (New York: Harper & Row, 1971), pp. 120–132.

Smith, Warren L., "Monetary Institutions and Policies," in *Perspectives in Economics,* Alan A. Brown, Egon Neuberger, and Malcolm Palmatier, eds. (New York: McGraw-Hill, 1971).

Part Two, Chapters 14-17

Friedman, Milton, *Monetary Correction,* Occasional Paper No. 41 (London: Institute for Economic Affairs, 1974).

Friedman, Milton, *Unemployment versus Inflation? An Evaluation of the Phillips Curve* (London: Institute for Economic Affairs, 1975).

Gurley, John G., "Have Fiscal and Monetary Policies Failed?" *American Economic Review,* Vol. LXII (1972).

Stigler, George, "The Economics of Minimum Wage Legislation," *American Economic Review,* Vol. 36 (1946).

Part Three

Bauer, Peter T., *Dissent on Development: Studies and Debates in Development Economics* (London: Weidenfeld and Nicolson, 1971).

Beckerman, Wilfred, *Pricing for Pollution* (to be published).

Dolan, Edwin G., *TANSTAAFL, The Economic Strategy for Environmental Crisis* (New York: Holt, 1971).

England, Richard, and Barry Bluestone, "Ecology and Class Conflict," *Review of Radical Political Economics,* (Fall/Winter, 1971).

Freeman, Myrick A., Robert H. Hareman, and Allan V. Kneese, *The Economics of Environmental Policy* (New York: Wiley, 1973).

Malthus, Thomas Robert, *An Essay on the Principle of Population; Text, Background, Contemporary Opinion, Essays,* Philip Appelman, ed. (New York: Norton, 1976).

Mills, Edwin S., "Economic Incentives in Air Pollution Control," in *The Economics of Air Pollution,* Harold Wuluzin, ed. (New York: Norton, 1966).

Power, Jonathan, and Anne-Marie Holenstein, *World of Hunger* (London: Temple Smith, 1976).

Weisskopf, Thomas E., "Capitalism, Underdevelopment, and the Future of the Poor Countries," in *Economics and World Order.* Jagdish Bhagwati, ed. (New York: Macmillan, 1972).

Part Four

Morgner, Aurelius, "International Economics: Theory and Policy," in *Perspectives in Economics,* Alan A. Brown, Egon Neuberger, and Malcolm Palmatier, eds. (New York: McGraw-Hill, 1971).

Pen, Jan, *A Primer on International Trade* (New York: Random House, 1967).

Stevens, Robert Warren, *A Primer on the Dollar in the World Economy* (New York: Random House, 1972).

Triffin, Robert, "International Economics, Monetary Reform," in *Perspectives in Economics,* Alan A. Brown, Egon Neuberger, and Malcolm Palmatier, eds. (New York: McGraw-Hill, 1971).

"The United States Balance of Payments: Exchange Rates—How Flexible Should They Be?" *Hearings before the Joint Economic Committee,* 88th Cong. 1st sess., 1963. Especially testimony by Henry Wallich (pp. 495-499) and Milton Friedman (pp. 451-456).

Index